RETHINKING WHO WE ARE

RETHINKING WHO WE ARE

CRITICAL REFLECTIONS ON HUMAN DIVERSITY IN CANADA

EDITED BY

JESSICA E. PULIS

AND PAUL U. ANGELINI

FERNWOOD PUBLISHING
HALIFAX & WINNIPEG

Editing and design: Brenda Conroy
Cover design: JVDW Design
Printed and bound in Canada

Published by Fernwood Publishing
32 Oceanvista Lane, Black Point, Nova Scotia, B0J 1B0
and 748 Broadway Avenue, Winnipeg, Manitoba, R3G 0X3
www.fernwoodpublishing.ca

Fernwood Publishing Company Limited gratefully acknowledges the financial support of the Government of Canada, the Canada Council for the Arts, the Manitoba Department of Culture, Heritage and Tourism under the Manitoba Publishers Marketing Assistance Program and the Province of Manitoba, through the Book Publishing Tax Credit, for our publishing program. We are pleased to work in partnership with the Province of Nova Scotia to develop and promote our creative industries for the benefit of all Nova Scotians.

Library and Archives Canada Cataloguing in Publication

Title: Rethinking who we are: critical reflections on human diversity in Canada / edited by Jessica E. Pulis and Paul U. Angelini.
Names: Pulis, Jessica E., 1978– editor. | Angelini, Paul U., 1962– editor.
Description: Includes bibliographical references and index.
Identifiers: Canadiana 20190064854 | ISBN 9781773631356 (softcover)
Subjects: LCSH: Multiculturalism—Canada. | LCSH: Equality—Canada. | LCSH: Canada—Ethnic relations. | LCSH: Canada—Social conditions.
Classification: LCC FC105.M8 R48 2019 | DDC 305.800971—dc23

CONTENTS

ACKNOWLEDGEMENTS

The editors would like to thank a number of people who helped bring this project to fruition: Fernwood publisher and development editor Errol Sharpe, for accepting this project and believing in a critical re-examination of Canadian identity; managing editor Beverley Rach, for her exceptional efforts in keeping the project focused and on time; and marketing managers Nancy Malek and Curran Faris for their expertise in getting the text "out there."

We also thank the freelancers for bringing their unique and essential skills to this project: copy editor and interior design and layout specialist Brenda Conroy, for her thoughtful and insightful comments and observations; and typesetter Debbie Mathers, cover designer John van der Woude and indexer Siusan Moffat, for their indispensable work and efforts.

I dedicate this work to my grandmother, Julie Camilleri, who came to Canada with the wisdom and courage of a generation who experienced the horrors of World War II; to my mother, Carmen Pulis, who reminds me that strength comes from never being complacent; and finally to my children, Olivia, Xavier and Sophia, who inspire me to challenge the nation in which they live.

— *Jessica E. Pulis*

I dedicate this work to my parents, Americo (1930–2017) and Venerina Angelini, and to my in-laws, Giovanni (1935–2009) and Maddalena Alba. Like the millions who came before and after them, they lived the immigrant experience and in doing so helped mould and shape Canada's ever dynamic identity.

— *Paul U. Angelini*

WHY STUDY HUMAN DIVERSITY IN CANADA?

Jessica E. Pulis and Paul U. Angelini

There are two important reasons to study human diversity in Canada. First, Canada's population differs widely. There are profound differences between Canadians living in different provinces and territories, and it comes as no surprise that definitions of what it means to be Canadian and what it means to be diverse also differ. Throughout this text, students are challenged to critically examine definitions of diversity in Canadian society and to reflect on the following questions. How do Canadian law, the Charter of Rights and Freedoms and human rights impact Canadian identity? How do sexual orientation, gender fluidity, social class and disability fit into conceptions of diversity? Why are the horrific abuses suffered by Indigenous Peoples only now being recognized? Why is there ongoing resistance to understanding Canada as a settler colonial country that continues to deny Indigenous Peoples their history and rights? How has Canadian identity been analyzed and treated by writers, storytellers and the mass media? Students are asked to think about Canadian diversity in the future. Who are we and where are we going? What will life in Canada look like for future generations?

The second reason to study human diversity is that it is a fact of life. All countries have unique populations that are diverse. Some countries, like Canada, have populations with a great deal of diversity. But what do you know about the history of colonization and immigration? Are you Indigenous? Are you an immigrant? With the exception of Indigenous Peoples, we are all immigrants. How many generations of your family have lived in Canada? If you are an immigrant, think about why your family came to Canada. Like the United States with the American Dream, Canada has a mythology surrounding opportunities and life for new Canadians. Since the mid-1970s, the dominant source of immigration to Canada has been the "developing countries."[1] These newcomers to Canada share three main characteristics: they are not white, they are not Christian, and they come from places that are economically underdeveloped. This text explores what changing diversities mean to individuals in Canada and to Canada as a whole.

We hope students will appreciate the differences that characterize Canadian life and develop a fuller understanding of what it means to be Canadian. The more we understand about ourselves and our settler colonial history, the more understanding we become. We hope this increased understanding will lead all generations of Canadians, new and old alike, to be less likely to repeat the sins of the past. Canadian identity is complex and multi-layered. So, who are we? Canada prides itself on being a country that embraces difference. Many years ago, the most anticipated public event in Toronto was the Santa Claus parade. Today, Gay Pride and Caribana are two of the most anticipated celebrations. People arrive from around the world to experience and revel in these proud celebrations of difference, spending millions of dollars on hotels, food, refreshments and entertainment.

This introductory text was conceived and written for students who have had little exposure to the issues surrounding human diversity in Canada. As a student-centred, topical text, it is designed to give readers a kaleidoscopic view of diversity in Canada framed within critical theoretical paradigms. For readers who have already examined diversity, this text provides up-to-date statistics and analyses of recent events. The text addresses diversity in its totality — that is, it includes diversities that are considered non-traditional and/or discusses diversities in a non-traditional manner. Topics range from law and human rights, regionalism, health, Indigenous storytelling and disability, to voice, literature and the mass media.

The first section of this text lays the foundation for the analysis of diversity in Canada, discussing law and human rights, regionalism and concepts of health, illness and disease. We call these national or "macro" diversities. The second section analyzes specific diversities in Canada and includes discussions of race and ethnicity, Indigenous storytelling, social inequality, gender, sexual orientation and disability. We call these specific or "micro" diversities. The final section explores how the idea and reality of diversity are treated by examining the topics of voice, literature and mass media.

The text employs the following pedagogical tools designed to highlight for students the essential components of diversity:

- Diversity in Action boxes contain additional information, case studies, current events reports and biographies.
- Think About boxes ask students to critically think about a selected area/topic/idea.
- Innov8 boxes represent particular areas of study and direct students to investigate documentaries, Ted Talks, flash mobs, art exhibits or other unique contributions to the subject area.

- Call-out text highlights essential policies, definitions, events or people.
- Key Terms are in bold typeface and are defined at the end of each chapter.
- Key Objectives begin each chapter.

Students are invited to examine the paradox of diversity in Canadian society: on the one hand, we see ourselves as champions of diversity and acceptance, yet on the other, we continue to participate in gross violations of Indigenous rights and in acts of hate, racism and prejudice, especially against those who live on the margins of society. Finally, students explore diversity through a critical lens, which both highlights and challenges their own understandings of diversity in Canadian society.

Note

1   In this text we use the term "developing world" or "developing countries" but there are problems and various opinions on what to call the countries that used to be called the Third World. See the NPR website for a discussion of this issue: <www.npr.org/sections/goatsandsoda/2015/01/04/372684438/ if-you-shouldnt-call-it-the-third-world-what-should-you-call-it>.

PART ONE

Part One adopts a macro approach to examining diversity in Canada. Using the analogy of a painting, these first three chapters are the canvass or foundation on which diversity in Canada unfolds in its own unique way. The canvas supports and absorbs the paint to stabilize the painting and hold it in place. Together the first three chapters allow for structured analyses of the specific diversities found in Part Two.

Chapter 1 examines how Canadian law and human rights impact human differentiation. Is there equity and inclusion in human rights and laws regardless of gender, race or ethnicity, sexual orientation, social status, religious beliefs? This chapter highlights the complex relationship Canada has both as enforcer and perpetrator of human rights violations.

Chapter 2 looks at regionalism. It begins with a definition of regionalism and outlines the competing theories that attempt to explain regional differentiation. It concludes by examining how the federal government in Ottawa has paradoxically increased inequality between regions while at the same time taking action to lessen the same inequality.

Chapter 3 lays the foundation or a basic understanding of how different cultures explain the nature of disease and illness. It also explains that one of the main differences between biomedicine and ethnomedicine is that in ethnomedicine mental illness is treated no differently from physical illness.

1

HUMAN RIGHTS AND THE LAW

DIVERSITY AND DISADVANTAGE

Jessica E. Pulis

> *Diversity is tolerated but only to the extent that everyone is different in the same way.* — Roger Maaka and Augie Fleras, "Engaging with Indigeneity"[1]

KEY OBJECTIVES

Understand human rights as social, civil, political, economic and environmental rights.

Explore how we balance individual rights and the rights of groups of people.

Understand human rights as a social construction.

Assess human rights as a paradox.

Explore rights violations of individuals and groups.

This chapter considers human rights within the context of a diverse nation. What are human rights? Do all people have human rights? Are human rights the same as legal rights? Do all people have the same human rights? Is there equity and inclusion in human rights and laws regardless of gender, race or ethnicity, sexual orientation, social status and religious beliefs?

Box 1.1 Diversity in Action

The Universal Declaration of Human Rights is reflected throughout the Canadian Charter of Rights and Freedoms of 1982, drafted under the tenure of Prime Minister Pierre Elliot Trudeau. The following are examples of similarities:

Security Rights

UDHR Article 5: No one shall be subjected to torture or to cruel, inhuman or degrading treatment or punishment.

CCRF Section 12: Everyone has the right not to be subjected to any cruel and unusual treatment or punishment.

Due Process Rights

UDHR Article 9: No one shall be subjected to arbitrary arrest, detention or exile.

CCRF Section 9: Everyone has the right not to be arbitrarily detained or imprisoned.

Basic Liberties

UDHR Article 20 (1): Everyone has the right to freedom of peaceful assembly and association.

CCRF Section 2 (c): Everyone has the freedom of peaceful assembly.

Rights of Democratic Political Participation

UDHR Article 21 (3): The will of the people shall be the basis of the authority of government; this will shall be expressed in periodic and genuine elections which shall be by universal and equal suffrage and shall be held by secret vote or by equivalent free voting procedures.

CCRF Section 3: Every citizen of Canada has the right to vote in an election of members of the House of Commons or of a legislative assembly and to be qualified for membership therein.

Equality Rights

UDHR Article 2: Everyone is entitled to all the rights and freedoms set forth in this Declaration, without distinction of any kind, such as race, colour, sex, language, religion, political or other opinion, national or social origin, property, birth or other status. Furthermore, no distinction shall be made on the basis of the political, jurisdictional or international status of the country or territory to which a person belongs, whether it be independent, trust, non-self-governing or under any other limitation of sovereignty.

CCRF Section 15 (1): Every individual is equal before and under the law and has the right to the equal protection and equal benefit of the law without discrimination and, in particular, without discrimination based on race, national or ethnic origin, colour, religion, sex, age or mental or physical disability.

Economic and Social Rights

UDHR Article 22: Everyone, as a member of society, has the right to social security and is entitled to realization, through national effort and international cooperation and in accordance with the organization and resources of each State, of the economic, social and cultural rights indispensable for his dignity and the free development of his personality.

CCRF: The Charter does not protect economic rights, like social assistance. Each province and territory is responsible for its own policies and regulations. [See Chapter 6 for a more detailed discussion of social assistance and economic rights in Canada.]

DEFINING HUMAN RIGHTS

When we think of human rights we might think about the Universal Declaration of Human Rights (UDHR), the Canadian Charter of Rights and Freedoms (CCRF), and the provincial and territorial human rights commissions (for example, the Ontario Human Rights Commission, the New Brunswick Human Rights Commission, the Northwest Territories Human Rights Commission). Canadian John Humphrey helped draft the first version of the Universal Declaration of Human Rights, which was adopted by the United Nations in 1948. The original declaration was not a set of legal obligations, but rather they were goals that United Nations member states were expected to strive for.[2] In other words, countries were not legally obliged by the United Nations or international law to comply with the declaration. It was a set of moral and social expectations that nations, to the best of their ability, would follow to acknowledge, address and uphold human rights. The declaration consists of a preamble and thirty articles aimed at protecting individuals and groups of people from existing and future rights violations.

We tend to think about human rights violations or human rights injustices as

Box 1.2 Think About...

Since the 9/11 attacks in the United States, due process violations of the rights of terrorist suspects were rampant in countries all over the world, as fear of terrorism and terrorist attacks were used to justify the denial of these rights (see Chapter 4 for a more detailed discussion). In 2017, the Canadian federal government awarded Omar Khadar $10 million in a controversial settlement after failing to uphold the Khadar's human rights as a Canadian citizen while the teenager was being held and tortured in the US prison at Guantanamo Bay.

things like mass murder, ethnic cleansing, violence, conflict and other harms. Many examples of such atrocities, both nationally and internationally, quickly come to mind: mercury poisoning in Grassy Narrows, genocide in Rwanda and Bosnia (now Bosnia and Herzegovina), ethnic cleansing in Syria, the Flint Michigan water crisis, mass incarceration and overrepresentation of racialized populations, systemic poverty and so on. This list highlights the fact that we often discuss human rights in terms of violations of those rights.

Definitions of **human rights** are complex. Human rights are designed to protect morally relevant and fundamental human interests, like human life, human freedoms, healthcare, access to education and so on. Definitions are often analogous with definitions of legal or civil rights that derive from the laws and customs of particular societies. For example, Article 3 of the UDHR states: "Everyone has the right to life, liberty and security of person." This is parallel to sections of the Criminal Code, a Canadian statute first enacted in 1892, which define the violation or termination of someone's life as illegal, an act punishable by the state. Both the UDHR and the Criminal Code place value on human life and emphasize its preservation. There is general consensus that human rights have two characteristics:

1. they are universal (each individual has rights); and
2. everyone has rights equally.

Human rights are the ethical, moral and fundamental characteristics of a society. They are universal and all people have them equally.

It is the social process of understanding human rights that leads us to conclude that human rights and legal rights are not mutually exclusive concepts. We must distinguish human rights from legal rights to other social demands, but they are interrelated concepts. We are exploring complex social phenomena that come through a multifaceted lens. A discussion of human rights is usually dominated by legal decisions that tell the government what they should or should not do. We rely on our legal system to decide which rights are human rights and not simply a social cause. For example, we often look to the justice system and government to define and construct human rights; that is, human rights and legal rights are dominated by discourse and decisions made through national and international law. Law plays an important role in advancing human rights through the ratification of new laws that address inequality and disadvantage (based on gender, race, poverty, sexuality, ability, etc.) and to challenge laws that reinforce or sustain oppression and inequality. In other words, human rights are often sought and cemented through legal decisions — and their strength, Judith Blau and Mark Frezzo argue, is dependent upon the ethical characteristics of a community or more broadly society.[3]

Blau and Frezzo define human rights as "a set of protections and entitlements held by all members of the human species — irrespective of race, class, gender, sexual orientation, cultural background or national origin."[4] One's existence in the human community is the only real eligibility condition for human rights. Therefore, we see and understand human rights as universal. Human rights exist in and of themselves, and they are afforded equally to all human beings. James Nickle argues that human rights are minimal standards by which societies and communities should live.[5] In addition, the human characteristics of gender, sexual orientation, race, etc. are irrelevant to whether a person has human rights — we all have them because we are human.

However, the central narrative appears to lie in the violations of these rights and that some groups of people (who are all **rights-protected people**) appear to be more vulnerable to **rights violations**. For example, marginalized sexualities have been subject to human rights abuses and atrocities (see Chapter 8 for a more detailed discussion of governing sexualities), and it is through human rights laws that those violations are addressed, reduced, mitigated or extinguished. Nickel calls human rights "high priority norms," not simply goals or aspirations or things we ought to have. Rather, human rights reflect legal and enlightened political moralities, which apply to and protect all people as members of the human community. These realities and rights priorities have developed and changed over time, yet the UDHR remains the most significant document that addresses violations of the rights of the marginalized.

Rights can also be thought of as positive or negative. **Negative rights** are rights that cannot be denied by the state or anyone in it: the right to life, individual safety and security, freedom from undue interference of the state, integrity, free speech, etc. **Positive rights** must be provided by the state: food, clothing, housing, healthcare, education, employment, social assistance, pensions for the elderly. Positive rights centre around several areas: examples are social rights (education, healthcare, social welfare, socioeconomic well-being and citizenship), civil rights (legally based), economic rights, political rights (freedom to participate in political systems, to assemble, to vote, to protest), cultural rights (protection of ancestral land and language, freedom to practice rituals and customs aimed at protecting the world's cultural diversity) and environmental rights.

Negative rights address our right not to have anyone or anything interfere with our lives. Positive rights address our right to have certain things provided to us as human beings.

Human rights apply to all humans, but they are limited to a legal, political, social and historical context. For example, in Canada we now have maternity leave protections for parents regardless of sexual orientation; adults have some rights that children in Canada do not (e.g., the right to vote); laws around discrimination in the workplace have existed for years but are only recently being widely enforced. We learn from history and witness a paradigm shift in social and political ideology as human rights become a priority of more societies. Canada abides by the UDHR, which requires that governments ensure that all people (not things or places) are treated equally regardless of their social position. For example, a human right of all Canadian children is equal access to education. However, the government spends less per child if the child is Indigenous.[6] This is a direct violation of that fundamental right, and we must ask ourselves how this is possible. This rights violation and inequality have persisted over decades and is reflected in the high school dropout rate for Indigenous Peoples, which is nearly 23 percent compared to roughly 6 percent of non-Indigenous Canadians.[7]

THE PARADOX OF HUMAN RIGHTS

A discussion of human rights from the perspective of the social sciences challenges the dominant social, legal and political discourse as largely neglecting human rights as a social movement. After the Second World War, when the UDHR was drafted, there

---

Box 1.3 Think About ...

The federal government announced that groups seeking funding through the Canada Summer Jobs program need to prove they respect the Charter as well as other rights, like reproductive and sexual rights, but an anti-abortion group in Toronto claims this policy violates their right to freedom of belief and expression. Michael Freeman argues: "Human rights are said to protect fundamental values from standard threats; however, human rights advocacy can itself be perceived as a threat to certain fundamental values." How does this example apply to Freeman's argument about competing interests within human rights?

Source: Michael Freeman, *Human Rights* (Boston: Polity Press, 2017).

> **Box 1.4 Think About...**
>
> In 2017, a Quebec teen refused a life-saving medical treatment for cancer based on religious beliefs. The teen, a Jehovah's Witness, refused a blood transfusion and argued she should not be forced to endure the procedure because it violated her right to religious freedom. Quebec Superior Court Justice Lukasz Granosik argued that the violation of her religious beliefs was warranted to protect her, a child, when decisions ultimately may be fatal or detrimental. This case sparked a debate about the rights of children and their ability to give consent and make decisions about medical treatment.

were many discussions about human atrocities, in particular the Holocaust. However, it was not until the profound and monumental **rights-oriented movements** of the 1960s that Western societies were exposed as perpetrators of significant rights violations. The civil rights movement, the women's movement, the LGBT2TQ (lesbian, bisexual, gay, trans*, two-spirited, questioning) and labour movements ignited a paradigm shift in the ways rights violations were perceived, documented and treated in Canada and the United States. These social justice causes became inexorably linked with human rights cases as social movements, which resulted in great social and legal changes.

The discipline of sociology investigates social problems that are likewise explored in consideration of human rights: examples include gender discrimination, racism, poverty, homophobia and transphobia. Sociologists uncover the social structures that reinforce and reproduce inequality, and they note how discourse serves to reinforce unequal treatment of some people (e.g., women, Indigenous Peoples, people who are LGBT2TQ or racialized). For instance, long-held stereotypical beliefs about women's essential caring nature (compared to men's competitive nature) were used to justify keeping women out of the paid labour force and relegated them to the private domestic sphere. Considering human rights as a social construction compels us to explain why human rights may be violated for some and upheld for others. We must acknowledge that human rights are influenced by political interests, by our history and our social structures, and by the socio/legal/historical reality of the time in which human rights as a social good were created.

In Canada in 1982, the Charter was enacted into law. Many of you were not born yet, but this was a time in society when the rights of women, Indigenous Peoples, racialized Canadians, LGBT2TQ women and men and girls and boys were clearly emphasized in the Charter. Yet continued and horrific rights violations persisted for decades after the Charter and implementation of section 15 (see Box 1.1). However, as we explore in this chapter, it may be that the lives of some are valued more than the lives of others.

Box 1.5 Think About...

How are human rights portrayed in the media? The factors that influence and shape society have a similar effect on human rights and perceptions of human rights — especially in terms of power relations and political interests.

As a social construction, human rights really are a reflection of political, social and legal interests of those with the most *vested* interests. If we consider, then, access to and protection of human rights of a wealthy, white man verses a young, queer Indigenous woman from a remote fly-in reserve community, without question, power and privilege will have a significant effect on the life of the man compared to the young woman.

Social and economic rights are often treated as aspirational and controversial. Anthony Woodiwiss argues that capitalism subverts human rights because it distributes freedoms unequally according to a person's social position in relation to labour. While many capitalist societies have sound human rights records, they often participate in unequal labour and social capital distribution.[8] Recall from Box 1.1 that economic rights are not protected under the Charter but are governed by each province and territory. It is up to each province and territory to decide who gets what, how often and how much. If we consider the lack of protections at the federal level, how might provincial and territorial variation and stereotypical beliefs about *who* accesses social assistance, and *how much* these benefits really provide, influence policy and regulation? Do you know how much a single mother with two children receiving social assistance would receive in your province or territory? Look it up. This number will surprise many of you (see Chapter 6 for a more detailed discussion of social inequality).

However, even a brief exploration of human rights violations in Canada tells an interesting narrative about the paradox of human rights. While human rights are universal and ought to equally apply to all human beings, explicit violations persist. On one hand, Canada condones other nations for their human rights atrocities, yet on the other hand, the Truth and Reconciliation Commission of Canada (TRC) (2015) highlights significant and continued human rights violations of Indigenous Peoples across Canada. Judith Blau argues: "Transformative social and economic processes have fueled human rights movements and increased people's demands for the realizations of their rights."[9] Think about current social movements like Idle No More and Black Lives Matter as transformative social movements (see Box 1.6).

Box 1.6 Innov8

Current social movements like Idle No More and Black Lives Matter demonstrate that while the Charter is nearly forty years old, significant rights violations of some of Canada's rights-protected peoples remains a central issue.

Human rights doctrines should reflect current social, economic, political, environmental and cultural innovations, and while there has been some meaningful social change in policy and attitudes and behaviours towards rights violations, many continue to persist. To put it simply, we cannot expect that human rights are universal in that all protected people will be satisfied: there are limitations to how protected diversity really is as we see through this chapter. If we consider the intersections of gender and gender identity, race and ethnicity, class, sexual orientation, disability, culture, religion, political ideology and social history, we begin to understand how complex an understanding of human rights and diversity can be.

HUMAN RIGHTS AND DIVERSITY

Diversity implies understanding and recognizing difference among individuals. As such, diversity reflects the individual but also lived experiences, social histories, belief systems and other ideologies. How do we explore human rights within the context of diversity? Human rights truly are reflective of all aspects of diversity, things like gender and gender expressions, race and ethnicity, social class, sexuality and sexual orientation, physical ability, age and political and religious beliefs. It is not surprising, then, that human rights policies, laws, treaties and discourse are policies, laws, treaties and discourse that also echo diverse ways of being, knowing and negotiating the world. What does it mean to be diverse? What do you think of when you think of Canada? Is Canada a diverse nation? See Box 1.7 for Prime Minister Justin Trudeau's understanding of Canada and diversity.

Blau and Frezzo pose the question: how do equity, diversity and human rights policies and practices respond to social inequality, social difference, unequal power relations?[10] The answer is as complex and multifaceted as the question. Let's explore some examples to help illustrate. The Canadian Human Rights Commission oversees the Employment Equity Act (1995), which is a legal obligation by all organizations or businesses regulated by the federal government to provide equal employment opportunities to four specific groups: women, Indigenous Peoples, persons with disabilities and members of racialized minorities. Employment equity was created to address disadvantage experienced by the four groups, who were significantly underrepresented

Box 1.7 Diversity in Action

Prime Minister Justin Trudeau spoke in London, UK, shortly after being elected in 2015. Here is an excerpt from his speech, entitled "Diversity Is Canada's Strength."

"Why diversity is important? It's easy, in a country like Canada, to take diversity for granted. In so many ways, it's the air we breathe. We've raised generation after generation of children who think nothing of hearing five or six different languages spoken on the playground. Because it's 2015, people around the world are noticing the diversity of our Cabinet, and our Parliament. But the diversity of our country is not news. An MP colleague of mine once told me a story that captures it perfectly. He was doing a parliamentary exchange program in Paris. There were elected representatives from around the world present. He was asked what Canada 'looks like.' He was accompanied by four other colleagues, none of whom except him were born in Canada. Among them were three women and two men. Two Catholics, an Ismaili Muslim, a Jew whose parents had survived the Holocaust, and a gay protestant minister. One was born in France, one in Portugal. Another was born in Argentina. Another in Tanzania. He pointed to his colleagues and said: 'Well, this. This is what Canada looks like.'... Just consider the words that people use to describe Canada: we're open, accepting, progressive and prosperous. There is a direct line between each of those attributes and Canada's success in building a more diverse and inclusive society. We're not the only nation that's tried to do it. But what's made it work so well in Canada is the understanding that our diversity isn't a challenge to be overcome or a difficulty to be tolerated. Rather, it's a tremendous source of strength."

Source: Government of Canada website <pm.gc.ca/eng/news/2015/11/26/diversity-canadas-strength>.

in varying degrees and at all levels of employment across Canada. Yet, a 2018 study by the Canadian Association of University Teachers reveals that racialized faculty comprise only 21.1 percent of all university faculty and only 15 percent of all college faculty. Indigenous professors make up less than 1.5 percent of all faculty, and Black professors represent 2 percent of all faculty (which has remained constant over the last decade).[11] In other words, equality, diversity and human rights policies tend to be drafted as reactionary measures to something or as a result of someone demonstrating that disadvantage exists within the structure. Equality, diversity and human rights policies are often created *after* inequality and rights violations are entrenched in employment, healthcare, criminal justice, education and other various systems across Canada.

For example, the *R v. Gladue* (1999) Supreme Court decision explicitly mandated Canadian courts to consider the unique circumstances of Indigenous Peoples and the impact of colonialism and the residential school legacy in its sentencing and treatment of Indigenous women and girls and men and boys in 1999. However, while the crime rates in Canada continue to remain at record low levels, the incarceration rate for Indigenous women has increased 112 percent in the last ten years, nearly twenty years after Gladue. More so, while Indigenous youth comprise 8 percent of the total youth population in Canada, they represent nearly 50 percent of all youth in custody in Canada.[12] This dramatic overrepresentation is not explained by factors like the nature of the offence or criminal history. In other words, it is not simply that Indigenous women commit more serious offences or have more extensive criminal histories. In fact, they are less likely to commit a violent offence compared to non-Indigenous women. While policies and laws are created, even as reactionary measures, to address the unequal treatment of Indigenous Peoples, discrimination and racism persist (see Chapters 4 and 5 for more detailed discussions).

Yet as with human rights, expressions of diversity remain expressions of social privilege and oppression, of marginalization, exploitation, violence, ethnocentrism, cultural hegemony and powerlessness. Multiculturalism (see Chapter 4 for a more detailed discussion) is presented as a concept to support and promote human rights and social inclusion. Think about the concept of multiculturalism. This concept is influenced by our socio/legal/political/historical realities; however, in reality the outcome of multiculturalism as an ideology infers sameness. As Roger Maaka and Augie

---

Box 1.8 Think About...

The following is an excerpt from a *Maclean's* magazine article exploring Canada's prisons as modern-day residential schools:

"In the U.S., the go-to example for the asymmetric jailing of minority populations, black men are six times more likely to be imprisoned than white men. In Canada, the Indigenous incarceration rate is 10 times higher than the non-Indigenous population—higher even than South Africa at the height of apartheid. In Saskatchewan, if you're Indigenous, you're 33 times more likely to be incarcerated, according to a 1999 report, the most recent available. This helps explain why prison guard is among the fastest-growing public sector occupations on the Prairies. And why criminologists have begun quietly referring to Canada's prisons and jails as the country's "new residential schools."

Source: Nancy Macdonald, "Canada's Prisons Are the New 'Residential Schools,'" *Maclean's* 2016. <macleans.ca/news/canada/canadas-prisons-are-the-new-residential-schools/>.

DIVERSITYINACTIONDIVERSITYINACT

Box 1.9 Diversity in Action

What Are Canadian Values?

In 2017, Kellie Leitch began a sensational and contentious campaign in her bid for leadership of the federal Conservative Party. Leitch's controversial plan to screen immigrants for "anti-Canadian values" ignited national debate about immigration policy and what it means to be Canadian. Leitch drafted a list of questions potential immigrants would be asked in their initial screening, including:

  Are men and women equal, and entitled to equal protection under the law? Is it ever ok to coerce or use violence against an individual or a group who disagrees with your views?

  Do you recognize that to have a good life in Canada you will need to work hard for yourself and your family, and that you can't expect to have things you want given to you?

  The questions and Leitch's campaign in general were largely touted as thinly veiled bigotry and left the now disgraced MP repeatedly having to defend what she meant by Canadian values and to defend herself against charges of being racist.

Fleras argue, diversity is an acceptable social outcome of multiculturalism as long as we are different in the same way.[13] Boxes 1.7–1.9 exemplify the inference of cultural sovereignty in narratives surrounding diversity: as Canadians *we* are all different but *we* have the same values, morals or beliefs. If multiculturalism "normalizes" our differences as similarities, it is easy to understand how and why many of our current rights violations go undetected or remain out of the dominant discourse.

Social Rights and Diversity

Social rights centre around rights that apply to things like education, healthcare, social assistance, socioeconomic well-being and citizenship. More specifically, they make the right to things like adequate housing, food security and clothing fundamental rights of all citizens. However, understanding diversity through the lens of human rights suggests that access to social rights is inconsistent and inadequate at best. Studies from across Canada indicate there is a significant gap in access to healthcare for those Canadians living in poverty or on the street, or for those who are Indigenous or elderly.[14] Sara Cumming discusses in detail the limitations and inadequacies of social assistance in Canada and how perceptions of need are affected by stereotypes of who accesses assistance and what social assistance benefits really are in Chapter 6 of this text. Social rights to housing, which physically translates into subsidized housing units, are usually underfunded, have extensive waitlists (some as long as ten years or have nearly 100,00 people in need of housing), and many are unsafe and require millions of dollars in repair.[15] Furthermore, food banks, year-after-year, indicate a growing need for support as more people access food banks across the country, yet they also report significant shortfalls in meeting the food security needs of their communities.[16]

As previously discussed, basic fundamental rights to education of Indigenous children varies greatly compared to non-Indigenous children. While the 2018 federal budget earmarks over $5 billion for "Indigenous and Northern Investments," only $10 million is dedicated to Métis postsecondary education. Elementary schools remain underfunded, understaffed and largely ignored. What monies have been dedicated to education do little to strengthen pathways for children from elementary school to high school to postsecondary school, regardless of where they live. As discussed in more detail below, perceptions of Indigenous communities as others or as a minority group within Canada reinforces the structure that limits opportunities for Indigenous children and justifies continued rights violations of Indigenous children.

Civil Rights

Rights violations and challenges of people's civil rights (or rights that are based on laws or legal decisions) have been well-documented in Canada over the last several years. Civil rights violations of those living on the margins and in marginalized communities persist and are further evidence that diversity often means disadvantage for many Canadians. Consider the following:

- Indigenous women, men, girls and boys are more likely to be questioned and documented by police, are more likely to be charged by police, are less likely to obtain counsel, are more likely to be denied bail, are more likely to be held in remand, are more likely to be sentenced to custody and are more likely to receive longer sentences of incarceration;
- the failure of police services across Canada to adequately investigate cases of missing and murdered Indigenous women and girls[17];
- the failure of police services to adequately investigate the disappearance of several marginalized men in Toronto, allowing alleged serial killer Bruce McArthur to prey on gay men for over a decade without detection[18];
- offenders in prison spending egregiously long periods of time in segregation, well-documented for mentally ill inmates and federally sentenced Indigenous women[19];
- racial profiling of racialized Canadians by judicial agents (see Chapter 4 for more discussion);

- continued violations of the "Mandela Rule" in prisons across Canada (United Nations Standard Minimum Rules for the Treatment of Prisoners).[20]

This list comprises only a few selected examples of continued civil rights violations to demonstrate how precarious lived experience and rights protections are for diverse Canadians.

Political Rights

When we consider political rights we often think about the right to vote or assemble or protest but when we once again consider diversity and human rights, we understand how navigating political rights and public spaces to assemble, protest or vote are often mitigated by one's social location. Analysis of social protests and social movements like Idle No More (which began in December of 2012) and Black Lives Matter (founded in July 2013) suggests a perpetuation of colonial and racist ideation and sometimes severely biased coverage. Christie Blatchford's racist column in the *National Post* in 2012 used words like "inevitable puffery and horse manure" in her column headline to describe the Idle No More movement and Chief Theresa Spence's hunger strike. An op-ed piece written by Jeffrey Simpson, which appeared in the *Globe and Mail* in 2013 entitled "Too many first nations people live in a dream palace" questions the lived "reality" of Indigenous Peoples and allies. In 2013, the Calgary *Sun* was accused of fuelling racism after publishing comments and polls from readers that perpetuated stereotypes, racism, hate and colonial mistruths about Idle No More.

The coverage of Black Lives Matter movements across the world were inundated with racism both implicitly and explicitly. Black Lives Matter Toronto co-founder Janaya Kahn discusses media coverage of Black Canadians:

> When language is being used like "hijacked," when language is being used like "bullied," when language is being used like "hostage," these are really problematic and very dangerous, particularly when we hosted a sit-in in a public place. So the question that always comes up is: would this have been different if we were six white men? Would they be using that language then? I don't think so. I've never seen that language used when white people have demonstrations. We didn't see the media cover Occupy the way that they covered BLMTO Tent City. We saw the police treat Occupy in a certain way. They were allowed to have tents and fire. We were not allowed to have those in the middle of winter at Tent City for all 15 days that we were there. So I think the media has been deeply irresponsible. I think the media has been anti-black in its practice.[21]

In their content analysis of American media coverage of Black Lives Matter, Mohamad Hamas Elmasry and Mohammed el-Nawawy conclude:

> African Americans, as well as other minorities, are more likely portrayed as violent and dangerous, while the white majority is portrayed as victim, and capitalized on investment of concepts like victimization and humanization in perpetuating negative stereotypes about African Americans, enforcing white privilege and downplaying white crime.[22]

It is clear that navigating public space and engaging in the right to assemble and protest is not always perceived as a universal right. The implications of racist, biased and stereotypical media coverage may negatively influence perceptions of political rights, and the "disrupters' validity" is questioned by the dominant discourse. For those Canadians living on the margins, accessing these political rights are presented in a way that ultimately distorts the cause of the movement or social protest.

Cultural Rights

Cultural rights expressly reinforce the protection of ancestral language, the freedom to practise rituals and customs and the protection of ancestral land. The United Nations Declaration of the Rights of Indigenous Peoples (UNDRIP) was first adopted by the General Assembly in 2007 and is a set of individual and collective cultural, economic and political rights. However, Canada remained one of four member nations who opposed the declaration, citing a conflict of interest with the Charter, mainly with Article 26 of the UNDRIP: "Indigenous peoples have the right to the lands, territories and resources which they have traditionally owned, occupied or otherwise used or acquired." Canada's ambassador to the UN, John McNee, argued that the declaration is "overly broad, unclear and capable of a wide variety of interpretations," which could lead to the resurrecting of settled land claims and existing treaties.[23] It took nearly ten years for Canada to support the declaration, which appears to be an intentional delay to address sovereignty, self-governance and land claims, rather than that the UNDRIP overlooks cultural rights to food, culturally specific healthcare and housing and self-determination. Cultural diversity and the discourse of cultural rights of Indigenous Peoples often suffers from **ethnocentrism**, whereby Indigenous cultural rights are evaluated against the dominate hegemonic cultural discourse.

The TRC provides overwhelming evidence of the role the Canadian government played in the cultural genocide of Indigenous Peoples through the creation of residential schools. Set up and maintained by the government and churches to assimilate Indigenous children into mainstream society, residential schools were essentially

Box 1.10 Innov8

Indigenous Language Rights

As part of its 2015 election platform to promote and protect Indigenous languages, the Liberal government engaged in a consultation with leaders from the Assembly of First Nations, Inuit Tapiriit Kanatami and Métis National Council to inform legislation to promote and protect ninety languages and dialects identified in Canada by the UN. This includes tabling legislation that will make the recognition of Indigenous languages a fundamental right under the Constitution. Natan Obed, president of the Inuit Tapiriit Kanatami, said legislation will go "beyond the symbolism" but suggests a factor in the success of the legislation is whether the government can ensure Indigenous speakers are able to access federal government services and education in their Indigenous language, saying: "It's an essential part of our ability to be Inuit within Canada."

Source: Alex Ballingall, "Ottawa Planning Law to Recognize Indigenous Language Rights," June 1, 2018 <thestar.com/news/canada/2018/06/01/ottawa-planning-law-to-recognize-indigenous-language-rights.html>.

designed to destroy Indigenous culture (for more detailed discussions of the residential school legacy, see Chapters 4 and 5). While some small strides have been made toward reconciliation (see Box 1.10), there are reminders that the recognition of cultural rights is still unjust and inconsistent in Canada. The federal government's 2018 announcement of intention to purchase of the Trans Mountain pipeline, the plans for which include developing on sacred lands that ought to be protected under cultural rights, is a reminder of how the federal government continues to justify cultural rights violations.

Economic Rights

Economic rights are seen as contentious by some and simply ambitious by others.[24] There is a deeply entrenched stereotype in the dominant discourse about *who* receives assistance or support and *why*: specifically, ideas that social assistance is usually accessed by newcomers or that people who receive assistance do so because they are "lazy" and will not work. While both are false, it is this stereotype that permeates conversations about economic rights and makes these provisions highly controversial. Immigrants, the poor, the homeless, women and low-income earners become easy targets of the stereotype, while facts about access and supports are ignored (see Chapter 6 for a more detailed discussion).

Economic rights are also seen as aspirational, in that our intentions to provide assistance are hindered by inadequate funding, inconsistent models of support (compare

Box 1.11 Innov8

The Living Wage

"A living wage is the hourly wage a worker needs to earn to cover their family's basic expenses within their community. It is calculated based on the needs of a two-parent family with young children, but would also support a family throughout the life cycle so that young adults are not discouraged from having children and older workers have some extra income as they age."

Living wages are not rights guaranteed by the Charter or provincial or territorial social assistance legislation. Advocates argue that the living wage be based on regional calculations of what employers pay their employees that is sufficient to maintaining a dignified standard of living. Living wage rates vary dramatically across Canada:

Victoria, BC - $20.50	Edmonton, AB - $16.31
North Central BC - $16.51	Waterloo, ON - $16.10
Winnipeg, MB - $14.54	Simcoe County, ON - $17.74
Whitehorse, YK - $18.26	Nipiwan, SK - $15.17
Calgary, AB - $18.15	

Source: Living wage rates come from communities across Canada that have calculated the "living wage rate" and publish these rates on <livingwage.ca>.

the platforms of your province's or territory's political parties and you will see they vary dramatically in terms of supporting and funding social assistance) and most importantly our current social assistance programs, which fall significantly short in providing comprehensive support. Paying all employees across Canada a living wage is seen as a more innovative solution to both these issues. The rationale is that if we pay people a wage that realistically covers housing, food and clothing expenses there would be less demand on social assistance programs to provide support. See Box 1.11 for a more detailed discussion of the living wage in Canada.

Environmental Rights

Environmental rights are the obligation of the state to protect all persons from environmental harms. These rights and the ability to protect people from environmental harms are also, at times, controversial. There is debate about what constitutes harm, the extent of environmental harm done and questions of how we effectively protect people when individual responses to harm are so varied? Do we all have equal access to the protection of environmental rights? In Canada, socioeconomic well-being hinders equitable access to environmental rights enforcement and protection from negative

> **Box 1.12 Think About...**
>
> **The Story of Grassy Narrows**
>
> For almost a decade during the 1960s Reed Paper dumped over 10 tonnes of mercury into the Wabigoon River, the lifeblood of the Grassy Narrows First Nation community in Ontario. While government officials became aware of the mercury poisoning in the 1990s, it was not until 2017 that residents and scientists exposed the cover-up and confirmed the continued contamination. Over forty years later the long term physical and mental health effects are profound, and Grassy Narrows residents have considerably worse health outcomes compared to any other Indigenous community in Canada. Watch the Toronto *Star* investigation "How mercury exposure has affected Grassy Narrows residents": <youtube.com/watch?time_continue=9&v=jVNJlPBjhFQ>.
>
> Source: Jayme Poisson and David Bruser, "Landmark Study Reveals 'Clear Evidence' of Mercury's Toll on Health in Grassy Narrows," May 24, 2018 <thestar.com/news/investigations/2018/05/24/landmark-study-reveals-clear-evidence-of-mercurys-toll-on-health-in-grassy-narrows.html>.

environmental outcomes. The narratives of the Grassy Narrows First Nation and the Neskantaga First Nation exemplify how being Indigenous is linked to continued and fractured environmental rights (see Boxes 1.12 and 1.13).

INDIGENOUS RIGHTS

The history of Indigenous Peoples and the horrific and enduring impact of colonialism, the residential school legacy (the last of which closed in the 1990s) and the Sixties Scoop on Indigenous communities and lands is well documented by the TRC. The Sixties Scoop refers to the government-designed and approved adoptions of Indigenous children from their families in the 1960s. The literal scooping of children from their homes was a byproduct of colonialism to assimilate Indigenous children into the mainstream.

Our systems of laws and human rights were constructed, developed and have been maintained largely through colonial ideologies and colonial institutions (e.g., government, politics, religion, education, criminal justice).[25] It is difficult to understand how rights designed to protect people are inexorably linked with the social institutions responsible for a cultural genocide and other horrors against Indigenous Peoples. Colonialism exists and persists to subordinate and disadvantage Indigenous Peoples and communities and questions Indigenous identity; as a result, Indigenous often becomes synonymous with minority. James Tully explains: "Indigenous people exist *within* the dominant societies as minorities, domestic, dependent nations, aboriginal

Box 1.13 Think About...

The Right to Clean Water

The Neskantaga First Nation, a northern Ontario community, has been without safe tap water since 1995. For over twenty years the Neskantaga have not been able to drink water from their taps or bathe in the water without getting sick. Neskantaga Chief Wayne Moonias contends: "Water is a basic human right, and it should not have taken this long to provide the people of Neskantaga with access to safe drinking water." Federal funding promised to the Neskantaga to end the boil water advisory in 2018 was still not complete upon publishing of this text. How can Canada violate basic human rights of its people? Would the boil water advisory have gone on this long if it had been a city like Montreal, Toronto or Vancouver instead of a remote First Nations community?

Source: Judy Porter, "Canada's Longest-Standing First Nations Boil Water Advisory Will End in 2018, Liberals Say," July 28, 2017 <cbc.ca/news/canada/thunder-bay/neskantaga-water-plan-1.4225889>.

Box 1.14 Think About...

Watch the CBCS news report about the Adopt an Indian and Métis program from 1968: <cbc.ca/player/play/1177224259554/>.

The cumulative impact of genocide, colonialism, the residential school legacy and the Sixties Scoop for Indigenous women, men, girls and boys has resulted in:
- intergenerational trauma;
- higher rates of victimization, violence, abuse, addiction and suicide;
- overrepresentation, in varying degrees, at all levels of the criminal justice system — applies to men and boys but is especially true for women and girls;
- exposure to higher rates of violent crime and more likely to suffer from intimate partner violence;
- an unknown number of women and girls missing and murdered;
- reduced access to healthcare;
- poorer health outcomes, including lower life expectancy, lower birth rates, higher rates of diabetes;
- reduced access to education (especially high school and postsecondary);
- the most frequent and longest boil water advisories on record in Canada;
- exposure to substandard living conditions; and
- higher rates of unemployment.

Source: The cumulative findings are presented in the Truth and Reconciliation Commission, Final Report, 2015 <trc.ca/websites/trcinstitution/index.php?p=890>.

peoples or First Nations *of* Canada and so on" and not as first peoples to the land.[26] This is done to maintain the construction of a false ideology where Indigenous Peoples are perceived as a minority group in comparison to the rest of non-Indigenous Canada. Roger Merino Acuña explains further: "These discourses stem from understanding Indigenous rights as ethnic minority rights, to ensure their inclusion within the political and economic framework of the state, 'tolerating' their cultural diversity."[27] The result is a society where intergenerational racism persists, and Indigenous Peoples are forced to interact and exist within systems deeply entrenched in colonialism.

Tully explains that the persistent strategy to extinguish the rights of Indigenous Peoples is undertaken in several ways, which maintains intergenerational racism and a belief system entrenched in explicit and implicit rights-denial. The first centres around the question of rights ownership and whether Indigenous Peoples should have self-governing rights or not. A public opinion survey of non-Indigenous Canadians reveals that Canadians are divided on whether they believe Indigenous Peoples have unique rights as the first inhabitants of Canada or have rights similar to other cultural or ethnic minority groups in society.[28] About half of those who responded supported the statement that Indigenous Peoples have unique rights as the original inhabitants of the land; however, these opinions varied greatly from the East Coast (more likely to support) to the West Coast (less likely to support). While opinions vary, it appears the state continues to wade in muddy waters, while making some decisions to uphold and create new rights (see Box 1.10 about Indigenous language rights) while others perpetuate a denial of rights (e.g., TransCanada Pipeline, centred on land and treaty rights). Rights are then extinguished through laws, decision-making, ideas about sovereignty or through treaties, agreements and partnerships with the state.[29]

Finally, Indigenous Peoples as unique rights-protected people are simply thought of as unnecessary if they are assimilated into the dominate, settler society (continuously achieved through colonialism) and this questions Indigenous status, personhood and subsequently rights. One could conclude that the need for Indigenous rights is superfluous if Indigenous Peoples are considered a minority group, part of a larger collective, sovereign state. The resistance to Indigenous self-governance and treaty claims is further evidence of colonialism and a continued effort to extinguish the rights of Indigenous peoples.[30] Rights-infringement continues to legitimize the settlement of Indigenous land, and resistance to such efforts are presented in a way that

Box 1.15 Innov8

Listen to the CBC podcasts "Missing and Murdered," which explore actual cases of missing and murdered Indigenous women and girls.

Box 1.16 Think About...

In 2017, Lynn Beyak, now-disgraced senator removed from the national caucus, made headlines when she claimed residential schools were "good" for some and went on to post racist and discriminatory letters of "support" on her website. Offering his support, Beyak's son, a city councillor in Dryden, ON, argued: "Whether anyone wants to admit it or not, the majority of Canadians agree with the comments Sen. Beyak has said.... How can you say that nurses and priests were bad people and did no good at those schools? How can a logical person say that and call a person who says that a racist? The connection is impossible." How are Beyak's actions and the words of her son evidence of intergenerational racism? How are these beliefs passed from one generation to the next?

Source: Andray Domise, "Lynn Beyak and the Real Danger of Racist Fabulism," *Maclean's*, January 9, 2018 <macleans.ca/opinion/lynn-beyak-and-the-real-danger-of-racist-fabulism/>.

---

questions legitimate status (who was here "first") and authority (proof of who you are — title, blood quantum, status) from legitimate land claims. Examples include Ipperwash, Caledonia, Oka, the Pinery, *R v. Caulder* (1973), *R v. Sparrow* (1990), and many more. As Manuhuia Barcham argues, the "problems of 'indigenous identity' are, in turn, symptomatic of a more fundamental deficiency in our current theories and praxis of indigenous rights: the recognition of difference in terms of the maintenance of prior identity."[31] While the current Liberal federal government proposes to work with Indigenous communities they are not obliged to get consent or partner with Indigenous communities (consider the federal government's purchase of the Trans Mountain pipeline and the ongoing struggle of Indigenous communities to block development that infringes on and destroys Indigenous land).

If we examine protections of individual rights through the Constitution or the Charter, we have to acknowledge that these are part of a larger colonial framework and that, despite explicit protections (e.g., section 35 of the Constitution Act and section 25 of the Charter [see Box 1.17]), violations of these rights persist. Social, political, economic and cultural legal safeguards designed to protect Indigenous individual and group rights are then problematized. In spite of a growing appreciation of Indigenous history and the positive impact of the TRC and its findings, decision-making and questions of self-governance remain heavily entrenched in colonial attitudes and ways of thinking about settler society. The call for cultural self-determination brings to light the difficulty in balancing individual cultural rights and human rights. Indigenous Peoples continue to be victims of gross human rights violations.

Box 1.17 Diversity in Action

Canadian Charter of Rights and Freedoms:
s. 25. The guarantee in this Charter of certain rights and freedoms shall not
be construed as to abrogate or derogate from any Aboriginal, treaty or other
rights or freedoms that pertain to the aboriginal peoples of Canada including
(a) any rights or freedoms that have been recognized by the Royal
Proclamation of October 7, 1763; and
(b) any rights or freedoms that now exist by way of land claims agreements or
may be so acquired.

GENDER AND HUMAN RIGHTS

Human rights, in theory, are equal for all individuals but we know this is not always
the case for some people, especially women. Women and girls are more likely to live
in poverty, more likely to be victimized, more likely to be paid a lower wage for equal
work, more likely to be the victim of a domestic homicide and more likely to suffer from
the stereotypes that limit them from jobs in science, technology, engineering and math.
Rights-based feminists argue that equality is achieved through equal participation, equal
pay and empowerment in decision-making. However, as we have seen throughout this
chapter, the creation of laws, policies and regulations does not necessarily translate into
meaningful social change for women and girls, especially marginalized women and
girls (see Chapter 7 for a thorough examination of gender and diversity).

SEXUAL DIVERSITY AND HUMAN RIGHTS

An examination of human rights and diversity compels one to examine how we balance
individual rights over cultural rights. This is no more evident than in a discussion of
sexual diversity and human rights. The UN dictates that there ought to be a priority
of human rights over cultural rights but similar to the examination of religious rights
and sexual reproduction rights (see Box 1.1), it is clear there is disconnect between
individual rights like sexual rights and heteronormativity as a cultural right. Michael

Box 1.18 Innov8

What is Indigenous activism? Watch the National Film Board documentary
"The Road Forward," a documentary/musical that explores the roots of civil
rights and Indigenous Activism in Canada.

Box 1.19 Think About...

In 2015, CBC reporter Shauna Hunt was interviewing spectators at a Toronto Football Club match when a man yelled an obscenity live on-air at the reporter. The incident was posted to Twitter by the reporter and was widely covered in the media. Search the incident online, and you will find out the man was originally fired from his job at Hydro One but appealed the decision and remains an employee of the publicly funded company. How does this example demonstrate the complex balance between human rights and gender?

Freeman writes: "How should we define the right to freedom of religion of those whose religion denies that all human beings are equal in rights? How can we make sense of human rights if the implementation of some human rights requires the violation of others?"[32] Freeman calls this quandary "compossible," whereby the protection of some rights may require the violation of others and vice versa. He uses the example of settler rights that did not include rights protection of Indigenous Peoples or women.

There have been significant social, legal and cultural changes surrounding the protection of sexual rights. However, Chapter 8 explores sexual diversity and how the dominant discourse and the desire to protect cultural rights over individual rights continues to problematize the sexual rights of all Canadians.

DISABILITY AND HUMAN RIGHTS

Human rights violations based on disability take many forms: unemployment, under-employment, institutionalization, social and political exclusion, violence and abuse, and a lack of access to social services and social supports. There is prejudice and discrimination embedded in the principal barriers to the participation of persons with disabilities in all rights: social, civil, political, economic and cultural. Section 15 of the Charter prohibits discrimination based on mental or physical disability; however, we see in Chapter 9 that violations of human rights because of disability have not been thoroughly addressed through legislation, policy or regulation.

CONCLUSION

This chapter explores human rights within the context of Canadian diversity and highlights the complex relationship Canada has both as enforcer and perpetrator of human rights violations. The paradox of human rights further problematizes human rights standards and current legislation as simply human rights protection in theory

Box 1.20 Innov8

Read more about government programs that resulted in significant human and sexual rights violations and perpetuated homophobia in Chapter 8. For more, watch the 2018 documentary "The Fruit Machine," directed by Sarah Fodey: <tvo.org/video/documentaries/the-fruit-machine>. Chapter 8 also details the story of Jim Egan, Canada's first gay rights activist. To learn more watch Canada's first LGBT2TQ Heritage Minute: <youtube.com/watch?v=rac4WiTDQHg>.

but not always in practice, which is especially true for Canadians living on the margins of society. Freeman argues that the backlash against extending rights or revisiting existing ones is a result of "rights inflation," where human rights as a concept is perceived as being extended to too many different causes, issues, events or circumstances. The remaining chapters in this book provide compelling evidence for human rights extensions, continued meaningful discourse and profound changes to the enforcement of rights protections for all Canadians.

CRITICAL REVIEW QUESTIONS

1. If you could create one human rights law, what would it be and why do you think it is needed?
2. How are human rights similar to legal rights? How are they different?
3. Look up examples of current human rights cases in your province or territory. How are they similar or different to historical human rights cases?
4. Despite the Charter and existing human rights laws, does the treatment of human rights vary in practice? Use specific Canadian examples to illustrate your answer.
5. How do you think human rights will change over the next fifty years as society changes?

RECOMMENDED READINGS

Canadian Charter of Rights and Freedoms (1982).

Peter Knegt, *About Canada: Queer Rights* (Halifax and Winnipeg: Fernwood Publishing, 2011).

Robyn Maynard, *Policing Black Lives: State Violence in Canada from Slavery to the Present* (Halifax and Winnipeg: Fernwood Publishing, 2017).

Lisa Monchalin, *The Colonial Problem: An Indigenous Perspective on Crime and Injustice in Canada* (Toronto: University of Toronto Press, 2016).

Senate Committee on Human Rights, *Life on the Inside: Human Rights in Canada's Prisons* (2017).
Truth and Reconciliation Commission Report (2015).
United Nations Declaration on Human Rights (1948, 2015).

KEY TERMS

ethnocentrism: evaluating the world from the perspective of a person's own culture.
human rights: the ethical, moral and fundamental characteristics of a society They are universal, equal and all people have them.
negative rights: cannot be denied by the state or anyone in it: the right to life, individual safety and security, freedom from undue interference of the state, integrity, free speech.
positive rights: must be provided by the state: food, clothing, housing, healthcare, education, employment, social assistance.
rights-oriented movements: social justice movements that emphasize human rights.
rights-protected people: all human beings in a society who have human rights.
rights violations: abuses of human rights.

Notes

1. Roger Maaka and Augie Fleras, "Engaging with Indigeneity: Tino Rangatiratanga in Aotearoa," in Duncan Ivison, Paul Patton and Will Sanders (eds.), *Political Theory and the Rights of Indigenous Peoples* (New York: Cambridge, 2000), 107.
2. For a detailed history of human rights development, see Michael Freeman, *Human Rights* (Massachusetts: Polity Press, 2017).
3. For a discussion of human rights as a moral system, see Judith Blau and Mark Frezzo (eds.), *Sociology and Human Rights: A Bill of Rights for the Twenty-First Century* (Los Angeles: Sage, 2012), 3.
4. Blau and Frezzo, *Sociology and Human Rights,* 3.
5. James W. Nickel, *Making Sense of Human Rights*, 2nd ed. (Malden, MA: Blackwell, 2007).
6. The exact difference in spending has been widely debated over the last several years, with some arguing different funding models make it impossible to compare Indigenous and non-Indigenous education. However, the 2013 policy report *The Debate on First Nations Education Funding: Mind the Gap*, by Don Drummond and Ellen Kachuck Rosenbluth, makes the differences clear. Their findings mirror the well-documented disparities that exist for all Indigenous People in funding for healthcare, education and income.
7. Scott Gilmore, "Canada's Race Problem? It's Even Worse than America's," January 22, 2015 <macleans.ca/news/canada/out-of-sight-out-of-mind-2/>; Statistics Canada, *Insights on Canadian Society: Young Men and Women Without a High School Diploma*, 2017 <150. statcan.gc.ca/n1/en/pub/75-006-x/2017001/article/14824-eng.pdf?st=-hOYIGBx>.
8. Anthony Woodiwiss, *Human Rights* (London: Routledge, 2005).
9. Judith Blau, "Going Forward," in Blau and Frezzo, *Sociology and Human Rights*, 273.
10. Blau and Frezzo, *Sociology and Human Rights*.
11. CAUT Online, "The Slow March Toward Equity," April 2018 <caut.ca/bulletin/2018/04/slow-march-toward-equity>.

12. Adult and youth correctional statistics in Canada, 2016/2017, released Tuesday, June 19, 2018 <150.statcan.gc.ca/n1/daily-quotidien/180619/dq180619a-eng.htm>.

13. Maaka and Fleras, "Engaging with Indigeneity."

14. Homeless Hub, "How Can We Improve Healthcare Access for the Homeless," n.d. <homelesshub.ca/resource/how-can-we-improve-healthcare-access-homeless>.

15. Jennifer Pagliaro, "Planned Closure of Hundreds of Social Housing Units Called 'Failure' of Governments as Waiting List Grows." April 25, 2017 <thestar.com/news/city_hall/2017/04/25/planned-closure-of-hundreds-of-social-housing-units-called-failure-of-governments-as-waiting-list-grows.html>.

16. S.J. Cumming, Michael McNamara, Jessica E. Pulis and Rory Sommers, *Housing Hurdles: Housing for Everyone,* Report for Halton Region (December 2016).

17. National Inquiry into Missing and Murdered Indigenous Women and Girls <http://www.mmiwg-ffada.ca/>.

18. A full investigation of the Toronto Police Service and the Bruce McArthur case will take place after McArthur's trial. At the time this chapter was written, McArthur has been charged with eight counts of murder; however, this number may increase as police continue their forensic investigation.

19. I. Zinger, "Annual Report," Office of the Correctional Investigator 2016–2017, 2017.

20. Zinger, "Annual Report."

21. Zane Schwartz, "How a Black Lives Matter Toronto Co-Founder Sees Canada," July 8, 2016 <macleans.ca/news/canada/how-black-lives-matter-co-founder-janaya-khan-sees-canada>.

22. Mohamad Hamas Elmasry and Mohammed El-Nawawy, "Do Black Lives Matter? A Content Analysis of New York Times and St. Louis Post-Dispatch Coverage of Michael Brown Protests," *Journalism Practice*, 11 (2016), 1–19.

23. CBC Online, "Canada Votes 'No' as UN Rights Declaration Passes," September 13, 2007 <cbc.ca/news/canada/canada-votes-no-as-un-native-rights-declaration-passes-1.632160>.

24. For a detailed discussion see Daniel Béland and Pierre-Marc Daigneault (eds.), *Welfare Reform in Canada: Provincial Social Assistance in Comparative Perspective* (Toronto: University of Toronto Press, 2015).

25. Lisa Monchalin, *The Colonial Problem: An Indigenous Perspective on Crime and Injustice in Canada* (Toronto: University of Toronto Press, 2016).

26. James Tully, "The Struggles of Indigenous Peoples for and of Freedom," in Duncan Ivison, Paul Patton and Will Sanders (eds.), *Political Theory and the Rights of Indigenous Peoples* (New York: Cambridge, 2000), 37–38.

27. Roger Merino Acuña, "Minorities or Nations? Discourses and Policies of Recognition of Indigenous Peoples' Rights," *Alternautas*, 1, 1, (2014): 41–47 <alternautas.net/blog/2014/7/8/minorities-or-nations-discourses-and-policie-of-recognition-of-indigenous-peoples-rights>.

28. Keith Neuman, "Canadian Public Opinion on Aboriginal Peoples," 2016 <nctr.ca/assets/reports/Modern%20Reports/canadian_public_opinion.pdf>.

29. For a detailed history of treaties and their continued treatment and impact refer to the Truth and Reconciliation Commission of Canada <trc.ca/websites/trcinstitution/index.php?p=3>.

30. Manuhuia Barcham, "(De)Constructing the Politics of Indigeneity," in Duncan Ivison, Paul Patton and Will Sanders (eds.), *Political Theory and the Rights of Indigenous Peoples* (New York: Cambridge, 2000).

31. Barcham, "(De)Constructing the Politics of Indigeneity," 137.

32. Michael Freeman, *Human Rights*, p. 5.

2

REGIONALISM

GEOGRAPHY MEETS SOCIAL-PSYCHOLOGY

Paul U. Angelini

> *Two things hold this country together. Everybody hates Air Canada coffee and everybody hates Ontario.* — late New Brunswick premier Richard Hatfield

> *Canada is like an old cow. The West feeds it. Ontario and Quebec milk it. And you can well imagine what it's doing in the Maritimes.* — late Saskatchewan premier and father of universal medicare Tommy Douglas

KEY OBJECTIVES

Define regionalism.

Appreciate regional identities as part of Canadian social life.

Discuss the possible causes of regionalism.

Examine the factors that intensify regional differentiation.

Make the case for a socio-psychological component to regional
     thinking.

Regional competition and conflict are as old as Canada. Along with language and culture, regional rivalry is one of the three great cleavages in Canadian political life. Canada exists as a political creation — politicians cooperated to intentionally create a country out of no fewer than a dozen disparate regions. "Diversity" certainly describes Canadian regions politically, socially, economically, culturally and linguistically.

The purpose of this chapter is fourfold: (1) to examine the meaning of **regionalism**; (2) to outline some theoretical explanations for regionalism; (3) to explain the role of the federal government in creating regional differences and their paradoxical attempts to ameliorate such differences; and, most importantly, (4) to make the case for the existence of a socio-psychological component to regionalism. This chapter does not attempt to establish the definitive causes of regionalism. Such attempts usually result in theoretical and ideological stalemates. These debates tell us little about the people living in specific regions and what they think about Canada and their place in it. We do, however, outline some of the general explanations of regionalism put forth by writers and researchers. It is important to do your own research to confirm the ideas you accept and discard the ones you do not.

Canada is characterized by its size and physical features. From east to west and north to south, there are differences in physical terrain, climate, population density, natural resource distribution, urban-rural living, culture, ethnicity, religion, language, occupation and income. These differences are visible to all Canadians. What about what is not so visible — the more subjective differences? How do people feel about the regions they live in, about people living in other regions and about the politicians who govern them federally and provincially? The answers to these questions are critical to understanding regionalism because they bring a more personal, human element to this study. *The Task Force on Canadian Unity* reported in 1979: "The country was originally brought together from disparate regional communities which remain strongly attached to their local identities."[1] After all, regions are made up of people and people make regions.[2]

WHAT IS REGIONALISM AND WHY IS IT IMPORTANT?

Delineating what constitutes a region in Canada has always been a problematic enterprise. In part this is due to Canada's huge geographic size, as it is the second largest country on earth. There are many ways to divide Canada into regions. One way to organize regions is according to time zones; Canada is home to five and half time zones. This method overcomes the principal weakness of defining regions according to provincial borders since provinces themselves can vary widely. For example, northern Ontario and northern Quebec are markedly different from the southern parts of those provinces and can be considered regions on their own. These northern regions have far fewer people, who live in more isolated communities with fewer economic opportunities and still fewer healthcare and post-secondary school choices. Life is much different for those living in North Bay, Sudbury, Thunder Bay, Atikokan and Chisasibi than for those living in Ontario's **Golden Horseshoe,** which stretches from

Niagara Falls, around Lake Ontario through Hamilton, Mississauga and Toronto to Oshawa. This is especially the case with respect to the quantity and quality of employment opportunities and access to healthcare and education. Driving one hour north from Hamilton and driving one hour north from North Bay produce radically different experiences. Drivers travelling north from Hamilton for an hour will pass no less than seven universities/colleges and at least that many hospitals. Perform an online search for driving in the same direction from North Bay. What do you find on that drive?

Regions could also be defined by specific geographic and physical characteristics. The cordilleran mountains isolate British Columbia from the rest of Canada. British Columbians generally regard their province as unique, completely different from the three other western provinces. This is reinforced by the fact that the economies of the four western provinces are so different: British Columbia is the centre of the Canadian lumber industry and possesses a significant fishing industry, while farming remains essential to the economies of Manitoba and Saskatchewan, and Alberta is the centre of Canada's oil and natural gas industry. Other provinces have similar ideas. Newfoundland and Labrador, the last province to join Confederation, considers itself to be distinct geographically and in other ways from the rest of the Atlantic region. Other physical features include the prairies, which separate Alberta, Saskatchewan and Manitoba from the remainder of Canada, the St Lawrence River and Great Lakes, which separate central Canada from the west and east, and the Arctic tundra, which separates much of Nunavut, North West Territories and Yukon from southern Canada.

"Regions usually have some concrete, physical foundation…
But to some extent regions are also a state of mind."
— political scientist Rand Dyck

CAN PROVINCES BE CONSIDERED REGIONS?

There is no consensus as to whether provinces can be considered regions.[3] As mentioned above, areas within provinces can differ greatly. This is especially the case from an economic perspective. The economic prosperity of the Greater Toronto Area (GTA), Golden Horseshoe and some parts of central Ontario does not extend to its northern regions. The Golden Horseshoe is aptly named. According to Statistics Canada, nine of the top twenty cities for median total income are located in Ontario, while just over half (eleven) are located in central Canada.[4]

In spite of interprovincial differences, most analysts agree that provinces can be defined as regions. Residents in particular regions believe their physical landscape makes them unique and are naturally proud of this distinctiveness. Yet, a sense of social-psychological isolation is entwined with the physical separation. The role of provincial governments is to defend and nurture these differences, and the federal government is expected to never forget them. People make up regions, and they elect provincial politicians to represent and protect their interests first and foremost. This is reflected in the historical rise of political parties to represent the interests of specific regions. Some of the more famous include the Parti Québécois (1976) at the provincial level and the Bloc Québécois (1992) at the federal level in the province of Quebec and the Reform Party (2002) in western Canada. As some parties disappear from Canadian political life, others eventually rise to express the discontent of certain regions. Residents expect both provincial and federal governments to act in their interests. They have specific ideas about how their region should change or stay the same and about what roles should be played by provincial and federal governments. Naturally, the core of provincial government responsibilities is to protect and promote the interests of their inhabitants. This very fact, that provincial/territorial governments are elected to protect specific, provincial/territorial interests (even though these regions vary internally) is what makes provinces an appropriate tool in the study of regionalism.

Regions may have geographic and physical foundations, but residents impart their feelings and passions onto these geographic differences and in the process become attached to them. In short, they make these physical differences their own; the differences become part of their personal identity. This attachment manifests itself as feelings of difference and uniqueness that separate them from other Canadians. This is also reflected in language. John Ralston Saul writes: "Languages are deeply unconscious expressions of place — of geography and climate.... People develop their cultures through their experiences of these places. You only have to look at the effect of large cities on language over the last hundred years to understand this."[5] Feeling unique and different is generally shared among regional inhabitants and is expressed in political, economic, social, linguistic and psychological forms. The core of regionalism, therefore, as a socio-psychological phenomenon, is the attitudes shared by those living in the same geographical area. More specifically, regionalism is primarily rooted in real historical and geographic experiences and can be defined as "an attitude that reflects a long, deep, certain feeling held by citizens of a specific geographical area that they have their own unique identity."[6] An essential part of this identity is that residents believe that successive federal governments have not recognized their past and current hard work and sacrifice in two specific areas:

1. building their modern region;
2. helping build this country called Canada.

Regional attitudes are framed by the belief that Ottawa has ignored their interests and has actively preferred some regions at the expense of others, resulting in noticeable economic differences and quality-of-life disparities. To those outside Ontario and Quebec, the central region of Canada has far too much influence on policy-making, especially monetary and fiscal policy, while the western and Atlantic regions have relatively little. The linguistic accommodation between Ontario and Quebec that characterized early Canadian political development is recognized in school curricula as essential to building Canada. This idea is not shared by other regions that have different linguistic and cultural roots.

THE CAUSES OF REGIONALISM

There are multiple theoretical explanations for why some regions prosper and others do not. What follows is a brief sketch of the four most prominent explanations.[7]

Natural Resource Approach

In Canada, the natural resource approach is more commonly referred to as **staples theory** and is based on the work of famous Canadian political economist and economic historian Harold Innis.[8] Generally, this theory asserts that the availability of natural resources is directly related to regional prosperity. Such natural resources include fur (primarily beaver pelts in the early years of Canadian development), coal, fish, grain, lumber, oil, natural gas, minerals and water. This approach asks some crucial questions: Does a region have an abundance of a particular resource? Can industry be enticed to extract/develop the resources in a cost-effective manner? Can the resource be sold on international markets for profit in the face of international price fluctuations? Different regions have been adversely affected by both price fluctuations and resource availability. The Albertan economy has suffered enormously since the depression of world oil prices beginning in 2012–13. Western grain farmers are also at the mercy of changing international prices. They are operating enormously expensive twenty-first-century farms (machinery, technology and seeds are not cheap) on twentieth-century grain prices. Similarly, small fishing communities across Atlantic Canada were devastated when the federal government issued the cod fishing moratorium in 1992. It is not surprising that provincial governments demand financial compensation from Ottawa to help offset the uncertainties of the international marketplace. This was evident when the lumber industry was hard hit by countervailing duties on imports of selected Canadian softwood lumber products into the United States. In response, Ottawa announced a $867 million investment to support those adversely affected[9] (see Box 2.1). In June 2018, US tariffs on incoming Canadian steel had the steel industry asking for similar treatment.

> ## Box 2.1 Think About...
>
> ### Softwood Lumber in Canada
>
> Softwood lumber is made up of spruce, pine and fir and is used primarily for framing in construction. Generating an enormous $22 billion in gross domestic product (GDP) in 2016, it is essential to Canada's forest industry. In 2015 the forest industry accounted for 201,645 jobs, including 9,500 jobs in Indigenous communities. More than 600 mills across the country produce softwood lumber, positively affecting the economies of over 170 rural municipalities. An astounding total of $3 million in softwood lumber passes from Canada to the United States every hour of every day!
>
> On April 24, 2017, the United States announced that it would impose countervailing duties on the import of Canadian softwood lumber products. Ottawa hopes to assist affected workers with a massive $867 million investment and loan guarantee programs. It also hopes to support negatively affected communities, which are largely rural, "reduce the risk of job loss, stabilize operations, diversify markets and promote innovation in the sector."
>
> Source: Adapted from Government of Canada, *Softwood Lumber Factsheet* <www.nrcan.gc.ca/19605>.

The criticism of the natural resource approach is, as the examples demonstrate, that there is no guarantee that being endowed with an abundance of natural resources will lead to regional economic prosperity. While this caution reflects many regions across the country, it is especially true of Atlantic Canada. Ralph Mathews notes that in spite of its wealthy base of iron ore, coal, gold, forests, fish and hydroelectric power, the Atlantic region has remained poor throughout most of the period since Confederation, while southern Ontario has become wealthy without a natural resource base.[10]

Free Market Approach

The free market approach to explaining regional prosperity in Canada focuses on the operation of the market and its impact on creating regional winners and losers. This approach detests government interference in regional economic activity. It asserts that the unbridled operation of the free market should determine whether or not to invest in a specific region. Whatever is necessary to make an industry profitable should be allowed to happen without government interference. Wages should be allowed to fall, corporate taxes reduced, regulations eased, environmental standards relaxed and unions discouraged or decertified. In short, capital should not be penalized for closing plants and affected workers should simply pack up and move to where the jobs are. The free market approach (also known as **neoliberalism**) has dominated Western (and world) economic thinking and behaviour since the early 1980s. The United States under President Ronald Reagan and the United Kingdom under Prime Minister Margaret Thatcher vigorously pursued these policies regardless of social outcomes. In Canada, Progressive Conservative premiers Ralph Klein of Alberta (1992–2006) and Mike Harris of Ontario (1995–2002) allowed these ideas to dominate government policy. Prime Minister Stephen Harper did the same at the national level for two terms, from 2006 to 2015. Despite campaign promises to the contrary, the behaviour of the federal Liberal government of Justin Trudeau indicates that Canada is in for more of the same economic policies.[11]

Interventionist Approach

The interventionist approach puts forward the idea that regions prosper or struggle because government intervention favours some regions at the expense of others.[12] The interventionist approach is the exact opposite of the free market approach. Generally, the interventionist approach argues that politicians and the relevant bureaucracies should cooperate with the private sector to assist poorer regions. This approach does not regard regional differences as "natural," as does staples theory, or the result of market forces, as does the free market approach.

The federal government has always been involved in regional economic development, especially since 1945. The most visible examples are the massive **transfer payments** from the federal government to the provinces. The importance to Canada's poorer regions can be seen in per capita differences. Poorer regions rely more heavily on federal transfers than wealthier ones (see Table 2.1). These massive payments, totalling $72.8 billion in 2017–18, are designed to provide poorer provinces with the necessary fiscal assets to deliver services to their inhabitants at similar qualitative levels as wealthier provinces.[13] This especially applies to healthcare and maintaining its five national standards: all healthcare must be delivered by public administration on a not-for-profit basis; healthcare must be comprehensive and cover all necessary health services; it must be universal and cover all insured people equally; all insured people must have reasonable access to services; and finally, healthcare must be portable from province to province.

Marxist Approach

The Marxist approach uses class analysis to explain regional differentiation. For Marxists, uneven economic development is a natural outcome of capitalist behaviour and the endless search for profit. This pursuit of profit results in exploitation of workers (pay them less than the value of the goods or services they produce), oppression of women (pay them even less), destruction of the environment (promote the burning

Table 2.1 Federal Government Transfer Payments to Provinces, 2017–18

Province	Total Transfers (millions of dollars)	Per Capita (dollars)
Nunavut	1,582	42,055
Northwest Territories	1,295	28,867
Yukon	972	25,884
Prince Edward Island	599	3,981
New Brunswick	2,813	3,709
Nova Scotia	3,096	3,243
Manitoba	3,677	2,749
Quebec	22,714	2,710
Ontario	21,058	1,489
Newfoundland and Labrador	738	1,388
Saskatchewan	1,620	1,388
Alberta	5,996	1,388
British Columbia	6,666	1,388

Note: Payments include health and social transfers, equalization payments, offshore offsets, Territorial Formula Financing, transfer protection and any additional payments. For explanations and details see <www.fin.gc.ca/fedprov/mtp-eng.asp>.

of fossil fuels) and the creation of conflict among workers (pit workers with stable, full-time jobs against those in precarious employment).

The Marxist approach regards regional economic differences as the natural outcome of capitalist behaviour in three ways.[14] First, capitalists regard workers in poorer regions as surplus, or a "reserve army of labour," to be hired and fired as the capitalist sees fit. Workers from around Canada flooded Alberta when oil prices were high and the economy was humming along. These same workers were the first ones laid off (and returned to their home regions) when oil prices began to plummet. Second, raw materials from poorer regions are transported to wealthier ones to be processed. This deprives poorer regions of lucrative processing jobs and profits. Third, much more expensive processed raw materials are then sold back to the poorer regions.[15]

Perhaps the most vicious exploitation recognized by Marxists is how capitalists use the existence of poorer regions as threats to demand concessions from workers (less pay, longer hours, fewer benefits) and all levels of governments (tax cuts, fewer regulations, more taxpayer subsidies) in wealthier regions. This is common capitalist global practice. Companies in developed countries threaten workers and governments with moving plants to the developing world if their demands for concessions are not met. This leads to the precarious nature of working-class jobs.[16] The Ford Motor Company of Canada alone has extracted well over a billion dollars from the different levels of government to keep operations in Canada. This is especially the case with respect to its Oakville, Ontario, manufacturing plant.

CAUSES OF REGIONALISM: CHICKEN OR EGG?

The federal government is in the paradoxical position of both causing regional social, political and economic differentiation and adopting policies that attempt to ameliorate these same differences. We can analyze the historical behaviour of the federal government by examining the operation of federalism itself, the impact of Canada's electoral system and finally, Ottawa's choice of economic development policies.

How Federalism Operates

The framers of Canada's constitution were determined to choose a form of government that would allow for the complicated nature of building a country, even while they ignored Indigenous Peoples, who were used and abused to help this new project to fruition. They concluded that nation-building could only be accomplished by a central government with political power in key development areas — those that impact the entire country, such as national defence and taxation. Yet, they had to ameliorate the concerns of provincial leaders that a powerful central government would ignore their interests. The solution was a government structure that would allow the central government to build the nation and provincial representatives to care for local populations. The framers of the constitution chose **federalism**, a structure of governance where two levels of government exercise power and authority over the same territory and population, with neither level having the authority to abolish the other. Relations between the two levels of government are characterized by negotiation and cooperation, with each level having authority over specific areas of jurisdiction, clearly outlined in the Constitution. Section 91 outlines the twenty-nine federal powers, while sections 92, 93 and 94 outline provincial ones.

The framers assigned the national government in Ottawa a set of responsibilities that would enable the national government to carve a country out of a disparate collection of geographic regions represented by provincial governments. These provincial governments were given responsibilities that were considered "local" in nature in 1867, such as healthcare, education, social services and natural resources. The strategic and national importance of some provincial responsibilities changed dramatically as Canada and the world changed. Can you think of any?

Federalism and Quebec

Federal governance comes with its own problems.[17] First, the national government will tend to gravitate to the provinces with larger populations; that is, concerns of the larger provinces — Ontario, Quebec and sometimes Alberta — will almost always be taken into account before those of other provinces. This is especially the case with the province of Quebec and is clearly evident in the emotional and divisive political conflicts over the Meech Lake (1988) and Charlottetown (1992) constitutional accords, discussed below, and the 1995–2002 sponsorship scandal. The federal government has spent billions of dollars trying to win the hearts and minds of all Quebecers. There is one sound reason for this. While issues such as racial profiling by police in Toronto, housing prices in Vancouver, world oil prices in Alberta and the size of fish stocks in the Atlantic provinces may occupy the minds of provincial and civic leaders, they do not threaten to break up the country. In response to the strength of the separatist vote during the 1995 sovereignty referendum in Quebec, Ottawa decided to spend $250 million on a sponsorship program, which began in 1995 and ended in 2002. The purpose of the program was to raise the profile of the federal government in the province of Quebec by "sponsoring" popular events and activities held across the province. In return for cash, the Canadian flag would be prominently displayed at every event from the high profile Canadian Grand Prix in Montreal to more local cultural activities. The program quickly spiralled out of control. When career civil servant in public works and government services Allan Cutler went public with evidence of financial improprieties, federal auditor general Sheila Fraser recommended the RCMP investigate how sponsorship money was handed out to advertising and communications agencies. Slowly a picture began to take shape of phony invoices, double billing and outrageous fees involving five crown corporations (Business Development Bank of Canada, Canada Post, Old Port of Montreal, RCMP and VIA Rail) and advertising and communications agencies across the province. Liberal Prime Minister Paul Martin succumbed to public pressure and appointed Justice John Gomery to head a public inquiry in 2005. The *Gomery Report*, submitted in November 2005, put the blame squarely on the shoulders of former Liberal Prime Minister Jean Chrétien and his senior advisors, members of Cabinet and the bureaucracy. Key players were charged and found guilty.[18] On May 5, 2006, Jean Brault was sentenced to thirty months in prison, and the very next day Chuck Guité was convicted of five counts of fraud and later sentenced to three and a half years in prison. In 2017, Jacques Corriveau, considered one of the prime figures in the scandal, was sentenced to four years in prison and fined $1.4 million.

Many Canadians believe Ontario and Quebec have always received special treatment from Ottawa. This is especially the case when the prime minister and Cabinet (together known as the executive), plus their important advisors, decide on policy with their provincial counterparts. This is known as **executive federalism**. Executive federalism contributes to regionalism by removing populations from having any impact on important political decisions, thereby favouring some provinces, almost always the larger ones, at the expense of the rest. Senior members of government and their advisors are likely to push the interests of their particular region and not the interests beneficial to the entire country. Citizens lose faith in their political leaders and the entire system when they are denied opportunities to express their concerns. Two important examples of this dynamic are the Meech Lake (1988) and Charlottetown (1992) constitutional accords.

Prime Minister Pierre Trudeau repatriated the original constitution, known as the British North America Act (BNA) 1867, by adding a Charter of Rights and Freedoms and renaming it the Canada Act 1982. During the repatriation process, provincial premiers asked for changes to the constitution and additions to the Charter that they believed would strengthen their hand when dealing with the federal government. In the end, every province except Quebec accepted the new, repatriated constitution. Parti Québécois (PQ) premier René Lévesque did not believe Quebec's unique or distinct characteristic — a French-speaking population with a noticeably different culture existing in a country dominated by English-speaking peoples and their cultures — was adequately addressed and protected. Trudeau preferred to enshrine individual rights in the new Charter of Rights and Freedoms and not group rights. Lévesque, therefore, withheld Quebec's consent and did not sign the new constitution. Without unanimous provincial support, Trudeau asked the Supreme Court to decide on the constitutionality of repatriation without full provincial consent. In a 5–2 decision, the court ruled in favour of the federal government. Trudeau moved forward without the consent of Quebec, his home province. For Quebecers, English Canada had once again ignored their important interests and concerns. Premier Lévesque publicly announced that Quebec, technically, was no longer part of the Canadian "family." Since 1982 successive federal governments have tried, with different levels of enthusiasm, to convince Quebec to sign the Canada Act 1982. The Progressive Conservative government of Brian Mulroney (1984–1992) was the most determined.

Mulroney's first attempt was the **Meech Lake Accord 1987**. The prime minister invited the premiers to a weekend retreat at his cottage, located on Meech Lake near Ottawa, for three days of talks. Mulroney did not communicate with the press until the details of the accord were released on Monday morning. This meant that Canadians awoke to an agreement that they were asked to accept without having any input. This is a pure example of executive federalism. Canadians in many regions vocally dissented once the details of the accord were released. In order to win the consent of each province, Mulroney ceded some federal powers and responsibilities to the provinces, in particular increased control over immigration, and to the dismay of many Canadians, each province was granted a veto over future constitutional change. In addition, Quebec received its coveted recognition as a "distinct society" within Canada.[19] Canadians generally believed the federal government gave up too much to win Quebec's signature. Indigenous Peoples, who were not invited to Meech Lake, believed their concerns were wholly ignored and vowed to fight the accord. In the end, the accord was defeated when the three-year ratification process expired, with Manitoba withholding its consent. This was the product of a legislative filibuster (talking in the legislature until a deadline passes) by Manitoba Indigenous Member of the Legislature Elijah Harper (1935–2005). Elijah Harper's impact on Canadian history was so important that the federal government placed his picture and an explanation of his actions in the foyer of the Peace Tower. In 1989, the new Liberal government of Newfoundland and Labrador, led by Clyde Wells, rescinded his predecessor's earlier acceptance. The accord was considered dead in June 1990. Undaunted, Mulroney vowed to try again.

"Canada, except by a mere play on words, is not a nation."
— Globe Newspaper 1871, later known as the Globe and Mail

Prime Minister Mulroney's second attempt came in 1992. Determined not to repeat past mistakes, he invited the premiers and Indigenous leaders to Charlottetown, Prince Edward Island. The choice of Charlottetown was not accidental, nor its significance lost on Canadians. The framers of Canada's original constitution first met in Charlottetown, and it is considered the city where Canada was born in 1867. On this occasion Canadians were not presented with a take-it-or-leave-it deal. Rather, a committee travelled coast to coast asking for input. The debates even found retired prime minister Pierre Trudeau briefly returning to the public eye to tell Canadians that the **Charlottetown Accord** deserved a resounding "No."[20] After a year of cross-country hearings, the final accord was subject to a national referendum on October 26, 1992. The accord was soundly defeated with significant regional differentiation (see Box 2.2). What do the results show? By the end of this constitutional cycle, Canadians had had enough and wished to move on. No federal government since 1992 has raised the issue of constitutional renewal.

Box 2.2 Diversity in Action

Results of Charlottetown Accord Referendum

Overall, 54 percent of Canadians voted "No."

No Votes	Yes Votes
Quebec	Ontario
Nova Scotia	Newfoundland and Labrador
Manitoba	Prince Edward Island
Alberta	New Brunswick
British Columbia	Northwest Territories
Saskatchewan	
Yukon	

For a brief analysis of the state of the Canadian mind leading up to the referendum, listen to "Will it be Yes or No to the Charlottetown Accord?" at the CBC archives: <www.cbc.ca/archives/entry/will-it-be-yes-or-no-to-the-charlottetown-accord>.

Canada's Electoral System

The constitution framers' choice of electoral system also contributes to regionalism. In order to build a new country, the framers believed elections should produce majority governments, which they considered more likely to be able to see their nation-building policies through to fruition. To this end they chose **single member plurality** (SMP), or what is more commonly known as the first-past-the-post electoral system.

In addition, Canada's electoral system is based on **representation by population**, the fundamental building block of democracy. This means that provinces with large populations are allotted more seats in the federal legislature, the House of Commons, than provinces with smaller populations. The number of seats per province is proportional to their percentage of the national population. Ontario, with one-third of Canada's population, receives one-third of the seats in the House of Commons. Quebec, with roughly 20 percent of Canada's population, receives 20 percent of the seats. This means Ontario has 112 of 338 seats and Quebec has 75. Having the two central provinces with over half of Canada's population means federal governments are more likely to pay attention to the concerns and grievances of central Canada. Being politically popular in central Canada makes winning federal elections more likely. Why would politicians pay acute attention to the needs and concerns of other regions when electoral realities dictate otherwise?

The single member plurality electoral system compounds the regionalism caused by representation by population. This is because the winning candidate in each constituency, or riding, only needs a "plurality" of votes to declare victory. In other words, the winner simply needs more votes than any candidate running against them; winning candidates do not need a "majority" of votes (50 percent plus 1). Therefore, the winning party is regularly elected with less than 50 percent of the popular vote, and it is likely to have far more seats in the House of Commons than the party with the next largest percentage of votes. In fact, the winning party is likely to have a majority of seats without winning the majority of votes. Indeed, it is common in federal elections for the winning party to have as little as 36–38 percent of the popular vote. In the 2015 federal election, Justin Trudeau's Liberal party won a majority of seats — 176 out of 320 — with just 40 percent of the popular vote. In the 2017 provincial election in British Columbia, the Liberals and NDP received 40.36 and 40.28 percent of the popular vote and received 43 and 41 seats respectively, while the Green Party received 16.84 percent of the popular vote yet received only three seats![21] This is the nature of the first-past-the-post system — it handsomely rewards the winners and viciously punishes the losers. This was also exemplified in the Nova Scotia election of May 2017. The Liberals received 27 of 51 seats in the provincial legislature with just 39.47 percent of the popular vote, the Progressive Conservatives were allotted ten fewer seats (17) with only 4 percent less of the popular vote (35.73), and the NDP received a meagre seven seats with a respectable 21.51 percent of the popular vote.[22]

Historically, representation by population and single member plurality have combined to preference some regions at the expense of others. For example, while Pierre Trudeau's Liberals governed from 1968 to 1982 (save for a short-lived Joe Clark–led Progressive Conservative government from 1979–1980), they did not have an elected member of Parliament west of the city of Winnipeg. This means that Alberta, British Columbia and Saskatchewan had no political representation in Ottawa for almost sixteen years! In order to have the three most western provinces represented in Cabinet, Trudeau used his constitutional powers to appoint senators to Cabinet who had previously been appointed by Trudeau to represent their province in the Senate.

Government Policy and Western Canada

Government policy can be analyzed by looking at the collective impact on some of Canada's regions: western Canada, Atlantic Canada, Quebec and Canada's northern regions.

The seeds of regional discontent were sowed shortly after Confederation with Prime Minister John A. Macdonald's **National Policy** of 1879. This policy had four goals: 1. strengthen the Dominion of Canada; 2. promote political unity; 3. promote trade and economic unity among regions; and 4. make the Canadian economy self-sufficient. Macdonald and his supporters were determined to build a strong manufacturing economy by encouraging east-west trade among the provinces. The promised national railway was crucial to the success of this plan. It was, however, equally important to limit cheaper manufactured goods originating in the United States from dominating Canadian purchases. Part of the National Policy was to attach a **tariff** — a tax on imported manufactured goods — on every incoming American-made product; this made American-manufactured goods artificially more expensive than Canadian ones. The tariff was raised from 15 percent to as much as 35 percent.[23] This forced western and Atlantic Canadians to buy more expensive "Made in Canada" goods. Specifically, western farmers and Maritime and BC fishers were forced to purchase their plows, implements and boats from Ontario and Quebec manufacturers. Western farmers, for example, purchased plows, mowers, mechanical reapers, thrashers and other farming implements from Massey-Harris Company, located in Brantford, Ontario. By 1891, the National Policy had helped Massey-Harris become the largest company of its kind in the British Empire. In short, the tariff made Canadian farming and fishing more expensive than they had to be. This confirmed the ideas espoused by the opponents of the National Policy, who believed that the protective tariff would raise the price of domestic manufactured goods and, above all, would favour industrial development in Ontario and Quebec, with the two biggest city winners being Toronto and Montreal. While central Canadian manufacturing was protected by the federal government, western farmers and Atlantic and BC fishers were at the mercy of international price changes. Finally, since the federal government used tariff revenue to partially fund the construction of the national railway, Atlantic and western Canadians were funding the railway twice: first, by actually contributing to its construction and second, by paying inflated prices for Canadian manufactured goods and/or paying the tariff on imported manufactured goods.

Another example of preferring central Canada over other regions is the Bank of Canada interest rate policy. Varying interest rates is a way to encourage investment and purchases to stimulate economic growth. Interest rate manipulation is also used to check the rise of inflation in order to slow down economies that are growing too quickly. A rapidly growing economy is known as a "hot" economy and results in rising inflation. In the early 1980s interest rates were allowed to rise to over 20 percent in an attempt to stop rising inflation. This was accomplished by making money more expensive to borrow. With less money available to spend, the demand for big ticket items like houses, cottages, cars and land quickly diminishes. The economy of Ontario was particularly hot at the time so interest rates began to quickly climb. Canadians in regions where the economy was not booming had no choice but to pay more to borrow money in order to slow down Ontario's accelerating economy. Once again, Atlantic and western Canadians were compelled to "prop up" central Canada: they paid artificially higher interest rates so Ontarians could be spared the ravages of inflation.

Still another example of federal government policy favouring central Canada was the fiasco over the process of awarding the CF-18 fighter plane maintenance contract. Canada contracted to purchase 122 new fighter aircraft for the Royal Canadian Air Force from American behemoth Northrop-Gruman in 1979. In 1981 the $1.2 billion maintenance contract for these high-tech fighters was put out to public tender. Three companies submitted bids, and the bidding was quickly whittled down to the two companies that had the necessary expertise, Bristol Aerospace of Winnipeg and Canadair of Montreal. The federal government concluded that the most cost-effective bid was submitted by Bristol Aerospace. In addition to their superior expertise, Bristol's bid was 10 percent cheaper. The situation became politically explosive after the Progressive Conservative government of Brian Mulroney won a landslide election in 1984, gaining 211 out of 282 seats. For the first time since the hanging of Louis Riel, a PC party dominated the province of Quebec, with 54 out of 75 seats. Mulroney was immediately inundated with demands from newly elected members of Parliament from Montreal and its surrounding areas reminding him of this fact and demanding the contract be awarded to Canadair lest future electoral support return to the Liberal Party. Mulroney eventually succumbed to the pressure and had the contract awarded to Canadair. Mulroney no doubt concluded that his party could win the next election without the support of Winnipeg (and Manitoba) but not without Montreal (and Quebec). This contract fiasco is an excellent example of just how representation by population and single member plurality can impact government decision-making.

Western feelings of alienation have deep roots.[24] The federal government always believed it was essential to Canadian existence to populate the west as quickly as possible especially given the loud and clear American talk of **manifest destiny**. Control of crown lands was essential to the successful completion of this task, and this resulted in the Dominion Lands Act in 1872. When the provinces joined Confederation (the date is after each province), the Act deprived Saskatchewan (1905), Alberta (1905), Manitoba (1870) and British Colombia (1871) of control over crown lands and natural resources in spite of provinces having constitutional jurisdiction over natural resources. Naturally, the provinces were not pleased with this arrangement, especially since Ontario, Quebec, Nova Scotia and New Brunswick were not subject to such federal interference in provincial affairs. Control of natural resources and remaining lands were finally transferred to the three western provinces when the federal government passed the Natural Resources Transfer Acts in 1930! One act was passed for each province.

Perhaps the most contentious western grievance with Ottawa was the Liberal government's 1980 National Energy Program (NEP). The program was designed to give the federal government a more active and visible role in Canada's oil and natural gas industry, with the hope of making Canada energy self-sufficient.[25] Part of the program involved Petro Canada buying Belgian company Petro Fina's Canadian operations in 1981. This purchase gave the federal government its much sought after "visible presence" across the country. Western Canadians, especially Albertans, regarded this federal program as a pure money and power grab to gain authority over provincial oil and natural gas resources just as international prices were exploding upwards. Prime Minister Pierre Trudeau believed these bountiful resources should be used for the good of Canada, which included selling Canadian oil (Albertan oil) to Canadians at below world prices. Alberta PC Premier Peter Lougheed (1928–2012) rightfully believed that these resources belonged to Alberta and that it would be unconstitutional for Ottawa to interfere, and he vowed to take the federal government to court. A Supreme Court decision later confirmed Lougheed's claims. Contentious negotiations with Ottawa finally led to an agreement in September 1981. Premier Lougheed maintained that Trudeau was acting in the best interests of Ontario and Quebec. Anger across Alberta was palpable (see Box 2.3). Indeed, many Albertans believe they have more in common with Americans in North Dakota and Montana than with Canadians on the other side of the country. Historically, this affinity with the US was particularly true of those involved in the oil and gas industry living in Calgary and Edmonton, who developed significant ties with their counterparts in Dallas, Texas, and Tulsa, Oklahoma.[26] Alberta remains at the mercy of international energy price fluctuations. The fall of oil and gas prices beginning in roughly 2015 have hit Alberta particularly hard.

Still another grievance involves the history of the Crow's Nest Pass Agreement of 1897.[27] The agreement allowed the federal government to subsidize railway freight rates for the benefit of its users. This was important to western grain farmers as it provided them with a cost-effective way to ship their grain to Canadian and international markets. The federal Liberals led by Pierre Trudeau reduced this subsidy

Box 2.3 Diversity in Action

One citizen was so angry about Trudeau's National Energy Policy that he called into a CBC radio show and stated: "If my voice is trembling, it's because I am terribly angry to the point where I would be happy to fight for our freedom and I literally mean with a rifle." The caller was obviously distraught with federal interference in Albertan affairs. When was the last time you heard an Ontarian express such emotional words directed towards Ottawa for interfering in Ontario's affairs? Most likely, never. Why?

Source: For a full account of the interview go to CBC Archives <www.cbc.ca/archives/entry/lougheed-retaliates-against-trudeau-for-nep>.

through the 1970s until it was finally eliminated in 1995 by Trudeau's successor, Jean Chrétien.

Western alienation is exemplified by the birth (and death) of several federal and provincial protest/separatist parties. The most recent and perhaps well know was the Reform Party, founded in 1987. Its official party platform was embodied in leader Preston Manning's declaration: "The West Wants In." In addition to wanting more influence in Ottawa and to advance its conservative economic ideas of lower taxes and privatization, the Reform Party's most famous political idea was a Triple E Senate: elected, equal and effective. Even though senators are appointed by the prime minister from provincial lists, the Reform Party believed such appointees were far more likely to put federal interests before provincial ones. Directly electing senators in their own province was believed to overcome this deficiency, allowing newly elected senators to more effectively represent and defend provincial interests. The Reform Party merged with the federal Progressive Conservative Party to create the Canadian Alliance. The merger was made final in 2003 with the creation of the Conservative Party of Canada. The party won two consecutive elections under leader Stephen Harper, governing from 2008 to 2016.

Other, largely right-of-centre, parties that were created as a form of protest included Social Credit (1935–1993), Western Canada Concept Party (1980), Western Independence Party of Saskatchewan (2003), Western Bloc Party (2005) and Alberta First Party (2013). One left-of-centre party was the Co-operative Commonwealth Federation (CCF), founded in 1930 to fight for the rights and liberty of farmers and labourers. In 1961 it merged with the Canadian Labour Congress to form the New Democratic Party of Canada. Saskatchewan CCF leader Tommy Douglas introduced Canadians to the idea of universal healthcare, and medicare was adopted as national policy in 1966. When the CBC asked Canadians to vote for the greatest Canadian of all time in 2004, the "father of universal medicare" finished a comfortable 50,000 votes ahead of second place finisher, Terry Fox.[28] Canadians do love their universal, publicly funded healthcare system.

Government Policy and Atlantic Canada

Canada's Atlantic region is the poorest in the country. In spite of this, as political scientists Stephen Brooks and Marc Menard observe, sentiments of Atlantic alienation or separatism have not manifested themselves in a political movement or party. This does not mean, however, that regional disenchantment with Ottawa and/or the rest of Canada is any less. The Atlantic region's alienation is compounded by the continued realities of economies that are among the weakest in Canada and the fact that the population as a share of Canada's total population continues to decline.[29] Per capita

Box 2.4 Innov8

In 2003 Prince Edward Island native and Sheridan College graduate Jeremy Carter produced a web series entitled *Just Passing Through*. The show is based on the lives of two islanders who find themselves stuck in Toronto on their journey to the tar sands in Alberta. Josh O'Kane of the *Globe and Mail* writes: "Beneath its vulgar script and crude humour lies a deep reverence for east coast culture and Canadian stories that you'd be hard pressed to find on conventional television." Watch a few episodes and tell the class what you think. A word of caution, viewer discretion is most certainly advised!

transfer payments from the federal government to the provinces are far more critical to Atlantic Canada than those to any other region. Only territorial governments receive more. Atlantic Canadians are aware of this fact.

Newspaper delivery is not immune to the narrow decision-making of central Canadian elites. On December 1, 2017, the *Globe and Mail* stopped sending its print edition to New Brunswick, Nova Scotia and Prince Edward Island, after first terminating delivery to Newfoundland and Labrador in 2013. The paper cited declining print subscriptions and the high cost of air freight. Shortly after the announcement, Errol Sharpe, co-founder of Fernwood Publishing, based in Halifax and Winnipeg, wrote to the paper and suggested it change its moniker "Canada's National Newspaper" since it clearly no longer applied. The paper has yet to reply.

> *"The opening up of the Saskatchewan would do to Canada what the prairie lands are doing now — drain away our youth and strength." — Prime Minister John A. Macdonald, 1865*[30]

Similar Atlantic stories can be found in the writings of some of the Atlantic region's and Canada's best authors. Perhaps the most famous is the iconic *Anne of Green Gables*, written in 1908 by Lucy Maude Montgomery. Other notable stories include Alistair MacLeod's *No Great Mischief* and David Adams Richards's *Mercy Among the Children* (see Box 2.5 for more).

The Atlantic region was particularly hard hit by the collapse of the cod fisheries in the early 1990s. In 1992, the federal government banned cod fishing. Entire communities were devastated as cod fishing virtually ceased, with processing plants closing or moving elsewhere. The chain reaction negatively impacted thousands of workers, particularly in Newfoundland. Between 1990 and 2010 Canada fell from third to

DIVERSITYINACTIONDIVERSITYINACTIO

Box 2.5 Diversity in Action

Atlantic Voices

Lisa Moore, *Caught:* David Slaney is 25 and in prison in Newfoundland for cannabis possession when he decides to break out and live life as a fugitive. One objective is to out-run the authorities; the other is to search for his former drug dealing partner, Hearn, and resume their business. As he moves across Canada, Slaney has to be inventive in his disguises — as student, lover, hitchhiker. When he reunites with Hearn, they are nearly caught by a detective ready for a high-profile arrest. Slaney heads to Mexico and Colombia, and back, in a quest fueled by luck and impetuous youthful conviction.

Wayne Johnston, *The Colony of Unrequited Dreams*: This is the big Newfoundland novel. Historical fiction based on the story of Joe Smallwood, a controversial political figure, this novel spans his lifetime, which coincides with Newfoundland becoming a part of Canada. Smallwood longs for world renown and works for a New York newspaper, a union and eventually as a politician. Interspersed with Smallwood's story is the story of Shelagh Fielding, his school friend and fellow journalist, who champions the poor and the workers with her acerbic wit and cynical columns.

Source: Dr. Jennifer Chambers, private correspondence, February 2018. See also Chapter 11.

seventh place in world fish and seafood exports in terms of overall value.[31] Many Atlantic communities suffered accordingly.

The discovery of oil and natural gas off the Atlantic coastline in the 1970s and 1980s has led to constant political friction between Ottawa and the provinces. Nova Scotia premier John Hamm remarked in 2001 that the equalization formula needed to be amended to allow the Atlantic provinces to keep more natural resource revenues.[32] Progressive Conservative premier Mike Harris of Ontario responded by comparing Hamm to a welfare cheat! Contentious negotiations turned into open conflict in early 2005. When negotiations between Ottawa and Newfoundland and Labrador stalled, Liberal premier Danny Williams ordered all Canadian flags to be removed from government buildings. This move was widely approved of across the province, with even Memorial University, traditionally neutral in such disputes, lowering its flag. As provincial revenues from oil and gas continued to grow, Ottawa eventually signed complicated agreements with Nova Scotia and Newfoundland and Labrador allowing them to keep 100 percent of offshore revenues without impacting equalization payments until 2012.[33] Specifically, Bill C-43 allowed Newfoundland and Labrador to keep an additional $2.6 billion per year in offshore oil and natural gas revenues. Other provinces, particularly Saskatchewan, wanted similar treatment for their energy reserves, while Ontario Liberal premier Dalton McGuinty complained that Ontario was now paying more for per capita program spending in "have not" provinces than it spent on its own citizens.[34] Like elsewhere, Newfoundland and Labrador have been hit hard with the fall in oil and gas prices. In fact, GDP fell 2.2 percent in 2015, marginally less than the 2.3 percent decline in 2014. The output of goods decreased by 6.1 percent, led by a noticeable decline in conventional oil and gas extraction, while lower oil prices have resulted in a significant decline in oil and gas extraction and engineering construction.[35]

Even with abundant energy resources, Nova Scotia, Newfoundland and Labrador, and Alberta are still at the mercy of international price fluctuations. In fact, in spite of Atlantic Canada's plethora of natural resources — oil, natural gas, coal, forests and hydroelectric power, it remains the poorest region in Canada. One of Canada's leading scholars on regional issues, University of Moncton professor Donald Savoie, argues that the Atlantic Provinces received a raw deal from Confederation and that "the region is not doing well because of federal government policy."[36] Savoie goes even further, believing that equalization payments are designed make sure the Atlantic region has just enough money to buy goods manufactured in Ontario and Quebec. In other words, the Atlantic region has been kept purposely poor by central Canada. Provincial tensions over the equalization formula erupted again in June 2018. Federal equalization payments to the provinces for 2018–19 will total $19.96 billion and will be transferred to six provinces: Quebec (receiving by far the most, $11.7 billion), Manitoba, Nova Scotia, New Brunswick, Ontario and Prince Edward Island, while British Columbia, Alberta, Saskatchewan and Newfoundland and Labrador will receive no transfers.[37] Saskatchewan premier Scott Moe and Newfoundland and Labrador finance minister Tom Osborne lobbied hard for changes to the formula, but it remained the same in the 2018 federal budget. The problems faced by the Atlantic region are compounded by the fact that its share of Canada's population continues to decline.[38]

FEDERAL RESPONSE TO REGIONALISM

The federal government has been actively trying to ameliorate regional social, economic and political differences since Confederation. It has pursued three main strategies to accomplish this goal: reducing travel time by investing in cross-country travel routes to physically link Canadians from coast to coast; educating and informing Canadians about each other by investing in and regulating communication technology — giving voice to all Canadians (see Chapter 10); and finally, transferring huge sums of money to the provinces in an attempt to make the quality of life of every Canadian as equal as possible in the fields of healthcare, education and the delivery of social services.

Reducing Travel Time

Prime Minister McKenzie King famously remarked that Canada has "too much geography" — a sentiment certainly not shared by Canada's Indigenous inhabitants. Canada's size has always occupied the minds of government officials. How do Canadians reduce the realities of space and time in order to build a functional country? One solution was for the federal government to massively invest in east-west transportation. The first and most famous of these investments was Prime Minister John A Macdonald's building of a national railway. Rail travel was considered essential to convincing different regions to join Confederation. In fact, British Columbia was promised a railway linking it to the rest of Canada as an enticement to join. So controversial was the pledge to build a national railway linking both coasts that Liberal leader Alexander McKenzie remarked in the House of Commons in 1871 that such a pledge was "an act of insane recklessness."[39] A national railway would bring western products (grain and timber) and Atlantic fish and timber to the population centres in central Canada and return with manufactured goods. The railway would also bring all Canadians' products to the appropriate cities and ports for export to Europe and the United States. In his immortal *The Last Spike*, Canadian historian Pierre Berton meticulously documented just how the construction of the railway consumed the early years of politics and development. Completed in 1885, in just four years and six months, the transcontinental railway was considered an engineering marvel and construction miracle, or as Berton wrote, Canada had "just accomplished the impossible."[40]

Much later, in 1977, Prime Minister Pierre Trudeau's Liberal government created VIA Rail as a **crown corporation** (a company owned by government) to provide coast-to-coast passenger rail service to unite all Canadians. Rail travel became especially popular with Canadians in the Quebec City to Windsor corridor. However, vicious cuts to VIA budgets and routes instituted by Brian Mulroney's Progressive Conservative government resulted in many towns, especially in the Maritimes, losing their only passenger rail link to neighbouring communities.[41] Atlantic Canadians were once again put at a disadvantage by the actions of the federal government. This is a vivid example of the paradoxical role of the federal government — after being helped with the creation of VIA Rail in 1977 by one federal government, many communities were disadvantaged by the cuts imposed by another.

With the popularity of car travel increasing, the federal government began construction of the TransCanada Highway in 1950. It was opened in 1963 and fully completed in 1971. It spans just over eight thousand kilometres, linking Canadians with one continuous road. The federal government also invested in air travel with the founding of TransCanada Airways in 1937. The original mandate of the airline was to serve remote communities not covered by private carriers, which were more concerned with profit.

Later renamed Air Canada, the airline was a crown corporation until it was privatized in 1989. The majority of shares are now owned by private investors.

Educating and Informing

The second tool used by the federal government to lessen regional differences was the creation and regulation of critical communication mediums designed to inform Canadians about each other in the hope of promoting more understanding and togetherness. The federal government hoped to solidify Canadian identity by connecting people living in distant regions emotionally and attitudinally. The Canadian Broadcasting Corporation (CBC) Radio was created in 1932, and CBC Television followed in 1953. From the outset, radio and TV were available coast-to-coast, allowing Canadians access to both national and regionally based programming. CBC national news aired at 10 pm across the country, followed by regional newscasts, and radio hosts established loyal audiences. Some hosts became hugely popular and had an enormously positive impact on what it means to live in such a large and diverse country. The late Peter Gzowski and the late Stuart McLean are two such towering figures (see Box 2.6).

CBC Radio also introduced Canadians to legendary *Hockey Night in Canada* host Foster Hewitt. It was Hewitt who described a goal being scored in the simplest and most memorable way: "He shoots, he scores!" Many a young Canadian has shouted these words in hockey games on arena ice, frozen ponds, streets, game tables and mom and dad's kitchen floor!

CBC TV allowed the regional to go national. From *Road to Avonlea, Kids in the Hall, The Beachcombers* and the many incarnations of *DeGrassi High* to *Hockey Night in Canada*, Canadians were introduced to each other's regional identities, attitudes, values, tastes, challenges and ways of life. This was on display for all Canadians to see in the follow-up to Canada's 150 birthday celebration on July 1, 2017. As part of the many celebrations, the CBC produced the historical docudrama, *Canada: The Story of Us*. It is unlikely that any private group would produce such work. Indeed, this was the case for the CBC's 2009 production, *Canada: A Peoples History*.[42] In spite of the fact that it was an immediate hit, averaging 2.5 million viewers each for the first six episodes, CBC TV producer Mark Starowicz could only convince one company to buy advertising time. The CBC went ahead with the series at a cost of $25 million without the support of corporate Canada. Canadians do want to know about each other. After all, it was the CBC that beamed the Tragically Hip's last concert from their hometown Kingston, Ontario, live from coast-to-coast.

Similarly, the federal government established the National Film Board (NFB) in 1939 with a mandate to document all things Canadian and to tell Canadian stories. NFB

Box 2.6 Think About...

Stuart McLean died on February 15, 2017. The unforgettable, quintessential host of CBCs *The Vinyl Café* radio show is sorely missed by millions of Canadians. The show was a unique mixture of stories, essays and music. So popular was *The Vinyl Café* that it spawned best-selling books of short stories. McLean was able to tell Canadians about each other in ways that will resonate for some time. Journalist Steve Milton, of the *Hamilton Spectator*, whose daughter Jessica produced *The Vinyl Café* for thirteen years, wrote, "Beloved Vinyl Café storyteller made us believe we all shape this vast land" and reminded us that "one of Stuart's core values was inclusion." McLean was professor emeritus at Ryerson University and an officer of the Order of Canada and received the Lifetime Achievement Award from the Canadian Booksellers Association in 2014.

Source: "Cancer Fells a Great Maple in the Canadian Arts Forest," *Hamilton Spectator,* February 16, 2017.

---

documentaries are standard fare in schools across the country, and most Canadians are at the very least somewhat familiar with the thirty-second historical vignettes broadcast on CBC TV. The NFB has garnered many international awards for its productions. Roughly 2,500 NFB films can be accessed free on the NFB website. In 2009–10, the federal government spent just over $2 billion on broadcasting, film and video, while total expenditures on "culture" exceeded a whopping $4 billion.[43]

Finally, the federal government uses **royal commissions** to investigate issues deemed critical to Canada. Royal commissions are usually headed by notable Canadians, often retired politicians and justices, appointed by the federal government. Commissions travel the country collecting information from all those who have an expertise in the area being investigated. They do not implement policy but rather suggest future direction to governments of the day. Two important royal commissions were the 1937 Royal Commission on Dominion-Provincial Relations, which examined the complex nature of fiscal relations (transferring tax dollars) between the federal government and provinces, and the 1981–85 Royal Commission on the Economic Union and Development Prospects for Canada, which recommended entering into a free trade agreement with the United States despite testimony by some experts that free trade would be harmful to Canada's poorer regions, especially the Atlantic provinces. Not all royal commission recommendations are accepted by federal governments. Such was the case of the 1997 Royal Commission on Aboriginal Peoples. Its report put forward almost 500 recommendations, the most important of which was to immediately increase spending by $2 billion per year for twenty years in addition to the more than

Box 2.7 Diversity in Action

Stompin' Tom Connors, a Canadian Original

Canadian folk music legend Charles Thomas Connors was born in Saint John, New Brunswick, on February 9, 1936, and died in Ballinafad, Ontario, on March 6, 2013. Better known as Stompin' Tom Connors for the stomping of his left foot while performing, he spent most of his adult life travelling across Canada writing and singing songs about the regions he experienced, people he met, cities and communities that welcomed him and largely forgotten, yet iconic, Canadian figures. Songs that have become legend in Canada include "The Hockey Song," "Sudbury Saturday Night," "Bud the Spud," "Roll On Saskatchewan," "Tillsonburg," "Moon-Man Newfie" and "Long Gone to the Yukon." He sang the truly Canadian stories of Joseph Monterrand, the Black Donnellys, Muk Tuk Annie, Robert Lyon, Wilfred R. May, Marten Hartwell and k.d. Lang to name a few. He paid homage to farmers, ironworkers, lumberjacks, miners, peacekeepers and unions. He reminded Canadians of the importance of maple trees, gold, wheat fields, tobacco, snowmobiles and ketchup to everyday Canadian life. Who but Stompin' Tom would sing about the Confederation Bridge and Algoma Central No. 69? Are you familiar with any of his music? Did you come across any of the above names and stories in history class? His autobiography, *Stompin' Tom: Before the Fame*, published in 1995, was runner-up for the Edna Staebler Award for Creative Non Fiction in 1996.

$5 billion already being spent. The Liberal government of Jean Chrétien announced in 1998 that it would spend a paltry $350 million.

Royal commissions are so popular with federal governments that there have been roughly 400 since 1867, an average of three per year.[44] Their popularity stems from their high-profile attempts — public and visible — to understand the plight of Canadians everywhere.

Spending and Transferring Money

Spending money is the final tool used by the federal government to lessen regional differences. This includes the billions of dollars transferred to the provinces every year. The most visible examples are **equalization payments** and **health and social transfer programs**. Equalization transfers are intended to help provincial governments deliver services to their populations in as uniform and equal manner as possible in the hope of ensuring Canadians experience the same quality of life wherever they may live. The amount transferred to each province is determined by a complicated formula based on the ways provinces are able to raise revenues. Once an average is calculated, the provinces that fall below the average receive a payment from Ottawa to elevate those provinces to the average. Equalization payments are so important to promoting regional equality that Prime Minister Pierre Trudeau enshrined them in section 36 of the Canada Act 1982.

Another transfer essential to provincial life and regional development are the Canada health and social transfer programs (CHT and CST). These transfers exceeded $50 billion for the 2017–18 fiscal year, while total transfers, including equalization payments, to provinces and territories were more than $72 billion. Box 2.8 shows that Canada's poorer provinces receive more money per capita (per person) from federal transfer payments than wealthier ones.

Canada is a political creation — a 150-year-old idea imposed on a disparate group of people living in geographically unique areas.

The federal government has historically used government departments/agencies to study and promote economic investment and growth in poorer regions. Ottawa creates new ones when necessary and disbands older ones it deems no longer useful. Important

Box 2.8 Think About...

Federal Support to Provinces and Territories (millions of dollars)

Major Transfers	2014–15	2015–16	2016–17	2017–18
Canada Health Transfer	32,113	34,026	36,068	37,150
Canada Social Transfer	12,582	12,959	13,348	13,748
Equalization	16,669	17,341	17,880	18,254
Offshore Offsets	196	125	44	-8
Territorial Formula Financing	3,469	3,561	3,603	3,682
Total Federal Support	64,029	68,013	70,943	72,826
Per Capita Allocation (dollars)	1,832	1,899	1,958	1,986

Note: Offshore offsets to Newfoundland and Labrador and Nova Scotia include cash amounts from the 1985 and 1986 accords and cash and notional amounts from the 2005 arrangements.
Source: Adapted from Department of Finance, "Federal Support to Provinces and Territories," <www.fin.gc.ca/fedprov/mtp-eng.asp>.

department/agencies/programs include the *Agricultural and Rural Development Act* (1965), Fund for Economic Development (1966), Department of Regional Economic Expansion (1969), Department of Regional Industrial Expansion (1982), Department of Industry, Science and Technology (1987), Atlantic Canada Opportunities Agency (1987), Western Diversification (1987), Enterprise Cape Breton (1987), Canadian Polar Commission (1991), Canadian Rural Partnership (1998), and First Nations and Inuit Health Branch of Health Canada (2000).

Canada's North

Canadians are largely unaware of the life lived by those in more northern regions. This is because roughly 80 percent of Canada's population is located within 320 kilometres of its border with the United States, with almost 63 percent being located within the Quebec City to Windsor corridor. This means most Canadians have a skewed sense of what it means to travel "up north." The city of Barrie is considered up north to those living in south-central Ontario in spite of the fact that the drive there is only a few hours. Torontonians venturing to their cottages in the Muskoka and Kawartha lakes believe the same. Yet, it is possible to drive a car for more than twenty hours and still be in the province of Ontario. Here is a quick quiz. What province is home

---

Box 2.9 Think About...

One-Industry Towns

One-industry towns — where the economy is dominated by one industry — are found in every province. When that industry closes or moves, the entire town suffers and, in some cases, completely collapses. Such was the case with Kirkland Lake, Ontario, a former mining town that is trying to reinvent itself as a retirement community. In Nova Scotia in June 2012, Resolute Forest Products closed its plant in Brooklyn, throwing 320 people out of work. In October of the same year, the paper mill in Point Tupper, NS, resumed operations under new management, with fewer than half of its former workforce. Roughly 135 people in a town of 1,160 lost their jobs, although about 40 people were offered jobs at a sister plant located elsewhere. Paper mills are not the only plants closing in the Atlantic region. Highliner Foods closed a fish processing plant in Burin, Newfoundland and Labrador, leaving 140 people jobless in a community of 2,400. The company claimed the isolated nature of the plant and its distance from the market made it too expensive to operate.

Source: *Huffington Post*, "Canadian Economy: One-Industry Towns Struggle as Economy Passes Them By" <huffingtonpost.ca/2012/12/17/one-industry-towns-canada_n_2314075.html>.

to Quetico Provincial Park? What Ontario city is farthest north, Sudbury, North Bay or Thunder Bay? What territorial capital is farther north, Whitehorse or Yellowknife? What Albertan city is farther north, Edmonton or Calgary?

Canada's northern reaches are so far removed from our daily consciousness that most Canadians are not familiar with the land and the experiences of those who live there. What is a "one-industry town"? See Box 2.9 for the answer. Here is another quick quiz. What is the name of Canada's newest territory? What is the dominant language of its inhabitants and what does the name of the territory mean to them?

THE SOCIO-PSYCHOLOGICAL DIMENSION TO REGIONALISM

The **socio-psychological dimension to regionalism** is clearly visible in the contempt felt across most of Canada for central Canada, and especially for metropolitan Toronto. There are also real interprovincial rivalries across the country, between Victoria and Vancouver, Edmonton and Calgary, Regina and Saskatoon. The same can be said of rivalries between big cities within a region. The rivalry between Halifax, Saint John and St. John's is one such example. Yet, these cities have one thing in common with cities across Canada; they resent the dominant role played by Toronto and central Canada in the political, economic and social lives of all Canadians. With the exception of the oil and natural gas sector, the Greater Toronto Area (GTA) is the centre of the Canadian economy. Most of Canada's largest and most powerful corporations have their head offices in Toronto and the Golden Horseshoe. With their logos perched atop some of the highest towers in the city, five of the six chartered banks call downtown Toronto home. The economic dominance of the Golden Horseshoe is obvious to all. According to the financialpost.com (2016), five of the top ten and a quarter of the top 100 corporations are located in Toronto. In fact, the Greater Toronto Area (GTA) is home to almost one-third of Canada's top 100.[45] The economic output of the GTA was $330 billion in 2013 — roughly equal to that of the entire province of Alberta, narrowly less than that of the province of Quebec and larger than the combined economies of Newfoundland and Labrador, Nova Scotia, New Brunswick, Prince Edward Island, Manitoba and Saskatchewan.[46] During 2016–17, housing prices skyrocketed in Vancouver and parts of the Golden Horseshoe. As drastic as the increases were, especially in Vancouver, according to the *Globe and Mail*, only a crash in Toronto's red-hot housing market could threaten a calamity. The simple mention of Bay Street conjures up images of power, money, wealth and dominance. Chicago, Los Angeles and New York, arguably the three most important American cities, do not, on their own, dominate American life in the same way that Toronto dominates Canadian life.

Central Canada's population ensures that its interests are paramount in Parliament.

> **Box 2.10 Think About...**
>
> **Canada's Supreme Court**
>
> Do Canadians believe their Supreme Court to be "objective" and "neutral" when adjudicating? Florian Sauvageau, David Schneiderman and David Taras believe the answer is "no." In other words, Canada's highest court is not immune to charges of regional favouritism. Quebecers regard it as a "leaning tower" that always leans in favour of English Canada. Guy Laforest goes even further and refers to the introduction of the 1982 Charter of Rights and Freedoms as the "updating of the [English] conquest [of Quebec]." Similar ideas are found in the western provinces, where Canada's highest court remains a powerful "symbol of the entrenched power of the East."

Winning big in Ontario and Quebec during a federal election is usually enough to form a majority government since 181 out of 320 seats are located in these two provinces. Powerful Cabinet posts are usually occupied by central Canadian MPs. This is especially true of the "inner" cabinet, the four or five most important posts, which include foreign affairs, finance, justice and international trade. Perhaps the most important Cabinet job, finance, is usually awarded to an elected central Canadian lawyer with connections to Bay Street who will return there once their political career is over, naturally with a hefty pay raise! Canada had to wait over a hundred years for its first non-Ontarian finance minister: Quebec's Jean Chrétien, who was appointed by Prime Minister Pierre Trudeau in 1979. The Liberal Party of Canada, long regarded as the "natural governing party" of Canada, has only ever chosen a party leader from Ontario or Quebec.

Toronto's media dominance is simple and complete. This is one of the themes of Peter Steven's cogent analysis of the media in Canada in Chapter 12 of this book. Toronto is the largest media centre in Canada and the fourth largest in North America! It is the home of the CBC, Global, City TV, Rogers and Bell and the publisher of the country's largest circulation daily/national newspapers, the *Globe and Mail, National Post* and Canada's largest circulation daily, the *Toronto Star*. Toronto is the centre of Canada's animation industry and has quickly established itself as one of the centres of the world's gaming industry. The GTA is also Canada's publishing hub, and along with Montreal, the centrepiece of Canada's fashion, entertainment and arts industries. In particular, Canada's Wonderland, the Canadian National Exhibition, BMO Field and the Rogers Centre (formerly SkyDome) are located in Toronto. Gay Pride and Caribana, two of the world's largest and most anticipated celebrations, happen in Toronto.

Culturally, Toronto is the home to a most enviable collection of theatres and museums, including the famed Massey Hall. Others include Roy Thomson Hall, Prince of Wales Theatre, Ed Mirvish Theatre, Panasonic Theatre, Sony Centre for the Performing Arts, Second City, National Ballet of Canada, Royal Ontario Museum, Casa Loma, Canadian Opera Company, Hockey Hall of Fame and countless others. The city of Toronto website reminds visitors that, after New York and London, it has the third-largest English-speaking theatre district in the world — quite an accomplishment since New York and London are both at least three times its size. Toronto is the only Canadian city and one of only a handful of cities in North America to have major league teams in the big five sports — hockey, baseball, basketball, soccer and football. The two largest universities in Canada (University of Toronto and York University) are located in Toronto, plus a third, Ryerson, along with four of Canada's largest colleges: Centennial, George Brown, Humber and Seneca — five if you include the GTA's Sheridan College. For all these reasons it is little wonder why many citizens across the country despise and envy Toronto specifically and the rest of central Canada more generally.

CONCLUSION

The study of regional diversity is critical to understanding the development of Canadian political and social life. In addition to regional differences, Canadians differ in many other ways, including but not limited to social class, ethnicity, gender, sexual orientation, income and the attitudes they have towards each other and the federal government. The last two differences confirm that regionalism does possess an important socio-psychological component.

What will future generations think of regional differentiation? What will the future hold? It is highly unlikely that the Canadian political system will change in any significant way. This is especially the case with the two key features that intensify regional feelings and differences — the nature of Canadian federalism and our electoral system. Prime Minister Justin Trudeau's electoral campaign promise to forgo our single member plurality electoral system in favour of some form of proportional representation was quickly abandoned when he took office. It is therefore unlikely that the behaviour of future federal governments will change. It is equally unlikely that capitalism will change its voracious profit-seeking behaviour. Money will move to where it can make more money regardless of the impact on people and the regions they live in. It is imperative that we remain vigilant and insist that all levels of government treat each and every Canadian, regardless of which region they inhabit, fairly and equally. Politicians need to be reminded that failure to do so will be remembered on election day.

CRITICAL REVIEW QUESTIONS

1. What is regionalism? Why is regionalism important to understanding the Canadian experience?
2. Briefly outline four theoretical explanations for regionalism. Which do you think makes the most sense? Would Canadians from different provinces choose different explanations? If so, why? If not, why not?
3. How do federalism and our electoral system compound and intensify regional differences?
4. What do we mean by the socio-psychological dimension to regionalism?
5. What roles has the federal government played in both creating and helping to reduce regional differences? Can you think of any current examples?
6. Is the idea of regionalism "real" to you? If so, why? If not, why not?

RECOMMENDED READINGS

Janine Brodie, *The Political Economy of Canadian Regionalism* (Toronto: Harcourt Brace Jovanovich, 1990).

Ralph Mathews, "Understanding Regionalism as Effect and Cause," in *Social Issues: Sociological Views of Canada*, 4th edition (Scarborough: Prentice-Hall, 1988).

Donald J. Savoie, *The Canadian Economy: A Regional Perspective* (Toronto: Methuen, 1986).

Lisa Young and Keith Archer (eds.), *Regionalism and Party Politics in Canada* (Toronto: Oxford University Press, 2001).

KEY TERMS

Canada health and social transfer programs: Canada Health Transfer (CHT) is a federal block transfer payment to provinces and territories in support of healthcare and health services. Canada Social Transfer (CST) is a federal block transfer payment to provinces and territories in support of post-secondary education, social assistance and social services along with early childhood development and early learning and childcare.

Charlottetown Accord 1992: the second attempt by Prime Minister Brian Mulroney to negotiate a constitutional agreement among the premiers to convince Quebec to sign the repatriated constitution. The accord was put to the citizens in a national referendum and was narrowly defeated. The referendum represented the opposite of executive federalism.

crown corporation: a corporation or regulatory body owned and operated by the federal government. They are used to achieve public policy goals such as national unity.

equalization payments: constitutionally mandated transfer payments from the federal government to the provinces based on a complicated formula designed to provide poorer provinces with the financial resources to deliver national quality services to their citizens.

executive federalism: refers to the political decision-making of prime ministers, premiers and their most important cabinet ministers, senior bureaucrats and advisors. Some argue this method of making political decisions is antithetical to democracy and an informed citizenry.

federalism: a system of governance where two levels of government exercise power and authority over the same population living within the same internationally recognized boundaries. Relations between the two levels of government are characterized by negotiation and cooperation since one level cannot abolish the other.

Golden Horseshoe: the cities that stretch along the coast of Lake Ontario from Niagara Falls to Oshawa and some parts of south-central Ontario. The centre of Canada's manufacturing, banking and wealth — hence "Golden."

manifest destiny: the nineteenth-century belief in American political thought that the entire North American continent was divinely granted to the United States and that its settlers should occupy the entire continent, carrying with them American ideas of freedom, democracy and capitalism.

Meech Lake Accord 1987: the constitutional accord negotiated by Prime Minister Brian Mulroney with provincial premiers to entice Quebec to sign the repatriated constitution. The accord was not ratified when it did not receive the necessary provincial support from Manitoba, Newfoundland and Labrador and New Brunswick. An example of executive federalism.

National Policy 1879: a conscious attempt by the government of John A. Macdonald to build an economy based on manufacturing and to lessen Canada's dependence on resource exports.

neoliberalism: extreme free market thinking that has dominated economic ideology, especially in the Western world, since the 1970s. The main tenets are cutting taxes and government spending, lowering inflation, reducing deficits and holding down wages.

regionalism: the attitude of the citizens of certain regions that they have not been given adequate recognition for their part in building Canada and have been penalized by the federal government in favour of other regions.

representation by population: the principle that allocates seats in the House of Commons to each province according to its share of the national population. For example, a province that has 10 percent of the population receives 10 percent of the seats. Frequently referred to as "rep by pop," it is the building block of democracy.

royal commission: an information-gathering committee used by the federal government to investigate issues deemed important to Canada. The commission travels across Canada, headed by people appointed by the federal government. A royal commission can only advise government; it has no authority to implement policy.

single member plurality: Canada's electoral system, where the candidate that wins the riding simply needs more votes than any other candidate running in the same riding. This is known as a "plurality" of winning votes. The candidate does not need a majority of votes to win. It is sometimes referred to as "first past the post."

socio-psychological dimension to regionalism: The unique feelings and attitudes held by citizens living in different regions about themselves and how these feelings and attitudes influence their actions toward each other, their community, other regions and the federal government.

staples theory: the theory that economic development is tied to the availability of natural resources. Associated with the work of famous Canadian political economist and economic historian Harold Innis.

tariff: tax applied to incoming goods from other countries. Used by John A. Macdonald in his National Policy (1879) to artificially increase the price of incoming manufactured goods to protect Canada's young and growing manufacturing industries.

transfer payments: name given to the billions of dollars that the federal government gives, or transfers, to the provinces and territories to help them deliver services to their populations. Key types of transfer payments are the health and social transfers, equalization payments and Territorial Formula Financing.

Notes

1. Jean-Luc Pepin and John P. Robarts, co-chairs, *The Task Force on Canadian Unity, Coming to Terms: The Words of the Debate* (Minister of Supply and Services Canada, 1979), 11.
2. Paul U. Angelini, "Regionalism in Canada: The Forgotten Diversity," in Paul U. Angelini (ed.), *Our Society: Human Diversity in Canada* (Scarborough, ON: Nelson Education, 2012), 4.
3. See the following discussions of this topic: Stephen Brooks and Marc Menard, *Canadian Democracy: A Concise Introduction* (Don Mills, ON: Oxford University Press, 2013), 77–104; Stephen Brooks, *Canadian Democracy: An Introduction,* 5th edition (Don Mills, ON: Oxford University Press, 2007), 101–21; Michael S. Whittington and Richard J. Van Loon, *Canadian Government and Politics: Institutions and Processes* (Toronto, ON: McGraw-Hill Ryerson Ltd, 1996), 47–88; Christopher Cochrane, Kelly Blidook and Rand Dyck, *Canadian Politics: Critical Approaches,* 8th edition (Scarborough, ON: Nelson Education, 2017), 41–66; Robert J. Jackson and Doreen Jackson, *Canadian Government in Transition,* 4th edition (Toronto, ON: Pearson Prentice Hall, 2006), 18–24, 100–29; Richard Simeon, "Regionalism and Canadian Political Institutions," in O. Kruhlak, R. Schultz and S. Pobihushchy (eds.), *The Canadian Political Process* (Toronto: Holt, Rinehart and Winston, 1979).
4. Statistics Canada, Table 11-10-0012-01 "Distribution of Total Income by Census Family Type and Age of Older Partner, Parent or Individual" <http://www.statcan.gc.ca/tables-tableaux/sum-som/l01/cst01/famil107a-eng.htm>.
5. John Ralston Saul, *The Comeback* (Toronto: Penguin Group, 2014), 147.
6. Angelini, "Regionalism in Canada," 4.
7. The explanations provided are drawn primarily from the following: Ralph Mathews, "Understanding Regionalism as Effect and Cause," in *Social Issues: Sociological Views of Canada,* 4th edition (Scarborough, ON: Prentice-Hall, 1988), 60–72; Ralph Mathews, *The Creation of Regional Dependency* (Toronto, ON: University of Toronto Press, 1983), 37–55; Janine Brodie, *The Political Economy of Canadian Regionalism* (Toronto, ON: Harcourt, Brace, Jovanovich, 1990), 21–36; and Donald J. Savoie, *The Canadian Economy: A Regional Perspective* (Toronto: Methuen, 1986), 9–24. The names of some approaches have been altered.

8. Perhaps Harold Innis's most famous work is *The Fur Trade in Canada: An Introduction to Canadian Economic History* (Toronto, ON: University of Toronto Press, 1930).

9. Government of Canada, *Softwood Lumber Fact Sheet* <www.nrcan.gc.ca/19605>.

10. Mathews, "Understanding Regionalism as Cause and Effect," 65.

11. For example, once in office Trudeau quickly gave the go ahead for the construction of two contentious oil pipelines; in June 2018 Ottawa moved to purchase the Canadian portion of the Kinder-Morgan pipeline.

12. This explanation is based on that provided by Brodie, *The Political Economy of Canadian Regionalism*, 27–34 and includes Keynesianism, regional science and developmental approaches.

13. Federal Support to Provinces and Territories, Government of Canada <www.fin.gc.ca/fedprov/mtp-eng.asp>.

14. See Angelini, "Regionalism in Canada," 10–11.

15. See Mathews, "Understanding Regionalism," 69.

16. For a quick and accessible analysis see R. Jamil Jonna and John Bellamy Foster, "Working-Class Precariousness," *Monthly Review*, 67, 11 (April 2016): 1–19.

17. For an accessible account of the history of Canadian federalism to roughly 1980, see Garth Stevenson, *Unfulfilled Union: Canadian Federalism and National Unity*, revised edition (Toronto: Gage Publishing, 1982).

18. For more detailed account, see <www.cbc.ca/news2/background/groupaction/>.

19. See Marjorie Montgomery Bowker, *The Meech Lake Accord: What It Will Mean to You and to Canada* (Hull, QC: Voyageur Publishing, 1990).

20. Pierre E. Trudeau, *A Mess That Deserves a Big NO* (Toronto: Robertson Davies Publisher, 1992).

21. *Times Colonist*, "Final Voting Results" <http://prod-admin1.glacier.atex.cniweb.net:8080/fileserver/file/1030559/filename/bc-election-final-2017.pdf>.

22. Elections Nova Scotia <http://results.electionsnovascotia.ca/Summary.aspx>.

23. Margaret Conrad, *A Concise History of Canada* (New York: Cambridge University Press, 2012), 159.

24. See Larry Pratt and Garth Stevenson, ed., *Western Separatism* (Edmonton, AB: Mel Hurtig, 1981); Roger Gibbons, *Conflict and Unity: An Introduction to Canadian Political Life*, 2nd edition (Scarborough, ON: Nelson Canada, 1990), especially Chapter 4; and Nelson Wiseman "The West as a Political Region," in Alain-G. Gagnon and James P. Bickerton, *Canadian Politics: An Introduction to the Discipline* (Peterborough, ON: Broadview Press, 1990), 308–324.

25. Conrad, *A Concise History*, 159.

26. Stephen Clarkson and Christina McCall, *Trudeau and Our Times Volume 2: The Heroic Delusion* (Toronto: McClelland and Stewart Inc., 1994), 167.

27. Adopted from Jackson and Jackson, *Canadian Government*, 123.

28. "And the Greatest Canadian of All Time Is…" CBC, Nov. 29, 2004 <http://www.cbc.ca/archives/entry/and-the-greatest-canadian-of-all-time-is>.

29. Brooks and Menard, *Canadian Democracy,* 125–26.

30. Source: "Just Passing Through Is a Remarkable Portrait of Canadian Regionalism," Globe and Mail, Feb. 11, 2016 <https://beta.theglobeandmail.com/arts/television/just-passing-through-is-a-remarkable-portrait-of-canadian-regionalism/article28727102/?ref=http://www.theglobeandmail.com&>.

31. Thai Nguyen, "Trade Agreements and Eastern Canada's Fisheries," *In Brief*, Library of Parliament No. 2014-05-E (February 19, 2014): 1.

32. See Angelini, "Regionalism in Canada," 30.

33. Jackson and Jackson, *Canadian Government*, 90–91.

34. "Equalization Being Used Unfairly, McGuinty Complains," *Globe and Mail*, May 10, 2006 <theglobeandmail.com/news/national/equalization-being-used-unfairly-mcguinty-complains/article1099417/>.

35. *The Daily*, "Gross Domestic Product by Industry: Provinces and Territories," Statistics Canada, May 12, 2016.

36. "Maritimes Kept Poor by Ontario," *Hamilton Spectator*, July 30, 2001.

37. "Equalization Debate Re-Emerges," *Hamilton Spectator*, June 26, 2018.

38. See *Globe and Mail*, March 20, 2015 <www.theglobeandmail.com/news/national/how-the-maritimes-became-canadas-incredible-shrinking-region/article23554298/>.

39. Pierre Burton, *The National Dream: The Great Railway 1871–1881* (Canada: Anchor Canada, 1970), 6.

40. Pierre Burton, *The Last Spike: The Great Railway 1881–1885* (Canada: Anchor Canada, 1970), 2.

41. For a detailed if depressing and disturbing account of the impact of these cuts, see Jo Davis, ed., *Not a Sentimental Journey: What's Behind the VIA Rail Cuts, What You Can Do About It* (Toronto: Gunbyfield Publishing, 1990).

42. See Angelini, "Regionalism in Canada," 28.

43. *Statistics Canada*, "Table 505-0003 — Federal, Provincial and Territorial Government Expenditures on Culture, by Culture Activity (dollars x 1,000)." <http://www5.statcan.gc.ca/cansim/a26?lang=eng&retrLang=eng&id=5050003&&pattern=&stByVal=1&p1=1&p2=31&tabMode=dataTable&csid>.

44. Keith Archer, Roger Gibbins, Rainer Knopff and Leslie Pal, *Parameters of Power: Canada's Political Institutions* (Toronto, ON: Nelson, 1995), 287.

45. "The Premier Ranking of Corporate Canada," *Financial Post* <https://business.financialpost.com/features/fp500-the-premier-ranking-for-corporate-canada>.

46. "Toronto's Bubble, Canada's Problem," *Globe and Mail*, April 8, 2017.

3

CONCEPTS OF HEALTH, ILLNESS AND DISEASE

A CROSS-CULTURAL PERSPECTIVE

Michelle Broderick

The quest for therapy all over the world is an important research issue since it reveals essential elements of people's social behaviour and provides insights into their perceived needs for different kinds of health services. — Axel Kroeger, "Anthropological and Socio-Medical Health Care Research in Developing Countries"[1]

Most healthcare providers working with people in or from different cultures inevitably experience a clash when their biomedical worldview collides with the worldview of their clients. — Patrice M. White, "Heat, Balance, Humors, and Ghosts: Postpartum in Cambodia"[2]

KEY OBJECTIVES

Understand how different cultures explain the nature of disease and illness.

Understand that, in ethnomedicine, mental illness is treated no differently than physiological illness.

Realize that plant-based medicines are used to treat a wide variety of illnesses.

Realize that a more comprehensive model of biomedicine incorporates complementary, alternative and ethnomedical practices.

Why study the nature of health and disease in different societies? Although the concepts of health, illness and disease are universal, the way they are understood and manifested varies depending on a person's culture. **Culture** is a system of shared beliefs, customs, behaviours and artifacts that members of a society use to cope with one another and with their world; these are transmitted from generation to generation. Studying different concepts of health, illness and disease among cultures not only gives us an appreciation for the variation inherent in human societies, but it can also lead to new types of treatments and approaches in healthcare. Since we live in a multicultural society, it is also important that healthcare practitioners develop cultural sensitivity in order to better serve a culturally diverse population. A crosscultural perspective is also useful in examining issues of health inequality, a global phenomenon.

MEDICAL ANTHROPOLOGY

Medical anthropology is the study of the socio-cultural dimensions of health, illness, disease and healthcare systems. **Health** is a state of physical, mental and social well-being; it is also a subjective state defined by cultural factors. **Disease** refers to the understanding of illness within a system of beliefs and practices of particular groups and practitioners — in other words, disorders as diagnosed by healthcare specialists. **Illness** refers to the learned and shared patterns of perceiving, experiencing and coping with symptoms, i.e., the manifestation of a disease.

    Healthcare systems encompass the people, institutions and resources which together provide healthcare services. Healthcare systems can be characterized as operating in two spheres or domains within which people experience and react to illness: the personal or popular sphere and the professional sphere. The **popular sphere** is the level where most of us experience illness and care, and this includes the family context, social networks

Box 3.1 Diversity in Action

As Canadians, we often look at what is happening in the United States in regards to racial unrest, limited access to and high cost of healthcare, and other social inequalities, and we think that things are so much better here. But are they really? Even if we do not acknowledge it, racism, social inequality and inequalities in access to healthcare still exist in Canada, and one of our biggest challenges is in providing healthcare to Indigenous communities. A YouTube video, posted by the National Aboriginal Health Organization (NAHO), discusses the need for cultural sensitivity in treating Indigenous Peoples in the biomedical setting: <youtube.com/watch?v=Bl-DU_9ukYg>.

and interactions within our larger community. Illnesses treated at this level tend to be relatively minor, for instance, a small cut or mild cold. The **professional sphere** centres around seeking health-related expertise from professional healing specialists. Through our experiences growing up in a given culture we learn which conditions and illnesses can be treated by ourselves, in the personal or popular sphere, and which are more serious and need to be treated by professional healthcare specialists.[3]

Healthcare systems, regardless of the culture in which they are found, possess several universal aspects. They are an integral part of the local culture and as such reflect that culture's worldview. Health, illness and disease are culturally defined. All healthcare systems have both preventive and curative aspects, and they provide not only a rationale for treatment but an explanation as to why a particular person is ill.[4]

NATURAL HISTORY OF DISEASE

The field of **paleopathology**, which examines diseases in prehistoric populations, has demonstrated that humans have always been exposed to disease stress in one form or another. Sources of information on prehistoric diseases include human remains that have been unintentionally preserved in ice or a peat bog or intentionally preserved though mummification. In these cases, intact soft tissues can provide evidence of disease, such as hardening of the arteries (arteriosclerosis), the eggs of parasites and disease-causing microorganisms. Coprolites, which are preserved feces, are another

---

Box 3.2 Think About...

The academic literature tends to describe three spheres within which people experience and react to illness: popular, folk and professional. The main distinction between the folk and professional spheres is that the folk encompasses ethnomedical healers while the professional encompasses biomedical healers. However, ethnomedical healers are professional in the sense that they undergo long periods of training and develop specialized knowledge. What they lack compared to biomedical healers is oversight by a government-recognized authority, such as a medical association. This distinction is ethnocentric and belittles the accomplishments and knowledge of traditional healers; therefore, both ethnomedical and biomedical healers should be included within the same sphere, i.e., the professional, as long as they are regarded as such within their own culture.

Source: Steven Polgar, "Health and Human Behavior: Areas of Interest Common to the Social and Medical Science," *Current Anthropology*, 3, 2 (1962): 159–205.

> **Box 3.3 Innov8**
>
> This chapter provides a brief overview of sources of information on the natural history of diseases in humans. Christina Warinner, an archaeological geneticist, looks at how the DNA of fossilized dental plaque can provide clues on diseases which affected ancient humans. Watch her TED Talk on this subject: <ted.com/talks/christina_warinner_tracking_ancient_diseases_using_plaque>.

source of information on the health of prehistoric populations. Coprolites provide information about diet since some parts of food — e.g., fish scales, animal hair and seeds — are not digested and therefore pass through the digestive system. Diseases can also be inferred from coprolites that contain the remains of intestinal worms or their eggs, or the remains of ticks, mites and lice, which can transmit disease.

The most common form of prehistoric human remains are skeletal (bones and teeth), which can provide evidence of congenital malformations (e.g., clubfoot), trauma (e.g., fractures), degenerative disorders (e.g., arthritis), infectious diseases (e.g., tuberculosis) and nutritional stress (e.g., scars indicating periods of arrested growth). When researchers have a large number of human skeletons from the same population, they can create a profile in terms of disease patterns and demography (age and sex composition, life expectancy, etc.). However, the main issue with relying on skeletal remains is that there are many diseases which do not leave their mark on bones, so we are not getting a complete picture of health in prehistoric populations.[5]

Although we have limited information on the health of prehistoric populations, there is even less direct information on how they may have treated illnesses. Just because a person survived an illness is not evidence of any deliberate attempt at treatment, because many illnesses and wounds eventually heal on their own. Instead, we often extrapolate information on disease and treatment by observing living pre-industrial populations. The drawback is that these are not true representations of prehistoric populations because they have not lived in a time vacuum and have therefore undergone change themselves. In fact, many pre-industrial populations have been forced into environmentally undesirable regions due to expansion of larger and more territorially aggressive industrial-based populations.[6] Another source of information used to infer how prehistoric populations may have treated illnesses is to look at animal behaviour, in particular that of non-human primates. Numerous monkey and ape species have been observed to ingest plants which have healing properties. From such indirect evidence it is possible to infer that prehistoric humans could also have had access to similar types of plants and have acquired the knowledge on how and when to use them effectively.[7]

Box 3.4 Innov8

This chapter cites a study which found that animals, including primates, self-medicate. It may surprise you to learn that insects do this too. For an insightful examination of this topic, watch the TED Talk by Jaap de Roode, a biologist who studies monarch butterflies: <ted.com/talks/jaap_de_roode_how_butterflies_self_medicate>.

THEORIES OF DISEASE

There are three basic elements seen in all medical systems: **diagnosis** (identification of a disease or the cause of illness), therapy (treatment of the disease or cure) and **prophylaxis** (prevention). Knowledge of diseases, their classification and their cause (**etiology**) are a part of every cultural system.

A theory of disease implies a theory of normality/abnormality. The concept of normality can be defined in several ways: statistically — those who deviate from an average are considered abnormal; functionally — the inability to function or cope is considered abnormal; and culturally — if we do not follow the rules of conduct, or norms, in our society we are considered abnormal. At the individual level, we judge ourselves to be in a state of abnormal health based on distress or lack of personal satisfaction.[8]

Theories of disease often reflect a culture's worldview (social and physical) and its place in the world, and can be categorized as either natural or supernatural causation theories.[9] **Natural causation theories** are those which account for illness as a physiological result of an event and include the following:

- infection — the human body is invaded by a foreign substance or organism (this does not necessarily imply the germ theory of disease);
- stress — exposure to physical or psychological stress such as over-exertion, severe dehydration or malnutrition, extreme temperatures or emotional distress;
- organic deterioration — a decrease in physical activity and function associated with the onset of old age, premature organ failure or the effects of inherited conditions;
- accident — an unintended physical injury that is also not caused by the supernatural. This is rarely seen as a major cause of disease due to the human tendency to personalize the cause of accidents and to associate them with supernatural causes. For instance, when you stub your toe, it is not unusual for you to blame the stool which got in your way; and

- overt human aggression — purposeful infliction of injuries on oneself or another human being.

Supernatural causation theories can be grouped into three categories: mystical, animistic and magical causations. **Mystical causation theories** are those which account for illness as a consequence of an act or experience caused by a punitive, impersonal, supernatural force. These include:

- fate — illness caused by astrological phenomena, an individual's destiny or bad luck;
- ominous sensations — illness caused by having powerful dreams or being exposed to particular sights or other sensations;
- contagion — illness caused by having contact with a contaminating item, substance or individual; or
- mystical retribution (also called taboo violation) — illness caused by violating a taboo or moral directive.

Animistic causation theories relate to illness being caused by a supernatural entity, such as a ghost, soul, spirit or deity. These include:

- soul loss — illness caused by the prolonged departure of one's soul from the body, which can be voluntary in nature or due to being frightened or captured by a supernatural entity; or
- spirit aggression — illness caused by the action of a malicious or angry supernatural entity. This is the most common cause of illness attributed to supernatural forces.

Magical causation theories are those which explain illness as the result of actions taken by a malevolent person who uses magical means to hurt another individual, and can be categorized as either sorcery or witchcraft:

- sorcery is when an illness is caused by a person who uses learned magical techniques either on their own or with the help of someone who possesses special supernatural abilities, such as a shaman; and
- witchcraft is when an illness is caused by the controlled or uncontrolled action of special type of person who is thought to possess supernatural powers coupled with a tendency for evil. Witchcraft is not something that can be learned, but rather is inherent in these individuals.

Of various cultures studied to date, the belief that illness is caused by supernatural forces is more common than the belief that illness is the result of natural forces. The most common explanations for illness are spirit aggression (animistic), sorcery (magical), punishment for violating taboos (mystical) and witchcraft (magical). It is also interesting to note that sorcery and witchcraft are rarely invoked as an explanation of illness within the same culture.[10]

BIOMEDICINE

Modern western medicine (**biomedicine**) is based on two assumptions: the first is the germ theory of disease, whereby many diseases are cause by germs or microorganisms; and the second is that illnesses can be prevented. The main elements of this medical system are that illness is firmly rooted only in natural causes; practitioners are formally trained and sanctioned by a governing body; diagnosis is based on the scientific approach, whereby practitioners locate the organic cause of the problem; and treatment is done in a formal setting, such as a hospital or clinic, using primarily drugs and surgery.[11] Biomedicine involves a hospital or clinical setting where healers work as a team, and where non-medical people, such as family and friends, do not play an active role in treatment. There are two main types of hospitals: general hospitals, which focus on organic or diseases of the body, and psychiatric hospitals, which focus on psychological or diseases of the mind. The main function of a hospital is to treat and restore a patient to health so they can return as an active participant in society.

Within hospitals there is a rigid role separation between the occupational groups of healthcare workers, which is related to the highly specialized services they offer. These include diagnostic specialists, such as x-ray and pathology technicians, pharmacists, physical therapists, social workers, and providers of more mundane services, such as dietary aides and housekeepers. Occupations such as housekeeping require little in the way of education or training, while most healthcare roles require college certification or university degrees and internships. Healthcare practitioners are required to undergo extensive training over a number of years and must maintain good standing in a related association in order to continue to practise in their field.

Patients' experience of the hospital setting often engenders stress, which can be similar to culture shock. They are removed from their familiar environment and often do not know how to react or behave; they have to learn new ways of interacting with healthcare professionals. They often encounter issues with communication because healthcare professionals use a specialized (and often foreign to the patient) language, which patients must adjust to. Such "hospitalese" includes phrases like: *Did you void this morning? I've scheduled you for an EEG. Do you regularly experience heart palpitations? Your vital signs are stable today.* There is also a lack of familiarity with and a need to learn how to use new cultural items. For example, patients have to push a button for service, and they may need to learn how to use a bedpan. Patients also lose their sense of identity and often suffer from depersonalization due to hospital policies which dictate that they must wear standard hospital gowns instead of their own clothing, have their identity certified by a plastic bracelet and become a "case" in room number X. Their normal life recedes as the role of "patient" is forced upon them. Patients also suffer a loss of control over their own bodies and their physical environment as they must submit to the authority of hospital staff 24/7. Their schedule is planned by hospital staff, who dictate when meals are served, when medications are taken and when other treatments are administered. Patients are under constant supervision and suffer from a loss of privacy, their mobility is often restricted, and they are forced to depend on others.[12] These rules and regulations are for the benefit of hospital personnel and not patients, and while there has been a general relaxation in some of the more rigid rules over time, the experience of being hospitalized is often still a demoralizing one.

Biomedical healers are mainly doctors, nurses and nurse-practitioners, and they are assisted by an array of paramedical healthcare professionals, such as physical therapists, osteopaths, chiropractors and massage therapists, to name but a few. Regardless of the variation of roles, the doctor is seen as having the ultimate authority to dictate treatment, especially in the hospital setting.

There is growing evidence of systemic gender and ethnic bias within the biomedical model. Health practitioners treat patients differently on the basis of their gender and/or ethnicity, which often results in poorer health outcomes for these patients.[13] Moreover, not only does gender and ethnic bias have a negative impact on health outcomes, it also affects the results of medical research. Take, for instance, genome-wide association studies, which are studies that focus on how the human genetic makeup can impact the efficacy of drug therapies. Such studies tend to draw genetic samples from individuals of European descent, with results therefore based on limited genetic diversity and of questionable value in the development of gene and drug therapies directed at other ethnic groups.[14]

Box 3.5 Diversity in Action

Generally, men have a reputation for not seeking medical intervention. What happens if you combine that tendency with men in particular ethnic groups who feel dismissed by biomedical practitioners? Watch the TED Talk by Joseph Ravenell, a physician who uses community engagement to tackle the issue of health inequality directed at African-American men: <ted.com/talks/joseph_ravenell_how_barbershops_can_keep_men_healthy>.

Box 3.6 Diversity in Action

People react differently to drugs based on their genetic makeup. As a result, biomedical treatments are becoming increasingly targeted to the genetic makeup of patients, which often makes them more effective. But what happens if the majority of genetic studies exclude most of the world's populations? Is this not a form of discrimination? Watch the TED Talk by Keolu Fox, a geneticist who argues that genetic research needs to be more diverse: <ted.com/talks/keolu_fox_why_genetic_research_must_be_more_diverse>.

Mental Illness within Biomedicine

Within the biomedical model, there are two sources of classification systems on mental illness: the *Diagnostic and Statistical Manual of Mental Disorders*, now in its fifth edition (DSM-5), which is published by the American Psychiatric Association; and the *International Classification of Mental and Behavioural Disorders*, now in its tenth edition (ICD-10), which is published by the World Health Organization. Both the DSM, which is more widely used in North America, and the ICD have many drawbacks compared to the diagnosis of physiological ailments, namely that the underlying causes of most mental illnesses are not well understood and that the identification of what constitutes a mental illness is subjective, influenced by culture and changes over time. (For example, in the DSM-1 and DSM-2 homosexuality was classified and regarded as a mental disorder, but in 1973 it was removed in the third edition of the DSM.) Since psychological illness is not well understood, syndromes are usually grouped together based on their symptoms rather than their underlying causes, as is usually the case in physiological illness. In the biomedical model, the treatment of mental illness focuses on psychotherapy and drug therapy, often in conjunction. Although treatment can be long-term, it is often effective.

Mental illness can be classified into five main categories of disorders: neurotic, psychosomatic, personality, organic brain and psychotic.[15] **Neurotic disorders** are related to anxiety and stress, things that we all deal with on a day-to-day basis. When a person's reaction to anxiety and stress has a negative impact on their behaviour and quality of life, i.e., they cannot cope with this anxiety, they have developed a neurotic disorder. For example, agoraphobia, or fear of open spaces, can engender panic attacks which are so severe that individuals become housebound.

Psychosomatic disorders are when physiological symptoms are caused by emotional stress and anxiety. Symptoms are varied and can affect numerous systems in the body and result in aches and pains, hyperventilation, high blood pressure, eczema and hives, heartburn and gastritis. If these persist, they can result in serious physiological damage to the individual.

Personality disorders refer to behavioural patterns that have a negative impact on interpersonal relationships, largely because individuals focus on meeting their own needs at the expense of the needs of others. One of the most well-known types of personality disorder is the antisocial personality. Individuals with antisocial disorder show no empathy for others, disregard social mores and laws, and cannot control their impulses.

Organic brain disorders refer to behavioural problems caused by physical damage to the brain, which can result from an infection such as encephalitis, a concussion, a stroke or tissue degeneration (as seen with dementia), as well as exposure to toxic substances, such as lead and carbon monoxide. Symptoms are varied and can include loss of memory, speech, vision and mobility.

Psychotic disorders result in a distortion of how an individual sees and interacts with people and the world around them. Of the five categories of disorders, this type is among the most disruptive to the individual and their family. For example, psychotic depression is characterized by a loss of interest in life and intense feelings of guilt; these individuals are often at risk of committing suicide.

ETHNOMEDICINE

Ethnomedicine refers to healthcare systems found in traditional, non-Western societies. As mentioned previously, there are universal aspects to all healthcare systems. They are an integral part of the culture, and disease classifications are often related to religious beliefs. They also reflect a culture's worldview. For instance, health is defined in many traditional cultures by the concept of equilibrium between hot and cold forces in the body and the surrounding environment; in these cultures, the general health of the community is also viewed in terms of equilibrium or balance. All healthcare systems have both preventive and curative aspects, and also function to provide a rationale for treatment and to explain why a particular person is ill. In many cultures, medical systems also play an important role in sanctioning and supporting cultural norms. For instance, if an illness is attributed to a taboo violation, that means the illness was sent as punishment for not following the rules of conduct. Fear of getting ill can therefore be seen as a mechanism of social control.[16]

Box 3.7 Innov8

How can you objectively measure the health of a population? There are several techniques used in demography (the study of human populations based on statistical analysis), such as the crude death rate and life expectancy at birth. The crude death rate refers to the number of deaths occurring in a year per 1,000 people, while the life expectancy at birth refers to how long a newborn can expect to live on average. These rates vary from population to population and over time. For a fascinating examination of how demographic variables and economic indicators can shed light on the history of global health, watch the YouTube video by the late Hans Rosling, who was a physician and professor of international health at the Karolinska Institute in Sweden: <youtube.com/watch?v=jbkSRLYSojo>.

Traditional Healers

Healers in non-Western cultures often play multiple roles in their societies. Through diagnosis they can uncover which individuals have violated cultural norms. Disease is thus seen as a social sanction, and diagnosis of an illness becomes a form of social justice. Because they reduce social tensions, traditional healers are often regarded as peacekeepers. In smaller scale societies, individuals are mutually dependent on one another and often interact closely with their neighbours. Overt social conflict in this type of setting can be devastating to the community at large. Healing can reduce or eliminate any perceived conflict. In such cases, an illness can be seen as a symptom of the larger problems in a society, and in treating the individual, equilibrium is restored to all. For this reason, healing sessions often occur in public. Traditional healers can also take on the role of entertainer, as rituals are often dramatic and help to validate the status of healers in their community.[17]

There is an association between the type of healer and the form of subsistence practised within a particular culture. Foragers who live in small nomadic bands tend to have only one healer, who has been trained to intercede with the supernatural, while agricultural-based and larger, more sedentary communities will have a variety of specialized healers.[18]

The most common type of traditional healer is the **shamanistic healer** (e.g., shaman, singer, etc.). This is an individual who acts on behalf of individuals or a society to intervene with the supernatural. They are recruited into this role either through inheritance or because they experienced an unusual event related to the supernatural. For instance, they may have survived a serious illness or exhibit a characteristic which is highly valued and believed to be rooted in the supernatural. These individuals are held in high esteem, but they are also feared because they can control certain aspects of the supernatural. They are not only believed to have the power to cure illness, but they are also thought to be able to cause illness. For these reasons, shamanistic healers usually live in a separate location outside of their community.[19]

Non-shamanistic healers are individuals who share the role of shaman, which is distributed among several healing specialists. They are often restricted to curing specific types of illnesses or assisting in particular life events. Non-shamanistic healers include spiritualists, diviners, herbalists and midwives. Unlike shamanistic healers, they focus on the problems affecting individuals and are not regarded as guardians of the well-being of their society. **Spiritualists** are able to communicate directly with supernatural beings. **Diviners** are healers who communicate indirectly with the supernatural. They interpret symptoms through prognostication and prescribe treatments. **Herbalists** are associated with non-supernatural illnesses (theories of natural causation) and prescribe plant-based treatments. **Midwives** are there to support the mother-to-be and to ease the birthing process; this can involve giving massages, preparing herbal teas and applying other treatments, as well as being prepared to deal with any complications which may arise.[20] The underlying rationale for non-shamanistic healers is to restore the body's internal harmony or balance. Each type of healer has their own rules of qualification, initiation and methods of practice. In all cases, traditional healers undergo long periods of training, not unlike practitioners in biomedicine.[21]

Treatment by traditional healers involves rituals, surgical techniques and a pharmacopeia. Rituals used in curing can serve multiple functions, such as reinforcing social norms. Sessions often involve not only the healer and the patient, but the patient's family and neighbours. In cases where an illness is linked to a taboo violation, part of the ritual involves extracting a confession. In this way patients take an active role in the healing process and help to reinforce the values and norms of their society.[22] Another common element of rituals involves a sacrifice on the part of the patient; this could be an animal sacrifice or the patient has to give up something they value. Surgical techniques used by traditional healers do not necessarily imply the cutting of flesh, as the word also refers to physical manipulation. This can take the form of massage, the setting of bones, blood-letting, bathing, suturing and cauterizing, to name a few.

Perhaps the most studied aspect of treatment by traditional healers is the use of a **pharmacopeia**, which is also a universal component of medical systems. A pharmacopeia refers to the knowledge on how to diagnose and treat illnesses; specifically, how to prepare medications, how much to use and in which situations to administer them. Sources of ethnomedical medications or treatments can include animal, mineral and botanical elements.

Cultures which have a strong belief in animistic disease causation will rarely make direct use of animal-based cures, as animals are believed to possess powerful and potentially dangerous spirits. Instead, they will be used indirectly on the spirit level and under strict ritual conditions. Some examples of animal parts used in traditional treatments include horns, organs and bones. Minerals used in traditional treatments can include different types of earth, ashes from a fire and stones, as they are thought to contain powerful spirits. Researchers have found in some cases that these materials possess pharmacologically active ingredients; for example, some muds contain soil bacteria with antibacterial properties.

Most cures used by traditional healers come from plants and are the culmination of experiments conducted over thousands of years, with knowledge passed from generation to generation through oral tradition. In biomedicine less than 1 percent of all known plant species have been tested for medicinal applications, and yet 25 percent of our medicines have originated from this small percentage. For example, taxol, which is derived from the bark of the Pacific yew tree, has been found to be effective in the treatment of ovarian and other cancers. Traditional treatments make use of a wide variety of botanicals, such as leaves, bark, seeds, fruits, roots and even fungus. A large proportion of non-Western herbal treatments (25–50 percent) have pharmacologically active properties.[23]

Botanicals used in traditional treatments can be categorized as anesthetics, narcotics or stimulants. Many are used in the treatment of illness, e.g., coca is used as an anesthetic. Others induce hallucinations, which have more of a ritual significance, as they are believed to alter the healer's state of mind to facilitate direct communication with supernatural elements and entities. Many botanicals have astringent properties and are effective in stopping bleeding, e.g., wild geranium root. Febrifuges are botanicals which can reduce or eliminate a fever, such as the bark of the dogwood tree. Cathartics are naturally occurring laxatives, such as mayapple root. Some botanicals are associated with childbirth and are used to ease labour, birth and recovery, e.g., the cotton root bark. Plants found to destroy intestinal worms are called vermifuges, and examples include the roots of the wild plum and cherry. Plants used to induce vomiting are referred to as emetics, e.g., ipecac, which is derived from the bark of a Brazilian tree. Numerous plants are also used as antibiotics (antibacterial, antifungal and antiviral); for instance, many of the plants for teeth cleaning around the world contain either antibiotic properties, tannins or fluorides, all of which inhibit the growth of microorganisms.[24] Another category of botanicals includes those considered to be contraceptives, as they can suppress ovulation and affect a woman's menstrual cycle, such as Chinese stone seed. The most feared category of botanicals are the poisons, such as curare, which is used as an arrow poison in hunting and is made from tree

DIVERSITY IN ACTION

Box 3.8 Diversity in Action

Why should we care about protecting the environment, rainforests, biodiversity and traditional, ethnomedical knowledge? Are we destroying future sources of medicine which may help to cure cancer and other life-threatening diseases? Watch the TED Talk by Mark Plotkin, an Amazonian ethnobotanist who is fighting to preserve traditional knowledge: <ted.com/talks/mark_plotkin_what_the_people_of_the_amazon_know_that_you_don_t>.

resin; curare is harmless if taken orally but fatal if it gets into the bloodstream; in biomedicine it is used as a muscle relaxant and to paralyze muscles during surgery.[25]

Despite the work of numerous ethnobotanists and anthropologists, ethnomedical knowledge continues to be lost with the passing of each generation. This not only impacts the quality of healthcare available to members of Indigenous cultures, but it also seriously threatens the future development of new drugs and treatments.[26]

The prevention of illness can come from traditional healers in the form of charms or rituals to restore and maintain harmony, but most prevention is practised directly by individuals in society (in the personal or popular sphere) and can be in the form of prayers, body painting, respecting taboos or the proper treatment of ancestral spirits and other spirits which inhabit the natural world. Other behaviours which are seen as helping to prevent illness include personal hygiene, such as cleaning teeth with small sticks or roots from particular trees and other plants and using soaps in cleaning. The disposal of waste products, such as feces, urine, soiled water and garbage, although often related to religious or magical injunctions, such as hiding waste for fear that it could be used against you in sorcery, also play a role in preventing the spread of disease. Food habits, both cooking and preparation, can have a huge impact and are often influenced by cultural beliefs. For example, in Ecuador, there is a folk belief that cooked food which has become cold is dangerous to eat and is only made safe through re-heating; needless to say, this would also serve to detoxify food by killing any harmful bacteria which may be present. Nutrition is another important factor affecting health and preventing illness. In general, the diet of people in traditional cultures is a healthy one; however, problems tend to occur with the introduction of processed Western foods, which are often viewed as prestigious. Housing and settlement patterns can also either promote or undermine health. For instance, since foragers and pastoralists are highly mobile, sanitation is not an important issue, but with prolonged sedentism sanitation can become an important factor affecting health.[27]

Mental Illness within Ethnomedicine

Ethnomedicine recognizes and treats not only physiological illness but mental illness as well. **Ethnopsychiatry** is the aspect of ethnomedicine in traditional societies which focuses on how individuals view and deal with mental illness. Biomedicine separates physiological and mental illness, but this separation does not exist in ethnomedicine. This is partly because supernatural disease causation theories explain both types of illness. All cultures have and recognize what constitutes for them abnormal behaviour. However, there is considerable crosscultural variation in what constitutes atypical behaviour, the degree or seriousness associated with it, and the accepted course of action.

Every culture exerts social control affecting the behaviour and activities of its members. This is important in order that society continues to function, as without it there would be chaos. Social norms of behaviour are first learned within the context of the family and later through interaction with peers and others. This is referred to as cultural conditioning, and it can influence how mental illness manifests. The majority of mental illnesses in traditional cultures are explained in supernatural terms. For example, it can be the result of possession (by a ghost, spirit or deity), as retribution for violating a taboo or due to witchcraft. Mental illnesses can also be inherited, transmitted from infected individuals (similar to the way you can catch a cold from others around you), the result of physical injuries (such as a blow to the head or severe blood-loss), or due to cosmic forces or experiences which cause emotional distress.

Treatment of mental illness in non-Western cultures usually involves a public ritual where the audience may play a significant role. There is often a special importance assigned to symbols, and treatment does not differ from that of physiological illnesses (the two are not separated). Non-Western therapy takes a practical approach which is aimed at achieving quick results and focuses on reducing or eliminating symptoms; therefore, treatment is typically short-term in nature. In general, traditional healers have been found to be quite effective in treating mental illness.[28]

Although mental or psychological illness is found in all cultures, the way it is manifested tends to be culture-specific, i.e., the characteristics of mental illness are influenced by culture. For this reason, researchers often refer to folk psychiatric or **culture-specific disorders**. These are indigenously perceived mental illnesses, which include changes in behaviour and of experience.[29] What follows is an overview of some of the more well-known culture-specific disorders, such as startle matching, sleep paralysis, sudden mass assault and running syndromes.

Startle matching syndrome consists of the presentation of a stimulus which, for a given individual, is so traumatic that it causes an episode of unusual and involuntary behaviour (a type of hysterical reaction). Symptoms can include hypersensitivity to sudden fright, hyper suggestibility, echopraxia (automatic repetition of the movements of others), echolalia (automatic repetition of words/sentences uttered by others), coprolalia (uttering obscenities), coprophagia (eating of filth) and a dissociative or trance-like state. Examples include *latah* in Malaysia and Indonesia and *imu* in Japan.[30]

The main symptom of **sleep paralysis syndrome** is the sudden feeling of not being able to move or speak when in a borderline sleep state, although the individual remains fully conscious of surrounding events and people. Individuals report feelings of anxiety or fear, being in a dissociative or trance-like state and experiencing hallucinations, such as someone sitting on their chest. Others report that the self or soul is dissociated from the body and is struggling to return. The episode is usually followed by exhaustion. Examples include *uqamairineg* among the Inuit and old hag in Newfoundland.[31]

Symptoms of **sudden mass assault syndrome** include dissociative or trance-like episodes, outbursts of violent and aggressive or homicidal behaviour directed at people or objects, persecutory ideas, automatism, amnesia and exhaustion after a return to consciousness following the episode. This syndrome has been observed in a variety of cases: in some, individuals were otherwise psychologically healthy; in others, individuals did suffer from a previous psychopathology. Examples include *amok* in Malaysia and Indonesia and *mal de pelea* in Puerto Rico.[32]

Running syndrome is characterized as a retreat from reality, literally or figuratively. Symptoms include brooding, depressive silences, loss or disturbance of consciousness during a seizure, tearing off of clothing, fleeing or wandering, echolalia, echopraxia and glossolalia (unintelligible speech). Following the attack, the individual is completely exhausted. Between attacks, the individual's behaviour is considered normal, and they are treated as such. Examples include *pibloktoq* or arctic hysteria among the Inuit and *grisi siknis* among the Miskito Indians in Nicaragua and Honduras.[33]

Box 3.9 Think About...

Can fear negatively affect your health? Barbara Natterson-Horowitz, a cardiologist who consults with veterinarians in the treatment of animals, argues that insights from vet research could be applied to humans, as both humans and animals suffer from many of the same diseases. Take, for instance, fear-induced heart failure; although a relatively new phenomenon in Western medicine, this is not the case in veterinarian circles — wild animals, captured for treatment due to an injury or other illness, have been found to be highly susceptible to fear-induced death, which they refer to as capture-myopathy. Watch Dr Natterson-Horowitz's TED Talk on this topic: <ted.com/talks/barbara_natterson_horowitz_what_veterinarians_know_that_doctors_don_t>.

Many of the culture-specific disorders examined in this chapter are found primarily in non-Western cultures; however, this does not mean that Western cultures are immune to culture-specific disorders. Take for example anorexia nervosa. This syndrome is characterized as an eating disorder whereby the individual fears gaining weight, even views themselves as overweight, and therefore severely restricts their caloric intake. In extreme cases, these individuals will become emaciated, and if left untreated anorexia nervosa can ultimately result in death. This particular disorder tends to be limited to Western cultures and is associated with unrealistic body images perpetuated by media and the fashion industry. Due to globalization and increasing Westernization of many cultures, the incidence of anorexia is increasing in non-Western cultures, such as Japan.[34]

MEDICALIZATION OF LIFE EVENTS

Over time, biomedicine has gained control over major life events, such as birth and death, to the extent that these are now considered to be medical problems in need of treatment.[35] This section examines this trend by comparing how these life events are viewed and treated in Western and non-Western cultures.

In many cultures birth is seen as a natural process, not a disease. Women normally give birth in their home or the home of a close relative. Usually, only women attend at births, and they support the pregnant woman and ease the process of giving birth.[36] Women are free to move around in the time leading up to delivery and usually deliver in an upright position, making use of gravity to help move the infant down through the birth canal.[37] In Western cultures, control over the birth process is no longer in the hands of women but rather in the hands of physicians. Pregnancy and the act of giving birth are treated as an illness, and birth occurs in the antiseptic hospital environment. Women often give birth in a supine position with their feet in stirrups, not to ease delivery, as in fact this complicates the birth process, but because it is a more comfortable position for attending physicians. However, this is changing. During the 1970s, Western perceptions of birth began to shift with the rise the home birth movement.[38] While most women still give birth in hospitals (at least in urban settings), they are usually attended by midwives in specially designed birthing rooms, not operating rooms; there is also less medical intervention, which often results in a faster recovery time for the mother.[39]

In Western cultures, as with birth, dying and death have been removed from the family setting to that of the hospital, nursing home or other type of long-term care facility. The dying patient is isolated from others and visiting is strictly controlled by staff. The conditions imposed on those who are dying are counter-productive as they create anxiety, uncertainty and frustration for both patients and their families. In traditional cultures, families tend to live in multi-generation households. The young grow up with elderly family members and witness their sometimes slow dissolution and eventual death. When it comes time to die, individuals are not removed to an institution but remain at home surrounded by family and friends, who help to support them and see to their comfort.[40] In the 1960s, the hospice and palliative care movement began to spread in Western cultures, which has helped to create a more supportive environment for people who are dying and for their families and friends; however, the majority still die in isolation and in an institutional setting.[41] Western cultures still have a lot to learn from traditional approaches to dying and death, the most important components of which are providing emotional and social supports.[42]

INTERSECTION OF BIOMEDICINE AND ETHNOMEDICINE

The biomedical model is not the most effective way to provide healthcare to the majority of the world's population, and this was recognized by the World Health Organization (WHO) in 1978.[43] Ethnomedicine is less expensive, more accessible (especially for rural populations) and more effective in the sense that patients are more satisfied with treatment.

In 1978 the World Health Organization incorporated traditional medicine in their efforts to deliver primary healthcare worldwide.

In Western cultures, the shift from the dominance of biomedicine to a more inclusive and holistic model is seen with the spread and acceptance of complementary and alternative treatments. One of the strengths of the ethnomedical model is that

---

Box 3.10 Think About...

What is wrong with our pharmaceutical industry and how can we fix it? In 2015 Martin Shkreli, chief executive officer of Turing Pharmaceuticals, increased the price of a life-saving HIV drug from $13.50 to $750 US. Shkreli faced no repercussions for his actions, although there was a huge public outcry. Why were his actions allowed? Can we not adopt a better, fairer system? Watch the TED Talk by Thomas Pogge, a philosopher who proposes a new way for medications to be developed and sold: <ted.com/talks/thomas_pogge_medicine_for_the_99_percent>.

> **Box 3.11 Diversity in Action**
>
> Using both biomedical and ethnomedical elements together in the delivery of healthcare programs can make them more effective, especially in Indigenous communities. In a TEDx Talk, Marcia Anderson-DeCoteau, a Cree-Saulteaux physician, discusses the gaps in healthcare in Indigenous communities and how these can be addressed: <youtube.com/watch?v=IpKjtujtEYI>.

treatment is based on the whole individual, where issues of the body are not separated from issues of the mind. This idea has permeated biomedicine and has developed into the concept of integrative medicine. The basic premise behind **integrative medicine** is to incorporate complementary, alternative, ethnomedical (traditional) and biomedical healthcare practices into one package, in order to provide more accessible and effective treatments.[44] Examples include treatments based on herbal medicine, massage therapy and chiropractic manipulation; therapies which recognize the importance of the mind-body connection, such as yoga, meditation and tai chi; treatments based on the flow of energy in the body; and treatments based on traditional Chinese medicine, traditional Indian medicine (Ayurveda), homeopathy and naturopathy.[45] Integrative medicine takes a more holistic approach to healthcare with an emphasis on preventative self-care.

CRITICAL REVIEW QUESTIONS

1. Can you have an illness but not a disease? Conversely, can you have a disease but not an illness?
2. Why is it important to not only preserve traditional healing knowledge but to encourage its practice?
3. How can a social policy intended to assimilate a culture, such as the residential school system in Canada, have a negative impact on the health of those being assimilated?
4. Can you think of any other culture-specific disorders found in Western cultures besides anorexia nervosa?
5. Have you or any members of your family sought treatment from a traditional healer or experienced complementary/alternative healthcare treatments? How did these experiences differ from treatment by a biomedical healthcare practitioner?

RECOMMENDED READINGS

Carol R. Ember and Melvin Ember (eds.), *Encyclopedia of Medical Anthropology: Health and Illness in the World's Cultures,* volumes 1 and 2 (New York: Kluwer Academic/Plenum Publishers, 2004).

Donald Joralemon, *Exploring Medical Anthropology*, 4th edition (New York: Routledge, 2017).

Andrew Strathern and Pamela J. Stewart, *Curing and Healing: Medical Anthropology in Global Perspective*, 2nd edition (Durham, NC: Carolina Academic Press, 2010).

Andrea S. Wiley and John S. Allen, *Medical Anthropology: A Biocultural Approach*, 3rd edition (New York: Oxford University Press, 2017).

Michael Winkelman, *Culture and Health: Applying Medical Anthropology* (San Francisco: Jossey-Bass, 2009).

KEY TERMS

animistic causation theories: theories in which illness is caused by a supernatural entity, such as a ghost, soul, spirit or deity.

biomedicine: modern Western medicine.

culture: a system of shared beliefs, customs, behaviours and artifacts that members of a society use to cope with one another and with their world; these are transmitted from generation to generation.

culture-specific disorders: psychological illnesses as perceived by members of a particular culture.

diagnosis: the identification of a disease or the cause of illness.

disease: the understanding of illness within a system of beliefs and practices of particular groups and practitioners.

diviners: non-shamanistic healers who communicate indirectly with the supernatural.

ethnomedicine: healthcare systems found in traditional, non-Western societies.

ethnopsychiatry: the aspect of ethnomedicine in traditional cultures which focuses on how individuals view and deal with mental illness.

etiology: the classification and cause of diseases.

health: a state of physical, mental and social well-being, which is defined by cultural factors.

healthcare systems: refers to the people, institutions and resources which together provide healthcare services.

herbalists: non-shamanistic healers who treat illnesses which are associated with natural causation theories.

illness: the learned and shared patterns of perceiving, experiencing and coping with symptoms of a disease.

integrative medicine: an approach to healthcare which focuses on the whole individual and which incorporates knowledge and treatments from complementary and alternative medicine, ethnomedicine and biomedicine.

magical causation theories: theories in which illness is caused by the actions of a living person who uses magical means to hurt others.

medical anthropology: the study of the socio-cultural dimensions of health, illness, disease and healthcare systems.

midwives: individuals who attend a woman during delivery and who provide support and ease the birthing process.

mystical causation theories: theories in which illness is caused by an impersonal, supernatural force.

natural causation theories: theories in which illness is caused by a physiological event.

neurotic disorders: psychological disorders which are related to having an extreme reaction to anxiety and stress.

non-shamanistic healers: individuals who share the role of shaman, which is distributed among several healing specialists who are often restricted to curing specific types of illnesses or assisting in particular life events. These include spiritualists, diviners, herbalists and midwives.

organic brain disorders: psychological disorders where behavioural problems are caused by physical damage to the brain.

paleopathology: the study of diseases in prehistoric populations.

personality disorders: psychological disorders whereby behavioural patterns have a negative impact on interpersonal relationships, largely because these individuals focus on meeting their own needs at the expense of the needs of others.

pharmacopeia: refers to the knowledge on how to prepare medications, how much to use and in which situations they should be administered.

popular sphere: a level where people experience illness and care; this level includes the family context, social networks and interactions within our larger community.

professional sphere: a level where people experience illness and care; this level centres around seeking health-related expertise from professional healing specialists.

prophylaxis: actions taken to prevent or protect from illness.

psychosomatic disorders: psychological disorders which are characterized by physiological symptoms caused by emotional stress and anxiety.

psychotic disorders: psychological disorders which result in a distortion of how an individual sees and interacts with people and the world around them.

running syndrome: syndrome characterized as either a literal or figurative retreat from reality.

shamanistic healers: the most common type of traditional healer; a person who acts on behalf of individuals or their society to intervene with the supernatural.

sleep paralysis syndrome: syndrome characterized by anxiety or fear caused by not being able to move or speak while in a borderline sleep state.

spiritualists: non-shamanistic healers who are able to communicate directly with supernatural beings.

startle matching syndrome: syndrome characterized by an extreme, hysterical reaction to a stimulus.

sudden mass assault syndrome: syndrome characterized by trance-like episodes during which an individual displays outbursts of violent and aggressive behaviour towards other people or objects.

supernatural causation theories: theories in which illness is caused by supernatural intervention.

Notes

1. Axel Kroeger, "Anthropological and Socio-Medical Health Care Research in Developing Countries," *Social Science & Medicine*, 17, 3, 1983: 147–161.
2. Patrice M. White, "Heat, Balance, Humors, and Ghosts: Postpartum in Cambodia," *Health Care for Women International*, 25, 2, 2004: 179–194.
3. Pamela I. Erickson, *Ethnomedicine* (Waveland Press, 2008); Arthur Kleinman, "Concepts and a Model for the Comparison of Medical Systems as Cultural Systems," *Social Science & Medicine*, Part B: Medical Anthropology, 12, 2 (1978): 85–93; Steven Polgar, "Health and Human Behavior: Areas of Interest Common to the Social and Medical Sciences," *Current Anthropology*, 3, 2 (1962): 159–205.
4. Frederick L. Dunn, "Traditional Asian Medicine and Cosmopolitan Medicine as Adaptive Systems," in Charles Leslie (ed.), *Asian Medical Systems: A Comparative Study* (University of California Press, 1976): 133–158.
5. Ann McElroy and Patricia K. Townsend, *Medical Anthropology: An Ecological Perspective* (Westview Press, 1985); Pat Shipman, Alan Walker and David Bichell, *The Human Skeleton* (Harvard University Press, 1985).
6. Susan Andreatta and Gary Ferraro, *Elements of Culture: An Applied Perspective* (Wadsworth, 2013).
7. Michael A. Huffman, "Current Evidence for Self-Medication in Primates: A Multidisciplinary Perspective," *Yearbook of Physical Anthropology*, 40 (1997): 171–200.
8. Charles C. Hughes, "Medical Care: I. Ethnomedicine," in David L. Sills (ed.), *International Encyclopedia of the Social Sciences*, vol. 10 (Macmillan Company and Free Press, 1968): 87–93.
9. George P. Murdock, *Theories of Illness: A World Survey* (University of Pittsburgh Press, 1980).
10. Murdock, *Theories of Illness*.
11. Lorna G.Moore, Peter W. Van Arsdale, JoAnn E. Glittenberg and Robert A. Aldrich, *The Biocultural Basis of Health* (C.V. Mosby Co., 1980).
12. George M. Foster and Barbara G. Anderson, *Medical Anthropology* (John Wiley and Sons, 1978).
13. David R. Williams and Ronald Wyatt, "Racial Bias in Health Care and Health — Challenges and Opportunities," *Journal of the American Medical Association*, 314, 6 (2015): 555–556; Elizabeth N. Chapman, Anna Kaatz and Molly Carnes, "Physicians and Implicit Bias: How Doctors May Unwittingly Perpetuate Health Care Disparities," *Journal of General Internal Medicine*, 28, 11 (2013): 1504–1510.
14. Susanne B. Haga, "Impact of Limited Population Diversity of Genome-Wide Association Studies." *Genetics in Medicine*, 12, 2 (2010): 81–84; Carlos D. Bustamante, Esteban G. Burchard and Francisco M. De La Vega, "Genomics for the World," *Nature*, 475, 7355 (2011): 163–165.
15. Jonathan P. Beard, David L. Hayter and Eric Shenkar, *The Diagnosis and Treatment of Mental Illness: An Introduction* (Wayne State University Press, 1989).
16. Francis J. Clune, Jr., "Witchcraft, the Shaman, and Active Pharmacopoeia," in Francis X. Grollig and Harold B. Haley (eds.), *Medical Anthropology* (Mouton Publishers, 1976): 5–10.
17. Corinne S. Wood, *Human Sickness and Health: A Bicultural View* (Mayfield Publishing Co., 1979).
18. Merrill Singer and Hans Baer, *Introducing Medical Anthropology: A Discipline in Action* (AltaMira Press, 2007).

19. Wood, *Human Sickness and Health.*
20. Brigitte Jordan, *Birth in Four Cultures: A Crosscultural Investigation of Childbirth in Yucatan, Holland, Sweden and the United States* (Eden Press, 1983).
21. Foster and Anderson, *Medical Anthropology;* Wood, *Human Sickness and Health.*
22. Foster and Anderson, *Medical Anthropology.*
23. Merrill Singer and Hans Baer, *Introducing Medical Anthropologyn.*
24. C.D. Wu, I.A. Darout and N. Skaug, "Chewing Sticks: Timeless Natural Toothbrushes for Oral Cleansing," *Journal of Periodontal Research*, 36, 5 (2001): 275–284.
25. Francis J. Clune, Jr., "Witchcraft, the Shaman, and Active Pharmacopoeia"; Robert A. Halberstein, "Medicinal Plants: Historical and Cross-Cultural Usage Patterns," *Annals of Epidemiology*, 15, 9 (2005): 686–699; Virgil J. Vogel, "American Indian Influence on the American Pharmacopeia," in George G. Meyer, Kenneth Blum and John G. Cull (eds.), *Folk Medicine and Herbal Healing* (Charles C. Thomas, 1981): 103–113; Krippner, Stanley and Benjamin Colodzin, "Folk Healing and Herbal Medicine: An Overview," in Meyer, Blum and Cull, *Folk Medicine and Herbal Healing*, 13–29.
26. Michael J. Balick, "Traditional Knowledge: Lessons from the Past, Lessons for the Future," in Charles R. McManis (ed.), *Biodiversity and Law: Intellectual Property, Biotechnology and Traditional Knowledge* (Earthscan, 2007).
27. Charles C. Hughes, "Public Health in Non-Literate Societies," in Iago Galdston (ed.), *Man's Image in Medicine and Anthropology* (International Universities Press, 1963): 157–233; Ethne Barnes, *Diseases and Human Evolution* (University of New Mexico Press, 2005); D.P. Mukherjee, "Industrializing Influence on Health, Care and Cure in Different Cultures,"in Buddhadeb Chaudhuri (ed.), *Cultural and Environmental Dimensions on Health* (Inter-India Publications, 1990): 363–368.
28. Foster and Anderson, *Medical Anthropology.*
29. Foster and Anderson, *Medical Anthropology.*
30. Ronald C. Simons, "The Resolution of the Latah Paradox," in Ronald C. Simons and Charles C. Hughes (eds.), *The Culture-Bound Syndromes: Folk Illnesses of Psychiatric and Anthropological Interest* (D. Reidel Publishing Co., 1985): 43–62.
31. Robert C. Ness, "The Old Hag Phenomenon as Sleep Paralysis: A Biocultural Interpretation," in Ronald C. Simons and Charles C. Hughes (eds.), *The Culture-Bound Syndromes: Folk Illnesses of Psychiatric and Anthropological Interest* (D. Reidel Publishing Co., 1985): 123–145.
32. John E. Carr, "Ethno-Behaviorism and the Culture-Bound Syndromes: The Case of Amok," in Ronald C. Simons and Charles C. Hughes (eds.), *The Culture-Bound Syndromes: Folk Illnesses of Psychiatric and Anthropological Interest* (D. Reidel Publishing Co., 1985): 199–223.
33. Zachary Gussow, "Pibloktoq (Hysteria) Among the Polar Eskimo: An Ethnopsychiatric Study," in Simons and Hughes, *The Culture-Bound Syndromes,* 271–287.
34. Raymond Prince, "The Concept of Culture-Bound Syndromes: Anorexia Nervosa and Brain-Fag," *Social Science & Medicine*, 21, 2 (1985): 197–203.
35. Adele E. Clarke, Janet K. Shim, Laura Mamo, Jennifer R. Fosket and Jennifer R. Fishman, "Biomedicalization: Technoscientific Transformations of Health, Illness, and U.S. Biomedicine," *American Sociological Review*, 68, 2 (2003): 161–194.
36. Brigitte Jordan, *Birth in Four Cultures: A Crosscultural Investigation of Childbirth in Yucatan, Holland, Sweden and the United States* (Waveland Press, 1992).
37. Wenda R. Trevathan, "Birth," in David Levinson and Melvin Ember (eds.), *Encyclopedia of Cultural Anthropology*, vol. 1 (Henry Holt and Company, 1996): 146–147.

38. Wendy Kline, "Communicating a New Consciousness: Countercultural Print and the Home Birth Movement in the 1970s," *Bulletin of the History of Medicine*, 89, 3 (2015): 527–556.

39. Margaret Macdonald, "Gender Expectations: Natural Bodies and Natural Births in the New Midwifery in Canada," *Medical Anthropology Quarterly*, 20, 2 (2006): 235–256.

40. Sharon R. Kaufman and Lynn M. Morgan, "The Anthropology of the Beginnings and Ends of Life," *Annual Review of Anthropology*, 34 (2005): 317–341.

41. Clive Seale, "Changing Patterns of Death and Dying," *Social Science & Medicine*, 51 (2000): 917–930.

42. Sjaak van der Geest, "Dying Peacefully: Considering Good Death and Bad Death in Kwafu-Tafo, Ghana," *Social Science & Medicine*, 58 (2004): 899–911.

43. World Health Organization, Primary Health Care, Geneva: World Health Organization, 1978.

44. Richard P. Petri, Jr. and Roxana E. Delgado, "Historical and Cultural Perspectives on Integrative Medicine," *Medical Acupuncture*, 27, 5 (2015): 309–317.

45. Ran Pang, Shihan Wang, Lin Tian, Mark C. Lee, Alexander Do, Susanne M. Chutshall, Guangxi Li, Brent A. Bauer, Barbara S. Thomley and Tony Y. Chon, "Complementary and Integrative Medicine at Mayo Clinic," *The American Journal of Chinese Medicine*, 43, 8 (2015): 1503–1513.

PART TWO

Part Two takes a micro approach to exploring and understanding diversity in Canada. Chapters 4 to 9 each examine a particular kind of diversity. The topics range from "traditional" diversities, such as race, ethnicity, social inequality and gender, to less traditional ones, including settler-sexual orientation, disability and the experiences of Indigenous Peoples through an exploration of Indigenous storytelling.

Continuing with our painting analogy, if Part One is the canvas and foundation of the painting, then Part Two is the details of what is actually on the canvass—the images, brush strokes, colours and lines. The text moves from the general, in Part One, to the specific, in Part Two.

Chapter 4 critically examines the effects of racism, discrimination and power relations. It seeks to distinguish between multiculturalism in theory and practice to help readers grasp the impact of immigration on Canada and to appreciate the immigrant experience. The chapter concludes by using Statistics Canada research to paint a picture of what Canada will look like by 2036.

Chapter 5 is unique in its approach to Indigenous realities in Canada. It analyzes Indigenous stories in the context of Canadian colonialism. In doing so, it establishes Indigenous storytelling as a practice of resistance and as an indispensable component to the process of truth and reconciliation in Canada.

Chapter 6 defines social stratification and describes various theoretical approaches to social class. The chapter also outlines the class system and the different ways social class is measured. It concludes with a look at which groups in Canada tend to be the most marginalized while clarifying the difference between blaming the system and blaming the victim.

Chapter 7 defines the language of gender studies and current social definitions of gender. It assesses the dominant sociological and ideological philosophies underpinning gender relations. This allows the reader to navigate the evolution of genders spheres and current issues with confidence.

Chapter 8 explains how sexuality is socially constructed. In doing so it helps navigate the tension between assimilation and visibility of sexuality in Canada. It also outlines the importance of decolonization to sexuality and helps explain the connection between race and sexuality.

Chapter 9 introduces models that explain disability in our society. In the process it presents designs which assist leaders in our society in creating an accessible space for all. The chapter also addresses the legislation which impacts disability and discusses issues related to employment of people living with impairment in our society. The citations for Chapter 9 differ slightly from the rest of the chapters. A decision was made to leave the citations as prepared in the style of choice by the author, Dr. Kate Hano, who uses sight-assist software when writing.

4

RACE AND ETHNICITY

DIFFERENCE AND DIVERSITY

Jessica E. Pulis and Paul U. Angelini

> *It's a nation with racism,*
> *Here since the start of it*
> *Hard to let go cause it's carved in the heart of it*
> *Relation to the land and our rise, we're a part of it*
> *Roots where I stand, I could never depart from it.*
> > — lyrics from "How I Feel," featuring A Tribe Called Red, Leonard
> > Sumner, Shad, Northern Voice, released 2016

> *The people of Canada do not wish as a result of mass immigration to make a*
> *fundamental alteration in the character of our population.* — Prime Minister
> William Lyon Mackenzie King, Policy Statement on Immigration, 1947

KEY OBJECTIVES

Define and understand race and ethnicity.

Recognize and understand racism and discrimination.

Critically examine the effects of racism, discrimination and power
relations.

Distinguish between multiculturalism in theory and practice.

Understand the impact of immigration on Canada, past, present
and future.

Appreciate the immigrant experience in Canada.

Human identity comprises many different factors, including gender and gender orientation, sexual identity, race and ethnicity, class, country of origin, language, profession and geographical orientation (where you live now, where your ancestors came from). This chapter asks you to think critically about what you know about race, ethnicity, racism, discrimination and immigration.

Because colonization treats Indigenous Peoples as one all-encompassing group, we see them not as many nations or peoples, but as a race or racialized minority. Bonita Lawrence explains:

> For Indigenous peoples, to be defined as a race is synonymous with having our Nations dismembered. And yet, the reality is that Native people in Canada and the United States for over a century now have been classified by race and subjected to colonialization processes that reduced diverse nations to common experiences of subjugation.[1]

The following discussion highlights the implications of such discourse in explicit and continuing manifestations of racism, prejudice and discrimination against Indigenous Peoples, amongst others, in Canada.

SOCIAL CONSTRUCTION OF RACE AND ETHNICITY

When you think of race or ethnicity what do you think of? Your answers will vary dramatically and may depend on your own race or ethnicity. When thinking about race, do you think of your genetic make-up or your biology, or do you consider your lived experience and the lived experiences of your family? It is a common notion, reinforced by popular discourse, politicians and pop culture figures, to support false claims that many of our human characteristics (behaviours, attitudes, level of intelligence, fiscal responsibility, athletic ability, etc.) are an outcome of our race. Such unsubstantiated, prejudiced and discriminatory beliefs are not in fact correct. Human beings, regardless of our country of origin, share almost the exact same genetic make-up. Geneticist Adam Rutherford explains:

> We now know that the way we talk about race has no scientific validity. There is no genetic basis that corresponds with any particular group of people, no essentialist DNA for black people or white people or anyone.… There are genetic characteristics that associate with certain populations, but none of these is exclusive, nor correspond uniquely with any one group that might fit a racial epithet. Regional adaptations are real, but these tend to express difference within so-called races, not between them.[2]

Scientific research continues to dispel myths around genetic differences across and amongst groups of people. As Rutherford confirms, there are no genes common to a group of people; rather genes and groups of genes are common to *all* people. Therefore, a biological understanding of race simply means that all people belong to the human species, while a sociological interpretation of race compels us to understand race and racial identity as social constructs.

Understanding race and racial identity as social constructs means these things are not static; they are fluid and change over place, space and time. Consider your own race. Now consider the race your great-great-great-great grandmother identified with. (Can you trace your ancestry that far back?) Is this the same race you identify with? Would your racial categorization have the same meaning in other countries across the world? It is not inevitable or natural that we recognize things like skin colour, eye shape, traditions, customs or language as socially important: we are conditioned and socialized to do so. As this chapter explores in greater detail, this conditioning results in criminal justice practices, education policies, healthcare treatments, Twitter hashtags, celebrity status and political rhetoric that propagate racism, prejudice, discrimination and bias.

Race

Race is a label used to describe and classify groups of people who share immutable and/or observable traits, including skin colour, eye shape, hair texture, ancestry, social role or name. However, while race is often presumed to be biological, and physical traits are used as indicators to determine someone's "race," it is the social meaning or implications of race that have become important. Augie Fleras argues that race has become an essential tool to control, exclude and exploit those who are racialized and to justify and maintain inequality.[3] It "means" something then to belong to a particular racial group. For example, **white privilege** refers to the social benefit of belonging to the "white race" and the advantages that come along with this "membership." Sociologist Jim Frideres defines white privilege as the "ability to make decisions that affect everyone without taking others into account, and White people set standards of humanity by which they are bound to succeed and others are bound to fail."[4] Fleras explains further that whiteness constructs people's lives by becoming symbols of dominance (not subordination), normativity (not marginality) and privilege (not disadvantage).

White privilege is deeply rooted in the history of European domination and colonial settlement of the Americas, Africa and Asia and the nineteenth-century practice and resurgence of "race science" justifying this power and domination.[5] The result is a set of profoundly embedded social, political and cultural beliefs and assumptions and practices based on the dominance of one group of people over others. The dominant discourse favours whiteness and "being white" over other racial identities and results in the unequal distribution of power and privilege. It also constructs social structures and systems which are then racialized (and also classed and gendered) to continue to reward those with power and privilege. Simply being white results in greater opportunity, less suspicion and scrutiny, both explicitly and implicitly, for individuals.

Race is important to our lived experiences and social histories because racial location is used to construct our identities, experiences and opportunities. Racial identity affects our lives and human interactions, so while race is not real, people believe it is, and the consequences of this perception are very real. Fleras argues that, while race did not give rise to racism (discussed in greater detail below), racism is used as a tool to justify the construction of race typologies to legitimize, control, dominate and exploit those who are racialized. This process of racialization reinforces the discourse that groups of people are defined as racially different by linking biological significance to these differences, perpetuates differential treatment based on stereotypes and forces racialized minorities into domains of poverty, crime, etc. because of limited opportunities. Our modern state is racist in that it maintains and replicates racist exclusions "by establishing and maintaining a system of racial domination and espouses colour-blind principles but tolerates colour-conscious discrimination."[6] The social, political and economic implications of racialization are explored throughout the rest of this chapter.

The Canadian Indian Act (1867) is one of the only pieces of legislation in the world based on "race" and it is still in effect today.

Ethnicity

Fleras defines ethnicity as "a principle and process in which shared awareness of a people's ancestral linkages and perceived commonalities serve as a basis for community, identity, and activity."[7] Ethnicity refers to identity or the means by which a group of people distinguish themselves and usually share a common ancestry, language or culture. Ethnicity also denotes shared traditions, norms and values and can include shared beliefs, customs and religion. Language is a distinguishing element to ethnic identity but not always required for membership. Consider that there are over ninety Indigenous languages and dialects identified across Canada but many are spoken only by elders and a few others.[8] While there are considerable efforts to save Indigenous languages there is significant concern that many will become extinct. For example, there are only about 190 native speakers of the Oneida language in Canada.[9]

Ethnic mobility refers to the changing of ethnic association, and there are many factors that influence ethnic mobility and how this happens. For example, a young Pakistani-Canadian no longer practices any of her traditional customs, no longer speaks the language and no longer has the same religious beliefs as her parents and grandparents. She now follows most of the dominant Canadian customs, including dress and food, and she speaks only French and English. On the 2011 census, her parents identified her ethnicity as East Indian, but as an adult she identified her ethnicity as Canadian when completing the 2016 census.[10] Her ethnic affiliation has changed as she associates her traditions, language and culture with being Canadian instead of East Indian.

Aside from social factors, other factors may influence ethnic mobility, including legislative changes. Previously, under the Indian Act, women who married non-status men would lose their legal "Indian status," and any children they had would also be deemed non-status. However, legislative changes in 1985 expanded the definition of status to include women and children previously excluded by non-status marriage, which resulted in thousands of Indigenous People changing their ethnic association. Furthermore, as populations of people practise mass migration and resettlement, and possibly have children, it is easy to understand how ethnicity may change over time. More than 250 ethnic origins were reported in the 2016 census, and more than 40 percent of Canadians recorded more than one ethnic origin.[11] The data also reveal that the longer an individual's family has lived in Canada, the more likely they are to report more than one ethnicity. Nearly 50 percent of third-generation Canadians reported more than one ethnicity compared to approximately 18 percent of foreign-born individuals. Therefore, ethnicity should be understood as something fluid that can change over place, space and time. Taken together, race and ethnicity are distinct aspects to our human identities, but an understanding of the social role these identities play is more complex and challenging.

RACISM

While definitions of race and ethnicity are fluid, the social, political and economic realities of being Indigenous, Black or white, for example, are very different. A perpetration and reinforcement of **racism** in ideologies, behaviours, practices, laws and regulations promote and support the wide breadth of the "validity" and continued justification of its utility. Fleras defines racism as

> those ideas and ideals (ideology) that are embedded within individual attitudes, cultural values, institutional practices, and those structural arrangements that assert or imply the assumed superiority of one social group over

Box 4.1 Think About...

Racism in Cultural Symbols

Search for images of the following logos and mascots and consider how they are illustrative of racism in cultural symbols: Cleveland Indians; Washington Redskins; Aunt Jemima; Uncle Ben; Miss Chiquita; Eskimo Pie.

another, together with the institutional power to put these perceptions into practice in ways that secure advantage for the mainstream but reinforce disadvantage for those racialized as different or inferior.[12]

Definitions of racism understand several dimensions or themes within racism, including biology, ideology, culture, structure and advantage. **Individual racism** refers to the behaviours, beliefs and assumptions of individuals that are prejudicial. **Systemic racism** refers to the entrenchment of prejudice and discrimination into the policies and practices of social, political and economic systems that results in inequality.[13] Below we explore the components of racism — prejudice, discrimination and power — in greater detail.

Prejudice

Prejudice can be understood as negative views of other people and other groups. Prejudicial beliefs are often blatantly simplistic, easy to dispel and highly dependent on stereotypes. For example, there are stereotypes that influence prejudicial beliefs around criminality, driving ability, alcoholism, drug use, frugality, intelligence, gang membership, etc. These value-laden generalizations and subjective racial prejudices are profoundly entrenched in stereotypical falsehoods — none of those stereotypes are factually or statistically correct. They are crude and demonstrate that even without evidence these beliefs permeate popular discourse, political rhetoric and the dominate narrative.

The manifestations of prejudice have significant and real-world consequences for those individuals who are being stereotyped. Consider Brian Sinclair (Box 4.2) and how prejudicial beliefs about Indigenous Peoples resulted in his tragic and completely preventable death.

Discrimination

While prejudice is the belief system of racism, discrimination is when action is taken based on these beliefs or attitudes or prejudgements. **Discrimination** occurs when prejudicial beliefs, attitudes and behaviours influence the unequal treatment of

Box 4.2 Think About...

Killed by Racism

In 2008, Brian Sinclair, a 45-year-old Indigenous man, was sent to a local Winnipeg hospital to have his catheter changed. Sinclair died in his wheelchair, in the hospital ER, after thirty-four hours without medical care. Despite four separate interventions by concerned citizens, dozens of hospital staff and security ignored Sinclair as he slowly died. An inquest into the death of Sinclair, which included testimony from over seventy-four witnesses, concluded that Sinclair had been visible in the waiting room but had been ignored because staff assumed he was intoxicated or homeless rather than in need of medical care. The racist assumptions about Indigenous Peoples the staff and security made ultimately led to Sinclair's death.

Source: "Out of Sight: Interim Report of the Sinclair Working Group." September 2017 <ignoredtodeathmanitoba.ca/index.php/2017/09/15/out-of-sight-interim-report-of-the-sinclair-working-group/>.

individuals and restricts their opportunities and full participation and membership in society. The Canadian Human Rights Commission defines discrimination as an action or a decision that treats a person or a group poorly for reasons such as their race, age or disability and states that reasons or grounds for discrimination can be based on any of the following: race, national or ethnic origin, colour, religion, age, sex, sexual orientation, gender identity or expression, marital status, family status, disability, genetic characteristics, or a conviction for which a pardon has been granted or a record suspended.[14]

Fleras explains further: "Discrimination can be defined as any restrictive act, whether deliberate or not, that has the intent or the effect of adversely affecting ('denying' or 'excluding') others on grounds other than merit or ability."[15] Discrimination becomes entrenched in organizational structure and rules, in social institutions and in normative functions.

Box 4.3 Think About...

In 2015, CBC closed online commenting for all stories related to Indigenous Peoples after noting that these stories draw a disproportionate number of prejudicial, hateful and ignorant comments, mainly "racist sentiments expressed in benign language." The CBC has not had to do this in any other circumstance.

Source: <cbc.ca/newsblogs/community/editorsblog/2015/11/uncivil-dialogue-commenting-and-stories-about-indigenous-people.html>.

There is a plethora of current examples of discrimination on social media, in the workplace, on the field, in the classroom, in Parliament, in parking lots and in many other spheres, so we know that discriminatory treatment of individuals is real for many in Canadian society. Some examples include a boss pays an employee less because she is a new Canadian; a landlord refuses to add a ramp for a tenant in a wheelchair; a retail employee follows customers in a store based on the colour of their skin; a pregnant woman is passed up for a promotion; a coach refuses to select an openly gay athlete; police stop and question racialized citizens more often (see Box 4.4).

Prejudicial beliefs, attitudes and behaviours become embedded in our social institutions and structures, which leads to discriminatory actions (police are more likely to stop and document racialized men), denials (a young Muslim-Canadian woman is denied a rental property, after being told it was available, after meeting the landlord in person), decision-making (Indigenous youth are significantly more likely to receive a sentence of custody compared to non-Indigenous youth convicted of the same offence) and/or exclusions (only a tiny percentage of Canadian firefighters are female).

Box 4.4 Think About...

Discrimination in Action

A restaurant in Toronto had to pay Emile Wickham $10,000 after staff ordered the man and his companions to pre-pay for their meal before being served in 2014. The group questioned other patrons only to find out they were the only ones asked to pre-pay. The restaurant, claiming no prejudice, believed the "non-regular" customers would "dine-and-dash." Wickham and his companions were the only Black patrons in the restaurant.

Starbucks locations in Canada and the United States were closed for "anti-bias" training in the spring of 2018 after an incident with two young African-American entrepreneurs was caught on camera and made national headlines. The men were arrested minutes after entering the Philadelphia Starbucks for a business meeting after being denied access to the washroom (it was company policy that washrooms were for paying customers only). One of the young men was a regular customer.

Think critically about both circumstances. How do prejudicial beliefs influence the discriminatory actions in both of these stories?

Sources: Nick Boisvert, "Toronto Restaurant Ordered to Pay Black Man $10K after Asking Him to Prepay for Meal," April 20, 2018 <cbc.ca/news/canada/toronto/hong-shing-tribunal-decision-1.4642009>; Andray Domise, "Starbucks Anti-Bias Training Is 'Racism 101' and Will Accomplish Little, Writer Says." June 11, 2018 <cbc.ca/news/canada/toronto/starbucks-anti-bias-training-toronto-community-advocates-1.4701182>.

Box 4.5 Diversity in Action

Carding Citizens by Police

Police forces across Canada continue to engage in the practice known as "**carding**." It involves the random stopping and questioning of citizens to build "profiles" and permanent data banks. Information is collected about factors such as name, address, age, skin colour (determined by the officer), estimated height and weight, and names of associates (if any). The practice has been revealed as largely a form of racial profiling, discriminatory and unnecessary. The impact of carding is illustrated in the following example: Knia Singh, a Toronto lawyer, has been stopped over thirty times by police. The information police collected in the many times Singh was stopped and documented included false and problematic information, such as that he is Jamaican (he was born in Canada) and that he is "unfriendly" and "resistant" to police, and his height estimations varied from 5'11" to 8 feet tall. Knia was *never* charged with a crime and does *not* have a criminal record.

Check out the *Toronto Star* series "Known to Police" for more about carding: <youtube.com/watch?v=mg3l1743gPA>.

Source: Jim Rankin, "Excuse Me Officer, Why Are You Stopping Me?" September 27, 2013 <thestar.com/news/gta/knowntopolice2013/2013/09/27/excuse_me_officer_why_are_you_stopping_me.html>.

One of the most visible outcomes of racism is racial profiling. **Racial profiling** is defined by the Ontario Human Rights Commission as any behaviour adopted for safety, security or public protection reasons that relies on stereotypes about ancestry, colour, ethnicity, race, religion, place of origin or any combination thereof rather than on reasonable suspicion of a single individual.[16] Racial profiling is most often directed at Indigenous Peoples, Black Canadians, Muslims, Arabs and West Asians and is often influenced by the particularly egregious negative stereotypes people in these communities face.[17] See Box 4.5 for an example of how racial profiling is a direct manifestation of racism into discriminatory action.

Power

Ultimately, it is power, power relations and privilege that reinforce prejudice and discrimination within a society. Power relations become deeply entrenched in organizational structures and laws, decision-making, social institutions, opportunities and norms, values and beliefs. Power, as a result, is institutionalized within social structures (organizations, rules, regulations) and embedded in our social fabric, where those in positions of power racialize difference (what Fleras refers to as "colour-conscious" discrimination) to protect privilege and power. Domination and suppression are normalized, so much so that those with the most privilege and power are often unaware of the power they have.[18] The dominant discourse and ideology further supports power relations that privilege some over others. As discussed in Chapter 1, expressions of diversity remain expressions of social privilege and oppression, of marginalization, exploitation, violence, ethnocentrism, cultural hegemony and powerlessness. Those with power and privilege continue to benefit socially, politically and economically from their racial advantage, while those who are racialized are disadvantaged.

UNDERSTANDING RACE AND ETHNICITY

Conflict

Conflict theorists view society as a complex structure wherein some people have power and privilege and others do not. This power differential results in significant inequalities and disadvantages between people in different class locations in society. Power originates from the ownership of resources and the production of goods, including land, food, structures, technology and knowledge. Those without power and ownership, or the working class, compete for scarce resources and the result is a society that is unstable and unequal. Structures and systems within this capitalist society are highly racialized, classed and gendered to maintain and reinforce power and privilege. In the context of race and ethnicity, conflict theorists argue that power and ownership of the means of production and resources usually results in exclusions and the maintenance and advancement of white, male privilege. Feminism, a branch of conflict theory, works from the premise that conflict in society is a result of male power, privilege and ideology, or patriarchy. Consequently, women and girls are forced to participate in a society that socially constructs them as unequal and inferior. Patriarchal normativity has profound implications for Indigenous, racialized and immigrant women and girls in Canada, who are further disadvantaged by biological, cultural and ideological racism. Racialized differences and inequalities, conflict theorists suggest, are part of the broader class struggle.

Conflict theorists challenge racism, patriarchal normativity and white supremacy and attempt to disrupt the current power imbalances and propose more equitable solutions. For example, the Canadian Centre for Justice Statistics has reported consistently over the last several decades that Indigenous women and men, girls and boys are disproportionately overrepresented, to varying degrees, at all levels of the Canadian criminal justice system (more likely to be arrested by police, more likely to have their case go to court, more likely to be denied bail, more likely to be sentenced to prison and twice as likely to be the victim of a crime, including murder and attempted murder).[19] Why do these inequalities (or "conflicts") exist? Conflict theorists argue that these findings are evidence of the history of colonialism, a continued power imbalance and systemic discrimination and disadvantage.

Symbolic Interactionism

Symbolic interactionists argue that society is in a constant state of flux, or is largely unstable. This instability, symbolic interactionists suggest, is a result of human interaction whereby we constantly construct and negotiate our own social realities. These interactions are socially constructed and depend on how each person defines their life and lived experiences. Our social realities, and our definitions of the world around us, are a result of all human interactions. Race and ethnicity become obvious factors in how people define and understand their social reality. Considering multiculturalism, racism and immigration, think about how you negotiate your own diversity and how disadvantage is constantly constructed and reconstructed within society.

Structural Functionalism

Structural functionalism works from the premise that society is a living organism, comprised of complex and interrelated parts. Different elements and structures work together to ensure social stability, consensus, social cohesion and most importantly social order. Everything then has an important role to ensure society runs smoothly and effectively. When there is a conflict or a disruption in the social order, functionalism suggests that some type of "corrective measure" is taken to return society to equilibrium. Racialized minorities and new Canadians are often blamed for creating conditions of economic instability. However, their international education and credentials are often denied or suppressed, and their limited English and/or French proficiency to communicate and engage "effectively" are more likely the reasons these Canadians are often economically disadvantaged.[20] In their analysis of race and ethnicity, structural functionalists concentrate on understanding how governance models such as assimilation (the subdominant group is expected to assume and conform to the culture, values, norms, authority, etc. of the dominant group) and policies such as multiculturalism (see below) contribute to social order.

OFFICIAL MULTICULTURALISM

Multiculturalism was first adopted as official government policy in 1971 and was included in the Charter of Rights and Freedoms in 1982. The **Multiculturalism Act** was passed into law in 1988. The goal of the policy is to manage cultural relations in

Canada, not as some believe, to eradicate cultural conflict. Rather, it is firmly rooted in the sociological belief of "**pluralism**," which accepts the fact that cultural conflict is a normal part of advanced, industrial, technological societies and that people tenaciously cling to their cultural identities. The role of government in pluralist thinking is to manage cultural relations to allow for the peaceful resolution of cultural disputes. Accepting the idea of pluralism leads to the acknowledgement that multiculturalism is beneficial to Canadian unity because it strengthens Canada's social fabric and enriches Canadian experiences in literature, the arts, health, music and countless other areas.

Ten goals are outlined in the 1988 Act (see Box 4.6). We can condense these objectives to three general principles that capture its overall intent and spirit. The first principle is to promote both official languages within the framework of multiculturalism. The second is to commit to assisting all members of cultural groups to overcome barriers to full societal participation, and finally, the third is to promote acceptance of cultural differences and understanding among different groups. Multiculturalism is not without its critics. Two broad criticisms are offered below — one from the perspective of the majority group, the other from the minority group perspective.

Tyranny of Multiculturalism — Views of the Majority Group

One interpretation of multiculturalism involves the idea that the policy is a bludgeon used to impose conformity on society at large. This view asserts that it is an all-encompassing, dogmatic piece of legislation that forces a worldview on Canadians that difference is good and beneficial without providing any evidence. "Difference" is regarded as morally good, forward thinking and socially progressive. Failure to support this idea renders one at the very least, intolerant if not totally prejudiced. In fact, many believe it is nothing but an election ploy aimed at recently arrived immigrants.

Still another part of this conformity argument negates the idea that Canadian culture is something new arrivals must adopt in order to fit in and become Canadian. It encourages groups to live in small enclaves, which limits their interactions with other groups.[21] The dominant group believes that multiculturalism puts all cultures on equal footing, forcing Canadians to subordinate "Canadian culture" to that of others. Most Canadians resist the idea of accepting cultural and religious differences when they are at odds with Canadian norms, mores and laws. This is certainly the case with Sharia Law for divorce proceedings, polygamy, female circumcision, eating dogs, the use of hallucinogenic drugs and having women wear veils in public places. To many in the Western world, female circumcision is regarded as female genital mutilation and the veiling of women as oppression masquerading as religious freedom. Ongoing debates dealing with religious dress/symbols such as turbans, hijabs, niqabs and kirpans remain divisive. Many believe official multiculturalism emboldens minority groups

Box 4.6 Diversity in Action

Goals of the 1988 Multiculturalism Act

3 (1) It is hereby declared to be the policy of the Government of Canada to

(a) recognize and promote the understanding that multiculturalism reflects the cultural and racial diversity of Canadian society and acknowledges the freedom of all members of Canadian society to preserve, enhance and share their cultural heritage;

(b) recognize and promote the understanding that multiculturalism is a fundamental characteristic of the Canadian heritage and identity and that it provides an invaluable resource in the shaping of Canada's future;

(c) promote the full and equitable participation of individuals and communities of all origins in the continuing evolution and shaping of all aspects of Canadian society and assist them in the elimination of any barrier to that participation;

(d) recognize the existence of communities whose members share a common origin and their historic contribution to Canadian society, and enhance their development;

(e) ensure that all individuals receive equal treatment and equal protection under the law, while respecting and valuing their diversity;

(f) encourage and assist the social, cultural, economic and political institutions of Canada to be both respectful and inclusive of Canada's multicultural character;

(g) promote the understanding and creativity that arise from the interaction between individuals and communities of different origins;

(h) foster the recognition and appreciation of the diverse cultures of Canadian society and promote the reflection and the evolving expressions of those cultures;

(i) preserve and enhance the use of languages other than English and French, while strengthening the status and use of the official languages of Canada; and

(j) advance multiculturalism throughout Canada in harmony with the national commitment to the official languages of Canada.

Source: Government of Canada <http://laws-lois.justice.gc.ca/eng/acts/C-18.7/page-1.html>.

to demand cultural and religious accommodation at the expense of Canadian laws and established ways of doing things. Multiculturalism becomes tyrannical when its ideas are reflected in law and enforced by the coercion and power of the state. Few tears were shed when in 1993 the federal Liberals under Jean Chrétien eliminated the Department of Multiculturalism and Citizenship.

Tyranny of Multiculturalism — Experiences of Minority Groups

The most important component of any culture and the key to its survival is language. It provides culturally unique worldviews, symbols and perceptions that are critical for minority group behaviour and survival. Yet, multiculturalism operates in an officially bilingual framework where English and French are Canada's official languages. This reduces multiculturalism to a "feel good" policy designed to give minority groups a false sense of cultural security while proclaiming unparalleled cultural acceptance. The dominance of Canada's two official languages is institutionalized in government, the bureaucracy and the most definitive assimilative institution of all, public schools. This became especially obvious in the 1990s. Stricken with "deficit hysteria," the federal government slashed and cut its way to a balanced budget on the backs of Canada's most disadvantaged groups — the poor, immigrants, women, Indigenous Peoples, students, people with mental and physical disabilities and the environment.[22] Ottawa drastically cut funding for minority group language retention programs and in 1993 permanently eliminated the Department of Multiculturalism and Citizenship. English and French Canadians politically, economically and socially dominate Canada, making minority group assimilation inevitable.

Minority groups have also come to realize that official multiculturalism is another tool used to stifle minority dissent and give them the illusion that they can negotiate with the English and French majorities on an equal footing. Yet minority groups have no history of negotiating on equal ground with majority groups. This is true of francophone minorities in Manitoba, New Brunswick and Ontario in addition to the Anglophone minority inside Quebec. Indigenous peoples also know this fact all too well. They regard multiculturalism as another colonial-settler policy designed to control Indigenous lives by acknowledging the reality of multiple Indigenous groups while simultaneously rejecting or putting barriers in place when Indigenous Peoples call for self-determination, settling land claims and honouring treaty rights. Majority groups respond by claiming that official multiculturalism (along with the Charter) are a panacea for all minority group concerns, questions and grievances. Consequently, it is not a stretch for minority groups to believe that official multiculturalism blocks minority group access to power and resources, further marginalizing them.[23] In the end it is easy for minority groups to regard the Multiculturalism Act as a tyrannical piece of government legislation adopted to permanently emasculate their cultures. Power imbalances cannot be remedied with multicultural solutions. How did Canada become the multicultural country that it is? Let us have a brief look at Canada's immigration history.

SHORT HISTORY OF IMMIGRATION TO CANADA

Debates surrounding immigration and Canadian identity go hand in hand — who is a Canadian? In spite of the existence of the myth that Canada has always been a "white" British and French country, a brief historical analysis of Canadian immigration paints a radically different picture. Book IV of the *Report of the Royal Commission on Bilingualism and Biculturalism* outlined four distinct stages to Canada's immigration history.[24] Let us examine them briefly.

Stage 1: Beginnings to 1901

Immigrants arriving in Canada prior to 1901 possessed many different skills and radically different work experiences. They were fishers, farmers, merchants, traders, soldiers, adventurers, enslaved labourers and fugitives. While French and British immigrants were numerically the largest two groups, they were not the only ones to arrive. The Canadian government, along with contracted steamship companies, openly advertised across Europe for able-bodied farmers to populate western Canada (see Box 4.7). Roughly 10 percent of Canada's population was not Indigenous, French or British. In fact, over two dozen cultures were reported in the 1901 census. German immigrants comprised more than half of all new arrivals during the nineteenth century. They settled in New France and in Nova Scotia, where they founded the famous Lunenburg settlement during the early 1750s. German religious minorities, including Mennonites, Moravians and Tunkers, predominantly from the United States, arrived from 1780 until well into the 1800s. Some settled in Ontario, particularly Waterloo County.

Roughly 10 percent of the **United Empire Loyalists** who settled in Canada after the American Revolution were African-American.[25] Some were still enslaved and arrived with their white owners. Contrary to popular belief, slavery did exist in Canada (see Box 4.8). Between 1815 and 1860, roughly 40,000 to 60,000 enslaved fugitives and

---

DIVERSITY IN ACT

Box 4.7 Diversity in Action

Immigrant Recruitment Posters, 1880–1897
Search online for immigrant recruitment posters from the Government of Canada in the late 1800s: <historymuseum.ca/cmc/exhibitions/hist/advertis/ads2-00e.shtml>.
What do you see? How are immigration patterns related to who was pictured in the recruitment posters?

Box 4.8 Think About...

Why is the existence of slavery in Canada not widely known? The first enslaved person was brought to New France from Madagascar in 1628. United Empire Loyalists continued to bring enslaved people to Canada during and after the American Revolution. No fewer than sixteen members of the first parliament of Upper Canada owned enslaved people. Informed of her owner's intent to sell her against her wishes, an enslaved African-descended woman named Marie-Joseph Angelique burned down part of Montreal in 1734.

Sources: Daniel G. Hill, *Human Rights in Canada: A Focus on Racism* (Ottawa: Canadian Labour Congress, 1977): 3, 7; Carl E. James, *Seeing Ourselves: Exploring Race, Ethnicity and Culture*, 2nd edition (Toronto: TEP, 1999): 161.

---

free people of colour arrived. The Dutch and Scandinavians were the only other large groups arriving in Canada, accounting for just under 1 percent of the total immigrant population.

Largely forgotten is the extinction of the Indigenous population of Newfoundland and Labrador, the Beothuk. The extinction was the product of a combination of starvation (being denied free access to traditional fishing grounds), tuberculosis (which exacted a heavy toll) and being hunted for sport by the European colonial-settler population.[26]

Stage 2: 1880–1918

The dominant feature of this stage is the massive departure of Europeans from their home continent. These years have been described as the "mightiest movement of people in modern history." Simply, millions and millions left the Old World for the New World. Many went to the United States, South America (especially Argentina and Brazil) and beginning in the 1890s, Canada. At this time the federal government decided to populate the western part of the country and encouraged immigrants to settle there. Other factors that made Canada a desired destination include the closing of the American frontier, the Yukon Gold Rush, the building of the transcontinental railway and new developments in farming technology.

In 1913 alone, more than 400,000 new people entered Canada. In the eighteen years prior to the beginning of the First World War, more than 3 million people came to Canada! Roughly 1.25 million came from the United Kingdom and about 1 million from the United States. Another important feature of this stage is the arrival of many from Eastern Europe: Ukrainians, Poles, Hungarians, Romanians and Russians. Italians and Jews saw their numbers rise roughly by a factor of six, to around 67,000 and 126,000, respectively. Greeks, Syrians, Lebanese and Armenians also experienced growth in immigrant numbers and, like the Italians and Jews, preferred to settle in the cities of central Canada rather than the farming communities of the west.

> *"Large scale immigration from the Orient would change the fundamental composition of the Canadian population."*
> — *Prime Minister William Lyon Mackenzie King*

This stage also witnessed the imposition of the racist head tax on Chinese immigrants. The head tax was intended to slow the pace of Chinese immigration, which was deemed too plentiful by Canadian immigration officials. In 1885, the tax was $50 and it was raised to $100 in 1900; but this had little impact on Chinese immigration. However, the pace was slowed when the head tax was raised to an enormous $500 in 1903 (see Box 4.9).

The racist workings of Canadian immigration were again on display in 1908 when Ottawa demanded that immigrants arrive directly without stopping in any other country during their journey. This was known as the "continuous passage" regulation, and in practice only applied to immigrants from India. In 1914, 376 Sikhs arrived in Vancouver aboard the S.S. *Komagata Maru*, which was made to wait in Vancouver harbour for three months before it was shamelessly turned away.[27] In fact, it was escorted back to sea by a Canadian warship!

Box 4.9 Think About...

Are Landing and Registration Fees the New Head Tax?

As of 2018, every immigrant to Canada must pay a variety of fees for applying to come to Canada as a permanent resident. A Business Class immigrant must pay a $1,050 processing fee, a right of permanent residence fee of $490, a spouse or partner processing fee of $550, another permanent residence fee of $490 and finally $150 for every dependent child less than 22 years of age. The sums are similar for Family sponsorship. Sponsoring your spouse or partner will cost $1,040, a right of permanent residence fee of $490, a dependent child is $150 each, and there is a $550 fee for every over-age dependent child

Source: <cic.gc.ca/english/information/fees/fees.asp>.

Stage 3: 1918–1945

The dominant feature of this stage is the restrictions put on immigration. Between the world wars the United States severely reduced the number of immigrants it accepted, making Canada a more popular choice for those seeking a life in the New World. The United States preferred to use a quota system to determine who entered, while Canada opted to implement a "list" system of "preferred" and "non-preferred" types of immigrants. These lists usually excluded Chinese immigrants and drastically cut back on immigrants from other areas in Asia.

The discrimination against Japanese and Chinese immigrants was so institutionalized and complete that it became known as the campaign against the "**yellow peril**." Low-income Chinese immigrants were banned from entering Canada by the "Chinese Exclusion Act," which was not repealed until 1947. The 1941 census showed that only 74,000 Asians had entered Canada since 1931. Throughout the 1920s, Black immigrants also felt the negative impact of Canada's racist immigration policy. In the middle of the decade, Ottawa decided that a "British Subject" could only be defined as coming from a Commonwealth country with a predominantly white population.

Immigration during the Great Depression essentially ceased. Only 140,000 immigrants entered Canada between 1931 and 1941. During the whole of this stage, Canada was reluctant to accept victims of terror from Nazi Germany.

"We were terrified of the cold land and the large amount of snow, where people were different and spoke a foreign language." — Anonietta Lanni nee Venditti, "Italian Trunk," Canadian Museum of Immigration at Pier 21 website.

Stage 4: 1945–1974

Immigration to Canada exploded after the Second World War. By 1961, 2.1 million people had arrived in Canada. This stage is the most prolonged period of immigration in Canadian history. Other important features of this stage include Toronto becoming the dominant destination; the arrival of just over 250,000 Italians between 1951 and 1960; and Italians, Greeks and Portuguese from rural areas choosing to live in cites. In fact, this group of immigrants shared important characteristics — they were largely from rural areas and therefore had no experience with city living (many turned their entire backyards into gardens!), had low levels of formal education and settled mostly in Toronto, where they built nationally recognized communities. The Italian population of Toronto CMA (Census Metropolitan Area) is estimated to be just over 400,000, making it one of the largest Italian communities outside Italy.

This stage is also infamous for the racist and brutal treatment of Japanese Canadians. At the conclusion of the war, 4,000 Japanese Canadians were forced to leave Canada as part of a benign-sounding "repatriation program." More than half had been born in Canada and more than two-thirds were Canadian citizens! The message to immigrants across Canada was and continues to be clear: your birthplace and citizenship mean nothing if the government decides to strip you of your basic human rights and individual liberties. A sobering thought to be sure. The experiences of Japanese Canadians sent to internment camps, primarily in British Columbia, are the basis for much of the analysis of internal Canadian policies during the war years. Deprived of their rights, they were sent to the camps with only what they could carry, the remainder of their property and livelihoods confiscated and auctioned off by governments. Upon release at the end of the war, most went to live in Toronto. By 1961, 8,000 Japanese Canadians were living in Toronto CMA.

The four stages mentioned in the royal commission report brought us up to 1974. We can add a fifth and sixth stage to Canadian immigration history principally as a result of the 1974 immigration policy change from a skill-set entry requirement to one focused on the needs of the Canadian economy and the dramatic events of the last two decades that have permanently altered international relations. As the Canadian economy evolves, so do the types of workers Canada is seeking and its treatment of new arrivals.

Stage 5: 1975–2001

The dominant feature of this stage is that the principal source of immigrants coming to Canada was the developing world. These immigrants generally share four characteristics: overwhelmingly not white; overwhelmingly not Christian; come from countries with low levels of economic development; and come from countries that lack Canada's political stability. The arrival of millions of new Canadians from the developing world has had a profound impact on Canada, especially the cities and particularly Toronto.

Between 1991 and 1996, China, India, the Philippines, Sri Lanka, Poland and Vietnam were the most reported source countries.[28] The racialized minority population grew steadily, from 9.4 percent of the total Canadian population (2.5 million) in 1991 to 16.2 percent (5 million) in 2006.[29] The 2006 census revealed that non-European immigration increased from 68.5 percent in 1981 to 83.5 percent by 2006. A 2017 Statistics Canada report notes that racialized minorities now make up over 20 percent of Canada's population, up from 16.2 percent in the 2006 census.[30]

Stage 6: 2001–Present

The tragic events of September 11, 2001, profoundly affected and continue to influence immigration to Canada. Legitimate and unfounded fears of international terrorists using immigration to Canada as a means of committing future terrorist acts in Canada and beyond quickly began to occupy the thoughts of Canadians everywhere. These concerns resulted in more intense screening of immigrants generally and of racialized minorities living in Canada more specifically. **Racial profiling** began to dominate the news. At its core racial profiling equates physical characteristics with specific behaviours that society at large deems unacceptable. Not surprisingly, racialized minorities leaving or returning to Canada have been subjected to racial profiling. While always a demeaning experience/process, some incidents were truly destructive to individual and family life. Such was the case for Maher Arar. Born in Syria, a Canadian citizen and living in Canada since the age of 17, he was returning from a family vacation in Tunisia when he was forcibly removed from his wife and children at New York's John F. Kennedy Airport. He was interrogated by American officials for supposed links to the Al-Qaeda terrorist organization. Against his will and consent he was flown to Lebanon, then Syria, where he was jailed, beaten, tortured and forced to sign a fabricated confession. One of the many disturbing aspects in the case was that American officials knew details of Arar's life that could have only been provided by Canadian officials. In the immediate aftermath of September 11, Washington pressured Ottawa to harmonize border/airport security and screening. Canadians regarded this as an affront to their sovereignty and independence. The public outcry when the Arar case made national headlines resulted in Ottawa establishing a commission of inquiry on January 28, 2004, to investigate the behaviour of Canadian authorities, including the use of racial profiling. Three years later the commission cleared Arar of any wrongdoing or membership in any terrorist organization and awarded him a total settlement package of just over $10 million. Both Prime Minister Stephen Harper and the head of the RCMP publicly apologized to Arar and his family in January 2007. Arar did not actually receive his settlement until it was finalized by Prime Minister Justin Trudeau in 2015.

Racial profiling is a manifestation of racism, and what makes it so problematic is the wide breadth of its use and the justification of its utility. This is especially problematic since Statistics Canada projects that racialized minorities will be the single largest component of new arrivals to Canada until at least 2036.

Canada continues to search for the best educated and the brightest immigrants. Generally, there are only four countries that consistently, as part of government policy, actively seek new immigrants: Australia, Canada, the United States and the United Kingdom. Since they all seek the same kind of immigrant, the developing world loses

Box 4.10 Think About…

While Muslim women and men account for a small percentage of the population in Western countries (e.g., the Unites States, Canada, Britain, France, Australia, among others), a majority of the media coverage centres around events that reinforce a rhetoric of fear that violent, extreme, radical, barbaric behaviours and beliefs are normalized in "other" countries in "other" parts of the world. It is also not surprising that, as a result of 9/11, international media sources have increased coverage of events and stories related to topics like terrorism, "honour killings" and the Muslim "other." This is just one indication of a growing international trend and evidence of Islamophobia in Western countries' policies and regulations. In 2014, changes were made to the Canadian citizenship study guide to state that Canada's openness and generosity do not extend to barbaric cultural practices that tolerate spousal abuse, "honour killings," female genital mutilation, forced marriage or other gender-based violence. In this example, violence perpetuated against Muslim women by Muslim men is treated as peculiar to Islam rather than part of the worldwide problem of violence against women, which cuts across culture, language, religion and country.

their best educated citizens. This is known as the **"brain drain"** for the developing world and the **"brain gain"** for the developed world. The Immigration and Refugee Protection Act 2002 and provisions set out in Bill C-36 reaffirmed the kind of immigrant Canada is interested in attracting: highly skilled, experienced, well-educated and fluent in English or French.[31] Many immigrants arrive with great expectations only to find out that their education and work experiences are not accepted on par with Canadian ones. This reliance on formal credentials is known as **"credentialism."** This leaves newcomers in the unenviable position of choosing between going back to school, with all of the financial implications, or seeking unskilled labour jobs to support themselves and their families. This results in the Canadian economy being populated with highly educated new Canadians working in unskilled labour for low pay.

WHAT WILL CANADA LOOK LIKE TOMORROW?

A wonderfully detailed account is provided by *Immigration and Diversity: Populations Projections for Canada and Its Regions, 2011–2036*, published in 2017 by the Demosin Team at Statistics Canada. Using the latest census data, the report paints a diverse narrative of Canada today with equally panoramic projections to 2036. We summarise the highlights below.

The ethnocultural composition of Canada's population has changed radically since the mid 1970s. The 2016 census reveals that immigrants now account for 21.9 percent of the population — the first time this number has rivaled the 22.3 percent recorded in 1921, the highest level since Confederation.[32] A total of 1,212,075 new immigrants arrived in Canada between 2011 and 2016, representing 3.5 percent of Canada's total population; just over one in five Canadians are foreign-born. This number greatly exceeds the 14–16 percent between 1951 and 1991 and the 19.8 percent recorded in the 2006 census. Statistics Canada reports that the numbers keeps rising due to a combination of low national fertility levels and a gradual rise in the number of deaths. In fact, if immigration levels remain constant in the coming years, between 24.5 and 30 percent of Canada's population could be foreign-born by 2036, a sizable increase from the 20.7 percent recorded in 2011. This will impact the number of second-generation Canadians (children with at least one parent born abroad), which is expected to rise to 19.7 percent in 2036 from 17.5 in 2011. Together, immigrant and second-generation Canadians could comprise 44.2–49.7 percent of the Canadian population in 2036, nearly one in two people!

Distribution of the Immigrant Population

The geographic distribution of immigrants across the country is not expected to differ from the 2011 estimates, which concluded that nine out of ten immigrants lived in a Census Metropolitan Area (CMA) and that could rise to as much as 93.4 percent in 2036.[33] Toronto, Montreal and Vancouver will remain the three principal destinations. In 2036, as many as 39 percent of all immigrants will live in these three cities, 14.6, 12.4 and 13.1 percent respectively. From 2011 to 2036 the proportion of immigrants living in almost all regions will increase while at the same time reinforcing existing regional difference. That is, the proportion of immigrants living in the Atlantic Provinces, Quebec (minus Montreal) and in non-CMAs will still be below the Canadian average by 2036. The five CMAs projected to have the highest percentages of immigrants as part of their populations are Toronto, Vancouver, Calgary, Montreal and Winnipeg, with the percentages as high as 52.8, 48.5, 40.8, 34.2 and 40.5 respectively.

Asia Dominant

By 2036 the continent of Asia will be the dominant source of Canadian immigration. As the source of the Canadian immigrant population changes, so does Canada's language and religious composition. Asian-born immigrants will comprise between 55.7 and 57.9 percent of Canada's immigrant population. At the same time the European-born number will decrease to between 15.4 and 17.8 percent by 2036, significantly down from 31.6 percent in 2011. South Asians will remain the dominant racialized minority group in 2036, followed by the Chinese. The long-term impact of the changes would see more than one-quarter of all Canadians whose first language is other than English or French. This could include as many as 30.6 percent of the Canadian population by 2036. Statistics Canada projects that the number of Canadians speaking English will increase from roughly 75 percent in 2011 to around 78 percent in 2036. At the same time the number of French-speaking Canadians will decline to under 21 percent from 23 percent. Simultaneously, racialized minority groups with the most rapid growth are Arab, Filipino and West Asian. This apparent paradox is explained by the fact that these groups comprise the higher proportion of the immigrant populations when compared to their percentages in the Canadian population as a whole.

These changes will also impact the religious composition of Canada's population. The number of Canadians in some way connected to non-Christian religions is expected to increase dramatically, to roughly 28.2–34.6 percent in 2036, compared to about 24 percent in 2011. This number would correspond to those affiliated with Catholicism (29.2–32.8 percent), leaving the Catholic Church as the single largest church in 2036. Muslim, Hindu and Sikh faiths will grow rapidly but still comprise only a modest share of the total Canadian population since these faiths are over-represented among immigrants compared to their numbers in the Canadian population as a whole. Finally, the percentage of Canadians reporting no religious affiliation continues to increase. By 2036 this percentage of the population is expected to rise to as much as 16 percent, from 9 percent in 2011.

Atlantic Canada

The majority of immigrants living in Nova Scotia, 64 percent, lived in Halifax in 2011. This is not expected to change by 2036, when as many as 76.3 percent of the immigrant population is expected to call Halifax home. The province-wide immigrant proportion of the population is expected to rise to anywhere between 7.7 and 10.7 percent. At the high end, this will be double the 5.5 percent recorded in 2011. As with the rest of the Atlantic region, the immigrant percentage of population is expected to remain significantly below the Canadian average of 20.7 percent. The continent of Asia will account for between 38.4 and 41.7 percent of immigrant arrivals. Immigrants from Northern Europe would account for only about 29 percent of the high end of the projections. Newfoundland and Labrador will remain the least ethnoculturally diverse province in Canada. The immigrant population will rise to between 3 and 4.6 percent in 2036, from 1.8 percent in 2011 (see Box 4.11).

DIVERSITYINACTION

Box 4.11 Diversity in Action

Immigrant percentage of Atlantic Region, 2011 and 2036 Projections

Province	2011	2036
Prince Edward Island	5.1	7.9–19.5
Nova Scotia	5.3	7.7–10.7
New Brunswick	3.9	3.1–4.6
Newfoundland and Labrador	1.8	3.1–4.6

Source: Adapted from *Immigration and Diversity: Populations Projections for Canada and its Regions, 2011–2036* (Statistics Canada, 2017): 53–57.

Quebec

The origin and composition of Quebec's immigrant population sets it apart from the rest of Canada. This is a consequence of a federal-provincial agreement, the Canada-Quebec Accord Relating to Immigration and Temporary Admission of Aliens, that allows Quebec to select its economic immigrants. Consequently, the province has the highest percentage of immigrants arriving from Africa and the Americas. By 2036, it is projected that as many as 30.4 percent of immigrants living in Quebec will be from Africa and 21.6–22.4 percent will be from the Americas. These numbers exceed the Canadian average (minus Quebec) of 7.6–8.4 percent and 12.6–13.2 respectively. The CMA of Montreal will continue to house almost nine out of every ten immigrants.

Ontario

The province of Ontario will remain the most diverse province in Canada, with potentially 36.1 percent of the population arriving from outside Canada by 2036, up from 28.5 percent in 2011. It is projected that by 2036, between 58.6 and 61.2 percent of immigrants living in Ontario will have been born in Asia, for a total of roughly three in five, while less than one in five will have been born in Europe. The main birthplaces will be South and East Asia. Almost 75 percent of all immigrants to Ontario will live in Toronto CMA. Toronto, Gatineau (Ontario side), the Tri-City region of Kitchener-Cambridge-Waterloo and Windsor will all have more diverse ethnocultural portraits than the rest of the province by 2036. In fact, similar to 2011, by 2036 the ethnocultural diversity in the remainder of the province (outside of the above listed cities) will be below the Canadian average, with the lowest numbers in Greater Sudbury, Peterborough and Thunder Bay. Projections indicate that the Toronto CMA will remain the most ethnoculturally diverse region in Canada.

Western Canada

Manitoba's immigrant population is projected to rise to roughly 22.4–32.6 percent of the population in 2036, up from 15.7 in 2011. By 2036 between 60 and 66.6 percent of the immigrant population will come from Asia. The vast majority of these immigrants, 77.1–81.8 percent, will be living in Winnipeg.

Saskatchewan will see its immigrant population will rise from 6.9 percent in 2011 to a high of 23.8 percent by 2036. While this number is below the Canadian average, Asian immigrants will account for between 62.1 and 72.2 percent. The dominance of Asian immigrants from Southeast and South Asia is a fact throughout the other Prairie Provinces. What sets Saskatchewan apart from most other provinces is that between 25 and 30 percent of the immigrant population will live outside a CMA.

The 2011 proportion of immigrants living in Alberta was 18.1 percent and is expected to rise to between 23.6 and 31 percent by 2036. In this same year, a high of 31.6 percent will have a mother tongue other than English or French and around 12–15 percent will be affiliated with a non-Christian religion. The vast majority of immigrants, well over 80 percent, will live in two CMAs, Calgary and Edmonton.

British Columbia's immigrant population is expected to grow to around 35 percent in 2036, from 27.5 percent in 2011. Immigrants from Asia will likely account for 69–70 percent of the immigrant population assuming the composition of immigration by country of birth remains the same throughout the 2011–2036 projection period. Roughly 80 percent are expected to live in Vancouver. Areas outside of Vancouver and Abbotsford will have ethnocultural diversity levels below the Canadian average.

Northwest Territories, Nunavut and Yukon

Projections for Canada's three territories are similar to the rest of Canada. Specifically, they will experience increased immigration from Asia, perhaps reaching a much as 55.8 percent of all immigrants, while immigrants tracking their ancestry back to Europe will represent between 20 and 21.7 percent of the total by 2036. By this time between 12 and 22 percent of Yukon's, 9–13 percent of the Northwest Territories' and between 3.3 and 4.4 percent of Nunavut's populations will be immigrants. All projections are based on settlement patterns established during the 2000–2005 period.[34]

CONCLUSION

The concepts of ethnicity and race are crucial to individual and group identity. It is impossible, therefore, to over-estimate their impact on individual and group relations in Canada. These relations form the core of Canadian immigration history with all of its triumphs and tragedies. Critically examining immigration history paints a realistic picture of group relations, allowing us the opportunity to expose national myths — always being a white country, that Indigenous Peoples were few in number and insignificant — and to celebrate unique accomplishments, such as official multiculturalism.

Canada is changing. By 2036 Asia will be the dominant source of immigrants and Canada will look much different. The Canadian mosaic is becoming more diverse and colourful!

CRITICAL REVIEW QUESTIONS

1. How are race and racial identity a social construct? Define and give specific examples.
2. What is meant by white privilege? How do we see this in Canadian society?
3. What is the significance of the fifth and sixth stages (1975 to the present) of Canadian immigration history?
4. Provide three criticisms of official multiculturalism. Give an example for each.
5. Describe what is meant by the term "racial profiling"? Why is racial profiling always detrimental to community cohesiveness?

RECOMMENDED READINGS

Ninette Kelly and Michael Trebilcock, *The Making of the Mosaic: A History of Canadian Immigration Policy* (Toronto: TEP, 2013).

Robyn Maynard, *Policing Black Lives: State Violence in Canada from Slavery to the Present* (Halifax and Winnipeg: Fernwood Publishing, 2017).

Lisa Monchalin, *The Colonial Problem: An Indigenous Perspective on Crime and Injustice in Canada* (Toronto: University of Toronto Press, 2016).

Ontario Human Rights Commission, *Under Suspicion: Research and Consultation Report on Racial Profiling in Canada* (2017).

David Tanovich, *The Colour of Justice Policing Race in Canada* (Toronto: Irwin Law Inc., 2006).

KEY TERMS

brain drain: developed countries that actively seek immigrants as part of government policy, especially Australia, Canada, the United States and the United Kingdom, all seek the same kind of immigrant — highly educated and skilled — thereby "draining" the developing world of their best and brightest citizens.

brain gain: developed countries "gain" the best educated and most skilled citizens from the developing world by actively recruiting them emigrate to the developed world.

carding: the random stopping and questioning of racialized minorities to build "profiles" and data banks of individuals statistically likely to commit crimes. Primarily used in racial profiling by police.

credentialism: reliance on formal credentials, faced by immigrants to Canada who discover that their education and work experiences are not accepted on par with Canadian credentials.

discrimination: occurs when prejudicial beliefs, attitudes and behaviours influence the unequal treatment of individuals and restricts their opportunities and full participation and membership in society.

ethnic mobility: changing ethnic association.

individual racism: the behaviours, beliefs and assumptions of individuals that are prejudicial.

Multiculturalism Act: federal act that officially sanctions multiculturalism. It became law on July 21, 1988.

multiculturalism: the federal government's official commitment to furthering national unity by promoting the positive aspects of cultural differences and the English and French languages.

pluralism: the belief that cultural conflict in society is a normal part of advanced, industrial, technological societies and that people tenaciously cling to their cultural identities. The role of government in pluralist thinking is to manage cultural relations to allow for the peaceful resolution of cultural disputes.

prejudice: negative views, attitudes and beliefs about other people and groups, largely based on negative stereotypes.

racial profiling: defined by the Ontario Human Rights Commission as any behaviour adopted for safety, security or public protection reasons that relies on stereotypes about ancestry, colour, ethnicity, race, religion, place of origin or any combination thereof, rather than on reasonable suspicion of a single individual, for greater security or differential treatment.

systemic racism: the entrenchment of prejudice and discrimination into the policies and practices of social, political and economic systems that results in inequality.

United Empire Loyalists: immigrants from the US who arrived after the American Revolution (1776) who wished to remain loyal to the British Crown. They settled principally in Atlantic Canada.

white privilege: the social benefits and advantages of belonging to the white race.

yellow peril: term used to describe the national feeling prevalent during Stage 3 (1918–1945) of Canadian immigration history that immigration from Asia, especially China and Japan, would negatively alter the ethnic and racial composition of Canada. This national feeling dominated federal immigration policies and resulted in the imposition of a head tax on Chinese immigrants and repatriation of Japanese immigrants and Japanese Canadians after the Second World War.

Notes

1. Bonita Lawrence, "Gender, Race, and the Regulation of Native Identity," *Hypatia: A Journal of Feminist Philosophy,* 18, 2 (May 2003): 5.
2. Adam Rutherford, "Why Racism Is Not Backed by Science," *Guardian,* March 1, 2015 <theguardian.com/science/2015/mar/01/racism-science-human-genomes-darwin>.

3. Augie Fleras, *Unequal Relations: A Critical Introduction to Race, Ethnic and Aboriginal Dynamics in Canada*, 8th edition (Toronto: Pearson, 2017).

4. James Frideres, "Being White and Being Right," in D.E. Lund, and P.R. Carr (eds.), *Revisiting The Great White North? Transgressions in Cultural Studies and Education* (Rotterdam: Sense Publishers, 2015).

5. < ryerson.ca/wpc-global/about/what-is-white-privilege/>.

6. Fleras, *Unequal Relations*, 93.

7. Fleras, *Unequal Relations*, 122.

8. <afn.ca/2017/07/16/assembly-first-nations-national-chief-perry-bellegarde-commits-action-indigenous-languages-act-protect-strengthen-first-nations-languages/>.

9. <passport2017.ca/articles/endangered-languages-of-canada>.

10. The census is a large-scale national survey undertaken by Statistics Canada every five years. It is a mandatory survey completed by every household (those living on the margins or in precarious or transient living arrangements are not included in the survey). The census collects data on variables such as education, ethnic diversity and immigration, income, labour, languages, population and demography. For more information, visit <12.statcan.gc.ca/census-recensement/index-eng.cfm>.

11. Statistics Canada, "Ethnic and Cultural Origins of Canadians: Portrait of a Rich Heritage, 2016 Census," *Census Year 2016*, Catalogue No. 98-200-X2016016, p. 4.

12. Fleras, *Unequal Relations*, 81.

13. Frances Henry, Carol Tator, Winston Mattis and Tim Rees, *The Colour of Democracy: Racism in Canadian Society*, 4th edition (Toronto: Harcourt Brace & Company, 2010): 56.

14. Canadian Human Rights Commission <chrc-ccdp.gc.ca/eng/content/what-discrimination>.

15. Fleras, *Unequal Relations*, 86.

16. Ontario Human Rights Commission, *Paying the Price: The Human Cost of Racial Profiling*, Inquiry Report 2004, p. 6. See also Charles C. Smith, "Crisis, Conflict, and Accountability: The Impact and Implications of Police Racial Profiling" (Toronto: African Canadian Community Coalition on Racial Profiling, March 2004), and Tom Wise, "Racial Profiling and Its Apologists," *Z Magazine*, March 2002.

17. Ontario Human Rights Commission, *Under Suspicion: Research and Consultation Report on Racial Profiling in Canada*, 2017.

18. Fleras, *Unequal Relations*.

19. <http://www.statcan.gc.ca/pub/85-002-x/2016001/article/14642-eng.htm>.

20. Fleras, *Unequal Relations*.

21. Neil Bissondath, *Selling Illusions: The Cult of Multiculturalism in Canada* (Markham, ON: Penguin, 2003).

22. Linda McQuaig, *All You Can Eat: Greed Lust and the New Capitalism* (Toronto: Viking 2001); *The Cult of Impotence: Selling the Myth of Powerlessness in the Global Economy* (Toronto: Viking 1998); and *Shooting the Hippo: Death by Deficit and Other Canadian Myths* (Toronto: Viking 1995).

23. Augie Fleras and Jean Leonard Elliot, *Multiculturalism in Canada: The Challenge of Diversity* (Scarborough: Nelson, 1992): 100.

24. "Report of the Royal Commission on Bilingualism and Biculturalism, Book IV, The Contributions of Other Ethnic Groups," in Howard Palmer, ed., *Immigration and the Rise of Multiculturalism* (Toronto: Copp Clark, 1975): 1–16. Unless otherwise noted, all statistics and examples of historical events are drawn from these pages.

25. Adrienne Shadd, "Institutionalized Racism and Canadian History: Notes of a Black Canadian," in Carl E. James (ed.), *Seeing Ourselves: Exploring Race, Ethnicity and Culture,* 3rd edition (Toronto: TEP, 2003): 165–168.

26. Ninette Kelly and Michael Trebilcock, *The Making of the Mosaic: A History of Canadian Immigration Policy* (Toronto: TEP, 2003): 36.

27. Daniel G. Hill, *Human Rights in Canada: A Focus on Racism* (Ottawa: Canadian Labour Congress, 1977): 10.

28. Statistics Canada, *The Daily,* 4 November 1997.

29. Statistics Canada, "Canada's Ethnocultural Mosaic, 2006 Census," *Census Year 2006,* Catalogue No. 97-562-X, p. 12.

30. Demosin Team, *Immigration and Diversity: Populations Projections for Canada and its Regions, 2011–2036* (Statistics Canada, 2017).

31. Yasmin Ai-Laban and Christina Gabriel, "Security, Immigration, and Post-September 11 Canada," in Janine Brody and Linda Trimble (eds.), *Reinventing Canada: Politics of the 21st Century* (Toronto: Prentice Hall, 2003): 299.

32. Statistics Canada, *The Daily*, November 25, 2017.

33. Information in this section is taken from Demosin Team, *Immigration and Diversity: Populations Projections for Canada and its Regions, 2011–2036* (Statistics Canada, 2017).

34. In fact, the report makes clear that the level of immigration will directly impact the speed of Canada's ethnocultural diversification and that the choice of immigrant settlement will similarly impact the speed at which each region will diversify.

5

INDIGENOUS STORYTELLING

ETHICS AND RESISTANCE

Alexander Hollenberg

The truth about stories is that that's all we are. — Thomas King, *The Truth About Stories*[1]

KEY OBJECTIVES

Understand Indigenous stories in the context of Canadian colonialism.

Understand Indigenous storytelling as a practice of resistance.

Understand the value of Indigenous stories in the process of truth and reconciliation in Canada.

Recognize the forms and consequences of censorship that affect Indigenous Peoples.

Appreciate one's own responsibility as an ethical listener in the process of reconciliation.

CREATION STORIES

Let me tell you a story. It's one I've picked up over the years. Lots of people tell it, and every time it's a little bit different. That's okay, though. Stories can change and the world won't end. But let's not think about ends. Let's think about beginnings.[2]

Back in the beginning — the beginning of imagination and thus the beginning of all stories — the world was water. All blue, no green. Somewhere far above this world was another, older world, and on that world, there lived a woman. I will call her Charm because that's what Thomas King called her the first time I heard this story, but some people call her Sky Woman.

If you're like me, and you like your characters to have single, defining traits, then you'll like Charm. Charm was curious. Questions were her thing:

> Birds, why can you fly?
> Because of the principle of lift, said the Birds.
> Grass, why are you green?
> Chlorophyll, said the Grass.
> Toes, why are there ten of you?
> Enough with the curiosity, said the Toes. Go find something else to do.

As it happened, Charm did have something else to do. She needed to find some food. But nothing she found seemed to satisfy her. When she saw Rabbit, he suggested eating some fish. Fish, alternatively, suggested eating some rabbit. Luckily for those two, she wasn't craving either of them. But she was craving *something*.

Maybe you're pregnant, said Fish. I always get strange cravings when I'm pregnant.

Maybe I am, said Charm. (I have it on good authority that Charm was, in fact, pregnant.)

So Fish and Rabbit told her about a special root underneath the oldest tree in the oldest forest that was sure to satisfy her.

Charm found the tree, and she started to dig for that root. And dig. And dig.

If I'm being honest, after a while she totally forgot about the root. She was more interested in the digging. She was more interested in what was on the other side. The animals warned her not to be so curious.

Stop digging, said Badger, if you know what's good for you.

Shush, said Charm.

Now we know what happens next, don't we? Charm dug right through to the other side of her world. Curious, she poked her head through. But all she could see was sky. So she wriggled her shoulders and arms through. Still, nothing but sky. So she wriggled her hips through. And then, well, she slipped all the way through and began to fall. Upwards, downwards, it doesn't matter. She fell and fell and fell. And as she fell, Charm noticed a pale blue dot. And that pale blue dot was getting bigger and bigger. It was, of course, not a dot at all, but the Earth. Well, the water.

Uh oh, said all the water animals on Earth. Someone's coming, and she's coming down fast. We should probably do something about this.

So the animals held a meeting as Charm was falling towards them. Whale thought they should just let her fall and see what happens. Dolphin was excited for the splash she'd make. Sturgeon wanted to see how deep she'd sink. But the consensus was that maybe she'd get hurt if she hit the water too hard, so the birds flew up and formed a great net with their wings and caught Charm just before she crashed.

Thank you, said Charm.

Now what, asked the birds. Can you swim?

Not especially well, said Charm.

Can you float, asked Trout?

For a moment or two, said Charm.

I don't suppose you can hold your breath for a while? asked Narwhal.

Maybe for a minute on a good day, said Charm. Why don't you find me something hard and flat that I can stand on?

Well, there was only one thing that anybody could think of that fit that description — the back of Turtle.

Hop on, said Turtle.

And that's how Charm lived for a month or two, but soon all the animals noticed that she was going to have a baby.

I'm going to need more space, said Charm. Where will the nursery go?

None of the animals really knew what to do.

Charm suggested that maybe it was time to find some dry land. Of course, none of the water animals really knew what dry land was. Charm, though, had an idea.

Who's the best diver? she asked.

That's easy, said Pelican, it's me!

Okay, all you have to do is dive to the bottom of the water and bring me back some mud.

No problem, said Pelican, though he didn't really know what mud was. He swooped high in the air and sliced straight down into the water. But when he resurfaced an hour later, Pelican was exhausted and mud-less.

Next up was Walrus. But even Walrus couldn't find the bottom. One by one, the water animals tried to find mud, and one by one, they all resurfaced tired and defeated. The only one left to try was Otter, and no-one held much hope for Otter since all she ever did was play play play.

Why not, said Otter. I like a good contest. So Otter took a big breath and dove down down down and wasn't seen for four days. When her body finally floated up to the surface, all the animals thought she had drowned. However, when Charm pulled her little body up onto Turtle's back, she noticed some dark, gooey substance clenched between her paws.

This is mud, Charm told the animals. It's magic.

Cough, cough, I like magic, whispered Otter, who wasn't drowned, just really really tired.

Charm placed the mud on the back of Turtle. She sang and danced, and the animals all sang and danced, and it was a pretty good time had by all. And then the mud started to grow. And it grew bigger and bigger until it grew into a world of mud and water. The animals sure liked the trick of the growing mud, but they spotted a problem — there wasn't enough room in the water anymore and some of them were going to have to live on land.

No-one really wanted to live in the mud though.

But as the animals were discussing what to do with all this mud, Charm gave birth.

It was twins. One girl, one boy. One light, one dark. One left-handed, one right-handed.

They were pretty great babies. And they loved the mud. One Twin smoothed the mud flat, so you could see for miles. Then the other Twin created piles of mud that were mountains and below them wide valleys. The first Twin dug deep, straight trenches that filled with water. The second Twin kicked at them and made those trenches into long winding rivers. The first Twin made forests with all the trees perfectly aligned so you would never get lost. The second Twin then jumbled the trees up randomly so there were some open spaces and some that were deep and dark.

One Twin created roses, the other thorns. One Twin made summer, the other winter. One sunshine, one shadows. And so forth.

It was a pretty beautiful world they created.

What's left? asked the Twins.

What about human beings? asked the animals. Would those be useful?

Sure, we can try, they said. The first Twin made women. The second Twin made men.

Not bad, said the animals. But will we get along with them?

Good question, said the Twins.

The stories we tell inevitably tell us something about ourselves. More than that, stories don't merely reflect values we already hold, they constitute values — they suggest to us ways of knowing our world and ways of being in our world. When Thomas King contends that "the truth about stories is that that's all we are,"[3] he offers an account of storytelling that transcends entertainment and diversion and instead implies that stories are the *sine qua non* of human existence — that we are, ultimately, story-creatures. But how can this be? Is story really so essential to life?

The story that I've just told you is a Haudenosaunee creation story. And as with all creation stories, whether you believe that this is what actually happened is, perhaps, beside the point. Rather, insofar as creation stories proffer a version of how the world came to be the way it is, they establish foundational imperatives for how we ought to think about our relationships with our world and with others. Values are not created in a vacuum; they are borne through stories that are told and retold over generations, and the more a story is repeated, the greater cultural weight it attains. When we tell stories — whether it is in the form of gossip with our friends, family anecdotes or mass-produced media such as novels and films — we are all at once creating, interpreting and judging our world. And when we hear stories, how we listen and how we respond tells us so much more about ourselves than we may realize.

The story of Sky Woman is an essential story not only because it is part of a long

---

Box 5.1 Diversity in Action

David Cusick

Though many different versions of the Haudenosaunee creation story have been recorded and many different nations share versions of the story, it was in 1827 that David Cusick became one of the first Indigenous People to record and publish the story in English. Cusick was born on the Oneida reservation in Madison County, New York, and he received a Christian education, which was common in the Tuscarora Nation during this period. Cusick's *Sketches of the Ancient History of the Six Nations*, of which "The Iroquois Creation Story" forms a small but significant part, was itself a response to the very real threat of American expansionism upon Haudenosaunee lands and people. Moreover, as a way of drawing the attention of a largely white audience to the fact of Indigenous presence, civilization and history on the continent, Cusick strategically blended Indigenous and Christian cosmologies. Notwithstanding this rhetorical triumph, very soon after his work was published, Andrew Jackson would be elected president and thousands of Indigenous People would be forcibly "removed" from their ancestral lands.

Source: David Cusick, "The Iroquois Creation Story," in Nina Baym et al. (eds.), *The Norton Anthology of American Literature*, Shorter 7th edition (New York: W.W. Norton & Company, 2008 [1827]): 17–21.

tradition of Indigenous storytelling on **Turtle Island**, but because it contains within it the bedrock of certain Haudenosaunee values. Who are we? Where did we come from? How should we act? These are questions that many, if not most, of us ask ourselves at some point in our lives, and we can conceive this story as one particular way of answering those questions. Consider, for instance, the character of Charm: Does Charm have all the answers? Is she an all-powerful deity? Is she an absolute authority figure? No, certainly not. Charm is magical, sure, but she needs help from the water animals. She could not survive without them. Far from absolute, her power derives from cooperation with the water animals. What about the Twins? A careless reader might be inclined to interpret them as representations of good and evil, a simplistic binary at best. While it may at first appear as though one Twin creates the world and the other ruins all those perfectly ordered creations, that's not really the case. The beauty of the storyworld is precisely in its variation — there is of course nothing inherently *evil* in the deep and dark corners of the forest or in the thorns of a rose. Indeed, as Charm does with the water animals, the Twins work together to create the world as we know it. There is no clear hierarchy, no single figure of dominance. And to that point, humans are almost an afterthought in this story: humanity is not afforded primacy of place. We, in other words, are not masters of the world, only fellow travellers on the back of the turtle.

So, it is a story of collaboration. Of partnerships. Of land for which we all share responsibility. But let's be clear: the story of Sky Woman bears relevance precisely because it is a *living* story. It is not simply a remnant of an ancient Indigenous past; in fact, much of its significance lies in its capacity to challenge other worldviews — other creation stories that construct other values and that envision our world in markedly different ways. Take the story of Genesis, for example. Of Adam and Eve. The story of man's dominion over nature (and woman). A story of law and punishment and blame. A story of a very different sort of fall and of, subsequently, a lost paradise. Whereas one story asks us to envision our relationship with the land and its inhabitants as cooperative, the other posits relationships of power and powerlessness. If both stories are premised through the question of how we ought to see ourselves in the world, King argues that they offer very different answers:

> What if the creation story of Genesis had featured a flawed deity who was understanding and sympathetic rather than autocratic and rigid? Someone who, in the process of creation, found herself lost from time to time and in need of advice, someone who was willing to accept a little help with the more difficult decisions?
>
> What if the animals had decided on their own names? What if Adam and Eve had simply been admonished for their foolishness?
>
> I love you, God could have said, but I'm not happy with your behaviour.

Let's talk this over. Try to do better next time.

What kind of a world might we have created with that kind of story?[4]

When King challenges the Judeo-Christian text, he does so through the lens of Sky Woman. The Haudenosaunee creation story — with its concomitant values of collaboration and shared responsibility — provokes a reconsideration of dominant Western values. To tell the story of Sky Woman, then, is also to resist dominant Western narratives and their cultural power. Thus, Indigenous storytelling is doubly significant: on the one hand, such stories communicate the singularity of Indigenous ways of knowing and being; on the other, they implicitly bear witness to the original and continued presence of Indigenous Peoples across Turtle Island.

Box 5.2: Think About...

Maps as Stories

Have you ever thought about how *maps* might be stories of colonization? Scholar Erika Luckert has thought hard about the way we have typically been taught to see the spaces that we now call Canada. In one exercise, she visited the Provincial Archives of Alberta and analyzed surveyors' notebooks from 1871 to 1917, which were ultimately used in the mapping of settler territory. Such journals contained detailed descriptions of landscapes and drawings of shrubs, rivers and trees, all of it bisected within a precise grid. "These notebooks were not journals of appreciation for the land," Luckert observes. "They were plans for the appropriation of it.... They were dividing the entire country into range and township lines, into a massive grid that would make it easier to map, and to control." As with any story, a map is not a neutral description of the world; rather, it contains values that are implied by how it represents the world. What is revealed? What is concealed? What names are used? Luckert's research shows us how settler maps continue to elide Indigenous spaces from the national consciousness. But Luckert also acknowledges that maps are not an exclusively colonial practice — there are many ways of seeing and knowing the land. One Indigenous map, for example, does not orient north as up, but instead uses certain mountain peaks as its point of orientation. Another map she describes is carved into a stick and plots a three-dimensional journey paddled downriver, all tributaries and turns precisely marked. Try taking a close look at a map of where you live. What histories and what values does it represent? How might you revise it?

Source: Erika Luckert, "Drawing Lines," in Danielle Metcalfe-Chenail (ed.), *In This Together: Fifteen Stories of Truth & Reconciliation* (Victoria, BC: Brindle & Glass Publishing, 2016): 39, 41.

TRUTH AND RECONCILIATION: THE NECESSITY OF STORY

The Canadian **residential school** system operated for over a century. From confederation in 1867 until the late 1990s, Indigenous youth were, through various means, forcibly separated from their parents and compelled to attend "educational" institutions administered by the federal government, as well as by the Roman Catholic, Anglican, United, Methodist and Presbyterian churches. At least 150,000 First Nation, Métis and Inuit students found themselves in the throes of this system. And though it is beyond the purview of this chapter to detail the litany of injustices and atrocities committed against Indigenous Peoples over this period, the Truth and Reconciliation Commission of Canada (TRC) describes the residential school system, powerfully, as an instrument of a larger policy of **cultural genocide**, which can be defined as

> the destruction of those structures and practices that allow the group to continue as a group. States that engage in cultural genocide set out to destroy the political and social institutions of the targeted group. Land is seized, and populations are forcibly transferred and their movement is restricted. Languages are banned. Spiritual leaders are persecuted, spiritual practices are forbidden, and objects of spiritual value are confiscated and destroyed. And, most significantly to the issue at hand, families are disrupted to prevent the transmission of cultural values and identity from one generation to the next.[5]

It is, unfortunately, still difficult for many Canadians to imagine that their country was founded not only upon the idealistic Commonwealth principle of "Peace, Order and Good Government,"[6] but also upon the eradication of Indigenous land and culture. Two stories. Two very different versions of Canada. If John A. Macdonald,

> **Box 5.3 Think About...**
>
> **Legislating Cultural Genocide**
> "Every Indian child between the ages of seven and fifteen years who is physically able shall attend such day, industrial or boarding school as may be designated by the Superintendent General for the full periods during which such school is open each year. Provided, however, that such school shall be the nearest available school of the kind required, and that no Protestant child shall be assigned to a Roman Catholic school or a school conducted under Roman Catholic auspices, and no Roman Catholic child shall be assigned to a Protestant school or a school conducted under Protestant auspices."
> Source: ch.50, s.10, An Act to Amend the Indian Act, 1920.

our first prime minister, has in the conventional narrative been lionized as a folk hero who connected Canadians from east to west, he is also the politician who spoke of Indigenous People as "savages," whose children "should be withdrawn as much as possible from the parental influence, and the only way to do that would be to put them in central training industrial schools where they will acquire the habits and modes of thought of white men."[7] Two characters. Two stories. One culturally dominant and oftentimes repeated. One traditionally marginal and provocative, but demonstrably true.

At the same time, it would be wrong to interpret residential schools as a historical anomaly, or some sort of deviation in the long, peaceable and progressive narrative of Canada; rather, they were a manifestation of a painful legacy of European **colonialism**. In the fifteenth century, the Roman Catholic Church granted Catholic nations sovereign rights over the lands they "discovered." Pope Alexander VI, for example, issued a series of papal bulls that gave the majority of North and South America to Spain. This is the basis of what came to be known as the "Doctrine of Discovery," a quasi-legal justification of empire-building, in which Christian nations brought "civilization" to non-Christian lands and their inhabitants. At the same time, non-Catholic empires, such as the British, simply asserted the right of first discovery — they laid claim to whatever lands they "discovered" first, deeming them *terra nullius* (nobody's land) and thus free for the taking. We know, of course, that Indigenous Peoples had inhabited Turtle Island for thousands of years before European colonists found them, but the language of discovery violently ignored this fact. But the myth of an empty continent was — and is — a powerful piece of rhetoric, because as soon as one declares that a

---

Box 5.4: Think About...

The Enduring Myth of the Empty Continent

If you look for it, the legacy of *terra nullius* is everywhere. One abiding example comes from Gordon Lightfoot's classic folk song, "Canadian Railroad Trilogy." The song's first two lines read: "There was a time in this fair land when the railroad did not run / When the wild majestic mountains stood alone against the sun."[10] Consider how such stories, which present the land before white settlers as empty and "alone," do harm to Indigenous cultures by imagining spaces as "made and founded by the dominant Anglo culture."[11] Can you think of any other examples of this myth persisting in popular culture?

Sources: Gordon Lightfoot, "Canadian Railroad Trilogy," *The Way I Feel* (United Artists, 1967): 1–2; Kamala Todd, "This Many-Storied Land," in Danielle Metcalfe-Chenail (ed.), *In This Together: Fifteen Stories of Truth & Reconciliation* (Victoria, BC: Brindle & Glass Publishing, 2016): 58.

land is empty, it makes the act of colonization — of religious conversion, of occupation, of genocide — appear non-violent and natural. It becomes a story, simply, of filling of an empty space.

By placing the residential school system within this context of colonial imposition and violence, we begin to understand the cultural attitudes from which it arose. Moreover, insofar as the rhetoric of discovery and *terra nullius* reimagined Indigenous existence as a non-existence and Indigenous civilizations as uncivilized, we begin to see the capacity of language and narrative to frame historical reality. This is, in a word, why Indigenous storytelling matters so much in the context of truth and reconciliation. The telling of a story is always an assertion of *presence*. When Elder Louis Bird explains his purpose for publishing the stories of the Omushkego people, he makes this plain:

> You just have a richer history in Canada when you know the truth about the past and can admit that these people lived here many years before the visitors came — and that they survived. If the Great Spirit had not liked them, they would have died many years before the European came — but these are stories about them surviving.[8]

The very act of telling is an act of resistance to the rhetoric of *terra nullius*. The land was never empty; it was always storied. To be clear, such stories are not only about survival; they *are* survival. Stories mark the fact of Indigenous civilizations long before European contact.

Truth and reconciliation are all about stories. The Truth and Reconciliation

---

Box 5.5: Think About...

Survivance

Anishinaabe scholar Gerald Vizenor employs the term "**survivance**" to describe a distinctive Native storytelling aesthetic. Though he describes the theory of survivance as "elusive, obscure, and imprecise," the practice of survivance is obvious in Indigenous storytelling, songs, traditions and customs. "Native survivance," according to Vizenor, "is an active sense of presence over absence, deracination, and oblivion; survivance is the continuance of stories, not a mere reaction, however pertinent." How do you understand this term through its connotations of *survival, endurance* and *resistance?* How does this concept subvert specific stereotypes of Indigeneity? Can you think of any stories in which an aesthetic of survivance becomes obvious?

Source: Gerald Vizenor, *Native Liberty: Natural Reason and Cultural Survivance* (Lincoln: University of Nebraska Press, 2009): 85.

Commission, which wrapped up its work in 2015 with the publication of its final report, was led by the Honourable Justice Murray Sinclair, Chief Wilton Littlechild and Dr. Marie Wilson, who, along with numerous statement gatherers, listened to nearly seven thousand witnesses share their personal narratives, accounts and testimonies about the residential school experience. Most of these witnesses were former students — survivors — of a system that incubated multiple forms of physical and sexual abuse. These stories are essential because they coalesce to tell a history of Canada that has long been excised from the national narrative. Truth, in other words, is borne through stories and storytellers.

The format of the TRC's work is important to understand. In addition to seven national events (Winnipeg, Inuvik, Halifax, Saskatoon, Montreal, Vancouver and Edmonton), there were regional events (Victoria and Whitehorse), as well as 238 days of local hearings across seventy-seven communities. At each of these events, the commission organized public sharing panels and sharing circles where participants' stories were gathered. More than 6750 statements from survivors, family members and others were collected between 2010 and 2014. The scope of this endeavour should not be underestimated: the thousands of stories told across the country each in their own way bears witness to recent colonial violence, and each, furthermore, stands as a powerful declaration of survival amidst overwhelming pressure to assimilate. Consider the statement of Simone, an Inuk survivor from Chesterfield Inlet, Nunavut:

> I'm here for my parents — "Did you miss me when I went away?" "Did you cry for me?" — and I'm here for my brother, who was a victim, and my niece at the age of five who suffered a head injury and never came home, and her parents never had closure. To this day, they have not found the grave in Winnipeg. And I'm here for them first, and that's why I'm making a public statement.[9]

Box 5.6 Think About...

"Any parent, guardian or person with whom an Indian child is residing who fails to cause such child, being between the ages aforesaid, to attend school as required by this section after having received three days notice so to do by a truant officer shall, on the complaint of the truant officer, be liable on summary conviction before a justice of the peace or Indian agent to a fine of not more than two dollars and costs, or imprisonment for a period not exceeding ten days or both, and such child may be arrested without a warrant and conveyed to school by the truant officer."

— from ch. 50, An Act to Amend the Indian Act, 1920

Pay close attention to Simone's words. She offers her personal story primarily as an act of remembrance for relatives no longer with her. Three times, she repeats the phrase "I'm here," and this repetition bears notice precisely because it is a statement of presence. She remains, and through her telling, so does her family. Simone's story is itself a refusal to vanish from history, a rejection of the way dominant narratives work to silence colonized peoples and an assertion of Indigenous existence, both past and present. To speak publicly is to resist erasure through storytelling.

If nothing else, the TRC report is an accumulation of such stories. When Florence Horassi was taken from her parents to the Fort Providence school in the Northwest Territories in a small plane, she tells of "a whole plane crying. I wanted to cry, too, 'cause my brother was crying, but I held my tears back and held him."[10] Raymond Hill, who was a student in Brantford at the Mohawk Institute, speaks of how "I lost my language. They threatened us with a strapping if we spoke it, and within a year I lost all of it. They said they thought we were talking about them."[11] The principal at the Brocket, Alberta, school told Evelyn Kelman that if she attended a Sun Dance during the summer, she would be strapped upon her return.[12] Bernard Catcheway recounts his time at Pine Creek, Manitoba, wherein he saw "other students that threw up and they were forced to eat their own, their own vomit."[13] In Lytton, British Columbia, Simon Baker's brother Jim died from spinal meningitis when the principal refused to take him to the hospital: "I used to hear him crying at night.... I pleaded with the principal for days to take him to a doctor."[14] Children who ran away frequently had their heads shaved. William Antoine tells of one such incident in Spanish, Ontario: "They cut all his hair off and they pulled, pulled his pants down and he was kneeling on the floor, and holding onto the chair."[15] Physical and sexual abuse was rampant and largely unreported. Multiple survivors, for example, recounted assaults that occurred within the church confessional.[16] These stories attest to the terror of the residential school system in Canada, and their sheer numbers amplify the multiple truths of survivors' experiences.

As appalling as these stories are, it would be a mistake to interpret these Indigenous storytellers as re-inscribing painful narratives of victimization. The term, *survivor*, is key: to survive connotes an experience beyond victimhood, beyond objectification and beyond powerlessness. In the very commitment to tell these stories — of actively recounting and representing events that were (and are) fundamentally traumatic — Indigenous People refuse to see themselves merely as victims. In telling a story, one *acts* as opposed to being *acted upon*. This is precisely why storytelling is such an essential instrument in the resistance against colonial institutions, because as soon as one becomes a storyteller — a narrator — one takes control of the discourse of representation. One can choose *what* events are represented and *how* events are

> ### Box 5.7 Innov8
>
> **Survivance the Game**
>
> Check out <www.survivance.org>. The makers of this site have designed a "social impact game" inspired by Gerald Vizenor's articulation of survivance as an aesthetic form of Indigenous self-determination (see Box 5.5). In this game, you are prompted to choose a quest (Orphan, Wanderer, Caretaker, Warrior, Changer), perform it, reflect on it and rest. Players are encouraged to post their results and creations to the website or to social media: #survivance.

represented. Rhetorical control is both a figurative and literal power: on the one hand, the capacity to control one's own story symbolizes one's agency and autonomy; on the other hand, by speaking and thereby reconstructing events that were once censored and ignored, one performs the dignity that was historically denied. Considering that the Department of Indian Affairs and the churches frequently ignored students' and parents' complaints of abuse within residential schools,[17] and thus effectively silenced Indigenous testimonials, it is no small thing that the work of the TRC centres upon a storytelling practice wherein rhetorical control is asserted by Indigenous speakers.

The stories of survivors expose truths about Canada that have gone unacknowledged for too long. Certainly, in the process of telling stories and revealing the far-reaching consequences of colonial violence, Indigenous people seek healing. There is resilience in the act of telling. Still, reconciliation does not automatically follow from the discovery of truth. What do we do with stories once they are told? What responsibility do we hold as listeners to stories? What exactly *is* **reconciliation**? According to the TRC,

> *reconciliation* [is] an ongoing process of establishing and maintaining respectful relationships. A critical part of this process involves repairing damaged trust by making apologies, providing individual and collective reparations, and following through with concrete actions that demonstrate real societal change. Establishing respectful relationships also requires the revitalization of Indigenous law and legal traditions. It is important that all Canadians understand how traditional First Nations, Inuit, and Métis approaches to resolving conflict, repairing harm, and restoring relationships can inform the reconciliation process.[18]

There are three critical aspects to this definition; first, reconciliation is a process, which means that once the truth is communicated and once Indigenous knowledge is recognized, it is our responsibility to somehow act — and to continue acting.

Second, a central feature of much Indigenous law is oral history. The stories of how one's ancestors resolved conflict and repaired communities contain practical and culturally relevant bases for reconciliation. Attempting to reconcile without engaging in storytelling conventions that are inborn to a particular Indigenous Nation would not only be fruitless but a reiteration of the colonial paternalism that reconciliation attempts to move beyond. Finally, the commission's definition makes it abundantly clear that reconciliation involves all of us, Indigenous and non-Indigenous alike. It is, in a word, born of a relationship between tellers and listeners. Stories make both explicit and implicit demands of their audiences, and reconciliation is ultimately dependent upon whether we acknowledge those demands. Survivor and reverend Stan McKay asserts:

> [There must be] a change in perspective about the way in which Aboriginal people would be engaged with Canadian society in the quest for reconciliation…. [We cannot] perpetuate the paternalistic concept that only Aboriginal peoples are in need of healing…. The perpetrators are wounded and marked in history in ways that are different from the victims, but both groups require healing…. How can a conversation about reconciliation take place if all involved do not have an attitude of humility and respect?… We all have stories to tell and in order to grow in tolerance and understanding we must listen to the stories of others.[19]

In this interpretation, *listening* is not a passive concept. By listening to stories, to oral histories and to testimonies, we too begin to bear witness and recognize that such narratives require a response. As listeners, we recognize that by sharing in the perspectives of others, we are implicitly being asked to take seriously our responsibility in the process of reconciliation.

Indigenous stories need to be understood for what they are — instruments of

---

Box 5.8: Innov8

Cree Storytelling

Watch Cree storyteller Megan Bertasson explain the nature, purpose and structure of Cree stories in her TEDx Talk about Helen Betty Osborne, an Indigenous woman who was kidnapped, assaulted and murdered in The Pas, Manitoba. Storytelling, Bertasson declares, is a tool of resistance and "one of the most important means of defence" for Indigenous Peoples against the multiple violences of the Canadian state. <youtube.com/watch?v=kFsioOa4nlk>.

knowledge and the foundation of reasoning. Louis Bird's introduction to *The Sprit Lives in the Mind* is revealing:

> We take the stories that have actually been brought down for generations because they have a value. Even though some of them sound horrible and terrible to different cultures, for the Omushkego culture it is a necessary type of teaching system. It saves lives. It saves the families. It saves the children. It allows people to have a serious understanding about where they live.[20]

Stories as a teaching system. Stories that save lives. If Indigenous stories comprise a *system*, it is because they are interactional. Bird's stories teach because they invite listeners to ask questions, to identify values and, more broadly, to respond to the teller. "Stories," as Val Napoleon and Hadley Friedland state, "are part of a serious public intellectual and interactive dialogue involving listeners and learners, and elders and other storytellers — as they have been for generations.[21] Reconciliation depends on an audience's capacity to actively listen and subsequently recognize their accountability within the cultural system of which Indigenous stories are a foundational part.

If stories reveal truth, they also point the way forward. Indeed, survivors' stories are at the centre of ninety-four separate Calls to Action published by the TRC. These calls are diverse in size and scope, and they cover almost every facet of Canadian society. They include demands to reduce the over-representation of Indigenous children in welfare care; that the federal government acknowledge Indigenous language rights; that governments close the health gap between Indigenous and non-Indigenous peoples; that the overrepresentation of Indigenous people in custody be addressed; that all faith groups adopt and comply with the UN Declaration on the Rights of Indigenous Peoples; that the Pope issue an apology to survivors for the role of the Catholic Church in the residential school system; that Indigenous issues such as residential schools and treaties be a mandatory part of K-12 curriculum; that families of children who died in residential schools be informed of the children's burial locations; that funding to the CBC increase so it can support reconciliation through greater Indigenous programming; and that the Canadian government replace the Oath of Citizenship to one that recognizes treaties with Indigenous peoples.[22] Though this list is, of course, just a small sample of the TRC's Calls to Action, it is important to remember that each of these demands arises from survivors' commitments to tell their stories. Every recommendation, every invitation to action, is a demand that we listen attentively to the Indigenous stories available to us. Canada has a long way to go in this respect: as of November 14, 2018, only eight Calls to Action were fulfilled; eighty-six remained incomplete.[23]

Box 5.9: Diversity in Action

The Dialogues Project

Many years before the TRC would formally call upon the federal government to revise the citizenship test and oath of citizenship to reflect the history and presence of Indigenous Peoples in Canada, Métis-Cree community planner and filmmaker Kamala Todd helped to create the Dialogues Project in Vancouver. Co-chaired by representatives from the Musqueam Nation, the Friendship Centre and the Chinese community, the Dialogues Project sought to foster the spirit of reconciliation by bringing newcomers to Canada in contact with Indigenous Peoples so they could garner a more comprehensive understanding of Indigenous stories within the context of colonialism. The project ran for nearly two years, and the Musqueam First Nation even hosted a citizenship ceremony.

Source: Kamala Todd, "This Many-Storied Land," in Danielle Metcalfe-Chenail (ed.), *In This Together: Fifteen Stories of Truth & Reconciliation* (Victoria, BC: Brindle & Glass Publishing, 2016): 64.

INDIGENOUS LITERATURE AND CENSORSHIP: THE CASE OF SHERMAN ALEXIE'S *THE ABSOLUTELY TRUE DIARY OF A PART-TIME INDIAN*

In collecting the stories of Indigenous Peoples, the TRC observed that the arts play a central role in repairing the damages of colonialism. Creative expression can certainly reveal injustice, but it can also provide a pathway to healing by "breaking silences, transforming conflicts, and mending the damaged relationships of violence, oppression, and exclusion."[24] Indigenous literature is one such mode of expression, powerful in its capacity to resist colonial ways of thinking through provocative narratives. Authors such as Thomas King, Eden Robinson, Katherena Vermette, Tracey Lindberg, Richard Wagamese, Leslie Marmon Silko, Louise Erdrich, N. Scott Momaday and hundreds of others, have all in their unique way created complex fictions that testify to the enduring presence of Indigenous discourse on the continent. Readers of these novelists are typically asked to engage in perspectives that challenge dominant settler ideologies, to spend significant time with Indigenous characters and contexts and to take seriously the value and breadth of Indigenous knowledges. For non-Indigenous readers, this may prompt modes of intercultural understanding, compassion and prosocial action. For Indigenous readers, such novels offer important opportunities to see themselves, their families and their ancestors represented — to be visible and to have a voice are critical to withstanding individual and collective histories of oppression.

Still, Indigenous novelists continue to face modes of discrimination that are as serious as they are pervasive. According to the American Library Association's Office for Intellectual Freedom, of the ten most frequently **challenged** books in America in 2015, nine of them contained "diverse content," which is to say literature by or about people of colour, LGBT2TQ people and people with disabilities.[25] Most notably, between 2010 and 2014, the most challenged novel in America was an Indigenous novel: Sherman Alexie's *The Absolutely True Diary of a Part-Time Indian*. This young-adult novel is narrated from the comic perspective of Junior, a teenager born with hydrocephalus, who grows up on the Spokane Reservation but decides to attend a primarily white high school off-reservation. It is a story that is just as much about the contemporary realities of growing up Indigenous in America as it is about the multiple forms of racism into which young Indigenous people are socialized daily. The social threats that confront Junior are manifold: he is poor; he has seizures and inadequate access to healthcare; he is bullied.[26] These forces intersect to create a complex web of vulnerability and disempowerment that Alexie asks his young readers to pay close attention to in order that they understand the weight of systemic racism upon Indigenous youth.

Why was this the most challenged novel in America? Why would certain groups censor a fictional story that bears witness to the lived experience of a Spokane boy who seeks education? The superficial reasons are as predictable as they are misleading. In 2011, for example, Alexie's novel was removed from library shelves and required high school reading lists in Dade County, Georgia, because of complaints about "vulgarity, racism, and anti-Christian content"; in 2013, the book was challenged on a tenth-grade reading list in Billings, Montana, because it is "shockingly, written by a Native American who reinforces all the negative stereotypes of his people and does it from the crude, obscene, and unfiltered viewpoint of a ninth-grader growing up on the reservation"; in 2014, it was removed from a high school reading list in Meridian, Idaho; after parents complained that the novel "discusses masturbation, contains profanity, and has been viewed as anti-Christian."[27] Canada, to be clear, is not immune to such censorship: in 2010, an educational assistant in a Manitoba school challenged Alexie's novel for its inaccuracy, age-inappropriateness and the fact that it would "make Aboriginals in the class feel bad if the book is taught."[28]

Each of these attempts to censor Alexie's novel, whether ultimately successful or not, leverages the language of impropriety and indecency to make its case. However, the censoring of Indigenous stories such as Alexie's is not about impropriety. It is about power. In writing for younger audiences, Alexie seeks to make injustice and vulnerability clear and present, because to influence young readers is to influence those who will one day have the power to change our world. His storytelling is as much an act of resistance as it is a form of entertainment. Furthermore, if the censoring of a novel is an attempt to control the breadth of communication through the realization of some quasi-specific value held by those in authority, then we might comprehend acts of censorship as attempts to both *hold onto social power* and *obfuscate* the locus of power in North America. In other words, by trying to censor stories that expose the unequal and inequitable access to power (to education, to resources, to economy, to healthcare, etc.) within a Western society that supposedly champions the neutrality of democracy and celebrates the equal availability of justice for all of its citizens, these moments of censorship effectively suppress the painful realities of living with systemic racism. When a writer for the *Wall Street Journal* sought to criticize contemporary young adult fiction in general, and Alexie in particular, for the ways such novels "constantly reflect ... back hideously distorted portrayals of what life is,"[29] Alexie responded in kind:

> Does Ms. Gurdon honestly believe that a sexually explicit YA novel might somehow traumatize a teen mother? Does she believe that a YA novel about murder and rape will somehow shock a teenager whose life has been damaged by murder and rape? Does she believe a dystopian novel will frighten a kid who already lives in hell?
>
> When some cultural critics fret about the "ever-more-appalling" YA books, they aren't trying to protect African-American teens forced to walk through metal detectors on their way into school. Or Mexican-American teens enduring the culturally schizophrenic life of being American citizens and the children of illegal immigrants. Or Native American teens growing up on Third World reservations. Or poor white kids trying to survive the meth-hazed trailer parks. They aren't trying to protect the poor from poverty. Or victims from rapists.
>
> No, they are simply trying to protect their privileged notions of what literature is and should be. They are trying to protect privileged children. Or the seemingly privileged.[30]

Here Alexie makes the point that censorship does not protect readers. It protects privilege, which is to say it conceals the lived experience of people who have been disempowered by historical and contemporary contexts of colonialism in North America. To wit, in *The Absolutely True Diary of a Part-Time Indian*, Alexie references the phrase, "Kill the Indian."[31] This is a direct allusion to a statement made by Richard Pratt in 1892 at the Nineteenth Annual Conference of Charities and Corrections. Pratt opened one of the very first off-reservation residential schools — the Carlisle Indian Industrial School — and the phrase, "Kill the Indian, save the man," was the basis of his proposed education policy for Indigenous peoples. Thomas King explains:

> ## Box 5.10: Think About…
>
> ### The Potlatch Law
> The following passage is taken directly from ch.7, s.3 of Canada's Indian Act, as it was amended in 1884; it came to be known as the Potlatch Law:
>
> > Every Indian or other person who engages in or assists in celebrating the Indian festival known as the "Potlach" or in the Indian dance known as the "Tamanawas" is guilty of a misdemeanor, and shall be liable to imprisonment for a term of not more than six nor less than two months in any gaol or other place of confinement; and any Indian or other person who encourages, either directly or indirectly, an Indian or Indians to get up such a festival or dance, or to celebrate the same, or who shall assist in the celebration of the same is guilty of a like offence, and shall be liable to the same punishment.
>
> Potlatch ceremonies are essential to the cultural fabric and community of many coastal First Nations. Though rituals differ from nation to nation, the Potlatch is generally an opportunity for the giving of gifts and exchange of wealth amongst community members of different social statuses. It may be held to mark births, naming, puberty, weddings and deaths. It involves special songs, feasts and stories. Consider, then, how the banning of the Potlatch relates to the contemporary censorship of Indigenous literatures, such as Sherman Alexie's novel. How do they similarly undermine Indigenous identity and to what larger effect?
>
> Source: "The Potlatch," *Native American Netroots*, August 13, 2010 <http://nativeamericannetroots.net/diary/tag/Potlatch>.

The Carlisle model called for schools to be situated as far away from Native communities as possible. The model insisted that personal contact between parents and students be greatly reduced or eliminated altogether. It prohibited the practice of Native traditions and the speaking of Native languages. The children were taught to read and write English, encouraged to join a Protestant Christian denomination, and given vocational training in such matters as farming, baking, printing, housekeeping, cooking, and shoemaking.[32]

Significantly, the forced assimilation and continued cultural genocide perpetrated by such policy specifically depended upon the censorship of Indigenous cultural practices. In Canada, too, amendments to the Indian Act banned a host of cultural practices, such as the west coast Potlatch and the Prairie Thirst-Dance. It is in this context that the attempted censorship of Alexie's novel is so painfully ironic: if one facet of "Indian policy" across North America was to eradicate Indigenous identity through censorship, then contemporary challenges to this novel are not unique; they are part of a much larger and longer historical continuum. To ban an Indigenous text is to participate in the same sort of cultural erasure that many people, in their complacency, believe is something of the past. Instead, it is an example of the same violations being perpetrated but with a slightly different face on them. To deny Indigenous lived experience — to deny the legitimacy of Junior's experience as a Spokane teenager — is to deny in one small but wholly significant way the possibility of Indigenous readers seeing themselves in North America.

CONCLUSION

In one of his many stories about shaman powers of the Omushkego people, Louis Bird reflects upon his own limitations as a storyteller:

> I can't explain in detail how a person got to be a shaman. I only know the basics because I was not born into a shaman's spiritual practice. I was born into Christianity — I was trained to believe in Christ and God. As a young boy I was not allowed to ask about our ancestral spiritual beliefs and practices. Christianity condemned them as heathen or as pagan. The only thing that I regret in this life is that none of our own people will know about these things. Those who imposed their culture on us never had to defend their own culture. Many are ashamed to be an Indian, without knowing why — without ever having information.… Other nations destroy their own land — this is what's happening today. And that is why I wanted to tell the story this way. It's not to condemn the European people, or to condemn their spiritual practice. No. But to record what was, and what is now so that our people will not be ashamed of being of First Nations descent.[33]

In the same moment that Bird affirms the power of storytelling to bear witness to and regenerate the knowledge, history and beliefs of his community, he also attests to the lingering power of colonialism in Canada. Having had Christianity imposed upon him and having been prohibited from asking questions of his ancestors' beliefs, Bird laments the cultural loss that he cannot fully recover. For as many stories as there are — as many stories as need to be listened to — there are other stories that have vanished. The TRC notes that the arts "restore human dignity and identity in the face of injustice."[34] We might push this idea further by recognizing that such dignity is also restored through one's capacity to resist. As with many Indigenous storytellers, embedded in Bird's narration is a rejection of those colonial practices, conditions and systems that have worked to silence Indigenous voices. To tell a story in this context is to attest to the integrity of one's life, one's family and one's nation.

Finally, if reconciliation is to become a reality, non-Indigenous citizens must ultimately recognize the risks of unethical forms of listening. Touting the virtues of respect is not enough, nor is falling back into comfortable-yet-naïve narratives of tolerance and multiculturalism. We must, as Paulette Regan contends, "risk interacting differently with Indigenous people — with vulnerability, humility, and a willingness to stay in the decolonizing struggle of our own discomfort ... to embrace stories as powerful teachings — disquieting moments that can change our beliefs, attitudes, and actions."[35] Central to such **decolonization** is recognizing which way the direction of responsibility must flow. It is not, in the end, the responsibility of Indigenous storytellers to educate non-Indigenous people about the legacy of colonialism; rather, our obligation towards healing is an obligation to educate ourselves, to actively seek out new modes of knowledge, and if we are gifted with a story, to listen as closely and carefully as we can.

CRITICAL REVIEW QUESTIONS

1. What values are constructed in the Haudenosaunee creation story?
2. What is the significance of Indigenous storytelling in the context of the truth and reconciliation?
3. How is storytelling a form of resistance?
4. Why is the censorship of Indigenous literature a critical social issue?
5. What is our responsibility when encountering Indigenous stories?

RECOMMENDED READINGS

Louis Bird, *The Spirit Lives in the Mind: Omushkego Stories, Lives, and Dreams* (Susan Elaine Gray ed.) (Montreal: McGill-Queen's University Press, 2007).

Thomas King, *The Truth About Stories: A Native Narrative* (Toronto: House of Anansi Press, 2003).

Kamala Todd, "This Many-Storied Land," in Danielle Metcalfe-Chenail (ed.), *In This Together: Fifteen Stories of Truth & Reconciliation* (Victoria, BC: Brindle & Glass Publishing, 2016): 53–66.

Truth and Reconciliation Commission of Canada (TRC), *Final Report of the Truth and Reconciliation Commission of Canada, Volume One: Summary*, 2nd edition (Toronto: James Lorimer & Co., 2015).

Gerald Vizenor, *Native Liberty: Natural Reason and Cultural Survivance* (Lincoln: University of Nebraska Press, 2009).

KEY TERMS

challenge: a form of literary censorship in which a person or group attempts to remove and/or restrict materials from a library or curriculum. Successful challenges result in various forms of book banning.

colonialism: the control, occupation, settlement and exploitation of lands and peoples by an entity foreign to those lands and peoples.

cultural genocide: according to the TRC, "the destruction of those structures and practices that allow the group to continue as a group. States that engage in cultural genocide set out to destroy the political and social institutions of the targeted group. Land is seized, and populations are forcibly transferred and their movement is restricted. Languages are banned. Spiritual leaders are persecuted, spiritual practices are forbidden, and objects of spiritual value are confiscated and destroyed. And ... families are disrupted to prevent the transmission of cultural values and identity from one generation to the next."[36]

decolonization: the formal process of restoring sovereignty and decision-making power to a formerly colonized peoples. More largely, decolonization refers to the long-term process of restoring Indigenous cultures, ways of knowing and customs, as well as reinterpreting Western history from Indigenous perspectives.

reconciliation: according to the TRC, "an ongoing process of establishing and maintaining respectful relationships. A critical part of this process involves repairing damaged trust by making apologies, providing individual and collective reparations, and following through with concrete actions that demonstrate real societal change. Establishing respectful relationships also requires the revitalization of Indigenous law and legal traditions."[37] True reconciliation involves recognizing and acting upon one's responsibility to decolonize Canada.

residential school: government-sanctioned religious schools designed to forcibly assimilate Indigenous children into Euro-Canadian culture. In practice, the residential school system routinely separated children from their parents, submitted many to a multitude of physical, sexual and psychological abuses, and fostered a legacy of intergenerational trauma.

survivance: an Indigenous storytelling aesthetic theorized by Anishinaabe scholar Gerald Vizenor, which he describes as "an active sense of presence over absence, deracination, and oblivion; survivance is the continuance of stories, not a mere reaction, however pertinent."[38]

terra nullius: nobody's land, the colonial myth of the empty continent, rhetorically used to justify the occupation, settlement and exploitation of Indigenous lands and people.

Turtle Island: an original name for North America that derives from the creation stories of numerous Indigenous cultures such as the Haudenosaunee.

Notes

1. Thomas King, *The Truth About Stories: A Native Narrative* (Toronto: House of Anansi Press, 2003): 2.
2. Though many versions of the story of Sky Woman exist, the version I am telling is based on Thomas King's telling. See *The Truth About Stories*, 10–20.
3. King, *The Truth About Stories*, 2.
4. King, *The Truth About Stories*, 27–28.
5. TRC (Truth and Reconciliation Commission of Canada.), *Final Report of the Truth and Reconciliation Commission of Canada, Volume One: Summary*, 2nd edition (Toronto: James Lorimer & Co., 2015): 1.
6. *British North America Act, Statutes of Canada*, 1867, Sec. 91.
7. Canada, Parliament, *House of Commons Debates*, May 9, 1883 (John A. Macdonald, Prime Minister). 15 September 2017. <http://parl.canadiana.ca/view/oop.debates_HOC501_02>.
8. Louis Bird, *The Spirit Lives in the Mind: Omushkego Stories, Lives, and Dreams* (Susan Elaine Gray, ed.) (Montreal: McGill-Queen's University Press, 2007): 5.
9. TRC, *Final Report*, 19.
10. TRC, *Final Report*, 38.
11. TRC, *Final Report*, 82.
12. TRC, *Final Report*, 83.
13. TRC, *Final Report*, 89.
14. TRC, *Final Report*, 98.
15. TRC, *Final Report*, 103.
16. TRC, *Final Report*, 107.
17. TRC, *Final Report*, 105.
18. TRC, *Final Report*, 16–17.
19. TRC, *Final Report*, 9–10.
20. Bird, *The Spirit Lives*, 4.
21. Val Napoleon, and Hadley Friedland, "An Inside Job: Engaging With Indigenous Legal Traditions Through Stories," *McGill Law Journal*, 61, 4 (2016): 725–54.
22. TRC, *Final Report*, 319, 321, 322, 324, 327, 330, 331,333, 335, 337.
23. Ian Mosby, "TRC Calls to Action Status," *Twitter*, November 14, 2018.
24. TRC, *Final Report*, 279.
25. American Library Association, Office for Intellectual Freedom, *Frequently Challenged Books* (n.d.), September 15, 2017.
26. Sherman Alexie, *The Absolutely True Diary of a Part-Time Indian* (New York: Little, Brown and Company, 2009).
27. American Library Association, Office for Intellectual Freedom, "Books Challenged or Banned: 2014–2015," edited by Robert P. Doyle (2015): 4–5.
28. Freedom to Read, Challenges to Publications in Canadian Libraries, "List of Challenges to Resources and Policies Reported by Publicly Funded Canadian Libraries" (Book and Periodical Council, 2013) September 15, 2017.
29. Megan Cox Gurdon, "Darkness too Visible," *Wall Street Journal*, June 4, 2011.
30. Sherman Alexie, "Why the Best Books Are Written in Blood," *Wall Street Journal*, June 9, 2011.
31. Alexie, *The Absolutely True Diary*, 35.

32. Thomas King, *The Inconvenient Indian* (Toronto: Doubleday Canada, 2012): 110–111.

33. Bird, *The Spirit Lives,* 61–62.

34. TRC, *Final Report,* 280.

35. Paulette Regan, *Unsettling the Settler Within: Indian Residential Schools, Truth Telling and Reconciliation in Canada* (Vancouver: University of British Columbia Press, 2010): 13.

36. TRC, *Final Report,* 1.

37. TRC, *Final Report,* 16–17.

38. Gerald Vizenor, *Native Liberty: Natural Reason and Cultural Survivance* (Lincoln: University of Nebraska Press, 2009): 85.

6

SOCIAL INEQUALITY

DIVERSITY AND SOCIAL STRATIFICATION

Sara J. Cumming

> *The history of all hitherto existing society is the history of class struggles ... society is more and more splitting up into two great hostile camps, into two great classes directly facing each other — bourgeoisie and proletariat.*
> — Karl Marx and Fredrich Engels, *The Communist Manifesto,* 1848

KEY OBJECTIVES

Define social stratification.

Discuss the theoretical approaches to social class.

Outline the class system in Canada.

Explain the ways that social class is measured.

Discuss which groups in Canada are most marginalized.

Clarify the difference between blaming the system and blaming the victim.

On February 28, 2017, *Maclean's* published an article by Scott Gilmore titled "The American Dream has moved to Canada." The so-called American Dream put forth the idea that everyone could "pull themselves up by their bootstraps" and achieve anything with a little grit and determination. Gilmore argues that Canada has now surpassed the United States as the land of opportunity. He highlights the fact that

Canadians live 2.5 years longer than Americans, are six times less likely to be incarcerated, have higher educational attainment and are more likely to be employed and to own a home as examples of the Canadian Dream. Furthermore, Gilmore argues that in Canada you are twice as likely to be able to move from the poorest quintile of the population to the wealthiest as you are in the United States. So, why you might ask, are you being required to read a chapter on social inequality in a Canadian textbook about diversity? It is fantastic news that we are doing "better than" the United States on many measures — but not all that surprising considering that we have many laws that protect our vulnerable populations (e.g., Employment Equity Act, Civil Marriage Act) and many programs and policies to help safeguard people against dire circumstances, such as social assistance, disability support, subsidized housing and childcare and student loans, to name a few. However, despite all of these measures, we continue to be a country that experiences a high level of social stratification. Some people do very well, while others experience **marginalization** on many levels.

The Employment Equity Act requires employers to engage in proactive employment practices to increase the representation of women, people with disabilities, Indigenous Peoples and racialized minorities in the workforce. The Civil Marriage Act makes same-sex marriage legal across Canada.

Marginalization is the process by which a minority or sub-group is excluded and their needs ignored. The term **social stratification** refers to the hierarchical arrangement of individuals based upon wealth, **power** and prestige. Almost every aspect of our lives is affected by social stratification — the street our house is on, the type of transportation we use, the brands of clothing we wear, our level of education and even our health and well-being. When we are talking about social stratification we are not focusing on individual circumstance; rather, we are concentrating on the ways that groups are layered in society according to their material wealth into social classes. A person's position within a social class is referred to as their social status. Our social status can be achieved or ascribed.

You are born into a number of circumstances beyond your control. We refer to these as your **ascribed status**. Your parents' socioeconomic status at the time of your birth, your race, sex, age, disability/ability are all factors that you did not choose or earn. In almost all instances, the factors that determine your ascribed status cannot be changed, although a few people do change their sex, and disabilities may appear or disappear over the life course. Our **achieved status** is generally a result of our accomplishments

> **Box 6.1 Think About…**
>
> Achieved statuses are not always open to everyone. If a female hockey player performs well in her younger years, it is highly unlikely she will achieve the status of "professional athlete" with the corresponding high income of her male counterpart.

and achievements. If a person goes to medical school and completes their residency, they earn the title of "doctor." A male hockey player who performs well throughout his younger years may achieve the status of "professional athlete" and earn the corresponding high income.

Although most of us would argue that a **meritocracy**, a system based upon achievement rather than ascribed status, is best, social status and social class are far more complex than equating successes or failures to individual strengths and/or weaknesses. In fact, there is a relationship between our ascribed status and achieved status that is very difficult to escape. For example, in a meritocracy, being accepted to post-secondary school should be a reflection of achieving the grades necessary to attend. The fact, however, is that the best predictor of university entrance is family income.[1] In addition, studies show that students who go to university are more likely to have university-educated parents.[2] Furthermore, if social status was mostly a result of our achievements, we would expect to see a high degree of social mobility — the ability to move between social classes — in Canada. Yet research shows that throughout their lifetime, most people remain in the social class into which they were born.[3]

Compared to other countries around the world, Canada is thought to have a relatively open stratification system. Although not easy, it is in fact possible for a young person who has grown up in poverty to earn a scholarship or to apply for a student loan to attend post-secondary school. Through hard work that student could earn their credentials and become a physician or an engineer, for example, thus changing their socioeconomic position.

Some systems of stratification are open — allow for a degree of social mobility — while others are closed — allow for limited or no possibility of social mobility.

From a global perspective, Canada offers more opportunity for upward mobility than many countries. However, we need to recognize the ways in which ascribed status limits opportunities for many groups in Canada. In this chapter, we discuss

Box 6.2 Diversity in Action

Closed System of Stratification — the Caste System

The caste system, found predominately in India, is an example of a closed system. Broadly speaking, the caste system is a process of placing individuals in occupational groups. In this system, a person's status is determined at birth and is lifelong. The practice is rooted in the Hindu religion. In India there are four major castes or varnas: priests, teachers, doctors and other scholars (Brahman); warriors and politicians (Kshatriya); merchants and artists (Vaishya); and workers in the service industry (Shudra). A fifth caste is referred to as the outcastes, dalits or "untouchables" and is considered so unclean that members have no place in the caste system. Each caste is clearly defined, and endogamy — marriage within one's own group — is required. This type of closed hierarchical arrangement leaves no room for social mobility. A person's caste determines every element of their lives — whom they can marry, what job they can perform, what houses they are allowed to enter, even what clothes they are permitted to wear. While the caste system was abolished in 1949, the system remains part of life in India. Centuries-old ideologies are difficult to eliminate in any society.

Source: Leslie Howard, "Untouchable Citizens: Dalit Movements and Democratization in Tamil Nadu," *Contemporary Sociology*, 35, 5 (2006): 521.

the disproportionate rates of poverty experienced by Indigenous Peoples, racialized minorities, immigrants, people with disabilities and lone mothers. It is important to also note that social class does not merely comprise income levels but also includes other factors. Factory workers, for example, may earn more money than teachers, and yet they are not viewed as holding the same social position as their jobs lack professional prestige. Many celebrities enjoy immense personal wealth — they live in expensive neighbourhoods, wear designer clothes and Rolex watches, and drive cars worth hundreds of thousands of dollars; however, they are rarely viewed as members of the upper class. Thus, our incomes and assets alone do not determine our social class. A number of theoretical approaches attempt to understand overall societal inequality.

CONFLICT THEORY: INEQUALITY IS BAD AND UNNECESSARY

Karl Marx

This chapter opens up with a famous quotation from *The Communist Manifesto*, written by Karl Marx (1818–1883). In the quote Marx notes two issues that underline his theoretical approach to the social world. First, he argues that society is characterized by class struggle. Second, he maintains that the shift from agricultural to industrial society brought in capitalism as the **mode of production** and resulted in the division of society into two distinct classes. Marx referred to these classes as the bourgeoisie and the proletariat. The **bourgeoisie** were the capitalists, who owned the **means of production** — the tools, factories, land and investment capital used to produce wealth.[4] The **proletariat** were those who worked for the bourgeoisie on their land and in their factories and businesses. Marx witnessed firsthand the suffering of working-class people during the Industrial Revolution in England. The bourgeoisie pursued ever-greater profits; thus, they exploited the proletariat, who had little choice other than to sell their labour to survive.

Mode of production refers to a specific economic system. Marx was examining the effects of capitalism as a mode of production.

Marx believed it was the desire to own private property that was mostly responsible for the creation of this two-class system. Under a capitalist mode of production, everyone needs to have an income in order to obtain property and ensure survival. Marx argued that this resulted in the **exploitation** of the proletariat, as the workers do not earn the value of the product they make. This system works for a number of reasons; the first is that unemployed people serve as a reserve army of labour, ready to be called upon if current workers complain about their exploitation. The second is that in the industrial economy, workers have no choice but to sell their labour power for wages, which are much less than the value of the products they produce. The bourgeoisie pays low wages to the proletariat to ensure that they earn **surplus value** for themselves. The proletariat are responsible for creating great amounts of wealth, while not reaping the benefits. The **reserve army of labour** is the term used by Marx to encompass the unemployed people in a society, who are thought to be "in reserve" until they are needed during high production times or when others are unwilling to take on the work. According to Marx's theory, surplus value is the money that the capitalist keeps as profit after paying the workers. This is profit is realized once the capitalist sells the product.

> **Box 6.3 Think About...**
>
> **Boycotting Exploitation**
> On January 1, 2018, Ontario saw an increase in the minimum wage from $11.60 per hour to $14.00. Many business owners argued against this raise, stating that the increase in costs would put them out of business. Minimum wage workers quickly found their hours cut across the service sector. It was, however, a Tim Hortons franchise run by the heirs to the famous hockey player's estate that caused the situation to go viral on social media. After the minimum wage increase took effect, Jeri-Lynn Horton-Joyce (Tim Horton's daughter) and her husband Ron Joyce Jr. sent out a memo to their staff stating that they were saddened to have to cut their employees' paid breaks and benefits due to the increase in wages. Particularly problematic was that the couple are estimated by Forbes to be worth over a billion dollars.
>
> This erupted in debates all over social media, with some arguing that the government needs to step in to ensure that businesses don't penalize low-waged labourers, and others arguing that the government has no right to limit profit. Do you think it is the government's place to help intervene in exploitative labour relations?

Marx maintained that the inequality this system produces is neither desirable nor inevitable.[5] He believed, however, that if the relationship between the bourgeoisie and proletariat continued on as it was during industrialization in England, the inequality between the two classes would continue to grow. Marx predicted that over time the proletariat would develop **class consciousness** — an awareness of workers' shared interests and their ability to act in those interests — and would overthrow the bourgeoisie, putting an end to capitalism as a mode of production.

Max Weber

Max Weber (pronounced *vay*-ber) (1864–1921) agreed with Marx that capitalism created class conflict. He also supported Marx's argument that ownership of property is a major source of inequality in society. However, Weber contended that social class and inequality are much more complex and require an analysis beyond economic production. According to Weber, in order to have a complete understanding of inequality we must examine three areas: class, status and power.[6] Most sociologists refer to these as property, prestige and power — the three P's of social class — as many believe these to be clearer terms.

Weber asserted that owning the means of production (factories, land, equipment) is only one part of what establishes a person's social class. In addition to property, or wealth, prestige and power play a role in determining a person's position within a social hierarchy. For example, the CEO of a Fortune 500 company does not actually own the company and yet still benefits immensely from its profits. In 2015 the average Fortune 500 CEO earned $13.8 million, with many earning well over $20 million.[7] In addition to high income, prestige can also come from sources such as athletic ability, intellectual prowess or even musical talent. Prestige may lead to property ownership; thus, for Weber, property and prestige are intertwined.

For Weber, social class is also a result of power — the ability of an individual to control others. Wealthy people tend to be more powerful than poor people, and prestige can be turned into power. Two famous actors, Ronald Reagan and Arnold Schwarzenegger, were able to leverage their prestige into American politics. Reagan became president of the United States, and Schwarzenegger became governor of California. Donald Trump provides an example of how property, prestige and power can become interrelated. Trump was viewed as a successful businessman (despite claiming bankruptcy six separate times) as his net worth in 2005 was said to be $2.6 billion. In 2005, Trump became a television personality as the face of the *Apprentice*, which ran until 2015. In 2017, much to the surprise of most Canadians, Donald Trump was able to parlay his property and prestige into the most powerful position in the United States.

STRUCTURAL FUNCTIONALISM: INEQUALITY IS NECESSARY AND INEVITABLE

Kingsley Davis and Wilbert Moore

In 1945 Kingsley Davis and Wilbert Moore released their publication "Some Principles of Social Stratification," which later became known as the Davis–Moore thesis. Davis and Moore argued that inequalities exist in all societies and thus must be necessary. They asserted that society must somehow distribute its members into varying social positions in order for society to function properly. There must be something in place that persuades people to perform the necessary duties of any particular position. Some positions are obviously more rewarding and pleasurable than others, and many require special training and are viewed as more important. According to Davis and Moore, the positions that are rewarded with the highest rates of pay and the most prestige are those that have the most importance for society and are also those that require the greatest training or talent. Thus, in order to compel people to undertake the work that is necessary to become a medical doctor or a judge, the rewards for these positions must be high. Likewise, in order to induce people to work as cleaners, or as fast food workers, they must be in need of the paycheque received from this work.

At first glance, the Davis–Moore thesis appears to be a reasonable explanation for social stratification. We do need people in society who are able to work in all of the available positions, and it is most likely that poor people will be the most willing to work in the undesirable positions. It also makes sense that people who put in the money, time and effort it takes to become medical doctors, for example, should be handsomely rewarded for that determination. However, the functionalist approach does not take into account that it is most often the people who were born into families with higher incomes that can afford to attend school for the length of time these higher status positions require. Thus, as discussed earlier in the chapter, it is money, not talent or determination, that is at the root of the success of some and the downfall of others.

Even more problematic is that regardless of educational qualifications there are substantial differences in who has access to the most prestigious jobs, with women and racialized minorities disproportionately represented in the lowest paid jobs. CEOs, movie stars and professional athletes earn millions of dollars a year, while people in the service industry and childcare generally make under $23,000 a year.

SYMBOLIC INTERACTIONISM: INEQUALITY ON DISPLAY THROUGH STATUS SYMBOLS

Thorstein Veblen

While the above theorists attempt to explain why inequality exists or how it creates conflict, symbolic interactionists are interested in how inequality is interpreted and represented in society. Symbolic interactionists focus on how meanings and symbols enable people to carry out uniquely human actions and interactions.[8] In reference to social stratification, they pay particular attention to the use of status symbols.

In *The Theory of the Leisure Class* (1899), one of the arguments Thorstein Veblen (1857–1929) makes is that the greed of business exists only for the purpose of earning

---

Box 6.4 Think About...

Gross Inequality or Achieved Status?

In 2017, 22-year-old Andrew Wiggins, number 22 of the NBA's Minnesota Timberwolves, became the highest paid Canadian athlete ever. Wiggins was reportedly offered a five-year contract worth $148 million. Should Wiggins and other professional athletes earn more than 100 times what an average physician earns? Is this reflective of a meritocracy?

Source: Jon Krawcyzynski, "Timberwolves Make Andrew Wiggins the Highest-Paid Canadian Athlete Ever," *Globe and Mail*, October 11, 2017.

Box 6.5 Think About…

Labelling Ourselves as Wealthy

Status symbols are apparent everywhere, although they may manifest themselves differently depending on culture and location. Look in your school parking lot and count the number of luxury cars you see. These symbolic statements of wealth are also noticeable in your post-secondary school hallways in brands such as Michael Kors, Yeezy, Supreme, Gucci and Apple, even though similar, less expensive items are widely available. Why do so many feel compelled to display wealth, even when their incomes and assets do not match the presentation?

---

profits for a leisure class. According to Veblen the main activity of a leisure class is the displaying of wealth. The leisure class spend their time engaged in **conspicuous consumption** — purchasing of expensive goods and services primarily for the purpose of putting wealth on display. These purchases are status symbols that help to identify people with a particular social and economic position. When Veblen was writing, the types of status symbols that the leisure class put on display were things like massive homes and a large number of servants. In drawing our attention to conspicuous consumption, he simultaneously highlighted the waste and excess that accompanies conspicuous consumption, while many live in dire poverty.

Veblen made an excellent contribution to discussions surrounding inequality by underscoring the ways that individuals embody social inequality through their practice of conspicuous consumption. Moreover, he stressed that most people in fact want to appear as though they are from a higher social status and as a result take part in consumption that is beyond their income level. Think of the ways that conspicuous consumption today has led to extraordinary rates of indebtedness. There are many multi-billion-dollar industries devoted to helping all of us live way beyond our means. Research shows that in the first three months of 2017, demand for credit in Canada had reached a record high, with credit inquiries rising by 3.6 percent over previous years.[9] The report indicates that Canadians carry on average $22,125 in non-mortgage debt, which includes credit cards and lines of credit, resulting in Canadians being more than $1.7 trillion in debt. Arguably, conspicuous consumption has become an epidemic.

FEMINIST EXPLANATIONS FOR SOCIAL STRATIFICATION

The theories so far discussed were written at a time when women mostly remained invisible in analyses of social class. Most likely, the **breadwinner ideology** — the assumption that a woman's role in the household was to provide unpaid work for her family while her husband provided the economic resources through his paid labour — resulted in women being excluded from class analysis.[10] Previous stratification research has consistently been accused of being **malestream** — excluding women from research studies on the basis of their secondary relationship to the labour market. During much of the time that early theorizing was taking place, it was assumed that women automatically take on their husband's social class.

Today, feminist scholars argue that it is important to understand that gender intersects in complex ways with social class (discussed in Chapter 7). As we discuss later in this chapter, the labour force continues to be segregated by gender, and women continue to bear the majority of household labour; thus, they are at greater risk of living in poverty. This **feminization of poverty** is important in understanding women's positions both within and outside of Canada. While there have been significant changes in women's access to wealth in the last sixty years, they remain disadvantaged both at work and at home. The **double ghetto**, first identified by Pat and Hugh Armstrong in the early 1990s, continues today.[11] Women who work full-time outside of the home, many in lower paid employment, are required to put in another full shift when they

Box 6.6 Diversity in Action

How might a gender-based analysis result in a more equitable Canadian society? In 2017 the Trudeau government announced that its next budget would reflect a gender-based analysis. Gender-based analysis examines the differential impacts on women and men by examining their different socioeconomic realities. The goal in this type of analysis from a government budgetary lens is to identify and reduce inequalities in how men and women are treated in public policy. Many people assume that budgets are gender neutral when in fact they are not. For example, tax cuts mostly benefit men as 38 percent of women do not make enough money to be taxable. In addition, tax cuts result in less money available for public services, which are used more by women than men (healthcare, affordable housing, childcare, public transit).

Source: Armine Yalnizyan, "Why the Federal Government Should Focus on Gender Equality," *Maclean's*, March 2017 <https://www.macleans.ca/economy/economicanalysis/its-time-for-a-gender-equality-budget-because-its-2017/>.

get home (taking care of their children and households). This is documented in the Canadian census, where women report taking on most of the domestic labour and sleeping fewer hours than their male partners while holding down paid employment.[12] Furthermore, despite employment equity legislation, women continue to be found at the lowest rungs of their professions and to be more likely to hold part-time rather than full-time jobs.[13] As a result, feminists argue for a more nuanced understanding of the complexities embedded in class and status inequalities.

THE CLASS SYSTEM

Researchers have taken several different approaches when describing the class system. Many follow the model proposed in 1996 by American sociologist Erik Olin Wright, who argues that classes are determined by three forms of social control:

1. economic ownership, which entails real control over the economic surplus;
2. command of the physical means of economic production. For example, owning and supervising the control over machines; and
3. supervisory control over other workers.[14]

Wright contends that the bourgeoisie have all three forms of control while the proletariat have none. He argues that there are two other classes in between the bourgeoisie and the proletariat — the petite bourgeoisie, who hold the first two types of control, and the managers, who hold the third type. Wright purposes, therefore, that there are four distinct classes: bourgeoisie, petite bourgeoisie, managers and proletariat.

Others follow the work of Dennis Gilbert, who argues for a six-class system:

1. capitalist — over $750,000 in cash and assets; the super rich capitalists at the top of the hierarchy;
2. upper middle — above $70,000; most are educated and work in professional jobs;
3. lower middle — approximately $40,000; most have high school education and some other formal training;
4. working — approximately $25,000; mostly semi-skilled workers whose tasks are habitual;
5. working poor — below $20,000; includes unskilled labourers and service industry workers.
6. underclass — below $13,000; under-employed individuals who usually suffer from low education, low employability and low income.[15]

Both of these class models are based the United States. In Canada, we use several measures to determine class, including whether one lives in a rural or urban setting and family composition. To simplify, we discuss three Canadian classes below — the wealthy elites, the middle class and those living in poverty. However, we recognize that the middle class includes upper, middle and lower middle classes. The middle class especially comprises a broad income range, $63,000–$189,199. Certainly, a family of four receiving the lower income level is not living close to the same quality of life as a family of four at the highest.

Table 6.1 Social Class by Deciles and Income, 2016

Social Class	Deciles	Income
Elite	Highest	$189,200 +
Middle Class	Middle Six	$63,000–189,199
Lower Class	Lowest Three	Up to $62,999

Source: Adapted from Statistics Canada, "Upper Income Limit, Income Share and Average of Market, Total and After-Tax Income by Economic Family Type and Income Decile, Canada and Provinces," CANISM Table 206-0031 (2017) <http://www5.statcan.gc.ca/cansim/a47>.

Wealthy Elites

When social inequality is discussed, attention often turns to those who are deprived and marginalized. The poor, homeless and low-income earners seem the natural targets of any such analysis. However, the opposite end of the continuum — those who hold disproportionate financial and other assets — are at least as significant in an understanding of patterns of social inequality.

Research on our elites shows the considerable gap that exists between the top and bottom of our economic hierarchy. Statistics Canada's income survey divides Canadians into deciles (one-tenths) and determines the average income for those occupying the wealthiest one-tenth all the way down to those at the bottom one-tenth. The latest data indicate that by 2016, families in the richest decile were receiving on average $189,200 in after-tax income and families in the poorest decile were receiving only $9,700.[16]

However, the issue here is not simply wealth inequality but also the presence of a very small number of Canadians who are extremely wealthy and, often, powerful. In 2015 the wealthiest 1 percent of Canadian tax filers held 11.2 percent of the total income.[17] The average total income of this group rose 12.2 percent from 2014, with an average income of $529,600. To grasp these levels of wealth, consider Linda McQuaig and Neil Brooks's suggestion: if one of Canada's wealthiest families — the Thomson family — started counting their wealth at $1 per second and counted non-stop day and night, they would have it all counted up in approximately 700 years.[18] This is wealth beyond the wildest imaginings of most Canadians.

The super wealthy are mostly born into wealthy families and raised in exclusive neighbourhoods. They vacation at expensive resorts and attend the most exclusive private schools. In the public domain, these families often sit with one another on corporate boards, university governing councils and political organizations. These experiences lead to friendships and marriages with other wealthy people. Thus, this group's ascribed status is very influential in determining their achieved status.

Table 6.2 Canada's Wealthiest People, 2018

Ranking	Name	Worth	Company
1	Thompson family	$41.4 billion	Thomson Reuters
2	Joseph Tsai	$14.36 billion	Alibaba
3	Galen Weston	$13.55 billion	Weston, Loblaws, Holt Renfrew
4	Rogers family	$11.57 billion	Rogers Communication
5	Saputo family	$10.41 billion	Saputo
6	Garnett Camp	$8.58 billion	Uber, Stumbleupon
7	Desmarais family	$8.38 billion	Power Corp of Canada
8	Irving family	$7.38 billion	Irving Oil
9	Richardson family	$6.55 billion	James Richardson and Sons
10	Jimmy Pattison	$6.41 billion	Jim Pattison Grocery Group

Source: Canadian Business, *Canada's Richest People* 2018 <http://www.canadianbusiness.com/lists-and-rankings/richest-people/top-25-richest-canadians-2018/>.

Middle Class

Most people believe themselves to be middle class. The median family income in Canada in 2015 was $70,363. Thus, only 20 percent of the population can truly be considered middle class, with an income that ranges between $63,000 and $77,000.[19] Middle class generally includes semi-professionals and managers who have post-secondary education (for example, teachers, police officers, human resource managers, social workers), as well as those in non-retail sales, such as insurance and financial services. Also included in this category are those with semi-skilled positions in areas such as manufacturing or clerical.

Box 6.7 Think About...

The Shrinking Middle Class

In 1980 there were only five very low-income neighbourhoods identified in Toronto. As of 2015 there were 88. This is in part attributed to the "disappearing middle-class." University of Toronto professor David Hulchanski compared the average Toronto income earners in 1980 to 2015 and found that there was an almost doubling of the number of both high and low income individuals, while the number of middle-income earners had decreased by more than 50 percent. His results were as follows: the number of high income earners went from 12 to 21 percent; middle income earners from 60 to 28 percent; and low income earners from 28 to 51 percent. What impact might a shrinking middle class have on our economy? Why do political platforms often focus on "helping the middle class"? Why might poverty experts also focus on the declining middle class in their research efforts?

Source: Ainsley Smith, "U of T Research Shows the Middle Class Is Disappearing," *Urbanized*, January 2018 <dailyhive.com/toronto/uoft-reasearch-toronto-middle-class-disappearing-2018>.

Poor and Economically Marginalized

Defining poverty is not quite as straightforward as one might imagine. "Poverty" is often used as an all-encompassing term to describe situations in which people lack many of the opportunities available to the average citizen.[20] In economic terms, income poverty is when a family's income fails to meet an established threshold that differs across countries.[21] Within Canada there is no consensus on how to measure poverty. The federal government has developed five measures, while many not-for-profits, individual researchers and social planning councils have developed their own

Box 6.8 Innov8

Dorothy O'Connell Monument to Anti-Poverty Activism

Dorothy O'Connell has been referred to as the poet laureate of the poor. A playwright and anti-poverty activist for many years, O'Connell helped establish Ottawa's first women's credit union and first legal aid clinic. She also co-founded the Ottawa Tenants Council and the Ottawa Council for Low Income Support Services. The monument, designed by C.J. Fleury, found on the south lawn of Ottawa City Hall, represents the interconnectedness of basic necessities of life, such as food and shelter. The monument incorporates visual symbols of bread and housing.

Box 6.9 Innov8

In 2012, TVO launched its Why Poverty? Campaign. A number of short documentaries exploring poverty in Canada can be found at: <tvo.org/programs/why-poverty-ontario-short-documentaries>.

measures.[22] The most common distinction between these definitions is whether they define poverty as "absolute" or "relative." **Absolute poverty** refers to a lack of basic necessities; **relative poverty** denotes an inability to maintain the average standard of living in the person's society.[23]

Outlining the differences between absolute and relative poverty, David Ross and Richard Shillington suggest that the first approach assumes that we can calculate an absolute measure of poverty by calculating the cost of all goods and services essential for physical survival. Alternately, the relative approach argues that any definition of poverty should take social and physical well-being into account. This approach argues that someone who has noticeably less than their surrounding community will be disadvantaged.[24]

Statistics Canada, which collects annual income data, relies on three measures to determine which Canadians are "poor" in that they live at or below low-income levels: the Low-Income Cut-Offs (LICOs), the Market Basket Measure (MBM) and the Low-Income Measure (LIM).[25] These are income-based measures that use a formula to calculate income "lines," with which analysts address low income and poverty. While Statistics Canada stresses that the LICOs are not a poverty measure, most anti-poverty researchers and advocates rely on the LICOs as a poverty line in Canada.[26] The LICOs are measured by calculating the point where an individual or family spends on average 20 percent or more of their income on shelter, food and clothing than the average family. In 2016 the LICO for a family of four living in a rural area was $25,572, and $33,060 if living in a large city.[27]

The Market Basket Measure (MBM) is a measure of low income based on the cost of a specified basket of goods and services representing a modest, basic standard of living. The Low Income Measure (LIM) is a measure of relative income. It is defined as 50 percent of median income, adjusted for family size.

Box 6.10 Think About...

2016 Yearly Rate of Social Assistance for a Single Mother with One Child

Province	Total Welfare Income
Newfoundland and Labrador	$22,908
Prince Edward Island	$20,116
Nova Scotia	$17,727
New Brunswick	$19,245
Quebec	$21,057
Ontario	$20,530
Manitoba	$20,815
Saskatchewan	$20,681
Alberta	$18,416
British Columbia	$19,120

Source: A. Tweedle, K. Battle and S. Torjman, *Canadian Social Report: Welfare in Canada 2016* (Caledon Institute, 2017): 50–53.

Many analysts argue that poverty is an issue that extends far beyond income. Amartya Sen makes a significant intellectual contribution to poverty discourse with his assertion that an impoverished life is more than just the lack of money: "Income may be the most prominent means for a good life without deprivation, but it is not the only influence on the lives we can lead." Arguing for a relational understanding of poverty and deprivation, he suggests: "We must look at impoverished lives, and not just at depleted wallets." For Sen, poverty is the lack of the capability to live a minimally decent life, which, in turn, limits the ability to take part in the life of the community.[28]

A single mother living in Oakville, Ontario, received a total welfare income of $20,530 in 2016. According to Rent Jungle, as of February 2018, the average one-bedroom rental in this city was $1527 a month, and the average two-bedroom was $3350. If this mother shares a bedroom with her child, she will spend $18,324 just on housing, leaving this family $2206 for the entire year for food, clothing, phone and entertainment. If she has no family supports and her child is under the age of five, how can she "pull herself up by her bootstraps" and carve out a better life for herself and her child? How can people in these types of situations change their status?

UNDERSTANDING POVERTY

Most people believe that we live in a meritocracy, that hard work and determination can result in obtaining a good life. This belief system is grounded in **classism** — bias, prejudice and discrimination on the basis of social class — and often results in **blaming the victim** rather than the system. Named by William Ryan in 1971, "blaming the victim" is a view that individuals are entirely responsible for their situations in life — economic and other.[29] The idea that we can all achieve anything in Canada leads to the belief that those who are not successful or who do not prosper in idealized ways are somehow at fault. Individuals are often criticized for lacking the motivation to make their lives better.

Some of these ideas were promoted by Oscar Lewis in his 1996 study on poverty.[30] He argued that people who live in poverty constitute a subculture with different value systems, morals and motivations from the rest of society. He contended that people who grow up in this culture of poverty are taught to feel inferior and helpless, which results in a defeatist attitude. In his analysis, the responsibility for changing impoverished circumstances lands completely on the individual. Lewis's analysis has contributed to a culture of "poor-bashing," where facts about systemic poverty are ignored and stereotypes are disseminated.

Blaming the individual overlooks environmental and systemic issues that create and sustain impoverished lives. For example, minimum wage increases that remain below the cost of living and abysmally low social assistance (welfare) rates continue to hold groups of people in poverty. Furthermore, this kind of individual-focused thinking about poor people — that they should transcend their social environment — "demands a higher standard of behaviour and sacrifice from people who are poor than from people who are not."[31]

An alternative view to poverty employs a perspective known as **blaming the system**. This view is consistent with a sociological view as it recognizes the systemic barriers that exist in society. Many people are poor for reasons that are beyond their control. Individuals have no control over the rising cost of living, the replacement

---

Box 6.11 Innov8

In *Seven Fallen Feathers*, award-winning author Tanya Talaga focuses on the lives of seven Indigenous high school students who died in Thunder Bay, Ontario. The author outlines the ways in which Canada has failed its Indigenous populations and does a remarkable job of highlighting the intersectional inequalities and discrimination that persist.

of manufacturing jobs with service-based jobs, the increase in technology, tuition costs, access to affordable housing or being born with a disability — all barriers to opportunities that exist outside of individual drive and motivation. Jean Swanson, a poverty researcher, urges society to stop blaming individuals for their impoverished circumstances so that "we can expose the policies, laws, and economic system that force millions of people in Canada and around the world to compete against each other, driving down wages and creating more poverty."[32]

Women

Women are the poorest of the poor, especially those raising children as lone parents and those living as unattached seniors. According to the 2016 census, Canada had 1,114,055 lone-parent families — 19.2 percent of all families.[33] That's two in ten families with children under age 16. Lone mother-led families accounted for 905,630 of that total. Thirty-nine percent of lone parent families lived in low-income households in 2015, with the rate much higher for mother-led families (42 percent) compared to father led (25.5 percent).[34] At this same time, 28.2 percent of women aged 65 and older living alone lived in poverty.[35] Women's low lifetime earnings in conjunction with their likelihood of living longer than men (83 years compared to 79) puts them at the greatest risk of poverty as seniors.[36]

Although pay equity legislation has come into effect in various jurisdictions in Canada, women continue to face barriers to employment and equal wages.[37] For example, women face inequities in their homes as they undertake the lion's share of household duties despite the number of hours they work, their paid work remains undervalued, and they are segregated into "female" jobs within the workforce. Even women working full-time still earn 20 percent less than men; and inequity is even greater for Indigenous, racialized and immigrant women.

Indigenous Peoples

There were 1.7 million Indigenous People in Canada in 2016, accounting for 4.9 percent of the population, a large proportion of whom live in poverty.[38] The average income of Indigenous individuals is 25 percent less than those who are not Indigenous.[39] Indigenous women experience the largest gap, with incomes averaging just 55 percent of non-Indigenous men's. Indigenous individuals also fared worse on average, with incomes 66 percent of non-Indigenous men.[40]

Four out of every five Indigenous families on reserves have incomes that fall below the poverty line. Statistics Canada reports that of the 367 reserves for which data was collected, 297 communities fell far below the Low Income Measure. At the lowest end, twenty-seven communities reported median incomes below $10,000.[41]

Box 6.12 Diversity in Action

Canada's Prisons — the New Residential Schools

Indigenous individuals feel the effects of poverty in many ways, including lack of appropriate housing, high rates of food insecurity, lack of education, difficulty finding employment, and unaddressed mental health and addiction issues to name a few. A major related issue is the rate of interactions between Indigenous People and Canada's criminal justice system. A 2016 article in *Maclean's* referred to Canada's prisons as the "new residential schools." Its author, Nancy Macdonald, reports that despite Canada's incarceration rate hitting a forty-five-year low, the number of people incarcerated reached an all-time high. The most troubling aspect is that a large proportion of those incarcerated are Indigenous People. The rate of Indigenous women incarcerated rose 112 percent over the last decade, and they now make up 36 percent of the incarcerated population. The intersection of poverty, gender and race results in Indigenous women being a particularly marginalized group in Canadian society.

Source: Nancy Macdonald, "Canada's Prisons the New Residential School," *Maclean's,* February 2016 <https://www.macleans.ca/news/canada/canadas-prisons-are-the-new-residential-schools/>.

New Immigrants and Racialized Minorities

Recent immigrants have long been more vulnerable to living in poverty than other Canadians.[42] They are at greater risk of low income and unemployment than comparable Canadians, despite having significantly higher education and more potential earners per household.[43] In 2015, the poverty rate for new immigrants and refugees was 31.4 percent.[44] The average total income of recent immigrants was 63 percent of non-immigrants, with recent women immigrants receiving 41 percent of non-immigrant men, meaning there is a 59 percent income gap between immigrant women and non-immigrant men in Canada.[45]

Intersecting with recent immigrant status is racialized minority identity. In recent years the overwhelming majority of Canadian immigrants have been racialized. Between 2006 and 2016, the racialized population in Canada increased from 5 million to 7.7 million. However, the income gap between the racialized and non-racialized Canadians isn't budging; rather, it has slightly widened. Racialized Canadians earn 26 percent less than non-racialized Canadians, and there are even larger differences when we add an analysis of gender. Racialized women earn on average 47 percent less than non-racialized men.[46]

Box 6.13 Think About...

Racism and Inequality

Canada is known for celebrating diversity and multiculturalism as it has more favourable immigration policies than most other developed countries. However, inequality and discrimination continue to plague our immigrant and racialized citizens. A study conducted by Diane Dechief and Phillip Oreopoulos found that employers across Canada prefer to interview "Matthew but not Samir." Resumes were sent to employers in Toronto, Montreal and Vancouver with racialized or European sounding names. Applicants with Chinese, Indian or Pakistani names were 40 percent less likely to get an interview than those with European names. This is especially disheartening when other research shows us that our immigrant population is more likely than our Canadian-born population to hold university degrees.

Source: Diane Dechief and Phillip Oreopoulos, "Why Do Some Employers Prefer to Interview Matthew than Samir," Working Paper 95, Canadian Labour Market and Skills Research Network, 2012 <http://www.bbc.com/capital/story/20160915-should-you-change-your-name-to-get-a-job>; Li Xue and Li Xu, "An Educational Portrait of Postsecondary Educated Immigrants," *Government of Canada*, 2010 <https://www.canada.ca/en/immigration-refugees-citizenship/corporate/reports-statistics/research/educational-portrait-postsecondary-educated-immigrants-2006-census.html>.

People Living with Disability

In 2012, 3.8 million Canadians (almost 14 percent of the population) relied on disability supports in order to live independently in their communities.[47] Despite these supports, 23 percent live in low income, although the percentage varies considerably by type of disability and by family composition. Seventeen percent of those with a physical disability, 27 percent with a mental or cognitive disability and 35 percent with a combination of both physical and mental disability live in low income. The low-income rate is over 50 percent for lone parents and persons living alone compared to 8 percent for those living with a partner or spouse. In fact, lone parents and unattached people aged 45 to 64 living with a disability account for a quarter of the total low-income population in Canada.[48]

CONCLUSION

Despite being known as a prosperous and welcoming country, Canada continues to experience high rates of social stratification and a persistent trend of increases at both the high-income and low-income ends of the continuum. Certain groups of people are more vulnerable to living in poverty: lone mother-led families, senior unattached women, Indigenous Peoples, immigrants and racialized people, and those living with a disability. The way in which we approach solutions to poverty is dependent upon whether we adhere to a blaming the victim or blaming the system framework. Our understanding of class inequality in Canada is extremely important as it helps to inform decisions not just about how empathetic or giving we are to those less fortunate than ourselves, but also on how we vote in elections, which types of policies we support or reject and our consumption patterns.

Current trends indicate that the gap between the haves and have-nots will continue to grow, especially in provinces where deindustrialization has taken place and there is a lack of natural resources. In the absence of significant government interventions and dramatic policy initiatives, our most marginalized populations will continue to be in dire circumstances and those living near the poverty line at great risk. In addition, individuals living in the middle class brackets are predicted to continue to live beyond their means, increasing their level of indebtedness and increasing their probability of also becoming financially insecure. The only people profiting in this type of climate are the already rich, who will continue to get richer and richer.

In the short term, investing in social programming such as social assistance, subsidized childcare, affordable housing, student loans, disability supports, increased access to food banks and improved, cost-effective transportation systems are all ways that government tax dollars and community organizations can help ameliorate some of the hardships faced by our most vulnerable. However, as a society, we need to shift focus to preventive measures of combatting poverty, such as increasing our minimum wages across Canada, instituting universal free education and daycare, and regulating housing costs. As Canada continues to grow and become even more diverse, we need to ensure that we have the proper processes in place to recognize the credentials of our immigrant populations so that they can effectively participate in all aspects of society.

CRITICAL REVIEW QUESTIONS

1. Compare and contrast the theoretical perspectives on inequality with an emphasis on the pros and cons of each approach. Which do you feel is the most accurate? Explain why.
2. Are there social policies that could lessen the gap between the haves and have-nots? What might some of these policies be and how might we fund them?
3. As you walk through your campus and look around your classrooms, what social class messages are you receiving? How do these messages relate to your own experiences?

4. Discuss some of the ways that election campaigns, both provincial and federal, draw on either blaming the victim or blaming the system ideologies to earn votes. Reflect on why some parties choose one approach over another.
5. A policy that has been piloted in Ontario is a "basic income," which models the idea of a guaranteed annual income. The idea behind this is that every citizen, whether employed or not, would be guaranteed a minimum living wage. What are the benefits and drawbacks of this approach?

RECOMMENDED READINGS

Rosemary Crompton, *Class and Stratification* (Cambridge: Polity, 1993).

Ralf Dahrendorf, *Class and Class Conflict in Industrial Society* (Stanford, CA: Stanford University Press, 1959).

Edward G. Grabb, *Theories of Social Inequality: Classical and Contemporary Perspectives*, 5th edition (Toronto: Harcourt, 2007).

Gerhard Lenski, *Power and Privilege: A Theory of Stratification* (New York: McGraw-Hill, 1966).

Peter S. Li, "Race and Gender as Bases of Class Fractions and Their Effects on Earnings," *Canadian Review of Sociology and Anthropology*, 29, 4 (1992): 488–510.

J.A. McMullin, *Understanding Inequality: Intersections of Class, Age, Gender, Ethnicity, and Race in Canada*, 2nd edition (Toronto: Oxford University Press, 2010).

John Porter, *The Vertical Mosaic: An Analysis of Social Class and Power in Canada* (Toronto: University of Toronto Press, 1965).

Erik Olin Wright, *Class Counts: Comparative Studies in Class Analysis* (Cambridge: Cambridge University Press, 1997).

KEY TERMS

absolute poverty: refers to a lack of basic necessities.

achieved status: features developed throughout life as a result of effort and achievement.

ascribed status: characteristics assigned at birth such as race, gender and sex.

blaming the system: recognizes the systemic barriers that exist in society and create impoverished circumstances.

blaming the victim: the view that individuals are entirely responsible for their situations in life — both economic and other.

bourgeoisie: the capitalists who own the means of production.

breadwinner ideology: the assumption that a woman's role in the household is to provide unpaid work for her family while her husband provides the economic resources through his paid labour.

class consciousness: an awareness of workers' shared interests and their ability to act in those interests.

classism: bias, prejudice and discrimination on the basis of social class.

conspicuous consumption: the purchasing of expensive goods and services primarily for the purpose of putting wealth on display.

double ghetto: recognition that women who work full-time outside of the home often also have a shift inside the home when they return.

exploitation: the difference between what the workers (proletariat) get paid and the wealth they create for their bosses (bourgeoisie).

feminization of poverty: the universal phenomenon whereby women are more likely to live in poverty than men.

malestream: refers to evidence that has solely been provided by men and is absent of any gendered analysis.

marginalization: the process by which a minority or sub-group is excluded and their needs ignored.

means of production: the tools, factories, land and investment capital used to produce wealth.

meritocracy: a system based upon achievement rather than ascribed status.

mode of production: the way in which we produce the things we need.

power: the ability for an individual to control others.

proletariat: the working class.

relative poverty: denotes a lack of ability to maintain the average standard of living in the society in which they live.

reserve army of labour: the unemployed people in a society who are thought to be "in reserve" until they are needed during high production times or when others are unwilling to take on the work.

social stratification: refers to the hierarchical arrangement of individuals based upon wealth, power and prestige.

surplus value: the difference between the cost that goes into the material and wages to produce a product and the money received for the product when sold.

Notes

1. Richard E. Mueller, "Access and Persistence of Students from Low-Income Backgrounds in Canadian Post-Secondary Education: A Review of the Literature," a MESA Project Research Paper (Toronto, ON: 2008) <http://higheredstrategy.com/mesa/pdf/MESA_Mueller.pdf>; M.R. Nakhaie, "Class, Breadwinner Ideology, and Housework Among Canadian Husbands," *Review of Radical Political Economics*, 34 (2002): 137–157.

2. Ross Finnie, Richard Mueller, Arthur Sweetman and Alex Usher, *Who Goes? What Matters? Accessing and Persisting in Post-Secondary Education in Canada*, Queen's Policy Studies Series (Montréal and Kingston, McGill-Queen's University Press, 2008); Dennis Gilbert, *The American Class Structure: In An Age of Growing Inequality* (Pine Forge Press, 2002).

3. Michael Greenston, Adam Looney, Jeremy Patashnik and Myxin Yu, "Thirteen Economic Facts about Social Mobiity and the Role of Education," *The Hamilton Project*, 2013 <https://www.brookings.edu/wp-content/uploads/2016/06/THP_13EconFacts_FINAL.pdf>.

4. Karl Marx and Fredriech Engels, *The German Ideology* (London: Lawrence & Wishart, 1964 [1846]).

5. L.L. Lindsey and S. Beach, *Essentials of Sociology* (Upper Saddle River, NJ: Pearson Education Inc., 2003).

6. Max Weber, "Protestant Sects and the Spirit of Capitalism," in H. Garth and C.W. Mills (eds.), *From Max Weber* (New York: Oxford University Press, 1946).

7. Ainsley Smith, "U of T Research Shows the Middle Class Is Disappearing," *Urbanized*, January 2018 <http://dailyhive.com/toronto/ uoft-reasearch-toronto-middle-class-disappearing-2018>.

8. George Ritzer, *Sociological Theory,* 7th edition (New York: McGraw-Hill, 2007).

9. Erica Alini, "Canadian Provinces Ranked by Average Consumer Debt: Equifax Report National Online Journalist," Money/Consumer, *Global News*, June 22, 2017.

10. M.R. Nakhaie, "Class, Breadwinner Ideology, and Housework among Canadian Husbands," *Review of Radical Political Economics,* 34 (2001): 137–157.

11. Hugh Armstrong and Pat Armstrong, *The Double Ghetto: Canadian Women and Their Segregated Work* (Oxford University Press, 1994).

12. M. Moyser and A. Burlock, "Time Use: Total Work Burden, Unpaid Work, and Leisure" (Statistics Canada, 2018) <https://www150.statcan.gc.ca/n1/pub/89-503-x/2015001/ article/54931-eng.htm>.

13. D.W. Livingstone, Katina Pollock, and Milosh Raykov, "Family Binds and Glass Ceilings: Women Managers' Promotion Limits in a 'Knowledge Economy'," *Critical Sociology*, 42, 1 (2016): 145–166.

14. Erik Olin Wright, *Class Counts: Comparative Study in Class Analysis* (Cambridge, UK: Cambridge University Press, 1996).

15. Dennis Gilbert, *The American Class Structure: In an Age of Growing Inequality* (Pine Forge Press, 2002).

16. Statistics Canada, "Low Income Cut Offs (LICO) Before and After Tax by Community and Family Size in Current Dollars," Table 206-0094 (2017) <http://www5.statcan.gc.ca/cansim/ pick-choisir?lang=eng&id=02060094&p2=33>.

17. Frank Dunn, "Canada's Wealthiest 1 Percent See Their Share of Income Increase," *Canadian Press,* November 16, 2017 <https://www.thestar.com/business/2017/11/16/canadas- wealthiest-1-per-cent-see-share-of-income-increase.html>.

18. Linda McQuaig and Neil Brook, *The Trouble with Billionaires* (Toronto: Viking Canada/ Penguin Books, 2010).

19. Statistics Canada, "Low Income Cut Offs"; "Upper Income Limit, Income Share and Average of Market, Total and After-Tax Income by Economic Family Type and Income Decile, Canada and Provinces," CANISM Table 206-0031.

20. Ruth Levitas, *The Inclusive Society? Social Exclusion and New Labour* (Basingstoke: Macmillan, 1998).

21. UNESCO, "Poverty," *United Nations Educational Scientific Cultural Organization*, 2017 <http:// www.unesco.org/new/en/social-and-human-sciences/themes/international-migration/ glossary/poverty/>.

22. Greg deGroot-Maggetti, "A Measure of Poverty in Canada: A Guide to the Debate about Poverty Line,s. *Citizens for Public Justice* (2002) <cpj.ca/sites/default/files/docs/A_measure_ of_poverty.pdf>.

23. Andrew Mitchell and Richard Shillington, *Poverty, Inequality and Social Inclusion* (Laidlaw Foundation, 2002).

24. David Ross and Richard Shillington, *The Canadian Fact Book on Poverty* (Ottawa: Canadian Council on Social Development, 1994): 3-4.

25. Statistics Canada, "Income Research Series Papers," *Statistics Canada,* 2015 <http://www.

statcan.gc.ca/pub/75f0002m/2012002/lico-sfr-eng.html>.

26. Chantal Colin and Bonnie Campbell, "Measuring Poverty: A Challenge for Canada," *Library of Parliament; Social Affairs Division* (revised October 17, 2008), PRB 08-65E.

27. Statistics Canada, "Low Income Cut Offs."

28. Amartya Sen, *Social Exclusion: Concept, Application and Scrutiny*, Social Development Papers 1 (Manila: Asian Development Bank, 2000): 3–4.

29. William Ryan, *Blaming the Victim* (New York: Pantheon, 1971).

30. Oscar Lewis, "The Culture of Poverty," in G. Gmelch and W. Zenner (eds.), *Urban Life* (Longrove, IL: Waveland Press, 1966/1996).

31. Jean Swanson, *Poor Bashing: The Politics of Exclusion* (Toronto, ON: Between the Lines, 2001): 3.

32. Swanson, *Poor Bashing,* 8.

33. Statistics Canada, "Census in Brief: Portrait of Children's Family Life in 2016," *Statistics Canada,* 2017 <http://www12.statcan.gc.ca/census-recensement/2016/as-sa/98-200-x/2016006/98-200-x2016006-eng.cfm>.

34. Statistics Canada, "Census in Brief."

35. Statistics Canada, "Income Research Series Papers," *Statistics Canada,* 2015. <http://www.statcan.gc.ca/pub/75f0002m/2012002/lico-sfr-eng.htm>.

36. Healthcare of Ontario Pension Plan (HOOP), "Women at Greatest Risk of Poverty in Senior Years," *HOOP,* August 2017. <https://hoopp.com/docs/default-source/newsroom-library/research/hoopp-research-article-women-at-greatest-risk-of-poverty-in-senior-years.pdf?sfvrsn=aabc1621_2>.

37. K. McInturff and B. Lambert, "Making Women Count," *Canadian Centre for Policy Alternatives* (March 2016) <https://www.policyalternatives.ca/publications/reports/making-women-count-0>.

38. Sheila Block, "Canada's Population Is Changing But Inequality Remains a Problem," *Behind the Numbers,* 2017. <http://behindthenumbers.ca/2017/10/27/population-changing-income-inequality-remains/>.

39. Statistics Canada, "Aboriginal Fact Sheet," *Statistics Canada,* Cat 89-656-X (2017) <https://www150.statcan.gc.ca/n1/pub/89-656-x/89-656-x2015001-eng.htm>.

40. Block, "Canada's Population Is Changing."

41. Statistics Canada, "Aboriginal Fact Sheet."

42. Naomi Lightman and Luann Gingrich, "The Intersecting Dynamics of Social Exclusion: Age, Gender, Race and Immigrant Status in Canada's Labour Market." *Canadian Ethnic Studies,* 44, 3 (2012): 121–145.

43. Rene Morissette and Diane Galarneau, *Labour Market Participation of Immigrant and Canadian-Born Wives, 2006–2014* (Ottawa, ON: Statistics Canada, 2016), Catalogue 11-626-X-No.055.

44 Citizens for Public Justice, "Poverty Trends 2017," *Citizens for Public Justice,* 2017 <https://www.cpj.ca/poverty-trends-2017>.

45. Block, "Canada's Population Is Changing."

46. Block, "Canada's Population Is Changing."

47..Sherri Torjman, *Disability Supports: Missing on the Policy Radar* (Toronto, ON: Caledon Institute of Social Policy, 2015).

48. Katherine Wall, "Insights into Person's Living With a Disability in Canada" (Statistics Canada, 2017), catalogue no. 75-006-X <https://www150.statcan.gc.ca/n1/en/pub/75-006-x/2017001/article/54854-eng.pdf?st=Le93AjgM>.

7

GENDER ISSUES IN CANADA

EVOLUTION AND REVOLUTION

Leslie Butler

> *Gender equality is more than a goal in itself. It is a precondition for meeting the challenge of reducing poverty, promoting sustainable development and building good governance.* — Kofi Anan, former secretary general of the United Nations

KEY OBJECTIVES

Understand and use the language of gender studies.

Understand current definitions of sex and gender.

Understand the evolution of gender spheres.

Understand the dominant sociological and ideological philosophies underpinning gender relations.

Participate in informed discussions of current gender issues in Canada.

The social world in all of its communication channels — classrooms, social media, the news, discussions around the water cooler and the kitchen table — is abuzz with hot-button gender issues. Are boys left behind in female-centred classrooms and women in male-dominated boardrooms? Should transgender people choose their own pronouns, and are they suffering disproportionately from mental and physical health problems? Is masculinity rewarded more concretely than femininity? What should we do about the pay gap for women, and judges who routinely deny men custody of their children after divorce? Will the #metoo movement finally liberate women from sexual harassment and male dominance, or will it unfairly victimize men?

Perhaps as much as any other aspect of human diversity, the concept of gender has undergone radical transformation in the past few decades. This is because we have come to understand gender as a changeable social role rather than a fixed biological condition. In other words, gender has been unpaired from sex, or as retired University of Toronto Professor Bernard Schiff says, "the relationship of gender to biology is not absolute."[1] People challenge traditional masculine and feminine roles in schools and workplaces. People are demanding the freedom to express an intensely personal and sometimes fluid range of gender traits in what they wear, what they do and whom they love. Women point out that gender-based male dominance in politics and power disadvantages them economically, while men say they are being shut out of meaningful roles in the domestic sphere of nurturing and raising children. **Transgender** people are struggling for recognition of their very existence. All are fighting for their rights as human beings to be accepted, to be treated equally and to be free from discrimination and social injustice.

This struggle has caused movements on all sides of the gender issue to flourish — MRAS (**men's rights activists**), new waves of feminism, LGBT2TQ and transgender rights groups. All exist to address pressing issues of social inequality related to gender — poverty, health, access to legal help, mental health, child custody, political participation and the list goes on. But before addressing the central issue of gender equality, we need to make some important distinctions.

The Canadian Men's Groups Directory lists more than seventy groups across Canada advocating for and supporting such causes as equal parenting, fair custody and single fatherhood.

DEFINING SEX AND GENDER

To begin with, sex and gender refer to different aspects of our physical, psychological and emotional identity. Sex refers to the reproductive organs we are born with, our genetic makeup (X and Y chromosomes) and the hormones that regulate our bodies. **Gender** is a social role that is determined by how our culture defines masculinity and femininity. Gender roles can and do change over time and from culture to culture. A man staying home to raise children or a woman working in construction would have shocked our Victorian ancestors; laws against women driving cars in Saudi Arabia seem oppressive to women in the West, while women who wear the burka might think bikinis are immoral or even a different kind of oppression.

Until relatively recently, sex was unchangeable, and with the exception of the statistically few who undergo **sex reassignment surgery**, it remains for most people — and for policy and lawmakers — a fact of life. By contrast, gender is more fluid as it accrues from our social experiences. The question of what we can and cannot change is central to discussions about gender and social justice. For example, if fathers don't get fair access to their children because society stereotypes men as being less capable than women to nurture children, we can decide to change our laws and redefine rigid gender roles. If women earn 87 cents for every dollar a man earns, we can legislate change. And if a transgender person is discriminated against in the workplace, we can educate people to change our attitudes about gender identity or put in legal protections. In this chapter, we will consider gender as a **social construct**, that is, something we can choose to change our attitudes toward in order to create a more just society.

Gender roles are expectations about behaviour based on a culture's ideas of what is masculine and feminine. And while some of these ideas may be rooted in the biological differences between men and women, gender roles are distinctly social. As Figure 7.1 shows, a masculine person is defined as being physically strong, aggressive, logical and protective, whereas a feminine person is defined as being physically weak, passive, emotional and in need of protection.

Our **gender identity** is a subjective feeling created by how closely our masculine and feminine traits align with our biological sex, our emotions and our experiences. The term **cisgender** (literally "on one side") describes a person whose gender identity fits closely with their biological sex: masculine men and feminine women. Such people may feel quite comfortable doing what society expects — finding gender appropriate work, dressing as they are supposed to and having heterosexual relationships, for example. The term transgender (literally "on the other side") refers to people whose biological sex is different from the way they feel and the gender traits they have. Some transgender people report knowing for a certainty at a very early age that they were trapped in a body that did not align with their gender. This lack of biological and psychological alignment is called **gender dysphoria**. A boy who *feels* feminine may experience deep conflict between the way he feels and what others expect of him. As a result of pressure to conform, his **gender presentation** — dressing and acting like boys are supposed to act — may obscure his actual gender identity. **Non-binary** individuals are those whose gender identity is not exclusively masculine or feminine and may include those who feel both genders or no gender at all. The dominant values that privilege cisgender people are called **heteronormal values** (heterosexuality over homosexuality, cisgender over transgender).

Figure 7.1 is one way of picturing the complex interplay of sex and gender.[2] The left-to-right axis shows sex and gender traits as existing on a continuum from female/hyper-feminine on the left to male/hyper-masculine on the right. On this same axis, sexual characteristics are plotted as distinct opposites — on the genetic level (xx or xy chromosomes), on the hormonal level (estrogen or testosterone), on the physical level (primary and secondary sexual characteristics) and so on. On this axis, the gender traits of masculinity and femininity are also seen as a set of opposites — or binaries — strong/weak, aggressive/passive/, logical/emotional and so on. The traditional view has been that a person is either one or the other — male or female, masculine or feminine— and that sex and gender are inextricably connected. But our understanding of gender has evolved past the binary as people feel freer to express gender ambiguity. The top-to-bottom axis includes those who are outside of the masculine-feminine binary because they identify, to some degree, with all (**pan-gender**) or even none (**agender**) of the defined gender characteristics. Those who find themselves on this axis are called non-binary. **Genderqueer** people may be uncertain or unwilling to be defined by gender. Transgender people are those whose sexual characteristics do not align with their feelings of masculinity and femininity. They are represented on the compass as moving from their biological sexual characteristics to socially constructed identities of masculine and feminine. Where we find ourselves in the gender compass depends upon the complex interplay of our biological and psychological traits.

So, is gender restrictive or liberating, oppressive or self-actualizing? Viewed one

Figure 7.1 The Gender Compass

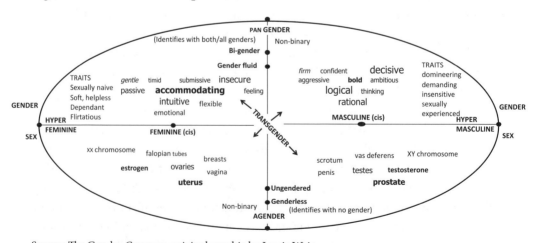

Source: The Gender Compass, original graphic by Lewis Wain.

> **Box 7.1 Think About...**
>
> In 2016, University of Toronto psychology professor Jordan Peterson gained international notoriety with his opposition to Bill C-16, an Act of Canadian Parliament that protects gender identity and gender expression under human rights and hate crime laws. Peterson refuses to use gender neural pronouns (they, ze) for students who request it. He claims that non-binary gender identities (trans, bi, pan and agender) are false, and forcing him to adopt this language violates his right to free speech by "radical political correctness authoritarians." Do you think Peterson's right to freedom of speech would be violated if U of T were to force him to use gender neutral pronouns? Or is Peterson simply using this claim to further intolerant and outdated views of gender?

way, gender roles help society function by setting clear expectations about how men and women should behave, what kind of work they are suited to do and how they interact in sexual and romantic relationships. Another view is that gender roles can be restrictive and demand a degree of conformity that can be emotionally and psychologically harmful. For transgender people, rigid gender codes can be downright dehumanizing. We return to this question later in the chapter.

LEARNING GENDER

Ideas about masculinity and femininity are deeply ingrained in our culture, and from the time their tiny bodies enter the world, babies are being taught how boys and girls, men and women behave. This process, called **socialization**, is society's way of passing on values, expectations and beliefs. As noted above, socialization into clear gender roles can be a warm security blanket or a restrictive straightjacket that does not tolerate the rich diversity of how humans actually express their personalities.

Generalizations about masculinity and femininity form **gender stereotypes**, which are a kind of cultural shorthand that oversimplifies what it is to be male and female. Gender stereotypes include images of boys playing with trucks and girls with dolls, the strong silent male and the overly emotional female, the man on the job providing for his family and the woman at home nurturing children. Other gender/sexuality stereotypes include the overly effeminate gay man with a lisp, the weak, confused and vulnerable transgender person and the flamboyant transvestite. Because stereotypes are oversimplified representations, most of us like to think we are not affected by them, but as we discuss later in this chapter, males and females still conform highly to traditional gender roles in the workplace, education institutions and leisure pursuits. This is because socialization comes with enforcement tools called **social controls**. Powerful forces such as ridicule, ostracism and workplace discrimination help enforce rigid gender behaviour codes. Despite the evolution of ideas about gender, effeminate men or "butch" women still pay a price for violating society's expectations. Gay and transgender people still face barriers in the workplace and in schools. We don't have to look far on television for examples of how violating gender norms brings laughter and derision. In real life, these social controls can affect our most important relationships. A man who prefers a domestic role in life may worry that his partner may find his femininity sexually off-putting. In the workplace, a decisive and unemotional woman gets labelled the "bitch" boss, which has real consequences for her career and workplace relationships. Transgender people are consistently **marginalized**, meaning that their concerns and experiences are trivialized or ignored — literally put in the margin of mainstream concerns. The plight of transgender people in our society demonstrates just how deeply ingrained our ideas about gender are.

Expectations about individual behaviour and beliefs about masculinity and femininity ultimately create identifiable areas of work, school and leisure called **gender spheres**. As the words suggest, gender spheres are physical and psychological spaces dominated by either men or women.

Gendered Workplaces

Traditionally, labour was divided into domestic work done by women — cooking, cleaning, raising children, looking after the elderly — and work outside the home done by men — paid employment, food production, infrastructure maintenance. Despite the many changes in modern workforces, many men and women often still find themselves concentrated in sex-typed workplaces that mirror their traditional

---

Box 7.2 Think About...

In 2011, Toronto couple Kathy Witterick and David Stocker stirred up a hornet's nest of controversy when they decided to keep their baby's sex and gender a secret. The parents believed they were giving little Storm the freedom to be what s/he wants to be, free from the constraints of gender. But they were severely criticized by those who thought they were setting the child up for ridicule and bullying. Still others said the parents were forcing their own values onto the child. What do you think?

Source: Jaymie Poisson, "Parents Keep Child's Gender a Secret," *Toronto Star*, May 11, 2011 <https://www.thestar.com/life/parent/2011/05/21/parents_keep_childs_gender_secret.html>.

Figure 7.2 Gendered Workplaces

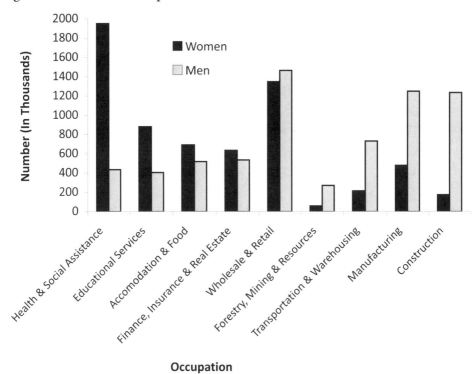

Occupation

Source: Adapted from Statistics Canada, Employment by Industry and Sex, Table 282-0008 (2017).

gender roles. As Figure 7.2 shows, the top three workplaces dominated by women are healthcare, social assistance and education services, reflecting the gender stereotype that feminine strengths are nurturing and caregiving. Similarly, men dominate in construction, fishing, forestry and mining, again reflecting the gender stereotype of physical work done outside of the home by men. Workplaces with roughly equal proportion of men and women include finance, real estate, retail and wholesale. Considering that before the mid-twentieth century, all paid work was dominated by men, women have made many gains in the area of paid work. Worldwide, the United Nations reports that greater gender equality leads to stronger economic prosperity in society generally.[3]

Glaringly absent from Statistics Canada data collection are transgender people. However, a comprehensive study of transgender people in Ontario called the TransPulse Project concludes that compared to cisgender, transgender people are more likely to be unemployed, underemployed, fired and discriminated against in hiring than non-transgender people. They have difficulty getting references for jobs and transcripts from schools that contain the proper gender designation. As a result of this and other factors, transgender people are overrepresented in the sex trade, with its attendant physical danger and criminal and health risks.[4] Here an intersectional approach is particularly useful in understanding oppression as the experiences of transgender people may vary widely depending on other identities, such as race, ethnicity and social class. It is important to note that despite the huge challenges faced by transgender people, they benefit significantly from family and social supports and legal protections. This fact argues strongly for social engineering — using law, policy and public resources — as a means to overcome social injustice.

Education

Given the persistence of gendered workplaces, it shouldn't surprise us to learn that gender spheres persist in the education choices people make that lead to certain jobs. College and university enrolments in education- and health-related disciplines are overwhelmingly female, while men are significantly overrepresented in engineering, math and computer and information sciences. Enrolments in business, the humanities and the social sciences are much more equally spread between men and women. It's worth noting that now women enroll and graduate from both college and university at a higher rate than men in Canada.

Leisure

Gender spheres persist in how men and women choose to spend their free time. Sport participation rates in Canada have been declining for both sexes, but overall men are more likely to participate in sports than women. When they do, men prefer competitive sports such ice hockey, golf, basketball, soccer and baseball. Women are more likely to choose individual sports such as swimming, golf, volleyball and downhill skiing. These gendered choices may be left over from a time when women were barred from playing physical team sports at all. In the late nineteenth century, when women were first permitted to play basketball, they had to stay in fixed areas of the court and their movements were severely limited. The sheer physicality of the game shocked many Victorians, whose ideas of femininity did not include a sweaty competition on the court.

Gendered Life Experiences

Figure 7.3 illustrates the kinds of life experiences that men, women and transgender people are more likely to have than their gender counterparts. Boys are more likely than girls to be diagnosed with ADHD, develop obesity and experience real-life bullying. Girls are more likely than boys to experience anxiety, family violence and online bullying. As

Figure 7.3 Gendered Life Experiences

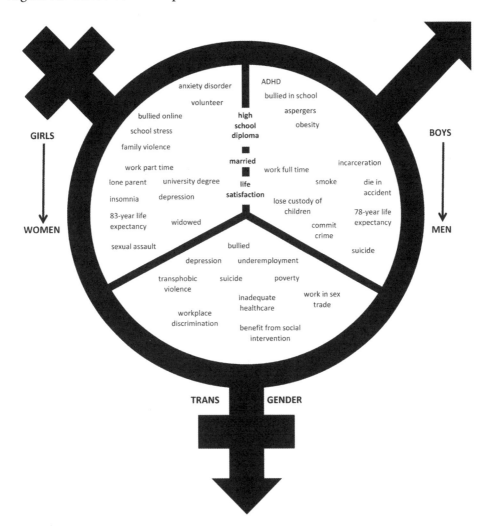

Note: rates of life experiences are relative to the other gender, not an overall statistical likelihood.
Source: Adapted from Statistics Canada data: Tamara Hudon, *Women in Canada: A Gender-based Statistical Report* (2017); G.R. Bauer and A.I. Scheim, "Transgender People in Ontario, Canada: Statistics to Inform Human Rights Policy," Trans PULSE Project Team (London, ON, June 1, 2015) <http://transpulseproject.ca/wp-content/uploads/2015/06/Trans-PULSE-Statistics-Relevant-for-Human-Rights-Policy-June-2015.pdf>, original graphic by Lewis Wain.

they grow up, men are more likely than women to drink heavily, be incarcerated, lose access to their children and die earlier. Women experience such things as depression, lone parenting and sexual assault at greater rates than men. Men and women are about equally likely to graduate from high school, be married and report life satisfaction.

> **Box 7.3 Think About...**
>
> What is the relationship between gender roles and sexual relationships? Consider these questions about traditional ideas about sex and gender. In your circle of friends, are men expected to initiate sex and to value it over other kinds of intimacy? Are women expected to value love over sex and to see love as a prerequisite for sex? Are women more likely than men to feel guilty about hook-ups that don't involve emotional commitments? Are women with multiple sexual partners still labelled "sluts" while their male counterparts are not? Is the masculinity of men with a low sex drive questioned?

Transgender people are more likely than both males and females to experience such things as poverty, underemployment, suicide and genderphobic violence.

Many more, less visible, gender biases exist. In what sociologist Arlie Hochschild calls the "double shift," women still do much more of the housework and childcare than men, even when both partners work full-time. They face invisible barriers to promotion due to something called the "glass ceiling," where masculine definitions of what constitutes success and leadership shut them out of senior roles. On the other hand, the "feminization of work," where the share of jobs requiring traditional male strengths is shrinking, has led some to conclude that traditional masculinity is in crisis. Still others have used the term "glass floor" to describe how men are discouraged from entering traditionally female-dominated professions.

The persistence of gender spheres is a sociological fact, but it's important to note that as society's attitudes toward gender evolve, the gender codes are indeed less rigid than in the past. As we discuss later in the chapter, ideas about gender sometimes change gradually through evolution and sometimes more radically through revolution. The movement has been toward greater parity and partnership between men and women. For transgender people, the first step toward social justice is in acknowledging their unique and legitimate existence.

Intersectionality

Gender is, of course, just one of our identities. Other characteristics such as race, ethnicity, age, physical ability, sexual orientation and social class are equally powerful determinants of the kinds of experiences we have and the factors that affect our lives. **Intersectionality** is the idea that each of us has an identity made up of these intersecting, or interconnected, characteristics. In understanding a social issue such as poverty, for example, we must not limit ourselves to looking at a factor such as gender in isolation. Canadian women may be more likely than men to live in poverty,

Box 7.4 Diversity in Action

Young men in Canada often bristle at the suggestion that their gender gives them a privileged life with more money, power and social status than women. After all, a male student who works two minimum wage jobs to put himself through college and who faces a bleak job market hardly feels as though he has it easy. As noted elsewhere in this textbook, poor, racialized, disabled young men from remote areas of Canada, for example, might face particularly strong barriers to success. Using the concept of intersectionality, explain why looking at the young man's gender alone does not tell the whole story. Consider how other identities might also come into play.

but disabled women may be particularly vulnerable, and white women less so than Indigenous women. Men may be overrepresented in Canadian parliament, but young men are woefully underrepresented. Transgender people may experience higher suicide rates, but wealthy ones may be far less vulnerable. And so on. Sociologists and cultural historians understand the interdisciplinary nature of studying the social world. Understanding issues requires looking though many lenses beyond gender, such as race, social class and ability.

GENDER AND SOCIAL ORGANIZATION

Gender has a powerful impact on individual experience, but it is also a significant factor in how our overall society organizes itself. And the principles that guide social organization are based on our deeply held beliefs about the role of biology and social forces. The heredity versus environment debate — nature versus nurture — is at the heart of many of our most pressing social issues. Are criminals born or created? Is addiction a genetic predisposition or a result of life experiences? Do boys have higher math scores than girls because of how their brains are wired or because teachers expect them to do well and therefore give them more attention? These are thorny questions that can split a room in seconds. But the answers to these questions will determine what, if anything, we can do about our life experiences. In this section, we look at how attitudes about gender relate to political and social organization, remembering always that what we can do about issues — sometimes called our **agency** — depends largely upon how we understand them.

Nature, Conservatism and Structural Functionalism

Biology and genetics clearly determine many of our characteristics, from eye colour to reproductive organs. But how much do they shape the more fluid and less fixed of our characteristics, such as personality and ultimately behaviour? Central to the nature argument is that most traits are innate, not learned, and they are largely fixed or immutable. Those who assign a big role to biology in gender traits say there is an inextricable connection between sex and gender, and therefore we have little individual control over our lives since we don't choose and can't change what we are born with. This is an inherently conservative view in the sense that things are more likely to stay the same when we don't have the power to change them. The term conservative means literally to conserve — or keep — things as they are. Conservatives would say that gender roles evolved out of the biological fact that women bear children, produce breast milk and are physically suited to nurturing and caregiving. Accordingly, male biology –testosterone, muscle mass, even brain structure — makes men more suited for hunting, building and protecting territory. While individuals may vary in their biological makeup, generally society is best organized when we exploit the strengths of each sex. Quite simply, why work against nature? Gender roles thus help organize society in order that it functions smoothly and efficiently. **Structural functionalism** is a social and political philosophy that emphasizes social cohesion and the tendency of humans to work towards social stability. Society is like a complex organism, and social roles evolve to keep the social body healthy. Recognizing that there are degrees of conservatism, functionalists would say that those who deviate from their natural roles threaten overall social cohesion and should be discouraged or even penalized. This explains why social conservatives tend to oppose such issues as gay marriage, transgender rights and challenges to patriarchal authority.

Nurture, Socialism and Conflict Theory

At the other end of the spectrum are those who assign a much greater role to social factors in determining human behaviour. Sometimes called progressives or liberals, these people point to the discoveries of social science — psychology, sociology, political science — that suggest gender roles are created by the social conditions in a culture. As noted above, gender is seen as a social construct produced by the process of socialization. Remember that socialization includes all kinds of influences, from family and peers to religion and media. While these influences may seem obvious to us, it wasn't until twentieth-century researchers such as B.F. Skinner and Ivan Pavlov discovered the notion of **social conditioning** that the nurture position began to take its central place in the social sciences. Once the genie was out of the bottle, it couldn't be put back. Boys could learn to be nurturing and develop their emotional side. Girls could thrive in jobs requiring physical strength and rational intelligence. The binary between the "weaker sex" (fragile, feeble, infirm) and the "stronger sex" (energetic, hardy, healthy) was breaking down. People could be free to choose their gender identity. Through social engineering we could create a society in which there was greater gender (as well as race and class) equality. Socialism uses the power of the state to create equality of condition not merely equality of opportunity.

GENDER AND POWER

Once gender was seen as a human and social construct, it wasn't a big leap to observe how the broader society is structured around **patriarchal values** that privilege masculinity and devalue femininity. A central theme of feminism is that society pays lip service to the value of women's work because that work does not receive as much of the usual rewards society confers — money, status and power. For centuries women did the grunt work of raising children, feeding families, looking after the elderly and sick, cooking and cleaning — all for free. One of sociology's founding fathers, Karl Marx, provided the framework for understanding gender relations — like class relations — as essentially a conflict of competing interests. **Conflict theorists** observe that in the competition for rewards, men have used the reins of power in government, business and law-making to subordinate women into roles that have negligible power. They point to the consequences of powerlessness for women, such as poverty, physical and sexual abuse, and pink-collar ghettos. For centuries in Western culture, women could not own property, vote or divorce themselves from abusive men. Conflict theorists say that far from promoting social harmony, rigid gender roles are a powerful tool in maintaining male power and dominance.

Box 7.5 Think About...

The idea that men need and want sex more than women is widely held and may be based on both biological and social factors. In Canadian society, people are protected against unwanted sexual advances; this gives a woman a lot of power since she has a legal right to say yes or no to a man's desire. And men seem to be willing to do a lot for sexual gratification. Literature and film abound with stories of women who use their sexual power to get what they want — money, power, marriage equality, self-actualization. Does this power to grant or withhold sex mean that women have power that is equal to men? How do you see sexual politics unfolding in your circle of friends and family?

Box 7.6 Diversity In Action

Statistics show that where both parents are seeking custody of children in a divorce, men are granted sole custody much less often than women. Access to children is a major issue in men's rights activism, with many websites providing a forum for both debate and venting of frustration. Many men feel that they continue to be valued only as a paycheque, often paying child support without getting fair access to their children. What attitudes about gender roles may have influenced the judges who make these decisions? Now, consider some diversities covered in other chapters. Are poor fathers who can't afford lawyers facing even stronger barriers? What happens in rural areas where the parents may be separated by long distances? Are disabled or fathers with mental illness or "male" diseases such as alcohol or drug abuse particularly vulnerable to discrimination in the courts?

Winners and Losers

If men have been winners in the economic and political spheres, we must acknowledge that women have been winners in the domestic sphere. They have experienced the special joys of raising children, the emotional fulfilment of close family ties, the creative potential of domestic pursuits. Men have paid a steep price for power — higher rates of stress-related diseases, alcoholism and drug abuse, emotional estrangement from children, higher death rates in war and conflict, and overall shorter life expectancy. If, as feminists have observed, women can be seen as sex objects, men can be seen merely as paycheques, or objects of material desire. Once again an intersectional lens puts this into particularly clear focus — poor, racialized or disabled men do not find themselves in positions of power as they slog it out in low-paying, physically exhausting jobs. Conflict theorists would acknowledge that women have also used gender to shut men out of the different rewards offered by domestic roles. To acknowledge this is perhaps to acknowledge that rigid gender roles have not been good for either sex, as famous twentieth-century feminist Betty Friedan did when she wrote in the *Feminine Mystique*:

> I now see the women's movement for equality as simply the necessary first stage of a much larger sex role revolution.... What had to be changed was the obsolete feminine and masculine sex roles.... It seemed to me men weren't really the enemy — they were fellow victims, suffering from an outmoded masculine mystique that made them feel unnecessarily inadequate when there were no more bears to kill.[5]

SOCIAL CHANGE

Societies are a work in progress, a story unfolding. The gender story in Western culture has, in its broadest strokes, been a narrative of increasing equality between men and women, more equal valuing of the masculine and feminine, increasing flexibility in gender roles for everyone and greater acceptance of transgender, bisexuality and homosexuality. Women have gone from being the property of men to achieving something much closer to parity. Men have gone from being all-powerful patriarchs to something much closer to partnership with women. Transgender people have finally been recognized and their rights protected in law, although there is a long way to go in practice. Gay men and women can marry, raise children and acknowledge their sexuality openly in work and leisure spaces. Along the way, much progress has been made in liberating people from the constraints of gender and recognizing its relationship to power.

Social change is often slow and uneven, and challenges to rigid traditional gender roles have historically existed in the margins of society. But as feminism (along with civil and human rights movements) gained traction in the twentieth century, people began looking at how gender roles maintain traditional power structures. As noted above, it soon became evident that masculinity and femininity were not separate but equal spheres. The work of men was valued more concretely than that of women, and masculinity was seen as the quality naturally suited for power, which left women largely shut out of business, politics and leadership roles. More radical feminists argued that the ultimate function of the **patriarchy** — a system dominated by men and masculine values — has been to control women's bodies and reproductive capacity.

The winds of change were blowing, and open expressions of gender fluidity came out of the closet to challenge the status quo, or the existing order. In the traditional realm of work, women were forcing themselves into male-dominated occupations, which ultimately allowed men to move into traditionally female jobs, such as nursing and primary education. Accelerating the rate of change were transvestites, transgender people, transsexuals, gays, lesbians and queer people who refused to accept their status as second-class citizens or even criminals. Homosexuality was a crime in Canada until 1967, when then Prime Minister Pierre Trudeau famously declared "there is no place for the state in the bedrooms of the nation." These challenges to rigid gender codes were much more than simple expressions of sex and gender fluidity — they were direct challenges to power, just as feminism was a direct challenge to the patriarchy.

Box 7.7 Diversity in Action

Identity politics have dominated discussions about social justice as more and more groups air their experiences of oppression. But some are concerned that the battle for equality has pitted groups within society against each other — men against women, Indigenous Peoples against whites, gays against straights. As such, it has fractured and weakened overall movements for social equality. A significant number of Black people and women, for example, do actually achieve power and wealth and therefore share little in common with poor, powerless members of their identity group.

Seen from this perspective, social class is the ultimate identity; it should unite all members of oppressed groups because material inequality is ultimately the root of all other forms of oppression. What do you think?

Regulate or Educate?

How does something as monumental as transforming deeply held beliefs about gender happen? How do we achieve social change on such a scale? Two schools of thought emphasize different approaches. The first says if we force change through law and regulation, new attitudes, beliefs and behaviours will follow. If our social institutions — schools, governments, the justice system, the media — are forced to include women and LGBT2TQ people, society's attitudes will ultimately change and equality can be achieved. Since these institutions are the very instruments that organize society, only they can change it. Early feminists who fought for the right to vote included a British woman named Emily Pankhurst. Around the turn of the nineteenth century, she and her comrades resorted to violence — putting explosives in public mailboxes — in order to force change. Shocking though it was, Pankhurst succeeded in getting the voting laws changed so women could participate in the politics. Less violent but equally effective was Canada's Persons Case. By 1927, most Canadian women had the right to vote, but they could not be appointed to the Canadian Senate. The British North America Act stated only persons could be appointed, and Canada's Supreme Court ruled that only men were persons under the Act. Five prominent feminists, including Nellie McClung and Emily Murphy, successfully petitioned the Privy Council of England, which in 1929 reversed the Court's decision. This paved the way for women to hold political office. Canada had its own version of the Stonewall riots, when police raided Toronto gay bathhouses in 1981 and laid more than 250 charges. This galvanized the gay community and within a few years, Canada's gay pride parades were known and copied around the world.

The second approach says we can't change social institutions until we change people's attitudes and beliefs. Therefore, education is the first and foremost weapon in the fight for gender equality. Change minds and hearts, and action will follow. This approach stresses that law should be an expression of a culture's values, so it is wrong to change the laws if the changes don't reflect society's values.

The same-sex marriage issue puts the two approaches clearly into focus. What do we do when a culture can't agree, when values are not widely or equally shared? Conservatives who opposed gay marriage in Canada were outraged and some felt their religious rights were being violated when Canada legalized gay marriage in 2005. Once the courts over-ruled the law defining marriage as exclusively between "a man and a woman," the Canadian parliament followed with legislation legalizing same-sex marriage. Progressives felt they had won a victory for minority rights. But should we require that a majority of Canadians need to support gay marriage for the law to be passed? Should groups facing discrimination need to wait until a majority supports them? The Canadian Charter of Rights and Freedoms protects both religious freedom and gender equality. What do we do when they are in direct conflict?

As long as people believed that patriarchy was a naturally occurring force that creates order and social harmony, written history, journalism and education institutions could do little to challenge it. History itself was seen as the true and accurate record of human experience, even though before the twentieth century women and LGBT2TQ people were nearly invisible in it. It's not as if people didn't know that women were treated as property with no human rights; it's that people believed that was the natural order of things. And even if some women objected, they were shut out of the very means by which they could advance their rights — education, law, politics and journalism. Homosexuals, bisexual, transgender and queer people were even more oppressed, prosecuted under the law, persecuted in daily life and living on the margins of society, especially if they were among the poorer classes.

Box 7.8 Think About...

Educate or regulate sex education? Some provincial governments in Canada use regulations to force schools to educate kids about sex, sexuality and gender issues. But not everyone is happy with government-mandated sex ed. They believe such regulation is immoral as families have the right to decide what and when their children should know about sex. Should the government or should families decide?

Ideology and Social Movements

Ideas die hard and entire sets of beliefs, called ideology, are particularly hard to change. But a convergence of forces, a veritable explosion of critical thinking, occurred around the world during the twentieth century that deeply wounded the ideological giants of the past — colonialism, capitalism and the patriarchy. To those of us in the twenty-first century, it may seem obvious that history can be revised and rewritten, that power structures are not "natural" but changeable, that law is merely an instrument wielded by those in power and does not arise naturally from the ether. But it's hard to overstate how profoundly the repercussions of revisionism affected those who had previously been invisible, in this context women and LGBT2TQ people. (It goes without saying that other groups who faced the oppression brought on by white, colonial, capitalist, patriarchal structures were busy revising their histories too — racialized persons, Indigenous Peoples, the disabled, homosexuals and the working class among them.) These were not called liberation movements for nothing.

Truly revolutionary ideas flourished in psychology, sociology, political science, literature, art, history and economics that fueled the great social movements of the twentieth century, such as feminism, the civil rights movement for racial equality, gay and transgender rights movements, working-class labour movements and socialism. In cultural studies, **critical theory** after emerged from the ideas of Marx (see Chapter 6) as scholars examined ideology and power relations in society with a view to liberating people from oppression. Among the oppressed were, of course, women and LGBT2TQ people.

All social movements ruffle feathers, and feminism was perhaps among the most vilified. After **first wave feminists** achieved such milestones as the vote and **second wave feminists** garnered equal rights for women in the workplace and education (equality rights in Canada's Charter of Rights and Freedoms), there was a considerable

---

Box 7.9 Think About...

In the #metoo movement, women around the world have brought their histories of sexual harassment and assault out of the closet with public accusations against some pretty powerful men. Perhaps predictably, the movement has been the object of a powerful backlash. From concerns that the careers of men are being ruined before there are even charges or a trial, to much more vitriolic posts about vicious women who make false accusations, #metoo has lit up the Internet. What do you think about the ease of using Twitter to make public accusations? What about the presumption of innocence as a basic right? Has Twitter helped or hindered our attempts to deal with sexual assault?

> ## Box 7.10 Innov8
>
> In a lively TED Talk called "Why gender equality is good for everyone — men included," sociologist Michael Kimmel argues that modern gender relations are not a "zero sum" game: <ted.com/talks/michael_kimmel_why_gender_equality_is_good_for_everyone_men_included#t-714431>.

backlash against feminists. By the 1980s and 1990s, those who were threatened by feminism sought to discredit and trivialize the movement. Everything from characterizing the very real threat of sexual assault as hysterical, to characterizing feminists as man-haters and home wreckers became prevalent in the media. It's interesting to note the men's rights activism has, to some extent, suffered a similar backlash. Some legitimate MRAs are ridiculed as women-haters and mocked on social media and in the blogosphere as merely weak or sexually frustrated men. We can certainly see the gender stereotypes at play here.

Like feminism, the men's rights movement has ignited controversy from its beginnings in the 1970s to the burning crucible of today's online world. For some, the idea that men need a movement at all seems absurd in light of the power men have traditionally held in the world of work and the halls of power. Others recognize the legitimate need for men to advocate in such areas as child custody, parenting, military conscription, men's health, circumcision and incarceration to name just a few issues. These people point out that men have paid a high price for power in many of the above areas of life. Still others see men's movements as existing at best in opposition to feminism and at worst as hotbeds of **misogyny**.

WORLDVIEWS

As noted above, ideology is difficult to change. At the core of every society is an all-encompassing worldview that explains how that culture understands and organizes its social world. Worldviews provide the basis for all social institutions. In the West for nearly a thousand years from the fall of Rome to the Renaissance, the worldview of Medieval Christian fatalism helped maintain the feudal system, in which the vast majority of people were starving serfs who worked themselves into an early grave (life expectancy was around 30). Christian fatalism taught people to accept their plight because suffering in this life would lead to eternal bliss in the next world. To rise up against your oppressors would be to commit the Sin of Pride in thinking you could be better off than you were, and would land you an eternal life of punishment. This worldview eventually gave way to another, equally powerful one.

Meritocracy

The worldview that has maintained the cornerstones of Western society — capitalism, colonialism, heteronormativity, the patriarchy — is called the meritocracy. Since social inequality is hidden in plain sight in our society, we need a founding principle to justify it, just as Medieval Europeans needed a story to justify serfdom. Arising from and solidified by Charles Darwin's notion of the survival of the fittest, the meritocracy pictures our social life as a competition for scarce rewards — money, power, social status, sexual fulfilment — in which those at the top of the heap, traditionally rich, white, cisgender, heterosexual men, have simply played the game better than anyone else. Either that or they are "naturally" better suited than everyone else. Or maybe some of both. Sound familiar? It's called a meritocracy because the characteristics that help us win the competition are called our merits, things of value, such as our physical abilities, intellect and sexual virility. A merit-based system is different from a needs-based system because rather than distribute rewards based on what people need (food, shelter, jobs, security), it gives rewards based on people's performance. At least in theory.

The meritocracy explains our social condition — where we are in the pecking order — and justifies the fact that there is a pecking order in the first place. If you are poor it must be because you've done a bad job of competing for good jobs. If an entire group is poor, say women or transgender people, it must be because as a group they don't have what it takes to climb the social ladder. Despite the revolutionary changes in our understanding of how societies work, the meritocracy is still the founding myth of our culture. But as society has evolved and the fact of inequality persists, we have modified the rules of the game in order to make the competition fairer. For example, employment equity laws (called affirmative action in the United States) establish hiring quotas for women and other minorities, and equal pay laws try to address the fact that women often make less than men for doing work of equal value. MRAS are trying to get laws and practices around child custody changed so that men are not discriminated against.

Playing Field and Barriers

These rule changes acknowledge the fact that in the game of life, the **playing field** is not always level. In other words, one side may have an uphill battle against a team that has a relatively easy downhill battle. What tilts the field against one side are barriers that prevent some individuals and groups from moving forward. These barriers include many of the intersectional identities discussed elsewhere in this book — race, gender, social class, sexuality, age, mental health. As Figure 7.4 illustrates, these characteristics

Box 7.11 Think About…

Even if employers do not consciously discriminate against men and women in highly gendered employment sectors, data show that underrepresentation and overrepresentation are real. Some people defend intentional discriminatory hiring based on such criteria as physical strength (policing, firefighting) or emotional intelligence (caregiving). Do you support laws that attempt to even out discrimination in hiring by establishing quotas? Which jobs are absolutely not suited to quotas? On the equal pay issue, which approach to achieving fairness is better — educate or regulate?

can be either a barrier or an advantage. Race is an advantage if you are white and a barrier if you are Indigenous, social class helps if you are wealthy and hinders if you are poor, and so on. Discrimination against disadvantaged groups in such areas of life as hiring, admission to education institutions, sports and labour unions exists, and such discrimination justifies laws and regulations to level the field. Sociologists have done a good job of identifying and proving the existence of **systemic barriers** (ones created by the rules of the system) and putting pressure on lawmakers to change them.

Historically, many gender barriers have been legal. An obvious example is **disenfranchisement**, in which groups are legally denied the right to vote or run for political office. It may surprise some to know that in ancient Athens, the much-vaunted birthplace of modern democracy, *most* people — women, enslaved people, foreigners, young men, men without property — were excluded from politics. There are many less obvious but nonetheless powerful examples of how law has been used to rig the game to favour some and exclude others. Consider licensing of professionals as a form of exclusion. For centuries in Europe women were the primary medical caregivers. With the rise of universities in the thirteenth and fourteenth centuries, a university degree became required, and women were excluded by law despite their deep knowledge of such things as midwifery, nursing and herbal remedies. Foreign professionals who enter Canada face the same kinds of barriers to having their education credentials officially recognized here. Our tendency to band together to protect our interests means we have found many and varied ways to game the system.

Other barriers may be psychological. Women who have never seen a female player on the field might never even think about the possibility of playing the game. This is called **self-selection**, the notion that in the process of socialization the powerful messages about who plays what game may cause us not to try out. Men who rarely see a man taking a paternity leave or being hired as a nanny might self-select out of those activities. Transgender people may shy away from professions such as teaching

Figure 7.4 Systemic Barriers

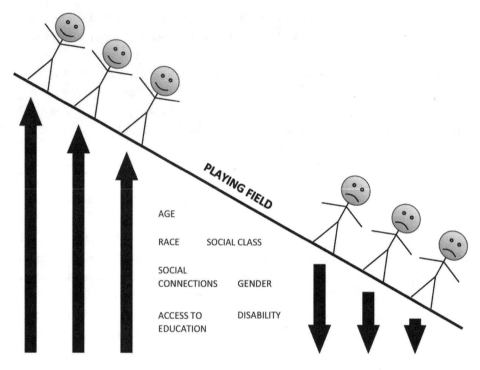

AGE

RACE   SOCIAL CLASS

SOCIAL
CONNECTIONS   GENDER

ACCESS TO   DISABILITY
EDUCATION

Source: Original graphic by Lewis Wain.

and childcare, where a backlash from some parents against gender fluidity might be strong. Self-selection answers the question of why people simply don't apply.

In 2014, Michael Sam became the first openly gay player in the National Football League. The National Hockey League has yet to have a player come out of the closet. Gay players may self-select out of pro sports, or may simply hide their sexuality.

Other Worldviews

Cultures around the world have diverse views about how sex and gender fit in the overall functioning of society. It's worth noting here that international bodies such as the United Nations have declared women's rights and gender equality as basic human rights requiring legal protection. Certainly not all cultures agree. Research

Box 7.12 Diversity in Action

In 2014, the province of Nova Scotia responded to new protections for transgender individuals in the province's human rights legislation. Halifax transgender substitute teacher Sylvia Mayers (not her real name) has faced transphobic slurs from her students as well as lack of acceptance from some school administrators. Despite the province's 2014 legislation, Sylvia keeps her transgender identity a secret because of what she calls "negative perceptions" from parents. Do you think transgender people are likely to self select out of jobs such as teaching? What more could school boards do to accommodate transgender teachers as well as students?

Source: Jessica Durling, "Transphobic Slurs in the Classroom," *The Coast,* March 8, 2018 <thecoast.ca/halifax/transphobic-slurs-in-the-classroom/Content?oid=13147899>.

by the International Lesbian, Gay, Bisexual, Trans and Intersex Association shows that homosexuality is illegal in seventy-four countries and punishable by death in twelve.[6] Women only recently won the right to drive cars in Saudi Arabia. The mutilation of female genitals continues in some countries. Ideas about gender are so deeply ingrained as part of our personal and cultural identity — our nationality, ethnicity, religious beliefs, traditions — that there is deep psychological resistance to change and a tendency toward **chauvinism**, or holding strongly to our identities.

Box 7.13 Diversity In Action

As the war in Afghanistan drags on, one of the main justifications Canadians give for our military presence has been that we are helping women and girls who are oppressed by Afghan men. Malala Yousafzai became an international symbol of this oppression when she survived being shot in the head by members of the Taliban and now travels the world speaking about women's rights. Should the West impose its values on other countries by invading them? Is gender equality a good enough justification for military intervention? Within Canada, is the province of Quebec justified in banning women who wear the burka from accessing healthcare?

CONCLUSION

Gender issues receive much-deserved attention in Canada and around the world. Gender-based social inequality, discrimination, income disparity and social role exclusion are pressing concerns. This is because real people suffer real harm due to rigid gender codes with all their political, social and economic implications. The outrage felt by the victims of oppression on all points of the gender compass is real and deserves action — the single mom struggling with a low-income job and expensive childcare, the father whose ex-wife has moved cross the country and who cannot see his children, the transgender student who is bullied online, the gay man who fears physical harm in his neighbourhood. The social, economic and psychological costs of rigid gender codes are also real. But solutions are complex and difficult. The guiding principles must be fairness and equality, but it's very difficult to get people to agree on how to achieve it. The means are there — education, law, social engineering — but we often get lost in the difficult and devilish details. Much progress has been made toward great gender equality, but it is important to remember that not all social change moves neatly in one direction. We can and do regress. The twenty-first-century challenge will be to press forward with ever more evidence-based solutions to thorny gender issues. Betty Friedan's message was prescient — cracking the gender codes may actually liberate not just women but people on all points of the gender compass.

CRITICAL REVIEW QUESTIONS

1. Sociologists use evidence-based methods of science such as data collection and analysis to draw conclusions about social justice issues. Sometimes these conclusions clash with widely held beliefs about social reality. Discuss the advantages and disadvantages of sociological inquiry.
2. Intersectionality has become an important tool in understanding the interconnected ways in which identifiable groups are disadvantaged or oppressed in society. List some questions you would ask when using intersectionality to understand an issue such as poverty.
3. Gender roles are so powerful that enforcement of rigid gender codes can lead to depression, anxiety and even suicide. Laws can be changed, but other social controls such as bullying are hard to stop. Discuss innovative ways to change people's attitudes about gender.
4. Sociologists have discovered that upward social mobility (getting good jobs, good income, higher social status) for oppressed groups such as women and transgender people is particularly hard. Using what you have learned about systemic barriers and the level playing field, discuss the particular challenges

women and transgender people face in the workplace.

5. Consider arguments for and against the meritocracy as an explanation for why some individuals and groups in society get a much smaller share of the rewards.

RECOMMENDED READINGS

G.R. Bauer and A.I. Scheim, "Transgender People in Ontario, Canada: Statistics to Inform Human Rights Policy," *Transpulse Project,* London, ON, 1 June 2015 <http://transpulseproject.ca/wp-content/uploads/2015/06/Trans-PULSE-Statistics-Relevant-for-Human-Rights-Policy-June-2015.pdf>.

Betty Friedan, *The Feminine Mystique* (New York: Norton, 1963).

Chris Hedges, "The Battle Over What it Means to Be Female," *Truthdig,* July 3, 2017 <https://www.truthdig.com/articles/the-battle-over-what-it-means-to-be-female/>.

Robert J. Sharpe and Patricia I. McMahon, *The Person's Case: The Origins and Legacy of the Fight for Legal Personhood* (University of Toronto Press, 2017).

Sharon Smith, "The Politics of Identity," *International Socialist Review,* 57 (Jan/Feb. 2008) <http://www.isreview.org/issues/57/feat-identity.shtml>.

KEY TERMS

agency: the ability of an individual or group to independently influence their circumstances in life.

agender: without gender identity; also called genderless, gender-free or non-gender.

backlash: generally, attacks on feminists from the 1980s and 1990s and attempts to undermine the feminist movement; also refers to attacks against the men's rights movement.

chauvinism: intense or excessive loyalty to one's own group.

cisgender: gender identity fits closely with a person's biological sex: masculine men and feminine women.

conflict theory: a social and political philosophy that stresses the tendency of groups in society to promote their own interests; because these interests conflict with one another, there is a perpetual struggle for power and dominance (men over women, rich over poor, etc.).

critical theory: a movement in sociology and literature that seeks to criticize the dominant ideology that sustains society with a view to liberating oppressed groups.

disenfranchisement: the practice of legally denying some groups the right to vote or run for political office.

first wave feminism: a political movement from the late 1800s to the 1920s in Europe and North America whose primary purpose was to remove the legal barriers that prevented women from getting access to power (e.g., voting, owning property, being admitted to university).

gender: a social role and set of behavioural characteristics determined by how our culture defines masculinity and femininity.

gender dysphoria: the psychological state a person is in when their biological sex does not line up neatly with how they feel and may in fact be the opposite.

gender identity: a subjective feeling and psychological state created by how closely our masculine and feminine character traits align with our biological sex, our emotions and our experiences.

gender presentation: all of the ways people express their identified gender — clothing, social role, behaviour, personality, etc.

gender role: expectations about behaviour based on a culture's ideas of what is masculine or feminine.

gender sphere: identifiable areas of work, school and leisure in which either typically masculine or feminine behaviour is expected and enforced.

gender stereotype: cultural shorthand that oversimplifies what it is to be male or female.

genderqueer: may be uncertain or unwilling to be defined by gender.

heteronormal values: the dominant values that privilege heterosexuality over homosexuality, cisgender over transgender.

intersectionality: the idea that individuals have many identities that "intersect" (e.g., a person may be young, female, black, poor, disabled, etc.); social justice studies focus on the idea that we experience oppression based on our intersectional identities, and they should not be studied separately.

level playing field: the idea that the competition for jobs, status and other social rewards should be a fair one; the game metaphor suggests the field should not be tilted to favour one group over another.

marginalized: trivializing or ignoring the concerns and experiences of a particular group; keeping them out of mainstream social and political discourse.

men's rights activists (MRAS): men and men's groups who advocate against the discriminatory treatment of men in such areas as child custody, men's health, military service.

misogyny: dislike, hatred or prejudice against women and all things feminine; attitudes and actions that attack women.

non-binary: gender identity that is not exclusively masculine or feminine, including identifying with both genders or with none.

pan-gender: identifying with more than one gender; refusing to be defined by one gender; pan-gender people reject the binary of male and female.

patriarchal values: the set of beliefs that value male traits and masculinity over female ones (reason over empathy, physical over emotional strength, etc.)

patriarchy: a political, social and economic system in which men hold power and masculine values dominate society.

second wave feminism: a political and social movement of the 1960s and 1970s whose purpose was to advance the rights of women beyond the legal victories won by the first wave feminists, including equal pay for equal work, access to birth control and abortions, affirmative action in hiring.

self-selection: gendered social roles and social controls cause males and females to choose to opt in or out of highly gendered work, education and leisure activities.

sex reassignment surgery: surgical removal and/or alteration of sexual characteristics in transgender people so that they align with their gender identity.

social conditioning: the process by which individuals can be trained to conform to society's expectations.

social construct: the idea that gender is a concept created and defined by society (versus arising naturally from biology).

social controls: tools that enforce society's ideas about acceptable behaviour; can be formal controls, such as laws against gay marriage, or informal controls, such as ridicule or ostracization.

socialization: the process by which individuals are taught the values, norms and behavioural expectations of the society they live in.

structural functionalism: a social and political philosophy that emphasizes the human desire for social cohesion and the tendency of humans to work towards social stability; functionalists study issues such as gender roles in terms of how they contribute to the overall functioning of society.

systemic barriers: laws, policies and practices that discriminate against some groups (versus individual acts of prejudice or discrimination); examples include eligibility criteria that exclude women from such jobs as policing and firefighting, or men from working in childcare or women's shelters.

transgender: refers to people whose biological sex is different from their gender identity and gender traits.

Notes

1. Bernard Schiff, "I Was Jordan Peterson's Strongest Supporter. Now I Think He's Dangerous," *Toronto Star*, May 25, 2018 <https://www.thestar.com/opinion/2018/05/25/i-was-jordan-petersons-strongest-supporter-now-i-think-hes-dangerous.html>.

2. The idea for this graphic is based on the Political Compass <https://www.politicalcompass.org>, which changed the standard conception of political ideology as existing on a spectrum of right and left wing. Similarly, this graphic re-conceptualizes the traditional gender binary of male and female to include non-binary identities on the vertical axis. This graphic was also developed from "Past the Binary, Beyond the Spectrum: The Gender Compass" <Fantasterik.wordpress.com>.

3. United Nations, "Facts and Figures: Economic Empowerment," *UN Women*, July 2017. <http://www.unwomen.org/en/what-we-do/economic-empowerment/facts-and-figures>.

4. G.R. Bauer and A.I. Scheim, "Transgender People in Ontario, Canada: Statistics to Inform Human Rights Policy," Trans PULSE Project Team (London, ON, June 1, 2015) <http://transpulseproject.ca/wp-content/uploads/2015/06/Trans-PULSE-Statistics-Relevant-for-Human-Rights-Policy-June-2015.pdf>; Erin Fitzgerald and Sarah Elspeth, "Meaningful Work: Transgender Experiences in the Sex Trade," December 2015. <http://www.transequality.org/sites/default/files/Meaningful%20Work-Full%20Report_FINAL_3.pdf>.

5. Betty Friedan, *The Feminine Mystique* (Norton, 1963): 68.

6. Susan Fenton, "LGBT Relationships Are Illegal in 74 Countries, Research Finds," *The Independent*, UK, May 17, 2016 <https://www.independent.co.uk/news/world/gay-lesbian-bisexual-relationships-illegal-in-74-countries-a7033666.html>.

8

GOVERNING SEXUALITIES

INTERROGATING SETTLER SEXUALITIES IN CANADA

Lee Easton and Shane Gannon

Both colonial control and Native resistance were shaped by struggle over gender and sexuality, in the establishment on the colonial frontier of modern methods for the colonial education of desire. — Scott Morgensen, "Settler Homonationalism"[1]

KEY OBJECTIVES

Understand how sexuality is socially constructed.

Understand the tension between assimilation and visibility of sexuality in Canada.

Understand the connection between race and sexuality.

Understand the importance of decolonization to sexuality.

We approached writing this chapter with a question about how we could capture the current debates in sexuality studies. Our thoughts quickly turned to the 2016 Pride Parade in Toronto, where Black Lives Matter activists staged a thirty-minute sit-in at the intersection of Carleton and Yonge Streets, bringing the Parade to a halt — much to the dismay of hundreds of thousands onlookers. The protesters produced thirty demands, including calls for more funding and space for trans*, Indigenous and Black queers and that Pride Toronto's organization better reflect the racial diversity of the LGBT2TQ community. Most controversially, the protesters demanded that officers of the Toronto Police Service not march in future Pride parades. Claiming that uniformed police officers marching contributed to an unsafe space for queers of colour, the Black Lives Matter activists highlighted how racializing and anti-Black police practices continue to fall disproportionately on queers of colour. In an effort to get the parade back on track, the Pride organizers agreed to the protesters' demands and the parade continued on to its end.

The fallout, however, did not end. For several weeks, in Toronto and across the country, mainstream media commentators excoriated the protesters for their demands that police be banned from participating in Pride marches. How dare queers be so excluding! Toronto politicians demanded that municipal funding be withdrawn to force Pride Toronto to allow the police to march: if public dollars funded Pride, then City Hall could insist the force march in uniform. Across Canada, other Pride organizations debated (and continue to debate) whether they too should ban uniformed police officers from their marches. These debates highlight that there remains a less sunny side to the "progress" that sexual minorities have made in the early twenty-first century — a progress most obviously understood in terms of same-sex marriage and the extension of other equality rights.

The Black Lives Matter protest, it seems to us, underlines the pressing questions about how sexualities shape individual identities today. How could it be, we queried, that for some lesbian and gay people, sexual identity seems less relevant than ever, while for others it remains a pressing concern? We also wondered how did Pride events, once political marches rooted in resistance to heterosexual norms, become a publicly "owned" event, where "everyone'" had a right to participate? The paradox here, we believe, is that many LGBT2TQ people have experienced material changes in their everyday lives, especially with the legalization of same-sex marriage in 2005. In fact, since then the percentage of same-sex couples getting married has increased faster than that of opposite-sex couples.[2] The prevalence of free dating apps such as Grindr, more social acceptance of sexual differences and decreases in overt homophobia have made some gays and lesbians feel that there is no longer the need for an overt political sexual identity.

However, many of these benefits are usually available to those who already enjoy other privileges, especially those related to being white and belonging to an urban middle class. In unpacking the paradox we see today, we underline what remains to be done to confront other forms of social inequity, most pressingly the challenge of persistent racism, especially anti-Black racism. The need for **decolonization** — a term that refers to the removal of European colonial institutions and an understanding of how contemporary settler practices rest on colonial assumptions that dispossess, disempower and disappear Indigenous Peoples — requires a close examination of how European settlers thought about sexuality. We aim to show how Canada, a settler-colonial state, has created a form of **settler sexuality**, which, according to Canadian anthropologist Scott Morgensen, draws on notions of whiteness and heteronormativity to regulate "Indigenous sexuality and gender by supplanting them with the sexual modernity of settler subjects."[3] The most pressing question for sexuality studies today, we contend, is how to reimagine settler sexuality to meet the demands of Indigenous Peoples and eliminate racism within Canada and its queer communities.

THINKING THROUGH SEXUALITY

Sex is not new: humans have been having sex and explaining it for millennia. Sexuality, on the other hand, is a more recent *topic,* which emerged in eighteenth-century Europe alongside **empiricism**, an approach to knowledge generation that privileged our senses and the application of reason to explain all natural processes. In fact, the word "sexuality" was first coined in the 1700s to name the property of organisms that possessed sexual attributes. Over time, the term became a way to talk about the physical sex differences between men and women. Then, as more studies focused on "aberrant" forms of desire, such as that between members of the same sex, sexuality became linked to sexual attraction to others. Although both **heterosexuality** (sexual attraction to the opposite sex; this term also denotes the institutionalization and normalization of such attraction) and **homosexuality** (sexual attraction to the same sex) are translated into in English in 1892, the term homosexuality was coined in 1869, *before* the term heterosexuality! And yet, until recently, only homosexuality was considered a disorder which required treatment.

Why do you think it is significant that the coining of the word "homosexual" preceded the creation of the term "heterosexual?"

As it happens, human sexuality has proven notoriously difficult to categorize. For example, how do we explain the fact that some people claim to have been aware of their sexual orientation from a very early age, while others come out much later in life after having married and raised children? People are able to have sex, and they often do, with members of the same sex even if they don't identify as gay, lesbian or even bisexual. Still others forego all sexual activity and intimacies, giving rise to the category of **asexuality**. In the attempt to explain these observations, two frameworks have come to shape our understanding of sexuality. One framework focuses on biological explanations of **sexual orientation**, or the direction of attraction to others based on sexual, gender characteristics rooted in physical, genetic or inherent psychological instincts. The other view centres on cultural and sociological forces that shape **sexual identity**, or a sense of self that is influenced by how one is sexually attracted to others. The dialogue between supporters of these two positions is commonly known as the **nature versus nurture debate**, or rather, a series of arguments over whether biology or environment plays a larger role in the person we become and the people we desire.

Biological Roots of Sexuality

While scientists agree that heterosexual reproduction offers the evolutionary advantage of developing immunity against diseases, there are other ways of reproducing a species than heterosexual sex. Some species of nematodes (worms) have both female and male reproductive organs, eliminating heterosexual reproduction, while both homosexual and heterosexual activity has been observed across many species. More to our point, human societies too have consistently identified hetero and homo sexual activities over our species' history. What has differed is how these acts have been incorporated or excluded in various societies across cultures and over time.

Biological arguments about sexual orientation were initially grounded in the belief that heterosexual attraction is inherently part of human makeup and cannot be changed except by wilful or sick individuals. In this account, heterosexuality is natural and homosexuality is a deviation that must be avoided (if not extinguished). According to some religious paradigms, homosexuality is against God's will. From a scientific framework, same-sex desire is "unnatural." Either way, to be attracted to members of the same sex is at best a "lifestyle choice" and at worse, a deviation that poses grave danger to a society as it is not natural or willed by God. Indeed, some believe homosexuals teach vulnerable young people to become like them — the so-called **homosexual agenda**. But in this view, nature and God's will could be restored; either through prayer, punishment or medical treatment, these tendencies could be "fixed." The case was not so easily made however. As some activists ask: If sexuality is learned or taught, how is it that heterosexuals have given birth to and raised homosexual children? Given the levels of **homophobia** (anxiety about or hatred of homosexuals or homosexuality) that still pervade North American society, why would a person choose homosexuality?

To answer such questions, scientists have attempted to locate the "cause" of homosexuality (but *not* that of heterosexuality). Studies of identical twins, for example, were an important focus since it was hoped that having genetically identical subjects might resolve the question of whether homosexuality is a biological fact or a product of upbringing. The results of these studies are mixed, without any clear resolution. In the 1990s, there was a flurry of studies examining the biological roots of sexual orientation. Simon Levay examined the brains of gay men and reported size differences between a section of the hypothalamus in gay and heterosexual men. Other studies looked at birth order to determine if indeed homosexuality might be a result of natal development and the role of hormones. For example, it is noted that that the chances of being gay are much higher if a boy is born after a brother, while a woman is more likely to be lesbian. One widely reported study in 1993 noted Dean Hamer's finding that "Xq28" was the **gay gene**, forming the genetic basis for homosexuality. Other studies suggested that gay and lesbian identities can be detected through fingerprints or finger size. Significantly, gay gene research has focused more on gay men and their same-sex desire; less research has been done on lesbians and the roots of same-sex attraction between women.

The more recent attempts to locate biological roots for homosexual behaviour are partly driven by the desire to show that homosexuality is not a choice, or a "lifestyle," but an orientation based on biology or genetics. In this argument, biology could be made to work politically *for* queers, not against them. If sexual orientation is biologically inherent in humans then there can be no basis to deprive lesbians and gays of basic human rights. But the biological approach has not been entirely successful either. Many criticisms were laid against Levay's research, and Hamer's findings have not been replicated in other experiments. Although the media and some activists used these findings to assert that homosexuality is innate, Levay, a gay man himself, cautioned against using his work to support such views since brain-size differences can also emerge as result of interactions with the environment.

Social Constructionism

In contrast to those who seek to find an answer in biology and unchangeable aspects of the human species, other theorists think about sexuality as connected and constructed through social institutions, including the family, the church and, of course, the media. What does it mean for identity to be socially constructed? To start with, social constructionists argue that identity, or the sense of self that people have, is not anchored in a fixed and unchanging source. Instead, they assert that we come to know ourselves through the already existing ways of thinking about ourselves, and these change over time and place. Language plays a central role here since it's through the meaning of the words that we begin to tell ourselves and others about our identity. For example, if I claim that I have a particular identity (whether it be white, male, queer, academic, etc.) then the meanings of these designations determine who I am. That is, the ways that we classify ourselves do not *reflect* who we are, but rather those categories *determine* who we are. For example, if someone identifies as "gay," then their identity becomes created through that term and all the social meanings that term brings with it; they understand their sexuality through the lens of gay-ness and not simply a series of sexual acts.

In this framework, identity is also contextual, shaped by the social historical contexts within which people find themselves. And more importantly, we have various identities that we draw upon, but not always consistently. Given that identity is contextual, a person might identify one way in one context and in a contradictory way in another context. For instance, a woman might identify as heterosexual in the context of her marriage and children and lesbian when she meets an attractive woman whom she desires. Instead of seeing these identities as contradictory and therefore impossible, social constructionists argue that identity is often contextual and inconsistent. This means that people can hold many different identities, some seemingly contradictory, and it is not a matter of which identity is correct; instead, they are all equally valid, but different. Social constructionist theories underline how heterosexuality is seldom questioned or challenged since opposite-sex attraction is presumed to be natural while other forms are seen as aberrant.

Beyond the Binary

So far we have focused on how the nature versus nurture debate has understood gay and lesbian members of the LGBT2TQ community. However, as gay and lesbian people have become integrated into mainstream Canadian life, issues affecting transgender people have come to the foreground. Transgender is a term used to denote individuals whose sense of core gender identity does not cohere with the gender to which they have been assigned. **Transgender** refers to a range of identities, including:

- those who present themselves as being of a gender even while feeling a part of another;
- those who present themselves as the opposite gender to which they were born and to which they feel they actually belong;
- **pre-operative transsexuals**, who have undertaken hormonal treatment to cohere to traits of the opposite gender; and
- **post-operative transsexuals**, who have undertaken various surgeries to align their gender identity with bodily appearance.

Trans* individuals can be either M->F transwomen or F->M transmen. In both cases, individuals undergo procedures, including hormonal treatments, phalloplasty, breast implantation and/or mastectomies to bring their sex characteristics into alignment with their gender identity. Trans* people face challenges on many fronts, from the everyday decision about which washroom to use, to being accepted within straight as well as gay and lesbian communities. Trans* people also challenge both our assumptions about the congruence of sex and gender and our notions about sexual orientation. For example, when individuals transition to their new sex/gender assignment, their orientation may remain the same. This means, for example, that a man who transitions to a woman may become a lesbian when he was previously heterosexual, or that as a woman, she might desire men, even if he was not gay before the transition. Similar outcomes are evident in female to male transitions, where a transman may find himself attracted to women or, alternatively, still be attracted to men.

Intersex people — formerly referred to as hermaphrodites — have also come to the forefront as they talk about how their experience of sex and gender is not perfectly aligned. Intersex people are those who present atypical sexual characteristics that do not match either those of males or females. Variations among intersex people make the identity complicated because the parameters are largely based on norms about gender and sex. Moreover, intersex individuals whose chromosomal makeup suggest they are biologically female may appear to be male or vice versa. About one in every 2000 people is intersex. In the past, when a child was born intersex, doctors and parents decided which gender the child would be and then performed sex reassignment surgery to assign a physical gender to the baby.

Intersex people remind us just how much of sex is about what humans decide. After all, at what point does a smaller penis start to be understood as a clitoris or what hormonal levels are required to be taken to be male or female? Some argue that gender assignment is necessary to allow the child to grow up "normally" as a boy or girl. As the Intersex Society of North America (ISNA) notes on its website, "Nature doesn't decide where the category of 'male' ends and the category of 'intersex' begins, or where the category of 'intersex' ends and the category of 'female' begins." If anything, intersex folks highlight precisely how normalizing our binary conceptions of sex and gender really are. Cultural norms often dictate when a boy's penis is so small that it has to become a clitoris. Humans decide whether a person with XXY chromosomes or androgen insensitivity counts as intersex.

Further complicating the sexual binary is that there is evidence that some men and women experience same-sex attractions and even sexual interactions without giving up a heterosexual or straight identity. The emergence of a "mostly straight" identity among heterosexual men provides an intriguing example of this phenomenon. Researchers have found that some men experience sexual and at times romantic attraction to other men but do not see their heterosexual identities compromised, nor do they identify as actively bisexual.[4] Similarly, some women report more flexibility in their sexual practices and desires while they too identify as heterosexual.[5] The Internet has also given opportunities for individuals to safely explore different sexual desires, especially with the easy availability of pornography and online social networks such as Reddit that allow for more fluidity in sexual identities.[6]

Those individuals who don't fit into a homo/heterosexual binary also underscore the problematic aspects of the nature versus nurture debate. Certainly, the debate is important insofar as it frames how we understand sexuality in popular culture. However, a binary approach is simply too simplistic. Sexuality is complicated and diverse and cannot be reduced to either nature or nurture. Indeed, the very existence of bisexual, intersex and trans* people complicate both biological determinism and social constructionism. How can someone who is not unequivocally male or female be considered homosexual or heterosexual when they do not fit into the two-sex binary of sexuality? For example, an intersex person may find men attractive; given that they are neither male nor female, how can their desire be labelled as either same-sex or other-sex desire? Likewise, transwomen may become lesbian or heterosexual, just as transmen may identify as gay or lesbian or heterosexual. Labelling one as homosexual or heterosexual is simply not that easy and is not based solely in biology. Moreover, some people feel from a very early age that they do not belong in the body in which they were born; that is, they do not identify with the sex of their body. Add in those who identify as bisexual—attracted mutually to both men and women—and those who identify as pan-sexual, and the social constructionism becomes much more complicated.

LOOKING AT SEXUALITY HISTORICALLY

Since its emergence as a category in the 1700s, sexuality has been studied and understood in a variety of ways over time. Focusing on whether sexuality is an *act*, that is, something one does with the body, or an *identity*, how we identify ourselves, has constituted one major debate in sexuality studies. Prior to the Western Enlightenment, for instance, Europeans tended to view homosexuality as a set of sex "acts," which in Christianity constituted a form of grievous sin. That is, sexuality was thought to be a range of sexual acts, some of which constituted actions against God and, possibly, nature. But according to historian Michel Foucault's *History of Sexuality,* which traces the different ways the West has conceptualized sexuality from ancient Greece to the twentieth century, the 1800s saw a major shift in how Europeans conceptualized sex practices. As empirical science began to enquire into the mysteries of sex, same-sex encounters were no longer sinful acts that anyone might do. Rather, they became the hallmarks of a particular type of person, one who had a past, a childhood and maybe even a person whose activities had been treated as a medical case history. In other words, sexuality became linked to a specific identity. As Foucault famously stated about this shift, "The sodomite had been a temporary aberration; the homosexual was now a species."[7]

In part this thinking resulted from applying the European Enlightenment's scientific gaze to the topic of sexuality, producing a field known as **sexology**. Of course, there had been investigations into sexuality before sexology. Augustine of Hippo (354–430 CE) and Thomas Aquinas (1225–1274 CE) had elaborate theories about desire and sex. In South Asia, we could point to a text such as *Kamasutra* (400–200 BCE), which posited extensive theories about sex. However, as European science itself became more organized, sexology became a specific field of sustained scientific examination of human sexuality. Those that made up the field of sexology — known as sexologists –included, among others, Richard von Krafft-Ebing and Havelock Ellis.

One of the main themes in sexologists' investigation of sex was heredity and degeneracy. The Viennese psychiatrist, Richard von Krafft-Ebing (1840–1902), asserted that homosexuality was a form of degeneracy. According to his most famous book, *Psychopathia Sexualis*, civilization is based on love and monogamy; any deviation from this mode of sexuality is representative of a degenerate stage of evolution, a perspective derived from the popular theory of evolution, often attributed to Charles Darwin. With Darwin's emphasis on sexual selection, authors such as Krafft-Ebing increasingly used science to understand certain sexualities as non-reproductive and, therefore, deviant.

Another common theme in sexology is the process of **normalization**, whereby certain aspects of social life — in this case, sexuality — become seen as "normal," not in a statistical sense, but rather as "common sense" arrangements found in everyday life. Many sexologists consequently focused on sexual variations, rather than sexual regularities. In other words, they were more interested in the differences between types of sexuality, rather than the commonalities. This perspective positioned homosexuality, lesbianism and other forms of sexual desire as aberrant and sources of potential illnesses subject to medical intervention. As sexology studies became better known, heterosexuality quickly became normalized, while other kinds of sexuality were seen as forms of illness or sources of criminality. Indeed, normalization positions sexual variation as aberrations that should be studied and understood, even as heterosexuality itself remains unexplained.

The nineteenth-century scientific study of sexuality also closely linked sexuality and gender, especially through the concept of **sexual inversion**, or when a person has the psyche of one gender, say a woman, in the body of another, say a man. Krafft-Ebing understood same-sex desire as a particular type of sexual inversion. Through his examination of skull shapes, postures, gestures and mannerisms, he argued that same-sex desire was based on biological factors.[8] For this reason, Krafft-Ebing advocated the examination of same-sex attraction through a medical perspective. Consequently, while same-sex attraction was thought to be similar to a disease, it was no longer viewed as a sin. British physician Havelock Ellis (1859–1939) shared Krafft-Ebing's belief in the biological nature of sexuality, but Ellis argued that homosexuals constituted a category of sexual inverts where hormonal irregularities played a factor in determining sexuality. However, Ellis also thought that sexual inversion could be affected by non-biological factors. Alas, these forces were not strong enough to overcome sexual inversion; for Ellis, the condition was incurable and, although not a disease, he still asserted that homosexuality was an abnormal behaviour, albeit not one that needed to be criminalized as was the case in the British Empire, including Canada.

The sexologists' work demonstrates that gender and sexuality were not originally conceptualized to be separate categories. Instead, they posited the two as necessarily intertwined. Crucially, since no consensus existed on whether sexuality/gender was a biological matter or not, the sexologists frequently addressed the nature/nurture question, with writers often allying themselves on the side of nature. By philosophically arguing that sexuality is based largely on biology, these thinkers could argue against punishing homosexuality. After all, if sexuality is biological, then one has no choice how it is manifest — an argument that re-emerges a century later.

Still, sexologists struggled with the idea of feminine women who had sex with women; they simply did not fit into their typology. To a far lesser extent, they grappled with masculine men who had sex with men. Sexual inversion could not explain those who did not conform to their models, so increasingly they separated gender and sexuality into distinct categories, thus creating our contemporary categories of heterosexuality and homosexuality.

The various contributions of the sexologists were not strictly academic in nature. Rather, they informed medical professionals in Europe and the United States. As doctors completed their training and put into practice the ideas espoused by the sexologists, they spread these ideas throughout the West. Doctors in Canada, for example, often received their medical education overseas and in the United States. These foreign-trained doctors then brought these concepts to nineteenth-century Canada, where they were eventually articulated to the legal system. As Canadian historian Stephen Maynard reports, Canadian judges often sent men charged with homosexual offences for psychiatric evaluations, which could determine whether a man stood trial or not.

Through these medical-judicial processes, sexuality became increasingly linked to a specific identity and to a disease and criminality. Sexuality was not what one did, but who one was. By normalizing sexuality as typical (heterosexuality) or deviant (sexual inversion/homosexuality), early sexologists created identities that were open to judgement and governance. In Canada, the resultant case histories and psychiatric discourses "laid some of the ground work for medical-legal regulation during and after the Second World War, most notably in the creation of sexual psychopath laws and their particularly devastating effects on gay men."[9]

Alfred Kinsey and Consequences of "The Kinsey Report"

Heterosexuality's normalization in North America continued unchallenged for many decades for two main reasons. First, the church was invested in the regulation of sexuality, especially in rural Canada, which constituted the majority of the nation. In this environment, challenging the normative construction of heterosexuality was strongly discouraged. Second, Canadian purity movements fervently sought to abolish forms of sexuality that were constructed as "deviant."[10] Organizations such as the Salvation Army, the Moral and Social Reform Council of Canada and the Canadian Purity Education Association actively deterred non-reproductive forms of sexuality.

However, American sexologist Alfred Kinsey (1894–1956) challenged the heterosexual status quo when he adopted an empirically based method and interviewed 4275 white males, finding that 37 percent of them had experienced at least one homosexual encounter in their lives.[11] Drawing on these findings and other data, Kinsey outlined a seven-point continuum of sexual desires from zero — exclusively heterosexual — to seven — exclusively homosexual (see Table 8.1).

Table 8.1 Kinsey Sexuality Spectrum

Rating	Description
0	Exclusively heterosexual
1	Predominantly heterosexual, only incidentally homosexual
2	Predominantly heterosexual, but more than incidentally homosexual
3	Equally heterosexual and homosexual (bisexual)
4	Predominantly homosexual, but more than incidentally heterosexual
5	Predominantly homosexual, only incidentally heterosexual
6	Exclusively homosexual

Source: A. Kinsey, W. Pomeroy and C. Martin, *Sexual Behaviour in the Human Male* (The Kinsey Institute, W.B. Saunders, 1948).

While his methodology and findings were significant to sexology, Kinsey's work also challenged the prevalent idea from earlier sexologists that sexuality was an identity. Rather, by focusing on sex as an act, he demonstrated that over a third of men had same-sex intercourse, making it difficult to maintain the contention that heterosexuality is normal and homosexuality is abnormal. Quite the opposite, Kinsey's findings indicated that homosexual experience was far more common than many had thought. Indeed, when he repeated his study with women, he found similar find-ings.[12] His dismissal of biology as determining sexual orientation also problematized the conceptions of the nineteenth-century sexologists. By challenging their biological determinism, he called for sexuality research to move out of the medical domain and into the psychological realm.

This shift in understanding sexuality had a number of unintentional effects. The revelation that homosexual acts were more widespread than thought coincided with the discovery that several homosexuals in Britain were Soviet spies. These findings, along with other underlying fears around national security and the postwar return to "normal," laid the ground for what sociologists call a **moral panic** — an intense feeling of anxiety promoted through mass media that a particular group threatens the social order. In postwar United States, one moral panic focused on the "Red Scare." Against the backdrop of the 1950s Cold War and fears of nuclear war with the USSR, Senator Joseph McCarthy stated that he knew of several — sometimes as many as 205 — names of Communists who had infiltrated the government of the United States. Consequently, he ordered several investigations to examine how such "Reds'" had come to positions of power. Many individuals were investigated and many were banned from jobs for their "Un-American" activities. Another less-well-known side to this moral panic was the "**Lavender Scare**," a term coined by historian David Johnson. This phenomenon saw accusations that paralleled McCarthy's comments aimed at homosexual men and women.[13] One politician claimed that there were 3,750 "homosexuals" in government positions. The worry stemmed from the fear that were a foreign government to determine a person was homosexual, the stigma could be used to blackmail the individual into giving up sensitive state secrets. The Lavender Scare affected thousands of Americans' lives.

Canada was not immune to the Lavender Scare; indeed, some scholars state that thousands of homosexual Canadian public servants were affected by this moral panic.[14] As noted, pre-Lavender Scare, same-sex sexuality was largely deemed a legal-medical problem. In fact, pre-existing Canadian legislation and judicial practices had created a legal framework to persecute homosexuals in Canada, even though post-Confedera-tion laws did not explicitly criminalize homosexuality. Instead, federal laws governed "gross indecency"; through the guise of controlling something as ambiguous as gross indecency, male/male sexual relations were criminalized.[15] This indirect regulatory approach, borrowed directly from British colonial legislation, led to little persecution until, according to public records from the time, the United States insisted that the Canadian government ferret out and discriminate against homosexuals.[16]

Working on the pretext of national security, the Royal Canadian Mounted Police security service took the project of monitoring sexuality seriously. In its most egregious

DIVERSITYINACTIONDIVERSITYI

Box 8.1 Diversity in Action

Canadian Prime Minister Apologizes

On November 27, 2017, Canadian Prime Minister Justin Trudeau rose in the House of Commons to issue an apology on behalf of the Canadian government to the LGBT2TQ community for the purge associated with the Lavender Scare. Trudeau also noted that imposing settler ideas about sexuality "saw the near-destruction of Indigenous LGBT2TQ and two-spirit identities. People who were once revered for their identities found themselves shamed for who they were. They were rejected and left vulnerable to violence." The government also introduced the *Expungement of Historically Unjust Convictions Act,* which proposed to permanently destroy the criminal records of those convicted of consensual sexual activity with same-sex partners. A class action suit related to the 1950s purge was also settled. For the full remarks and a video of the apology go to: <https://pm.gc.ca/eng/news/2017/11/28/remarks-prime-minister-justin-trudeau-apologize-lgbtq2-canadians>.

form, the RCMP deployed an instrument called the **Fruit Machine**, invented by Carleton University psychology professor Frank Robert Wake. The fruit machine exposed its subjects to pornographic photos, many of which were designed to elicit same-sex arousal. If a man were stimulated by the machine, he was adjudged to be gay (or a "fruit," derogatory term of the time). Most disturbingly, the subjects were not forced to take the test, but were asked to do so under the guise of a falsehood; they thought they were taking a stress test.

Even after the Lavender Scare, other homophobic government policies remained in place, especially in the Canadian armed forces, where openly gay and lesbian people could not legally serve until 1992. Immigration laws were also homophonic until 1977, when the *Immigration Act* was amended to remove the prohibition of foreign homosexuals from entering Canada. In the same year, the Quebec National Assembly became the first legislature to recognize equal rights for lesbians and gays in Quebec's provincial Human Rights Code. As a result of pressure from LGBT2TQ activist groups, the federal government recognized the damage it did to LGBT2TQ people during the Lavender Scare and by the homophobic practices of the Canadian government. Prime Minister Justin Trudeau formally rose in the House of Commons and issued a formal apology to those LGBT2TQ people whose lives were irrevocably altered.

Early Liberation Movements: From Assimilation to Visibility

Our narrative so far has focused on how settler sexuality has been socially constructed in post-Confederation Canada. Initially, Canada remained primarily a rural agricultural society where sexuality was policed through the church and through the various purity movements that mobilized in the late 1800s and early 1900s. In the early 1900s the medicalization of sexuality resulted in an increased reliance on doctors' psychiatric evaluations as a way to regulate homosexuals' lives. This practice established the ground for the psychosexual laws that later allowed for many Canadian men to be persecuted and imprisoned. Calgary city bus driver Everett Klippert is a case in point. After being charged with violation of the *Criminal Code*, Klippert was forced to undergo several psychiatric assessments. These evaluations determined that he would not stop his practice of aberrant sexual behaviour. As a result of the medical determination, the Canadian legal system declared Klippert to be a "dangerous offender" and sentenced him to life in prison, an outcome the Supreme Court of Canada upheld upon appeal. Partially because of the outcry against the Klippert sentence, in 1969, the *Criminal Code* was amended through Bill C-150 (also known as the Omnibus Bill), repealing the law criminalizing "buggery" in private. Despite this change, Everett Klippert was only eventually released from prison in 1971.

The postwar period saw another shift. With increasing urbanization and the growing awareness of the Kinsey Report and its ramifications, Canadians became more aware of homosexuality and homosexuals. As the moral panic about homosexuality and its putative dangers to home and country took shape, the state also began to take a more immediate and personal interest in the sexual activities of its citizens in Canada. In the US, resistance to these intrusions gave rise to the Mattachine Society and its female counterpart, the Daughters of Bilitis, the most prominent organizations in the **homophile movement.** Countering the position of gays and lesbians as dangers

---

Box 8.2 Innov8

Legislating Love: The Everett Klippert Story

In March 2018, *Legislating Love: The Everett Klippert Story* had its world premiere at Sage Theatre in Calgary, Alberta. Natalie Meisner wrote the play to explore the legacy of Everett Klippert, the last man charged and jailed for being a homosexual. The play features Maxine, a lesbian university professor precariously employed, and Tonya, a Métis woman who is also a standup comic. Meisner explores Klippert's life in Calgary while also exploring how queer lives have changed fifty years after Klippert's release from prison.

to society, these organizations drew parallels between homosexuals and heterosexuals, arguing that homosexuals really wanted the same things as heterosexuals: family and loving relationships. As for sex, they asserted that sexual practices were a private matter and the state had no place, as Pierre Trudeau would later famously say, "in the bedrooms of the nation." The homophile movement focused on **homonormativity**, the argument that homosexuals just want to "fit in" to the existing heterosexual society. Even when homophile arguments about privacy expanded to include demands for freedom from police attempts to survey and entrap gay men having sex in public settings or in communal spaces such as bars and bathhouses, the core message of the homophile movement remained the same.[17] If only heterosexuals better understood that all sex was a private matter, gays and lesbians would be free to assimilate into (North) American society.

Similar assimilationist arguments dominated Canadian thinking until the mid-1970s.[18] An early Canadian gay activist group called the Association for Social Knowledge (ASK), founded in Vancouver in 1964, aspired "to help society understand and accept variations from the sexual norm."[19] The group offered public lectures to the Vancouver community to that end. In Toronto, too, gay activist groups "strongly believed in the ability of scholarly research to provide accurate, and more positive, information about homosexuals," which showed how homosexuals were the same as heterosexuals.[20] These organizations often opposed the existence of gay bars and bathhouses and were not enthusiastic supporters of public sex. According to gay activist Charles Hill, "public sexual activity was symbolic of the shame and self-loathing experienced by homosexuals because of the attitude of mainstream society."[21] Hill argued that those who engaged in washroom sex were forced to do so because of "society's anti-homosexual prejudices," which made it necessary for people to "compulsively hide their homosexuality."[22] Public sex and communal bathhouses robbed conforming gay men of their respectability, an important concept that underpins homonormative discourses today.

Creating Communities: "Come Out and Be Proud"

Several Canadian metropolitan areas today feature visible queer urban spaces such as Rue St. Cathérine in Montreal, Davie Street in Vancouver and the Church-Wellesley area in Toronto. All are marked (and marketed) with rainbow banners and other symbols of sexual identity to claim the street as a "gay village." While official statistics about individuals who identify as members of the LGBT2TQ community are not kept, the 2016 Canadian census did show that 50 percent of same-sex couples lived in Canada's five major metropolitan areas.[23] However, not all queers necessarily live in these big cities. The census data suggest that although a smaller percentage of queers now live in rural Canada than in 2011, more LGBT2TQ people are living in suburbs and in smaller metropolitan areas, such as Halifax and Quebec City.

The need for gay villages (or "ghettos") and the need for visibility has long been debated within queer communities. Much has been written about eighteenth-century molly houses in London where homosexual men commingled socially and sexually. Gay historian John D'Emilio relates the emergence of urban gay spaces in the early twentieth century to growing industrialization and urbanization, which saw the breakdown of extended family structures. The Second World War played a crucial role in gay spaces since the war brought many gays and lesbians from across the country together for the first time. In the postwar period, many demobilized military personnel decided to live in larger urban centres where they could continue to live discreetly among other like-minded individuals. Although gay spaces existed, they were often hidden from public view.

By the 1970s, a shift in conceptualizing sexual identities in North America was underway. Heralded by the galvanizing resistance of drag queens, trans* people and gay men to a police invasion at New York City's Stonewall Inn on June 28, 1969, the new focus of 1970s sexual identity politics was to become visible. Pride marches were an important feature of expressing visible sexual identity. Formed in the wake of Stonewall riots, Pride marches were both political acts of defiance and celebrations of different sexual identities. The first Canadian Pride march was organized in Toronto for June 1971, and it was followed by events in Montreal and Vancouver. These marches created a visible way for lesbians and gays to reject the stigmas that heterosexuals had placed on them and to celebrate pride in their identities.

Stonewall marks an important if contentious moment in queer settler-colonial history: it operates as a coalescing moment that inspired the **gay liberation** movement, which also drew on experiences from the American civil rights movement and precepts from the 1960s counterculture, as well as important insights from the women's movement. Gay liberation sought to resist **compulsory heterosexuality**, or the institutionalized belief that everyone must be heterosexual, and asserted the importance of sexual desire in social relations. The *Gay Liberation Manifesto* declares that gay bathhouses, bars and gay casual sex in public spaces constitute a fundamental challenge to heterosexuality's insistent divisions between public and private space.[24] More importantly, these practices provide queers with a model of sociality that opposes heterosexuality's claim that the only way to organize social, affective and sexual relationships is based on monogamous, gendered dyadic relationships cemented in state-sanctioned marriage.

For most of their settler-colonial histories, Canadian cities have been largely organized as heteronormative spaces. But, there is a history of queer spaces within those

Box 8.3 Diversity in Action

In 2007 in Montreal, a woman sued a bar that refused to serve her on the grounds that she was a woman in a gay bar. The bar was ruled out of order, and now, gay and lesbian spaces cannot discriminate on the basis of gender. The ruling, along with many women considering gay spaces as safe spaces, free of the pressures of straight bars, has resulted in an influx of women into gay bars. This has led to some backlash from gay men, who see their spaces being assimilated (some might say colonized) by heterosexual women.

Source: Jaime Woo, "Drag Shows Aren't Free-for-Alls for Straight Women Letting Loose," April 26, 2017 <theglobeandmail.com/arts/theatre-and-performance/drag-shows-arent-free-for-alls-for-straight-women-letting-loose/article34821238/>.

heteronormative places. The first recorded gay establishment in North America was Montrealer Moise Tellier's "apples and cake shop" on Craig Street (now St-Antoine) in Old Montreal in 1869, where men met and had sex.[25] With more gay men and lesbians moving to urban centres, by 1966 Toronto had become known as the "homosexual capital" of Canada.[26] Post-Stonewall, queer-identified spaces in Canada often became the site of conflict between older assimilationists, who disliked gay ghettos, and gay liberationists, who fully endorsed them. These tensions became evident in Toronto during a moral panic which followed the murder of 12-year-old shoeshine boy Emmanuel Jacques. In the wake of the homophobic media responses, those advocating for assimilation and respectability were even more reluctant to associate themselves with the disreputable bars and bathhouses that existed in and around Yonge Street. According to some historians, the Jacques murder led to even more policing of the gay community and eventually to the 1981 Toronto bathhouse raids, which saw 286 people arrested, the largest mass arrest in Canada since the *War Measures Act* was invoked during the FLQ crisis in 1970.[27]

Like Stonewall a decade or so earlier, the bathhouse raids galvanized and politicized the Toronto community at a time when gay communities gained further importance with the AIDS crisis. Gay and lesbian community centres provided spaces where the lesbian, gay and bisexual communities could organize political action and social support networks for those suffering from the disease. As the AIDS epidemic captured national attention, fear was rampant and a particular caricature of AIDS emerged. It was a "homosexual disease," known as gay-related immune deficiency (or GRID). Later, medical officials changed the name to acquired immune deficiency syndrome (or AIDS) to more accurately capture the nature of the disease; after all, it was not unique to the gay population. However, even with a change in name, it was still understood as a "gay disease." For example, despite some changes to the policy, it is still illegal for gay men to donate blood in Canada, because of a fear of the transmission of AIDS.

Coming Out for All? Films such as Love, Simon *dramatize coming out to peers and parents. How important is it for LGBT2TQ people to come out? Should heterosexuals have to come out too? What are the advantages and disadvantages of everyone having to come out?*

Parliament's passage of Bill C-150 marked an early acceptance of the homophile argument that sexual acts were primarily private and the state had no role in regulating them through the Criminal Code. This legislative achievement, among the first in the world, meant Canadian queers were now freer to express themselves — but only to a point. Decriminalization did not bring an end to the myriad forms of discrimination to which many gays, lesbians and other sexual minorities were legally subject. Nor did it end state policing of sexuality. Indeed, the police used the new public/private divide and continued to lay charges of gross indecency against gay men and to use common bawdy house laws against gay establishments.[28] In Toronto, the police raided and attempted to close gay bathhouses such as The Barracks, an establishment associated with the BDSM community. Indeed, it was precisely the ongoing harassment and interference by police in gay establishments that fueled the riots following the Toronto Police's raid on gay bathhouses in February 1981. Ironically, these police actions had the effect of shifting many in the gay community away from the assimilationist arguments of the early 1970s to more liberationist ones that claimed gay sex practices posed a challenge the norms of compulsory heterosexuality.

THEORIZING SEXUALITIES

The AIDS epidemic presented another moment where thinking about sexuality needed to urgently change. In (North) America, AIDS gave new impetus to discrimination against gay and bisexual men, who were fired and barred from employment, as the film *Philadelphia* portrayed. More urgently, even as people were dying in increasing numbers, governments (and other social institutions) stayed silent and even actively promoted the eradication of homosexual men. Indigenous communities were often ignored in the early debates about the crisis. In the face of the health crisis, the state again asserted greater control over those in the settler homosexual community. Some politicians spoke of quarantining all gay men, while AIDS-phobic violence became

Box 8.4 Diversity in Action

Toronto Bathhouse Raids

In February 1981, the Toronto Police raided five bathhouses in and about the gay village. Seen by some historians as the culmination of the campaign to "clean up" Yonge Street, the Toronto Police staged raids which saw hundreds of men charged with being or operating a common bawdy house. In the wake of the raids, the LGBT community took to the streets in what the media called "rioting," smashing police cars. The bathhouse raids galvanized the LGBT community similar to the ways that Stonewall had a decade earlier galvanized and radicalized the New York gay community. In 2016, the Toronto chief of police formally apologized for the bathhouse raids.

common. As a response to the AIDS crisis, activists and academics undertook theorizing the operation of homophobia and the structures that maintained sexual minorities in subordinate, often lethal, positions.

Feminist Interventions

Fortunately (if we can use that word), some prominent feminist writers had taken the perspective that sexuality must be thought in terms of its intimate relationship to power. We highlight feminist Gayle Rubin's intervention, which addresses the problem of erotic injustice and sexual oppression. Through a close examination of our cultural milieu, she argues that a "charmed circle" of sexual stratification has been created that understands male-female sexual relations within a monogamous marriage as the pinnacle of a sexuality hierarchy (see Figure 8.1). Rubin places these relations in the centre of the circle while on the outer limit of the circle are "bad" or "unnatural" sexualities. The main difference between the inside and outside of the circle is the degree to which a sexuality is reproductive and respectable. For her, earlier feminisms often viewed sexuality as negative for women living in patriarchal societies and consequently, tend to champion a conservative version of sexuality. In response, Rubin calls for an analytic separation of sexuality and gender, arguing that people who are oppressed by sexuality are not dominated in the same ways that those who are subjugated by gender.

Rubin's "charmed circle" of sexuality helps us understand the concept of **heteronormativity**. Gay/queer theorist Michael Warner states that heteronormativity is "the normalising process which supports heterosexuality as the elemental form of human association, as the norm, as the means of reproduction without which society would not exist."[29] This definition usefully recalls the importance of normalization, discussed earlier. Moreover, Warner emphasizes that heterosexuality constitutes the primary

Figure 8.1 The Charmed Circle

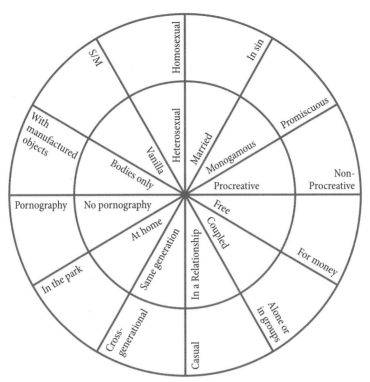

Source: Gayle Rubin (1984) *Thinking Sex: Notes for a Radical Theory of the Politics of Sexuality*

form of human relationships — human society is based on the union of a man and a woman. According to this narrative, without heterosexuality, humans could not procreate and human society would end.

Warner's move to a focus on control is captured by Jacqui Alexander, who uses Lynda Hart's concept of **heteropatriarchy** to capture how the processes of heteronormativity and patriarchy combine to explain "a moment of crisis when state-sponsored violence moved to foreclose desire between women."[30] In other words, the parallel operations of heteronormativity and patriarchy control not only sexuality but also many aspects of social life. Specifically, the state created itself as the only entity that protects women from patriarchal violence. In doing so, the state also controlled how women were treated; it became a paternalistic institution that women could only turn to for justice. Yet, at the same time, the state used patriarchal values such as the nuclear family and heterosexual union to justify a rule that positioned the ideal citizen as heterosexual and male. Through heteropatriarchy, non-citizens were constructed as women and those with marginalized sexualities.

Troubling the Sex/Gender Divide: Queer Theory

Alongside these feminist investigations, there emerged a new but not always clearly defined field in the 1970s, lesbian and gay studies, which focused on revealing the often-hidden lives of lesbians and gay men. Paralleling earlier feminist arguments based on the identity categories of "women" and "men," scholars in lesbian and gay studies based their analyses on identities such as "lesbian" and "gay man." Still, as the AIDS epidemic continued and dissatisfaction with the limitations of fixed identities of feminism and lesbian/gay studies grew, another different field of theory emerged to examine sexuality. Coined "queer theory" in 1990 by Teresa de Lauretis, this approach largely defined itself against feminism and previous lesbian and gay studies with its emphasis on fluid identities. For queer theorists, desire and identities are unstable and socially constructed.

Often deeply influenced by the work of Michel Foucault, queer theorists tend to focus less on the identities of sexual persons *per se*, and more on how these identities are constituted through various sexual acts. Thus, the focus is on how desire is created. Desire does not function along a binary that is implicit in many conceptions of sexuality. In other words, desire is not just about heterosexuality/homosexuality; desire is the subject of our wants. Capturing that there are many ways of being sexual, this idea of desire allows queer theorists to examine a plethora of different forms of sexuality without the risk of assessing any of them as "right" or "wrong." Thus, they can value difference in such a way as to avoid evaluating such difference. As a consequence, queer theorists see sexuality as in flux, diverse and complicated. Certainly, they took the feminist concerns with power to heart but challenged the idea of identity as something that is static and single.

Box 8.5 Diversity in Action

Jim Egan, Social Activist

Jim Egan is a prominent activist in Canadian LGBT history. Egan was the first publisher of *Gay!*, the first gay publication in Toronto and in Canada, predating Vancouver's ASK newsletter by a few months. However, Jim Egan was best known for his court case against the Canadian government's refusal to grant CPP spousal benefits to his long-time partner, Jack Norris. The case, which started in 1991, reached the Supreme Court of Canada in 1995. The Court upheld the government's denial of spousal benefits to Egan and Norris but at the same time "read into" the Charter of Rights and Freedoms freedom from discrimination on the basis of sexual orientation. Egan and his partner were subjects of a documentary, *Jim loves Jack*. Egan died in 2002.

SEXUALITIES IN TWENTY-FIRST-CENTURY CANADA

In many ways the legalization of same-sex marriage and the granting of other legal rights have led some to view the identitarian (i.e., identity-based) approaches of the late twentieth-century as *passé*, the residual of the now-won battles over social differences, especially now that Canadians seem to inhabit a post-feminist, post-capitalist, post-racial society where *all that* just doesn't matter. Although these individuals elsewhere in the world remain at risk, these risks seem less in Canada where members of the LGBT2TQ community enjoy the benefits of the extension of civil and human rights. In this new context, gay villages and businesses seem less important even as the proliferation of online sexual communities of interest and online dating apps such as Grindr have challenged the traditional role of bars and bathhouses as safe meeting places. In short, being gay or lesbian is now just part of the new normal where sexual diversity is tolerated if not entirely accepted.

Objecting to Normal

But not all were happy with the new normal. Lisa Duggan's essay "The New Homonormativity," argues that the 1990s equality debates created a "new homonormativity." Duggan notes that civil rights discourses, echoing the 1950s homophile argument, emphasized how LGBT people simply want the same choice heterosexuals had about access monogamous marriage, children, privacy and as Bruce Bawer's book suggests, *A Place at the Table*. Equality advocates such as Bawer disavowed sexual promiscuity and dissidence, those aspects of queer culture that seemed disruptive and disreputable. In this iteration, the "new homonormativity" also expressed the sexual politics of neoliberalism, which Duggan argued, is not just an economic theory, but a form of Foucauldian governmentality that "produces and validates subjects with marketized understandings of the relations between public and private."[31] Drawing on neoliberal notions of individual choice and personal responsibility, the new homonormativity argued that LGBT2TQ people had the right to individual autonomy, equality and supposed free choice.

Duggan's critique also underlined how same-sex marriage, adoption rights, pension and medical benefits were rights available primarily to middle-class gays and lesbians who were often white. The new homonormativity posited an inclusive but non-political approach to sexual difference, one we see in the proliferating of positive images of gays and lesbians in mainstream media. The gay couple in *Modern Family*, Ellen DeGeneres' talk show, and even the steamier representations found on *How to Get Away with Murder* ultimately endorse homonormative values of monogamy, family and privacy, which are mirrored by an inclusive heteronormativity. Framing the case through Gayle Rubin's model, we observe that insofar as LGBT2TQ people renounce allegiances to the outer limits of polyamorous relationships and intergenerational sex, they have access to a charmed circle.

As gay activist/theorist Jeffery Weeks states, it's crucial to "never underestimate the importance of being ordinary."[32] Still, we must also remember that even with the extension of same-sex marriage and legal injunctions against homophobia, the Canadian social landscape remains an uneven experience for LGBT2TQ people. The Black Lives Matter protest underscored the hard work that queer communities must still do to reduce social inequities. As cultural geographer Julie Podmore observes, the new normal means that queers, especially those with privilege, must still question how "neo liberal capitalism, patriarchy, colonialism and racism work to empower some queer subjects and further marginalize others."[33]

Sexualities and the Colonial Nation

Podmore's work points to a needed development in sexuality studies, one to which the Black Lives Matter protesters indirectly drew attention: the need to recognize "Indiqueer" peoples, a term that highlights the settler bias in how Canadian sexualities have been mainly conceptualized. Before we consider the specifics of the Canadian context, we must understand how colonialism has shaped sexualities in the world generally. Although colonialism is officially over in many countries, the range of permissible sexualities is controlled through legal and judicial systems, many of which still maintain laws created in the colonial period. For example, anti-sodomy legislation continues to exist in the penal codes of formerly colonized countries. In many Commonwealth countries, sodomy was criminalized under British rule. For example, the Indian Penal Code of 1860 included section 377, which dealt with sodomy. Only in 2009 did India dismiss legislation against sodomy but this dismissal was repealed in 2014, criminalizing sodomy again. Ironically, the legislation against same-sex sexuality is a byproduct of colonialism. Even as European nations have removed strictures against homosexual sex, many non-European nations have maintained the same prohibitions inherited from the colonizers.

Colonialism's legacy is also evident in how leaders of formerly colonized nations legitimate their leadership through espousing a particular conception of sexuality. As Jacqui Alexander famously argued, in an international context of economic competition and political instability, national leaders vie for authority.[34] However, the form of authority that has become synonymous with legitimate leadership is one that privileges "moral rectitude." Only leaders who embody this moral rectitude, one that privileges heteronormative sexuality, are seen as fit to lead the nation.

Even though the origins of this legitimate nation-state (i.e., colonialism) are largely gone, the role of morality has been incorporated into global capitalism. Instead of valuing a particular type of morality *per se*, nations in the global context must compete with others. Consequently, only those citizens who aid in the productivity of the nation are valued. Since those who do not procreate are not considered productive, they are not considered important. As a result, those who are deemed "sexual deviants" (i.e., those who do not engage in reproductive intercourse, such as prostitutes, unwed mothers, gays and lesbians) are blamed for many of the social ills.

In Canada, the form of colonialism that still continues is settler colonialism, a formation that promotes types of sexuality that are evident in other colonial contexts, and what we termed earlier, settler sexuality. When the French and English, as well as the Dutch and Spanish, settlers arrived in the Americas, they brought with them a particular conception of sexuality that Indigenous Peoples and settlers had to follow. Failure to abide by this model meant Indigenous Peoples could not benefit from the institutions of modernity that settlers purportedly brought with them: government, rights and freedoms, law and technologies.

Settler sexuality is evident in the Indian Act, passed by Parliament in 1876. While the Indian Act claimed to consolidate earlier policies that governed all aspects of Indigenous Peoples' lives in Canada, the Act has specific effects on sexuality. First, a settler-derived sexual division of labour was imposed onto Indigenous Peoples: men were expected to engage in farming and women were taught domestic proficiency. This imposition of gendered norms served to make the colonialists' way of understanding gender seem to be common sense. Moreover, deviations from those gendered norms were defined under the guise of law such that an Indigenous "cross-gendered individual was seemingly confronting legislative regulation if not vigilant policing."[35] Second, the Act set out the control of Indigenous Peoples' sexualities with a goal of assimilation: women lost their status as "Indians" — as did their children — if they married a non-Indian; this did not apply to Indigenous men. This mechanism effectively institutionalized both "patrilineal descent and heterosexual marriage."[36] Colonization through sexuality was also evident in how authorized settler sexualities labeled sexual practices that deviated from settler norms as perverse. While this labelling referred to distinct sexual conventions, it also was applied to Indigenous gender practices. That is, Indigenous people often had gender categories that did not map onto colonial understandings of gender.

This disjunction is reflected by a term that was applied to those Indigenous individuals who deviated from European notions of proper sexuality: *berdache*. In the words of Morgensen:

This orientalist term arose to condemn Middle Eastern and Muslim men as

Box 8.6 Innov8

Artist Kent Monkman

Kent Monkman is an Indigenous painter/visual artist whose paintings pose challenges to Canadian viewers about the relationship between Indigenous peoples and Canadians. In his 2017 show, *Shame and Prejudice: Canada at 150*, Monkman draws on his perspectives as a queer and two-spirited artist to question the role of colonialism in dispossessing Indigenous Peoples of their land. Monkman's paintings often deploy his alter ego Miss Chief, a two-spirited trickster who is capable of time travel, to comment on the colonial practices that still pervade Canada's relationships with Indigenous Peoples. In 2017, Monkman received the Bonham Centre Award from the University of Toronto Sexual Diversity Program recognizing his work around sexual identities. Here are two links to interviews with Monkman: <youtube.com/watch?v=NsdaAwIrKgE> and <youtube.com/watch?v=up3XLJcMEeo>.

racial enemies of Christian civilization, by linking them to the creation of berdache (in translation) as "kept boys" or "boy-slaves" whose sex was said to have been altered by immoral male desire.[37]

This term, which came from Persia, was a common word to indicate people who deviated from settler sexuality; the term illustrated how Europeans both understood and devalued Indigenous sexuality. This homogenizing word also erased the great variation across Indigenous cultures throughout North America. The various groups — for example, the *badé* (by Crow people), *kwiraxame* (by Maricopa people), *okitcitakwe* or *agokwa* (by Ojibwe people), *chelxodelean(e)* (by the Ingalik people), *sakwo'mapi akikwan* (by the Blackfoot people), *a-yahkwew* (by the Cree people), *Geenumu Gessalagee* (by the Mi'kmaq people) — used these terms to capture specific local differences about gender and sexuality. These differences were erased, reduced to a single category, the deviant *berdache*.

Indigenous People who did not follow settler gender norms were stigmatized, had their hair cut to fit gender norms and forced to wear what the colonial government thought were gender appropriate clothes. According to one report: "In the 1880s for instance, as part of this mission [to criminalize transvestism], Canadian police forced a *berdache* to wear men's clothes and to cut his hair."[38] Canadian residential schools played a key role in the eradication of Indigenous sexual identities: these "undesirable customs" were to be corrected through a curriculum that established European values and traditions as the only valid ones. In the words of Richard Pratt, at the Carlisle

Box 8.7 Diversity in Action

M versus H

In 1999, the Supreme Court of Canada ruled in the case known as *M vs H* that the exclusion of same-sex couples from the definition of common-law spouse under section 29 of the Ontario Family Law Act was in violation of equality rights under section 15(1) of the Canadian Charter of Rights and Freedoms, and could not be justified under section 1 of the Charter. Although the appellants' identities were unknown at the time, the case revolved around the separation of a lesbian couple, Joanne Mitchell (M) and who went to court over the division of assets from their relationship.

Indian School, the goal was to "Kill the Indian and save the man."[39] This mission included erasing Indigenous gender and sexual identities.

Were the colonialists racists and homophobes? While many certainly were, the project of collapsing a range of sexualities into a single binary was not necessarily so. As Andrea Smith argues, the European settler's understanding of sex and sexuality was premised on a binary. In contrast, Indigenous cultures were composed of multiple genders and sexualities. The two simply were not compatible. With colonialism, and its corresponding violence, Indigenous sexuality became reframed within Western terms. In Smith's words, "it is not surprising that the first peoples targeted for destruction in Native communities were those who did not neatly fit into western gender categories."[40] So, while there was certainly intention to racialize and sexualize the Indigenous population, there was also a structure that existed through colonialism that supplanted Indigenous sexualities with a Western one.

Through colonialism, then, the nation-state controlled sexuality. Reminiscent of the Fruit Machine's deployment, colonialism served as a mechanism of control that was based on sexuality. Through such technologies of power, the nation-state posited an ideal citizen, which entailed characterizing what such perfection did not include: the non-heterosexual citizen. The practices established the nation-state as heteronormative. In other words, by locating heterosexuality as the norm, nation-states privilege a particular form of reproductive sexuality as central for citizenship. Echoing Alexander, not just any(body) can be a citizen.

Yet, nation-states appear to be more accepting of non-heterosexuality in recent times. Canada, for example, changed the legislature around marriage in 2005 to allow for same-sex couples to wed. Moreover, between 2010 and 2018, the number of nations that have legalized same-sex marriage in some form has more than tripled. This would lead one to think that nation-states are more accepting of non-heteronormative sexualities.

In spite of these advances, authors such as Jasbit Puar argue that this progress is illusory. Coining the term **homonationalism**,[41] Puar asserts that countries that appear to support the rights of LGBT2TQ folks are doing so in such a way as to allow for exclusion of other groups. By positing that same-sex accepting nations are more egalitarian than other (mostly Muslim) countries, these virtuous nation-states represent the other nations as intolerant and homophobic. In other words, nation-states include diverse sexualities into the nation only insofar as it allows for them to claim a moral high ground even as they exclude others from citizenship rights. Locating such inclusion of queer bodies can only be understood within the context of race, gender, nation, class and ethnicity.

Why do you think that so many more countries criminalize male homosexuality than female homosexuality? Can this relate to the process of colonialism?

However, the relationship between the queer citizen and the racialized non-citizen is by no means a simple one. Only certain forms of non-heterosexuality are acceptable in the nation. This is referred to as homonormativity: the assumption that non-heterosexual people want to be just like heterosexual folks. For example, although same-sex marriage has been legal in Canada since 2005, it only allows for two people to be married. Other forms of queer marriage — most notably, polygamy — are still illegal. In opposition to this homonormative citizen is the racialized non-citizen, who is represented as sexualized. This form of homonationalism "frame(s) the terrorist as a monster who can be read as queer."[42] Thus, homonationalism not only allows for the construction of racialized terrorists, but conflates it with those queer bodies who deviate from homonormativity.

CONCLUSION: SEXUALITY STUDIES TODAY

In the aftermath of the Black Lives Matter protest, Pride organizations across Canada continue to debate whether uniformed police should participate in Pride marches. In Halifax, the police force decided against participation in the 2017 parade. However, Fredericton Pride continued to welcome uniformed officers, while Pride Calgary welcomed the police to march, albeit not in uniform. In Toronto, police-community relations remain strained. In 2016, Marc Saunders, the Toronto chief of police, apologized to the community for the bathhouse raids in 1981, although some community members noted that it was a qualified apology. The 2018 discovery of an alleged mass murderer at large in the community undetected for several years has highlighted how prejudice about gay men of colour, trans* people and sex workers still shape police responses to crimes against community members.

This chapter set out to explore the issues underlying these events. Working from a critical sexualities perspective, we have shown how Canada's history of regulating sexuality helped to produce the Black Lives Matter protest in Toronto. We reviewed how contemporary settler sexualities emerged as an identity, beginning with debates about *sexual* desire in the European Enlightenment. These debates often took place in light of European colonization underway in the Americas and elsewhere. As those European forms of sexual identity took shape, they were imposed on Indigenous Peoples through legislation, most notably through the Indian Act, which among other actions, imposed compulsory heterosexuality on Indigenous Peoples, eliminating pre-existing ways of conceiving sexualities. This legislation also worked to contain Indigenous Peoples *outside of* but *subject to* Canada. Although sexual minorities have long existed in settler communities, these identities were also contained. The variously heterosexist and homophobic cultural practices and beliefs of the early post-Confederation period and the early twentieth century meant that sexual difference was suppressed and certainly, largely invisible. The Second World War, however, reshaped the opportunities for sexual others to meet and socialize, giving rise to a range of manifestations of homosexual identities in the postwar period and debates about whether gays and lesbians should assimilate to heterosexual norms or resist them. These debates, which continue today, must be placed in relation the development of queer theories' insistence on plural and shifting sexual identities and the urgent need to consider how these same sexual identities remain deeply tied to settler colonialism and deep-seated attitudes about race. Coming to grips with these demands is the work of sexuality studies today.

CRITICAL REVIEW QUESTIONS

1. What is the relationship between transgender individuals and settler sexuality?
2. How did the Indian Act serve to create contemporary sexuality in Canada?
3. What is the relationship between the homophile movement, homonormativity and homonationalism in Canada?
4. Is heteropatriarchy compatible with decolonization?
5. What is the relationship between medical discourse, psychiatry and sexuality?
6. Lesbian in/visibility has been a contentious issue in both feminism and gay/lesbian theory. How does this chapter replicate the absence of lesbian presence in its writing?

RECOMMENDED READINGS

Lisa Duggan, "The New Homonormativity: The Sexual Politics of Neoliberalism," in Russ Castronovo and Dana N. Nelson (eds.), *Materializing Democracy: Toward a Revitalized Cultural Politics* (Duke University Press, 2002).

Gary Kinsman, *The Regulation of Desire: Homo and Hetero Sexualities*, 2nd edition (Black Rose Books, 1996).

Scott Morgensen, "Settler Homonationalism: Theorizing Settler Colonialism within Queer Modernities," GLQ: *A Journal of Lesbian and Gay Studies*, 16, 1–2 (2010) 105.

Carl Wittman, *The Gay Manifesto* (Red Butterfly Publication, 1969).

KEY TERMS

asexuality: category of sexuality that is defined by an absence of sexual activity and intimacies.

compulsory heterosexuality: The institutionalized belief that everyone must be heterosexual.

decolonization: removal of European colonial institutions in post-independence nations in Africa and Asia. In Canada, decolonization has the additional meaning of cultivating an understanding how contemporary settler practices have colonial assumptions that dispossess, disempower and disappear Indigenous Peoples.

empiricism: approach to knowledge generation that privileges our senses and the application of reason to explain all natural processes.

Fruit Machine: instrument that the RCMP used to determine the sexual orientation of a subject.

gay gene: Xq28 gene, which some suggest causes homosexuality in men.

gay liberation: movement that sought to resist compulsory heterosexuality; it drew on experiences from the American civil rights movement and precepts from 1960s counterculture, as well as important insights from the women's movement,

heteronormativity: "normalizing process which supports heterosexuality as the elemental form of human association, as the norm, as the means of reproduction, without which society would not exist."

heteropatriarchy: the way that heteronormativity and patriarchy are used by the state to exclude some from the rights of citizenship.

heterosexuality: sexual attraction to the opposite sex; also denotes the institutionalization and normalization of such attraction.

homonationalism: practice of the nation-state to include diverse sexualities into the nation only insofar as it allows for them to exclude others from citizenship rights.

homonormativity: belief that queer folks wish to be just like heterosexual people.

homophile movement: organized campaign to understand homosexuals as just wanting to be like heterosexuals.

homophobia: literally, fear of homosexuals; also refers to reactions that suggest anxiety or hatred of homosexuals or homosexuality.

homosexual agenda: strategy imputed onto homosexuals that understand them as teaching vulnerable young people to become like them.

homosexuality: sexual attraction to the same sex.

intersex: person who has intermediate or atypical sexual or reproductive characteristics that usually differentiate male from female.

Lavender Scare: persecution of homosexuals in the mid-twentieth century in the United States federal government.

moral panic: intense feeling of anxiety that the social order is threatened, often because a group is perceived to be a threat.

nature versus nurture debate: argument over whether biology or environment plays a larger role in the person we become.

normalization: process through which certain neutral actions become constructed as normal or abnormal.

post-operative transsexuals: individuals who have undergone gender reassignment surgery.

pre-operative transsexuals: individuals who are undergoing hormonal treatments to bring their gender identity into alignment with their physical bodies.

settler sexuality: white national heteronormativity that regulates Indigenous sexuality and gender by supplanting them with the sexual modernity of settler subjects.

sexology: sustained scientific study of sexuality.

sexual identity: sense of self that is shaped by how one is sexually attracted to others.

sexual inversion: reversal of gender traits in which a person of a specific sex performs the gender of someone from a different sex; in nineteenth-century sexology, a term for homosexuality.

sexual orientation: direction or pattern of attraction to others based on sexual, gender characteristics; used to suggest that there are physiological as opposed to sociological forces at work; replaced gender preference.

transgender: those whose gender identity is not aligned with their physical bodies.

Notes

1. Scott Morgensen, "Settler Homonationalism: Theorizing Settler Colonialism within Queer Modernities," GLQ: *A Journal of Lesbian and Gay Studies*, 16, 1–2 (2010): 113 (DOI 10.1215/10642684-2009-015).

2. H. Lathe, *Same-Sex Couples in Canada in 2016 — Census of Population, 2016* (pp. 1-9) (Statistics Canada, Ministry of Industry, 2016): 2.

3. Morgenson, "Settler Homonationalism," 106.

4. For example, R.C. Savin-Williams, *Mostly Straight: Sexual Fluidity Among Men* (Boston: Harvard University Press, 2017).

5. James Joseph Dean, "Being Straight in a Post-Closet World," *Contexts,* 14, 3: 68–69 (DOI 10.1177/1536504215596951).

6. Brady Robards, "'Totally Straight': Contested Identities in Social Media Site Reddit," *Sexualities* 2 1–2 (2017): 49–67 (DOI: 10.117/13634607/6678563).

7. Michel Foucault, *History of Sexuality: An Introduction, Volume One* (Vintage Books, 1990): 43.

8. Nikki Sullivan, *A Critical Introduction to Queer Theory* (New York University Press, 2003).

9. S. Maynard, "On the Case of the Case: The Emergence of the Homosexual as a Case

History in Early-Twentieth-Century Ontario," in M. Fitzgerald and S. Rayter (eds.), *Queerly Canadian: An Introductory Reader in Sexuality Studies*, (Canadian Scholars Press, 2012: 155).

10. Gary Kinsman, *The Regulation of Desire: Homo and Hetero Sexualities*, 2nd edition (Black Rose Books, 1996).

11. Mona Nag, "Sexual Behaviour in India with Risk of HIV/AIDS Transmission," *Health Transition Review*, 5 (1995): 298.

12. Jennifer Terry, "Anxious Slippages between 'Us' and 'Them': A Brief History of the Scientific Search for Homosexual Bodies," in Jennifer Terry and Jacqueline Urla (eds.), *Deviant Bodies: Critical Perspectives on Difference in Science and Popular Culture* (Indiana University Press, 1995): 157.

13. David L. Johnson, *The Lavender Scare: The Persecution of Gays and Lesbians in the Federal Government* (University of Chicago Press, 2004).

14. Gary Kinsman and Patrizia Gentile, *The Canadian War on Queers: National Security as Sexual Regulation* (University of British Columbia Press, 2010): 93.

15. Although sodomy was no longer punished by death, one could still suffer corporal punishment or imprisonment. See *Criminal Code and Selected Statutes, 1955,* The Queen's Printer (1955: 47).

16. Reg Whitaker, "'We Know They're Out There': Canada and Its Others, With or Without the Cold War," in Richard Cavell (ed.), *Love, Hate, and Fear in Canada's Cold War* (University of Toronto Press, 2004).

17. Lisa Duggan, "The New Homonormativity: The Sexual Politics of Neoliberalism," in Russ Castronovo and Dana N. Nelson (eds.), *Materializing Democracy: Toward a Revitalized Cultural Politics* (Duke University Press, 2002): 181.

18. Catherine Jean Nash, "Toronto's Gay Village (1969–1982): Plotting the Politics of Gay Identity," *The Canadian Geographer / Le Ge´ographe canadien*, 50, 1 (2006): 1–16.

19. Rick Bebout, "The Origins of the *Body Politic:* False Starts and Food for Fodder," Rick@Rickbebout.

20. Nash, "Toronto's Gay Village," 5.

21. Hill, cited in Nash, "Toronto's Gay Village," 5.

22. Hill, cited in Nash, "Toronto's Gay Village," 5.

23. Lathe, *Same-Sex Couples,* 3–4.

24. Carl Wittman, *The Gay Manifesto* (Red Butterfly Publication, 1969) <http://www.againstequality.org/files/refugees_from_amerika_a_gay_manifesto_1969.pdf>.

25. Richard Burnett, "Looking Back at Quebec Queer Life Since the 17th Century," *Xtra* Daily Xtra.com., Dec. 7, 2009 <https://www.dailyxtra.com/looking-back-at-quebec-queer-life-since-the-17th-century-30878>.

26. Cited in Nash, "Toronto's Gay Village," 5.

27. Ed Jackson, "The Fallout of a Murder," in Stephanie Chambers (ed.), *Any Other Way: How Toronto Got Queer* (Coach House Press, 2017): 170.

28. Jackson, "The Fallout of a Murder," 169.

29. Michael Warner, "Introduction," in Michael Warner (ed.), *Fear of a Queer Planet: Queer Politics and Social Theory* (University of Minnesota Press, 1993): xxi.

30. Jacqui Alexander, *Pedagogies of Crossing: Meditations on Feminism, Sexual Politics, Memory, and the Sacred* (Duke University Press, 2005).

31. Gavin Brown, "Homonormativity: A Metropolitan Concept that Denigrates 'Ordinary' Gay Lives," *Journal of Homosexuality*, 59, 7 (2012): 1065-1072 (DOI:

10.1080/00918369.2012.699851).

32. J. Weeks, *The World We Have Won* (Routledge, 2007): 9.

33. John Podmore, "Critical Commentary: Sexualities Landscapes beyond Homonormativity," *Geoforum*, 49 (2013): 264.

34. Jacqui Alexander, "Not Just (Any) Body Can Be a Citizen: The Politics of Law, Sexuality and Postcoloniality in Trinidad and Tobago and the Bahamas," *Feminist Review*, 48 (1994): 5–23.

35. Martin Cannon, "The Regulation of First Nations Sexuality," *The Canadian Journal of Native Studies,* 18, 1 (1988): 10.

36. Cannon, "The Regulation," 12.

37. Morgensen, "Settler Homonationalism," 111.

38. Kinsman, *The Regulation of Desire,* 73.

39. Cited in Morgensen, "Settler Homonationalism," 113.

40. Andrea Smith, *Conquest: Sexual Violence and American Indian Genocide* (South End, 2005): 108.

41. Jasbir Puar, *Terrorist Assemblages: Homonationalism in Queer Times* (Duke University Press, 2007).

42. Morgensen, "Settler Homonationalism," 105.

9

IMPAIRMENT AND DISABILITY

THE SOCIAL PERSPECTIVE

Kate Hano

> *My disability is that I cannot use my legs. My handicap is your negative perception of that disability, and thus of me.* — Rick Hansen

KEY OBJECTIVES

Explore models that explain disability in our society.

Explore designs that assist leaders in creating an accessible space for all.

Understand legislation which relates to disability.

Understand issues related to employment of people living with impairment.

People who have impairments live in a world of able-bodied individuals. The social and geographical environment is commonly designed for able-bodied persons, to which the impaired group needs to adapt. This chapter explores the concepts of abilities verses impairments by drawing on the social perspective on disability and feminist theory, as well as other concepts that shed light on the experiences of the impaired, and how, by making certain provisions, everyone can live in harmony. People in our society do not live in isolation, but together, and by making policy and attitudinal changes people who have impairments are going to be able to live full and successful lives. This chapter speaks to some perspectives which will assist us in understanding social attitudes towards people with impairments and present the concept of **universal design**, which can be applied in many areas of social life to include the impaired in the social mix, as well as discuss current policies regarding the impaired. The example of employment is used to show how people with impairments can be involved in our society and make their contribution. There is not enough space to discuss every topic in relation to the impaired; however, the concepts presented here give an understanding and tools that can be used in creating positive change and embracing diversity rather than resisting it. We are all very different, and by embracing the differences in ourselves we are able to celebrate our uniqueness, since life would be very boring if we were all the same. Our differences make our society exciting and dynamic.

DEFINITIONS OF IMPAIRMENT AND DISABILITY

Many different definitions of **impairment** and disability have been used by researchers who study and theorize about **disability**. Those who study disability from the social perspective differentiate between disability and impairment and these definitions are often used while discussing disability from social and attitudinal points of view. From this perspective, impairment is a physical limitation whereas disability is a social construct, and this is the perspective adopted in this chapter. These definitions of impairment and disability are consistent with a social perspective because emphasis is placed on the ability of an individual with impairment to function in society, rather than on the impairment itself.

"Impairments are defined as 'any loss or abnormality of psychological, physiological or anatomical structure or function.' Disability is any restriction or lack of ability to perform an activity in the manner or within the range considered normal for a human being" (Edwards 11).

Impairment and disability can be studied from a variety of perspectives, including legal, economic, medical, psychological, etc. This discussion utilizes a social approach to explore impairment and disability. This lens is considered to be an approach that can potentially lead to the greater empowerment of those with impairments.

For the purpose of this chapter, the definition presented in 1976 by the Union of the Physically Impaired against Segregation (UPIAS) is used. UPIAS defines impairment as "lacking all or part of a limb, or having a defective limb, organism or mechanism of the body." Disability is "the disadvantage or restriction of activity caused by a contemporary social organization which takes no or little account of people who have physical impairments and thus excludes them from the mainstream of social activity" (Butler and Bowlby 411). Since the social environment is designed mainly by those who are able-bodied, the social space they design may be difficult for those with an impairment to use. Those who have mental/physical impairments are rendered disadvantaged by the economic, political and other systems, including social groups that fail to take this group's interests into account in the creation of the built environment. Some may view the impaired body of a person as being a problem, but it is actually the society in which the person lives that is the problem that results in disability. People who have an impairment are often viewed by society as being ill. However, often these individuals are healthy and their only medical restriction is their impairment, which may cause them difficulties in the built environment because of the way that it is constructed. For example, a person who is in a wheelchair due to an accident may be healthy; it is the paralysis which is causing them to be in a wheelchair. This person, however, is able to enjoy daily activities similar to the non-impaired group and often only sees a doctor or members of the medical profession when they feel unwell (French).

THE SOCIAL PERSPECTIVE ON DISABILITY

The **medical model of disability**, according to Ruth Butler and Sophia Bowlby, is based on the idea that biological differences are the basis for explaining the inequalities between the able-bodied and the impaired. More specifically, Vera Chouinard (2012) suggests that the medical model equates impairment and disability and regards the person with an impairment as "defective" and, insofar as is possible, needing to have the defect "fixed" through medical intervention.

The **social perspective on disability** can be seen as a reaction to the medical model and can be traced to British disability theorists in 1976. Until that time, according to Butler and Bowlby, the medical model dominated the writing and views of disability theorists. The disability movement at that time recognized the importance of society in an impaired person's life. Thus, the social perspective on disability rejects the medical model and focuses on the interaction that people with impairments have with others in society and the attitudes which able-bodied people hold toward the impaired. Furthermore, the social environment/context plays a significant role in how impaired people are viewed in society and the impact that has on handicapping them versus integrating them into the mainstream society (Shakespeare, Barnes and Mercer). This, in turn, has implications for the design and construction of the built environment.

Under the medical model, it was the able-bodied group that isolated the impaired into separate schools, housing and day care, separating them from mainstream social life. They were segregated both socially and physically by the dominant and more powerful members of society (Omansky Gordon and Rosenblum; French). Being segregated spatially as well as socially, the impaired groups were unable to become integrated into society, for several reasons. First, the built environment outside of their segregated one was unprepared to welcome this group of people, whose needs were not addressed adequately for them to enter the built space. For example, ramps were needed in order for people in wheelchairs to enter a building, and cut curbs were necessary in order for people in wheelchairs to cross streets and maneuver in the physical space. Thus, upon leaving the segregated environment, it was very difficult to become integrated into the mainstream of social life and, as well, to become contributing members of society (French).

The dominant group, that is, the able-bodied, has a vested interest in maintaining the status quo. It holds society together by imposing its norms on society. Certainly, there would be short-term costs, both financial and otherwise, in giving greater recognition to the needs of those with impairments and attempting to accommodate them. Moreover, keeping a hold on the current system is central not only to policies, but also to practices, ideologies and livelihoods. The dominant group is currently not only in charge of all aspects of social life, but it includes many individuals who greatly fear impairment, for it is a state which cannot be predicted by an individual and which could embrace them at any time. This fear and uncertainty encourage them to turn away from the issue, resulting in a lack of understanding and discrimination against those who are impaired. This differs from relationships with some other disadvantaged groups, where some activists will never become members of that disadvantaged group, such as a male activist fighting for women's rights. This, however, is not the case with impairment. At any moment, an able-bodied person can become impaired. For this reason, disability is resisted and these groups are marginalized. It is the able-bodied persons in society who have the status, can establish memberships in the in-group and thus deny others, potentially those with impairments, entrance into that group.

DIVERSITY IN ACTION

Box 9.1 Diversity in Action

"At Apple we believe the most powerful technology in the world is technology that everyone, including people with disabilities, can use. To work, create, communicate, stay in shape and be entertained. So we don't design products for some people or even most people. We design them for every single person."
— Apple website

This can be accomplished through having an inaccessible society, negative attitudes and exclusionary practices (Omansky Gordon and Rosenblum; French).

Many current disability theorists believe that it is not the body's impairments that play the largest role in contributing to the problems which impaired people face; rather, it is the society and the able-bodied people who create the majority of the obstacles. There is a complex interaction at play between society's able-bodied persons and their attitudes, and the experiences of impaired individuals. The negative attitudes of many able-bodied persons instigate the creation of inaccessible space for the disabled groups, which, in turn, results in impaired individuals having a hard time living their lives and having negative experiences in the different facets of public life (Butler and Bowlby).

Furthermore, many in the able-bodied community do not understand impairment/ disability. If they are asked to simulate being impaired, it is very difficult for them to live their normal lives. By not understanding the diverse methods which impaired people adopt in order to make their lives easier, or by failing to appreciate the different tricks used by impaired people to live normal daily lives, the able-bodied community makes the impaired dependent on society for their daily needs (French).

Many in the able-bodied society strongly believe that a person is either able or disabled (Barnes and Mercer; Omansky Gordon and Rosenblum; French; Imrie and Hall): there are only two large categories and all members of society fall into one or the other. In fact, people do not fall neatly into one category or another, many fall in between; that is, people have varying degrees of impairment. For example, someone who does not have any night vision may be categorized as blind, even though during the day they are sighted. Furthermore, conditions such as obesity, pregnancy or a broken leg may render the able person impaired/disabled; however, those individuals would not see themselves or speak of themselves as having impairments or being disabled. Furthermore, all impaired people in society are often grouped into one category, even though there are many different types of impairments and therefore, many different levels of impairment. The built environment may not be made ready for this diverse group of people because those who design the built environment may not take into consideration adequately the needs of those people who may be temporarily impaired (Omansky Gordon and Rosenblum; Barnes and Mercer; French; Imrie and Hall).

Although it is also made up of people with extremely varied attributes, the able-bodied group is the powerful and dominant group in society that controls the design of physical space. Theories of design clearly illustrate this point. Buildings are designed not only for their use by the public, but also based on their ornamental appeal to the human eye (Imrie and Hall). Building designers, who are mostly able-bodied people, may view the impaired group as not living normal lives. For example, they may be thought not to shop or spend money in the same way as able-bodied persons do, living in a way different from able-bodied people. Instead, they may be seen as living in specialized homes which are designed in ways to directly cater to their needs, where support staff helps them with daily chores and activities. Thus, it may be thought that creating accessible environments is not economically feasible since few will use such places. It is commonly viewed that the only people who will benefit from the provision of accessible space are the disabled groups, who may not have the immediate need to use the facilities. The elderly and families with small children are seldom seen as being groups who would also benefit from such provision. Such a view is demeaning, and the outcome is that it makes it more difficult for impaired people to live independent lives. Furthermore, it may be invalid to claim that accessible design is more expensive, especially when incorporated from the beginning. It is much more expensive to add accessibility after the fact (Imrie and Hall). Thus, for impaired people to gain greater access to public facilities and more social acceptance, the able-bodied community, along with the developers and designers, need to accept and welcome this group of people, known as the impaired, into mainstream society.

As previously stated, impairment is not static and, at any moment, an able-bodied person can become impaired; yet those who design physical spaces commonly do not take this into consideration. Therefore, not only are public buildings often not accessible, but private homes are not designed to be accessible and few options are created for people to choose an accessible design if they want one. Often, families with an impaired person, or who live with elderly parents, must spend much money on their private home to make it accessible. If architects created an accessible design at the outset, it would make this process much easier. Moreover, more impaired people might then have the option of living independently since their homes would be designed to meet their needs (Imrie and Hall; French).

The social perspective on disability suggests that it is the able-bodied persons in society who not only have the power to rule and establish norms, but also have the resources to create change. Disabled persons have not been passive victims of the able-bodied, and they have also worked to promote change. Nevertheless, given prevailing attitudes, such as fear and lack of understanding of the role of society in making the impaired disabled, this perspective helps to explain why the change to an accessible society is occurring so slowly. This perspective is important for the current discussion, since it explains why impaired individuals may still have a difficult time gaining full entrance to all aspects of social life (Omansky Gordon and Rosenblum). Since able-bodied people have created this problem, it is possible that they can eliminate it by establishing a more inclusive society. For example, building codes have not always included minimum accessibility standards. In the last thirty years, the National Building Code of Canada has included accessibility standards in recognition of the growing impaired population and their desire to live independent lives. The social perspective on disability gives the impaired group a sense of self-worth, as well as a collective identity. It does this by placing the blame for disability on society, rather than on impaired individuals and, in doing so, unites them in a common cause to improve their opportunities and lifestyles. The social perspective refutes the claims of the medical model, which viewed the problems experienced by impaired persons as being caused by their own bodies and not by the actions of the society of which they are a part (Butler and Bowlby). It did this by changing the perspective on impairment, potentially allowing those who were impaired to be integrated into society, as well as providing the means of acquiring greater independence for the impaired. The social perspective, by reinterpreting the causes of disability, can give greater confidence to those with impairments and potentially empower them to advocate for changes that will enable them to live independent lives. However, many in society have yet to embrace this perspective, and thus changes in the situation of those with impairments are occurring only slowly.

Making changes to the physical environment, such as ensuring that buildings are accessible, is only one aspect of social life. The reluctance of able-bodied people to accept impaired individuals fully into social life/activities is another important aspect of this perspective. Excluding a group from taking full part in social activities may be compared to the past practice of denying entrance to racialized persons. Posting signs which are written in small print or located in very high places has the effect of exclusion and segregation. The elderly, as well as those who are visually impaired, are unable to read signs which would inform them of important facts, such as the types of stores in a given building or the change of a bus route (Shakespeare; Omansky Gordon and Rosenblum; Barnes and Mercer). Thus, the social perspective of disability puts emphasis not only on adjusting physical spaces, but also on the roles that individuals play in society. By empowering the impaired, such individuals will have the confidence and ability to take on roles that able-bodied people hold in society, such as parenting, and being employers and employees. Once impaired people are able to control their lives, to have jobs in society and to guide the disability movement, changes in communities may happen very quickly. For example, as more impaired people gain entrance to higher education and become architects, engineers and health professionals, they will be able to assist able-bodied professionals in making changes that will benefit all, not only those with impairments. Education of impaired people and education of the public by the impaired group are important in creating an inclusive society, as well as accessible spaces (French; Imrie and Hall).

The relationships which are built by people living in social spaces are also very important. People do not live in isolation and need to build relationships with each other. If the attitudes and social environment built by able-bodied people do not change, impaired individuals will not be able to become full participants in society. It is also important to allow the impaired groups to speak of their needs and requirements, since able-bodied people may not have the full knowledge or understanding to create accessible space, meaning a space that all people may use regardless of their abilities. In the past, the medical model did not encourage dialogue between the able-bodied and the impaired, which led to segregation rather than integration. Although people with impairments can take action individually in their own lives and collectively to increase awareness and understanding of their circumstances, disability, which is imposed on the impaired population, is ultimately socially constructed and designated. Since this is the case, it is the responsibility of the able-bodied to eliminate the social and physical barriers experienced by the impaired groups in order to integrate them into mainstream society (Shakespeare; Oldman).

Society itself is complex and social change needs to involve many of its representatives, including educators, designers and politicians, for movement is required on many fronts if greater inclusion of the impaired population is to be realized. The social perspective on disability espouses a view that can help to integrate the impaired and give them the power to think of themselves in very different terms than they commonly have in the past. No longer would they need to rely on the charity of able-bodied persons, but they could take control of their lives and move forward. They can mobilize themselves to act together to create social change rather than wait for able-bodied people to change social attitudes for them. For example, the Americans with Disability Act (ADA), which came into effect in 1991 in the United States, has had important implications and positive effects on stimulating accessibility changes in countries around the world. The Accessibility for Ontarians with Disability Act (AODA) based its integration of disabled persons into mainstream society on the ADA and created recommendations which would protect impaired people from discrimination (Shakespeare; Oldman). Indeed, by empowering the impaired and instilling the belief that they are not the problem but that society is, impaired individuals would be able to engage different social groups in positive attitude change. This would occur by impaired people wanting to gain access into different social groups, including the government, and thereby changing the system. Many impaired people have already taken charge of their lives and are very involved in creating positive attitudinal changes in society (Imrie and Hall; French). Thus, the social perspective on disability is important for the current discussion, since it explains why the medical model has not enabled impaired individuals to become involved in the disabled movement. Under this model, individuals are reluctant to appear to others in society as if they are impaired. The social perspective, by placing disability outside of individual responsibility, can potentially empower them to take collective action to make their needs more widely appreciated. Furthermore, light has been shed on the reasons for creating accessible space and fully integrating impaired persons into all aspects of social life. It also helps to explain why society is changing so slowly and reluctantly in addressing the needs of impaired persons.

FEMINIST PERSPECTIVE

Many claims made by proponents of the social perspective on disability parallel those of advocates of feminist perspectives. Arguing by analogy, the ideas are very similar to those of some feminist researchers who worked to identify, document, make society aware of and change the status of women. Women's ability to bear children, for example, often renders them "impaired" for a short period of time because pregnancy may cause physical and social limitations. In order to counter such ideas, feminist researchers needed to redefine women's experiences, make a clear distinction between biology, sex and gender, and address the distinction between the feminine and masculine in more nuanced ways. Somewhat similarly, the impaired need to make clear the distinction between impairment and disability, and show that there are two distinctive factors at play: impairment and society's responses to it (Shakespeare). Feminists challenged the notion of the female being weak and physically incompetent, by asserting the beauty and strength of the female body. However, society is now fixated on the perfect body and thus many women have worked, and still are working, to achieve that "perfection."

Both impaired individuals and feminists have struggled to redefine how the human body is perceived and evaluated. Many feminists have complained about the objectification of female bodies and the pressure to conform to norms of beauty. In much the same way, since many impairments are visible and render the body "imperfect," people with such "imperfections" are deemed to be less desirable than those without such "flaws," with resulting implications for access to opportunities. Consequently, many impaired individuals try to hide their impairments by trying to appear normal and non-impaired. This is often done at great personal risk and pain. For example, someone who is diagnosed with chronic pain may have pain and difficulty walking up stairs. However, after coming back from a break with co-workers, this person, instead of taking the elevator and avoiding discomfort, may take the stairs in order to appear normal. This person may experience pain, but they will not say so, since the act of doing so may result in their being categorized by others as impaired/disabled (French).

Females in our society have struggled with such issues and, very similar to some impaired individuals, have tried to change their body to fit the social image of perfection. Young girls and women have dieted and, in some cases, used extreme measures

Box 9.2 Diversity in Action

In Canada, CBC was the network that brought the 2018 Winter Olympics into people's homes. The broadcaster provided over 3100 hours of coverage over different platforms. A few weeks after the closing ceremony, the Para-Olympics began. Impaired athletes from all over the world came to compete. Once again, CBC provided coverage of this event; however, this time the coverage was only about 600 hours and a special Para-Olympic media platform was not available. This major discrepancy in the media portrayal of the Olympic Games may have a significant impact on the future athletes in our society.

to become thin and socially desirable. Furthermore, the media portrayal of women in society as thin and beautiful, as seen on many TV shows and constant advertisements for female beauty products, lead many women to feel inadequate and undesirable (Butler and Bowlby; Moss and Dyck; Dyck). The impaired are often portrayed in the media as helpless and dependent, and rarely as strong independent role models. Thus, the message which may be sent by the media to society is that women and impaired people require help if they are to lead independent and happy lives (French).

The concept of objectifying the body is well established in the feminist literature. Some women will gaze in the mirror and worry about looking good. They take into serious consideration what others think of how they look. Impaired persons experience the able-bodied population looking at them as objects of sympathy or as a social or medical curiosity. This may impact the social experience which impaired people have and how they view their own body. The impaired person may look in the mirror and see a body that is broken or disfigured, which in turn, may lead them to feel inadequate and undesirable. They are often unable to change their appearance and, thus, are unable to meet the socially desirable look of beauty and success. The body which is disfigured or different may be seen by some able-bodied people as undesirable and will be stared at and scrutinized. The body of an able-bodied person, which is not disfigured or different in any way, may be used as a measurement by the main group in society to judge who has the normal and desired body and who does not (Butler and Bowlby; Shakespeare; Omansky Gordon and Rosenblum; French).

The impaired person's self-concept is formed through social interaction with others, and, mostly, the others are members of the able-bodied group. Impaired people can accept or reject the concept but they cannot escape its implications. However, they can have a significant impact on how the able-bodied group views them, based on their own self-concept. Thus, not only does the able-bodied group help the impaired person to form their self-concept, the able-bodied, in turn, will be affected by the view which the impaired person presents. For this reason, eliminating negative socially constructed views of impairment and disability will help the able-bodied group to create a more positive image/concept of impaired individuals. One way in which this can be accomplished is by creating public spaces which are accessible. The impaired, then, would have a greater opportunity to interact with the able-bodied persons in society, thereby demonstrating their abilities rather than their impairments. This perspective provides further understanding of why it is so important to have accessible space available (Barnes; Butler and Bowlby).

By looking at environment, body and identity formation through the lens of feminist perspectives, it is very clear that location, environment and people play a role in developing an individual's identity. People's lives in society are woven together through the place in which they live, experiences they have and the type of body which they possess. The relationships which are created do not exist separately but form an interconnected whole. The experiences a person has related to the type of body they have are crucial in creating identities within relationships which are grounded in oppression of gender, sex or disability. Both able and impaired individuals live together in society and their lives are interconnected. However, it is those in the position of power who will dictate the general image and identity for both the able-bodied and impaired groups (Moss and Dyck).

Impaired people will often deny their identity as an impaired person in order to fit in better in the able-bodied world. This may cause them much stress, pain and difficulty, but they will see it as worthwhile if society views them as being able-bodied. Otherwise, they may be viewed as being inactive, unadventurous, non-competitive and dependent on others for support. The truth is much different, since often the impaired are courageous, adventurous and active. Lack of accessible space, however, may make them appear to be inactive and dependent on others. This is especially true in unfamiliar environments. By adopting the social perspective on disability, impaired individuals may be able to shake off their perceptions of a negative disability identity and adopt a more optimistic and healthier one (Moss and Dyck; French). This may be possible since it is society that constructs the deviant identity that marks disability as a social problem and overlooks individual/personal abilities.

The language which the able-bodied society uses while addressing impaired persons reflects the social attitudes towards them. For example, ordinary events may be viewed as extraordinary when an impaired person engages in them (Chouinard 2001: 188). The able-bodied perception of impaired individuals who try to blend into society and strive to fulfill their professional and life goals may be expressed in awe and wonder. It is especially interesting that able-bodied women, who have struggled against many similar issues and still do, may turn around and view the impaired group in a similar

> Box 9.3 Think About…
>
> Ordinary events in life may seem extraordinary when an impaired person
> does them. Think about trying an ordinary event in your daily life from the
> perspective of someone with an impairment of some kind. For example, as
> you wake up in the morning, blindfold yourself and go through your morning
> routine. Get dressed, have breakfast and move around your space without
> vision. Similarly, go through your morning routine while in a chair on wheels,
> to simulate being in a wheelchair, and move around your space while getting
> ready for the day. If you like you can also tie one arm behind your back and go
> through the routine.
> After you complete the exercise, think about how you felt, what you struggled
> with or what felt impossible. Were your clothes colour-coordinated? Could you
> access all areas of your living space?

way as they were seen in the past. Women experienced the dominant group in society
looking at them with awe when they broke social norms and were combining professional work with motherhood. Furthermore, women experienced difficulties with
gaining entrance into various communities based on their social status as women.
Some professions were closed to them, not because of their inability to perform the
tasks, but because they were women. Women who broke the social norms were seen
as courageous and adventurous for stepping out and speaking or acting to change the
negative social norms (Chouinard 2001).

The able-bodied society views impaired people as a problem and as people who
need help or a cure. This attitude prevents the impaired community from pursuing
careers, which, in turn, creates low self-esteem/self-worth. It is not the impairment
which prevents this group from working but rather the attitudes of the able-bodied
community (Barnes and Mercer; French). Combined with feminist ideas of the social
perception of beauty and body, the social perspective on disability provides an explanation for why impaired people have been excluded from mainstream society. The
feminist perspective informs this discussion by providing a possible explanation of
why impaired people are having experiences that parallel women's treatment by society.
The feminist experience over the decades not only informs the disability movement of
how hard it may be to change attitudes, but also that while change is possible, it may
take time. These ideas are very important for the current discussion since much has
already been done to achieve integration of impaired people into social life, yet there
is still much to be done. Women have challenged social norms for years in order to
gain access to areas of social life that were closed to them, and they are still doing it

and will continue to do so in the future. Impaired people and the disability movement can learn from that, and understand that change may occur slowly, and that there may be aspects in the future which will need to be challenged in order for advancement to occur. Moreover, women have made many strides in recent decades which are similar to what the impaired are striving to achieve. Able-bodied persons are in positions of power, and thus are able to restrict and control the access and integration of impaired persons into mainstream society. By addressing problems such as physical access and negative attitudes, which have created difficulties for impaired people, the latter will be able to reach positions of power and create further change. Integrating impaired people into the able-bodied society would allow the two groups to be able to work together in order to create change which will be beneficial for all, especially since an able-bodied person can never know if or when they may become impaired. This realization could be an important step towards merging the two social groups. Instead of resisting each other, they could work together towards the common good. Creating accessible physical space, as well as having people with positive attitudes in all social areas, could be very important steps towards greater integration.

Such approaches are important for current as well as future discussions since, in order to empower impaired individuals, not only does the world need to become more accessible, but social attitudes also need to change. Currently, society places much emphasis on aesthetics and looks. In order for impaired individuals to become fully participating members of the community, social attitudes and norms need to change. Discussion that examines both physical accessibility and attitudes to impaired individuals could lead to social change, which will affect the impaired population positively. By allowing the impaired to have greater access to all aspects of life, social attitudes toward people with physical impairments can be changed.

UNIVERSAL DESIGN

For people with impairments to make use of all social and physical spaces, they need to be made accessible. Universal design could be an effective tool to prepare the various aspects of social life for impaired individuals. Many people in the world do not fit the category of the average person, yet many architects design facilities with a "mythical" average person in mind. Instead of designing spaces and facilities for an average user, universal designers create buildings and facilities with a broad group of people in mind: groups such as children, the elderly and the physically impaired. Universal design means that products are designed for all people to the greatest extent possible. Universal designers create spaces that will be used by large and diverse groups of people, and that will not need to be changed in the future, since they take the needs of all people into consideration. This makes universal design very economical, as well as very practical (Mace, Hardie and Place; Centre for Universal Design; Trachtman, Mace, Young and Pace).

Both buildings and some outdoor environments can be designed in such a way that people of all ages and abilities are able to participate in all activities and access all commodities. Since no design can take everyone's needs fully into consideration, universal designers do their best to meet the needs of most people. Each project needs to be viewed individually within universal design, because each has different challenges (Mace et al.; Centre for Universal Design). For instance, universal designers create many adaptable and flexible fixtures, which can easily be changed or removed. All elements are designed to fit the decor and to allow people of all abilities to be a part of a wide variety of activities. By creating such interior and exterior spaces, universal designers make public facilities more accessible, without the investment of more capital than is necessary. This is especially true today when people who are aging and may be losing some of their physical abilities still have the desire to participate in different aspects of social life and require spaces that will accommodate their needs (Trachtman et al.).

The origins of universal design reflect changes in society. Initially, universal design was developed to accommodate war veterans and, later, impaired people (Centre for Universal Design; Trachtman et al.). Therefore, universal design originally reflected the current social attitudes towards these groups. Due to new medical innovations, victims of war, who used to become impaired, can now live fuller lives. Social attitudes towards impaired individuals are changing, and some may even be able to make changes to their homes in order to make them universally accessible. This not only assists impaired individuals but also people with small children and the elderly (Trachtman et al.). The stigma associated with impairments/disability has been lifting gradually, and people of various ability levels now take part in many aspects of social and public life. With this trend, new legislation has been established in many parts of the world to create more opportunities for the growing group of people with impairments. Furthermore, with legislation came the need to create designs that are barrier-free and, using the assistance of new technology, universal design was born (Centre for Universal Design).

After the first examples of universal design came into existence, it became apparent that it not only benefitted the impaired population but other groups as well. With globalization, individuals have greater access to travel, and people with a variety of language barriers visit and stay in many locations. Able-bodied travellers may become handicapped when visiting a different culture, or country, and see signs they cannot understand. Thus, universal design can serve this seemingly able-bodied group of

Box 9.4 Innov8

D2L is an international company which provides online-learning platforms for educators at different levels of education, as well as for governments and other public and private companies to enhance people's learning. Its founder, John Baker, wanted to answer the question of how we can use technology to transform learning. His strong belief is that the best thing that we can do for each other is to ensure that we have the best possible access to learning opportunities. Accessibility is integrated into D2L's technology in order to provide learning opportunities to all learners and educators despite their level of ability: <www.D2L.com>.

people in addition to those with a physical impairment. Moreover, universal design may be perceived by some as less stigmatizing since it focuses on the space being used by all, as well as presenting information in many formats, which makes it much easier for all members of society to understand and access the space (Iwarsson and Stahl). Accessibility to and within our built environment is very complex however, and universal design is only one approach to creating physical space which is more usable by all people in society.

Universal design has also been successfully applied in other areas of social life, such as education. By applying the principles of universal design to education, instructors are able to address the needs of the majority of learners in their groups, since not every student learns in the same way. Educators have realized that their classrooms not only may have students with different types of impairments, but also students who learn in different ways. In order to successfully teach all those students, some educators have turned to universal design to create an inclusive learning environment (National Center on Universal Design for Learning).

This universal design for learning not only allows abled-bodied students to learn in optimal environment, but it also includes those students who may not want to share their invisible disability with the instructor or the classroom. Students with learning disabilities which are not visible would be successful in pursuing their educational goals, along with students who may be visually or physically impaired.

In order to make universal design more tangible, there are seven principles that can be used by architects to create plans for new facilities (Centre for Universal Design). The seven principles of universal design can also make it easier to assess a facility for its level of accessibility. Those same principles have been used in creating materials for learning. The first principle of universal design deals with equitable use. It urges planners to create spaces that are usable by a diverse group of people. Doors that open automatically allow those with an impairment to enter and exit a facility with ease and efficiency. Non-impaired individuals can use the same door with ease. People who carry many bags or have young children would also be assisted.

The second principle addresses the need for flexibility of use. It refers to designing objects in a way that would give the user choice in the method of use. A bank machine with visual, tactile and auditory feedback, located in a place to allow access for people in a wheelchair or for people of small stature, would enable the impaired to access their money independently. Moreover, in bad lighting conditions, or under disabling circumstances, all individuals would be able to access money from the bank machines with ease.

The third principle refers to simplicity in use. It refers to people being able to understand and experience an activity regardless of their knowledge, ability to concentrate or language skills. For example, creating moving sidewalks in places such as airports, which require individuals to do a lot of walking, would benefit all people. Similarly, it would be beneficial to adopt an international signage system that can help to direct people to different places quickly and efficiently, including signs that are both verbal and visual.

The fourth principle addresses multiple ways of repeating the same information for the public. Using multiple ways to convey information, such as print, pictorial images and auditory channels, would benefit everybody. In a resort or hotel setting, displaying daily activities visually, through printed word, in a pictorial format and through announcements, would ensure that all individuals are able to access the information and can respond to it.

The fifth principle encourages tolerance for error. Individuals are prone to making mistakes and, at times, it may not be possible for them to re-do the same action. For example, a key card could be developed for use in hotels that can open doors regardless of the way it is inserted, which would allow individuals to access their rooms easily and quickly, regardless of the dexterity of their hands.

The sixth principle encourages designers to create objects or items that a person can access without much physical effort, such as automatic and touch sensitive water faucets and lamps. When no physical effort is required to use water faucets, washrooms and other appliances, buildings become more accessible to all individuals.

The last principle deals with creating a large physical space that allows easy approach, manipulation and reach for the user. Wider gates in subway stations would allow not only a physically impaired person to pass through easily, but also a large person or an individual with luggage.

The seven principles of universal design could be incorporated into the design of all public facilities to allow physically impaired individuals to access all aspects of the

> **Box 9.5 Think About...**
>
> Now that you have learned about universal design and its principles, think about a building on campus that you like very much or frequent often. Once you have a building in mind, assess it for compliance with the seven principles of universal design. What aspects of the building need to change to fit the concept? How would you change the physical space?

facilities with ease and independence. Many public spaces would probably need only minor changes to make them universally accessible to all people. By examining all aspects of social life through the lens of universal design, educators and employers could ensure that their accommodation, transportation, eating and drinking establishments, and recreational sites are easily accessible to people regardless of the level of their physical ability.

Despite the ever-increasing number of physically impaired people, and the provisions taken by the different levels of governments, many, perhaps most, public facilities are still not accessible to the physically impaired. Moreover, the social attitudes towards these individuals are often not only unfavourable, but also discriminatory, and may create segregation rather than inclusion. Education, empathy training and greater acknowledgement of the new and ever-growing group of impaired people would ensure an increase in social participation and economic benefits. It would also provide a much higher quality of life for the impaired population.

LEGISLATION: THE AODA

Universal design and other international initiatives were fundamental in creating the AODA. For example, the Americans with Disability Act of 1990, a civil law that prohibits discrimination based on disability, was a leader and a guide upon which other countries, including Canada, based their legislation. The new Ontario legislation has taken every aspect of life into consideration, and introduces, in five-year intervals, different areas of the Act into public life. The goal of the Ontario government is to create an accessible province by 2025, at which point people living with impairments will be fully integrated in to every aspect of social life. Furthermore, the Ontario government has created sanctions for those who do not comply with the legislation, ensuring cooperation from those who may not have felt that they could comply, such as small businesses.

The main objectives of the Accessibility for Ontarians with Disabilities Act, or AODA, are to identify, remove and eliminate barriers for people with disabilities (information in this section is from the Access Ontario website). The AODA became law on June 13, 2005, and applies to all levels of government, nonprofits and the private sector, and businesses in Ontario that have one or more employees (full-time, part-time, seasonal or contract) are also included in the Act.

The AODA includes requirements that all businesses and organizations must meet with deadlines specific to an organization's type and size. The AODA is made up of five parts or standards and deadlines for compliance started on January 1, 2010, and will continue until 2025. Thus, Ontario has already introduced many of the standards into public life. Since our society is not static but fluid and keeps changing and evolving, once all standards are fully introduced and implemented in 2025, it will be time to assess the effectiveness of the legislation and to make changes.

The AODA is made up of five standards, as well as some general requirements. The AODA is very complex and inclusive, and this chapter describes it only in broad terms. The legislation includes standards in the following areas: customer service, information and communication, employment, transportation, and design of public spaces. The AODA standards are detailed and contain direct guidelines for all the sectors. Furthermore, the AODA is a part of the Integrated Accessibility Standards Regulation (IASR), which includes, in addition to requirements specific to each standard, the following general requirements: to provide training to staff and volunteers; to develop

Box 9.6 Diversity in Action

Many impaired individuals take advantage of the assistance that service animals are able to provide for them, whether it is a guide dog, a hearing dog or a special skills dog, who assists individuals in wheelchairs. These dogs are specially selected and trained, and impaired individuals who seek assistance of these animals undergo a screening and qualification process. Emotional support animals is another category of service animal has recently become common; they are usually small dogs, but may be other animals, like cats or chickens. These dogs/animals are not specially trained but are assisting impaired individuals, and their owners insist that their presence is necessary while traveling. These animals have been allowed on public modes of transportation such as airplanes; but, due to their distractive behaviour, Delta Airlines created new regulations which impacted all users of service animals. Their first proposal was very restrictive, and only after much discussion did they alter their policy. Now, Delta has made it easier for passengers flying with trained service dogs and emotional support animals.

Source: Delta Airlines website.

an accessibility policy; to create a multi-year accessibility plan; to update the plan every five years; and to consider accessibility in procurement and when designing or purchasing self-service kiosks.

The AODA legislation recognizes that every aspect of social life may change and therefore has made provisions for that. Moreover, it is important that training and compliance policies are updated in order to keep social places accessible at all times. Many businesses may not have had customers or clients who are impaired for many years, or on a regular basis, but once such a situation occurs, both staff and business will be ready to embrace this group of customers.

One example has been identified by businesses who provide their customers with the option of online-shopping. Since their websites are regulated by the AODA and thus comply with accessibility standards, many visually impaired individuals have turned to online shopping to satisfy their needs.

I spoke to some visually impaired families and couples, and they expressed relief and satisfaction with online shopping. One said, "I can shop from the comfort of my own house and my computer, without having to wait for a store clerk to come and help me with reading the tags, sizes, and all the other details that I would like to know. Furthermore, I do not need to worry about walking to a wrong store, or trying to find the one store that I am really looking for. Most people are very nice and they really want to assist us, but online-shopping is so much more time efficient and most importantly I can do it independently." Thus, it is clear that the current legislation has already benefitted the impaired population in Ontario. As time goes by the legislation will become updated and revised, and impaired individuals will have greater control over their lives.

As discussed above, both the private and public sector, as well as various company sizes, have compliance reporting requirements. Just as there are different compliance requirements there are different penalties for non-compliance, depending on the type and size of the company. The AODA gives government authority to set monetary penalties to enforce compliance with accessibility standards. The maximum penalties under the AODA include:

- a corporation/organization that is guilty can be fined up to $100,000 per day
- directors and officers of a corporation/organization that is guilty may be fined up to $50,000 per day.

With such steep penalties the AODA is really hoping to ensure that corporations/ organizations take this legislation seriously and do everything in their power to comply, thus creating a greater inclusion for the impaired. Moreover, the Ontario government has prepared calendars, workshops, timeline checklists and newsletters to assist companies during this transition period. This will help ensure compliance at all organizational levels and also that implementation will occur on time and in the correct fashion.

DISABILITY AND EMPLOYMENT

As the AODA becomes deeply embedded in Ontario society it is important to look at and examine the employment market in Canada and see where people with impairments fit in. According to website of the ODEN, currently almost 16 percent of Canadians identify themselves as having some kind of a disability. For comparison, this is equal to the combined populations of Alberta, Saskatchewan and Manitoba. It is the largest minority in the country. When you add family and loved ones, 53 percent of the Canadian population is directly affected by disability.

Internationally, there are 1.3 million people who report having a disability. When those numbers are combined with family and loved ones, they control over $8 trillion US in disposable income (information in this section is from the Ontario Disability Employment Network website). This is a very large market sector both nationally and internationally, and as our society grows and evolves those numbers are expected to grow as well. Statisticians are projecting that over 20 percent of the population in Canada will have a disability by 2020. Couple that with the Conference Board of Canada's prediction that by the same year, there will be a shortfall of a million workers, and it is clear that business will need to enhance their understanding of disability to increase market share and meet future labour needs.

When presented with such numbers, employers and corporations may take notice, since it is their bottom-line which may be affected. At first there is going to be much resistance; however, as more and more impaired individuals enter the workforce and prove their worth, future generations of impaired people will have an easier time seeking and obtaining employment.

As many employers have already discovered, people with impairments have much to contribute to any organization. They will make it more productive, more diverse and more human. It does not matter if one operates a small to medium sized enterprise or a multi-national corporation, or if the business is in the private, public or nonprofit sector, impaired individuals have much to contribute and can have a positive impact on the bottom line.

One may question how that is possible and how impaired individuals may have so much to contribute to our employment sector. According to a survey conducted by the US company DuPont, employers who hired impaired individuals reported performance ratings of average or above average for 90 percent of workers with impairments.

Furthermore, a Harris poll of 920 employers found that 88 percent of workers with impairments earned performance ratings of good or excellent. The same research shows that 33 percent of employers say that people with impairments work as hard as other employees. About 46 percent of those employers say this group of individuals actually work harder than those without impairments.

Another study was conducted in the United States and more specifically by Walgreens and analyzed in thirty-one distinct locations in three distribution centres, where 40 percent of the workforce comprises employees with impairments. The results showed that in eighteen locations, the difference in productivity rates was statistically insignificant. In three locations employees without any impairments were more productive. In ten locations employees with impairments were said to be more productive. Higher productivity of these companies' employees translates to higher profits for the business, and greater efficiency of work. This means that the work gets done faster, which reduces wait times, and may increase overall satisfaction that is experienced by the public. Furthermore, the company costs go down, since their employees are so productive.

Another finding by the DuPont researchers, showed that 86 percent of employees who are impaired have average or above average attendance records. People with impairments not only want to work but are showing their satisfaction with their employment by attending work as often as they possibly can. Sickness or family obligations may take these employers away from work, but not more so than those employees who live without impairments.

The following are examples of employers who have hired people with impairments, and their experiences. They are national chains; however, the businesses are located in Ontario. One such business is a Toronto-based Tim Hortons. Its owner, Mark Wafer, reported that his employees with impairments have an 87 percent better attendance record than his employees who don't have impairments. In other food industry businesses, such as Pizza Hut and Taco Bell, research indicates that employees with impairments were five times more likely to stay on the job. Furthermore, those same businesses also reported an average annual turnover rate of 38 percent in an industry where the average turnover can be as high as 120 percent.

People with impairments stay on the job when they obtain employment and become loyal to their employers, despite the fact that they may be in low paying jobs. For some it may be the only type of job they are able to perform, and they do it to the best of their ability while being satisfied to contribute to society. People with impairments may have limited mobility, or other physical, mental and sensory limitations, yet they take great care with their own safety, as well as others, while on the job. What this translates into is employers rating 97 percent of workers with impairments as average or above average in terms of safety. In the case of one particular workplace, after twenty-one years in business and over 150 employees with impairments, the company has never filed a workers' compensation claim for any of their employees with impairments.

In addition to the above discussed reasons for which hiring people with impairments is beneficial to employers there is another incentive. Just like abled-bodied persons, people with impairments do not live alone or in isolation in our society. They have friends, families and acquaintances who believe in them and support them, as well as companies and businesses who support impaired people. This means that people with impairment and their family members comprise 53 percent of the marketplace. This creates a strong emotional connection to impairment, demonstrated in a 2008 COMPAS research poll which indicated that 78 percent of Canadians said they were more likely to buy a product or service from a business that has a policy of hiring people with impairments. In another research study, conducted in 2006 in the United States, the results showed that 92 percent of consumers reflect favourably on businesses known to hire persons with impairments, and 87 percent prefer to do business with these same companies. People with impairments are not only loyal, safe and thoughtful employees but they also bring with them another large loyal customer group, which rewards businesses that hire impaired individuals with their own business and loyalty.

Since people with impairments are generally happy in their roles and experience job satisfaction, employee morale and engagement is less of a problem than in companies where impaired individuals do not work. Thus, when many businesses lament the high costs associated with poor employee engagement and are initiating employee engagement programs and processes because of the 55 percent able-bodied turnover rate, it is interesting to note the rate for people with impairments is less than 1 percent. Employers who hire impaired individuals suggest that employee engagement is enhanced due to their diverse hiring practices. This is why, for example, Kitchener, Ontario-based Dare Foods engaged a hiring strategy to include people with disabilities in their workforce. One human resources recruiter remarked: "When managers are attuned to the specific skills and practices required for guiding a diverse team, and when all employees understand the workplace's culture and values and their role within it, a better 'fit' is achieved and employee engagement increases." Therefore, those organizations that take diversity seriously and implement effective integration strategies have greater success in achieving optimal employee performance and retention of staff.

Many of the examples in this section of the chapter focus on employees who work in customer service type of positions; however, the impaired are not only very diverse in their talent but also in education and employment goals. Therefore, it should not come as a surprise that a 2012 study by Human Resources and Skills Development Canada

> *Box 9.7 Innov8*
>
> Dolphin is a Canadian company which provides work to those individuals who may not be able to find employment elsewhere, despite being qualified, such as people with disabilities. It also is involved in Disability Mentoring Day, during which people with impairments are paired with employers in our society to create contacts, links, connections and find employment. See Dolphin's website: <www.dolphin.ca>.

showed that almost half — 48 percent — of working age people with impairments have a postsecondary education. According to the Ontario Chamber of Commerce, in a 2013 report highlighting the need to connect employers with graduates who had a disability, 29 percent of Ontario's small and medium sized enterprises are having difficulty filling job vacancies due to the absence of qualified individuals. Yet, there exists a skilled labour pool of postsecondary graduates with impairments in our own backyard who are disproportionately unemployed, underemployed and have lower earnings than their abled-bodied counterparts. Diversity in the workforce and inclusion of talented people from different backgrounds fuels innovation and growth.

Myths and Facts about People with Disabilities

After reading this last section of this chapter, you may ask yourself, is there really still a problem? Do people living with impairments/disability experience much discrimination, or exclusion from social life? The answer is unfortunately still yes. Below are some of the **myths** which people with impairments still face in our society. Once these myths are eliminated and attitudes are changed, and they are combined with current legislation and accessibility provisions, people with impairments will become fully integrated into our social life. First, let's turn to the discussion of myths and how they are defined in relation to disability:

> Myths are roadblocks that interfere with the ability of people with disabilities to have equality in employment. These roadblocks usually result from a lack of experience and interaction with persons with disabilities. This lack of familiarity has nourished negative attitudes concerning employment of persons with disabilities. (National Service Inclusion Project)

The National Service Inclusion Project lists some common myths and the facts that tell the real story:

MYTH	Hiring employees with disabilities increases workers' compensation insurance rates.
FACT	Insurance rates are based solely on the relative hazards of the operation and the organization's accident experience, not on whether workers have disabilities.
MYTH	Employees with disabilities have a higher absentee rate than employees without disabilities.
FACT	Studies by firms such as DuPont show that employees with disabilities are not absent any more than employees without disabilities.
MYTH	People with disabilities are inspirational, courageous and brave for being able to overcome their disability.
FACT	People with disabilities are simply carrying on normal activities of living when they work at their jobs, go grocery shopping, pay their bills or compete in athletic events.
MYTH	People with disabilities need to be protected from failing.
FACT	People with disabilities have a right to participate in the full range of human experiences including success and failure. Employers should have the same expectations of, and work requirements for, all employees.
MYTH	People with disabilities have problems getting to work.
FACT	People with disabilities are capable of supplying their own transportation by choosing to walk, use a car pool, drive, take public transportation or a cab. Their modes of transportation to work are as varied as those of other employees.
MYTH	People with disabilities are unable to meet performance standards, thus making them a bad employment risk.
FACT	In 1990, DuPont conducted a survey of 811 employees with disabilities and found that 90 percent rated average or better in job performance compared to 95 percent for employees without disabilities. A similar 1981 DuPont study, which involved 2,745 employees with disabilities, found that 92 percent of employees with disabilities rated average or better in job performance compared to 90 percent of employees without disabilities.
MYTH	People who are deaf make ideal employees in noisy work environments.
FACT	Loud noises of a certain vibratory nature can cause further harm to the auditory system. People who are deaf should be hired for all jobs that they have the skills and talents to perform. No person with a disability should be prejudged regarding employment opportunities.

MYTH   Considerable expense is necessary to accommodate workers with disabilities.

FACT   Most workers with disabilities require no special accommodations, and the cost for those who do is minimal or much lower than many employers believe. Studies by the Job Accommodation Network have shown that 15 percent of accommodations cost nothing, 51 percent cost between $1 and $500, 12 percent cost between $501 and $1,000, and 22 percent cost more than $1,000.

MYTH   Employees with disabilities are more likely to have accidents on the job than employees without disabilities.

FACT   In the 1990 DuPont study, the safety records of both groups were identical.

CONCLUSION

This chapter discusses several perspectives on disability which shed light on the experiences of the impaired in our society. The discussion showcases universal design, which embraces the diversities in our society by taking most people's needs into consideration, rather than the mythical few. Furthermore, our society is not static but fluid, thus legal changes currently occurring in Ontario are discussed, along with indepth information about the employment sector as it relates to people with impairments.

CRITICAL REVIEW QUESTIONS

1. Define and explain the terms impairment and disability and how they differ.
2. Explain the medical model of disability and the social perspective on disability.
3. What is universal design and what are its principles?

Box 9.8 Innov8

Before leaving the discussion of impairment and disability in our society one idea needs to be restated and repeated. We are all different, and our diversity is the beauty of our society. It enriches our lives and experiences. The next time you encounter someone who may be perhaps different from you, with different ideas, perspectives or abilities, use the experience as a learning opportunity to enhance your knowledge and enrich your life. See Rick Hansen in this YouTube video "Changing the conversation about disability.": <youtu.be/Hha9XkXa0qM>

4. Discuss the new Ontario legislation. What is it, and how does it affect the lives of people living in Ontario?
5. Discuss the employment challenges experienced by people living with impairments in our society.

RECOMMENDED READINGS

Ruth Butler, and Sophia Bowlby, "Bodies and Spaces: An Exploration of Disabled People's Experiences of Public Space," *Environment and Planning D-Society and Space*, 15, 4 (1997): 411–433.
S.D. Edwards, *Disability: Definitions, Value and Identity* (Abingdon, UK: Radcliffe Publishing, 2005).
R. Imrie and P. Hall, *Inclusive Design: Designing and Developing Accessible Environments* (New York: SponPress, 2001).
J. Swain, S.Y. French, C. Barnes and C. Thomas, *Disabling Barriers: Enabling Environments* (Thousand Oaks, CA: Sage Publications, 2004).
R.S. Upchurch and J.W. Seo, "Civic Responsibility and Market Positioning: Complying with the Americans with Disabilities Act," *Facilities*, 14, 5/6 (1996): 48–56.

KEY TERMS

disability: disadvantage or restriction of activity caused by a contemporary social organization which takes no or little account of people who have physical impairments and thus excludes them from the mainstream of social activity.
impairment: lacking all or part of a limb, or having a defective limb, organism or mechanism of the body.
medical model of disability: biological differences are the basis for explaining the inequalities between the able-bodied and the impaired.
myths: roadblocks that interfere with the ability of people with disabilities to have equality in employment.
social perspective on disability: disability is created by the interactions that people with impairments have with others in society and the attitudes which able-bodied people hold toward the impaired.
universal design: a way to design built structures and products that are accessible for all people to the greatest extent possible.

References

Access Ontario. 2018 <www.accessontario.com/AODA>.
ADA. 2002. "Accessibility Guidelines for Buildings Facilities." September <http://www.access-board.gov/adaag/html/adaag.htm>.
Barnes, C. 1991. *Disabled People in Britain and Discrimination*. London: Hurst Press.
Barnes, C., and G. Mercer. 2005. "Disability Work and Welfare: Challenging the Exclusion of Disabled People." *Work Employment and Society*, 19, 3: 527–545.
Butler, Ruth, and Sophia Bowlby. 1997. "Bodies and Spaces: An Exploration of Disabled People's

Experiences of Public Space." *Environment and Planning D-Society and Space*, 15, 4: 411–433.

Center for Universal Design. 2006. <http://www.design.ncsu.edu/cud/>.

Chouinard, Vera. 2001. "Legal Peripheries: Struggles over Disabled Canadians, Places in Law, Society and Space." *Canadian Geographer*, 45, 1: 187–192.

___. 2012. Personal communications.

Church, R.L., and J.R. Marston. 2003. "Measuring Accessibility for People with Disability." *Geographical Analysis*, 35, 1: 83–96.

D2L webpage. <www.D2L.ca>. D2L.

Delta Airlines webpage. <https://www.delta.com/us/en/accessible-travel-services/service-animals>.

Dyck, I. 2003. "Feminism and Health Geography: Twin Tracks or Divergent Agendas?" *Gender, Place and Culture*, 10, 4: 161–168.

Edwards, S.D. 2005. *Disability: Definitions, Value and Identity*. Abingdon, UK: Radcliffe Publishing.

Eichhorn, V., and D. Buhalis. 2007. "The Accessibility Requiring Market in Europe: Socially and Economically Important." *e-Review of Tourism Research*, 5, 2: 34–36.

Figaroa, H.T.B.J. 2002. "Our Building Codes, Archaic or Not?" *Chamber News and Views*, 13, (September/October) <www.arubachamber.com>.

French, S. (ed.). 1994. *On Equal Terms: Working with Disabled People*. Oxford: Butterworth-Heinemann.

Gleeson B. 1999. *Geographies of Disability*. London, UK: Routledge.

Imrie, R., and P. Hall. 2001. *Inclusive Design: Designing and Developing Accessible Environments*. New York: SponPress.

International Disability Rights Monitor (IDRM) Publications. Disability Rights Community. <http://www.ideanet.org/content.cfm?id=5B5C74>.

Iwarsson, S., and A. Stahl. 2003. "Accessibility, Usability and Universal Design — Positioning and Definition of Concepts Describing Person-Environment Relationships." *Disability and Rehabilitation*, 25, 2: 57–66.

Mace, R.L., G.J. Hardie and J.P. Place. 1996. "Accessible Environments: Toward Universal Design." The Center for Universal Design, North Carolina State University, Raleigh, NC.

Moss, P., and I. Dyck. 1996. "Inquiry into Environment and Body: Women, Work, and Chronic Illness." *Environment and Planning D-Society and Space*, 14, 6:. 737–753.

National Center on Universal Design for Learning. 2015. June <www.udlcenter.org>.

National Service Inclusion Project. *Myths and Facts about People with Disabilities*. 2018. <http://serviceandinclusion.org/index.php?page=myths>.

Oldman, C. 2002. "Later Life and the Social Model of Disability: A Comfortable Partnership?" *Aging and Society*, 22: 791–806.

Omansky Gordon, Beth, and Karen E. Rosenblum. 2001. "Bringing Disability into the Sociological Frame: A Comparison of Disability with Race, Sex, and Sexual Orientation Statuses." *Disability and Society*, 16, 1: 5–19.

Ontario Disability Employment Network. 2018. <https://odenetwork.com>.

Ontario Ministry of Community and Social Services. 2006. "About the Accessibility for Ontarians with Disabilities Act, 2005." <http://www.mcss.gov.on.ca/en/mcss/programs/accessibility/index.aspx>.

Rains, S. "2004. "Universal Design and the International Travel and Hospitality Industry." Paper presented at Designing for the 21st Century conference, Rio De Janeiro, Brazil. <www.

designfor21st.org/procedings/spocedings/precon_rains.html>.

Shakespeare, T. 2006. *Disability Rights and Wrongs*. London, UK: Routledge.

Swain, J., S.Y. French, C. Barnes and C. Thomas. 2004. *Disabling Barriers: Enabling Environments*. Thousand Oaks, CA: Sage Publications.

Titchkosky, T. 2003. *Disability, Self and Society*. Toronto: University of Toronto Press.

Trachtman, L.H., R.L. Mace, L.C. Young and R.J. Pace. 2000. "The Universal Design Home: Are We Ready for It?" *Physical and Occupational Therapy in Geriatrics*, 16, 3-4: 1–18.

Upchurch, R.S., and J.W. Seo. 1996. "Civic Responsibility and Market Positioning: Complying with the Americans with Disabilities Act." *Facilities*, 14, 5/6: 48–56.

PART THREE

Part Three examines how diversity is treated in the media and is perceived in literature. Continuing with the painting analogy, if Part One is the canvass and foundation and Part Two the details, the actual picture, then Part Three is the picture frame. It "frames" the discussion of the painting, how people view it—that is, how they perceive it, assess it, value it and treat it.

Chapter 10 examines the critical and creative approaches to voice as they relate to your own language, culture, identity and experience. It also discusses artistic and literary representations of voice in Canadian contexts and considers the role of voice, listening and silence within the context of social change.

Chapter 11 sketches the origins and development of Canadian literature. It looks at ways in which voice and power are related in Canadian literature and publishing. Current debates about appropriation of voice and diversity in Canadian literature are also examined. The readers will come to appreciate the diversity of experiences, voices and characterizations in Canadian literature that mirror its culture.

Chapter 12 describes the four major theories about media and the important issues confronting Canadian media today. The chapter makes the reader aware of the economic, political and technological forces that shape our media and how the various forms in which Canadian news is delivered to its readers, viewers and listeners impact reporting across the country.

10

DIVERSE VOICES

CRITICAL PERSPECTIVES
IN CANADIAN CONTEXTS

Tamara Wasylenky-Stern

> *A voice is a human gift; it should be cherished and used, to utter fully human speech as possible. Powerlessness and silence go together.* — Margaret Atwood

KEY OBJECTIVES

Analyze critical and creative approaches to voice as they relate to your own language, culture, identity and experience.

Discuss artistic and literary representations of voice in Canadian contexts.

Consider the role of voice, listening and silence within the context of social change.

Assess the value and efficacy of voice within a variety of circumstances.

This chapter is an introduction to the critical analysis of voice: its meanings, its uses, its development, its persistence and its value. What is voice? And what does it mean to use your voice? There are many different meanings and uses of the word "voice" in the humanities and social sciences, and we connect these definitions to

Box 10.1 Think About...

Examine and discuss the following definitions of voice.

1 a: sound produced by vertebrates by means of lungs, larynx or syrinx; sound so produced by human beings

   b: (1) musical sound produced by the vocal folds and resonated by the cavities of head and throat

   (2) the power or ability to produce musical tones

   (3) singer

   (4) one of the melodic parts in a vocal or instrumental composition

   (5) condition of the vocal organs with respect to production of musical tones

   (6) the use of the voice (as in singing or acting); studying voice

   c: expiration of air with the vocal cords drawn close so as to vibrate audibly (as in uttering vowels and consonant sounds as \v\ or \z\)

   d: the faculty of utterance: lost my voice

2: a sound resembling or suggesting vocal utterance

3: an instrument or medium of expression; the party became the voice of the workers

4 a: wish, choice, or opinion openly or formally expressed: the voice of the people

   b: right of expression; also, influential power

5: distinction of form or a system of inflections of a verb to indicate the relation of the subject of the verb to the action which the verb expresses, active and passive voices

6: with one voice; without dissent: unanimously

Match the examples below of the use of the word "voice" with the definitions above. Discuss the assumptions that arise from its use in each sentence.

He has a deep voice.

"Can we speak privately?" she said in a low voice.

A voice on the radio

We heard voices coming from the next room.

She does the voices for several cartoon characters.

I shouted so much that I lost my voice.

She has a terrific voice.

Town meetings give people a voice in local politics.

Listen to the voice of the people.

Please vote and make your voices heard!

Source: Definition adapted from the Merriam Webster Online Dictionary.

their theoretical bases. This chapter examines voice as a concept which, though it has been investigated in many disciplines, continues to puzzle and fascinate us. Primarily examined through the fields of ethnomusicology, literary criticism and cultural anthropology, voice is now also considered in fields such as linguistic anthropology, media studies and sociology.[1] This introduction begins with a discussion of the evolution and anatomy of the physical voice and examines it as sound. It moves on to consider voice in literature, and then as project, as participation and as performance. It addresses questions about the nature and elements of voice, the degree to which our voices are our own and the ways they can be used to affect change. Lastly, this chapter celebrates the diversity of voices throughout Canada and connects issues of voice to our stunning cultural landscape.

HUMAN VOCAL ANATOMY: VOICE AS SOUND

Humans have a long tradition of appreciation for the aesthetics of the voice and for its function as a vehicle for the transmission of meaning.[2] As culture initially evolved and was passed on orally, free from written texts, voice was at the centre of cultural transmission. In fact, even when writing systems were developed, it was not to express the creative aspects of culture, but to log exchanges of goods, land purchases and taxes.[3] Because the information, knowledge and memories were passed on through folk tale, ballad, chant and song, they were viewed as embodied within the speaker or singer and could not be passed on without the person. This may seem like a simple concept, but its implications are far-reaching, especially in a text-based society such as ours. Throughout history, many cultures have recorded large bodies of literature written primarily in poetic form; for example, in Asia, the *Vedas*, a collection of religious texts including myths, poems, hymns and prayers is dated between 1500 and 1000 BCE, and in Greece, the epic poems *The Iliad* and *The Odyssey* are dated around 750 BCE. It is important to remember, however, that these texts were first passed on orally to local audiences, often by travelling bards responsible for their accurate and aesthetically pleasing performance. Additionally, we do not have to look very far to find cultures still steeped in oral tradition throughout Canada; many Indigenous cultures rely heavily on the oral transmission of history, knowledge and worldview. This is, in part, why the impact of the residential school system instituted across the country has been so devastating to Indigenous Peoples. Sharing knowledge from generation to generation through language and voice is central to culture and is connected to our cumulative history.

Voice can therefore be considered as a sound that we produce in order to create beauty or to express meaning. But what are the necessary anatomical structures used to

Box 10.2 Diversity in Action

Indigenous Languages in Canada

According to Statistics Canada, there are currently over sixty Indigenous languages and at least twelve language families across Canada. The largest language family is Algonquian, which includes Cree, Ojibway, Innu-Montagnais and Oji-Cree. The most frequently reported spoken languages are Inuit and Athapaskan. First Nations languages throughout Canada are extremely diverse in both sound and structure; the most linguistically diverse area is British Columbia. Due to aggressive assimilation policies of the Canadian government, the most devastating of which was the residential school system, many Indigenous languages are endangered. It has been projected that of the many Indigenous languages spoken in Canada, only three, Cree, Ojibway and Inuktitut, have the possibility of surviving long term. Despite this grim projection, the number of Indigenous language classes at all levels of education is on the rise, and there is a renewed effort to ensure their survival. For example, the University of British Columbia has introduced a bachelor of arts program in First Nations and endangered languages. Furthermore, Indigenous communities are actively using any available resources to encourage language learning. For example, in Iqualuit, Nunavut, a new app, entitled Uqausiit Pinnguarutiit has been created to teach children simple words in three varieties of the Inuktitut language. The app, named Playing with Words, was developed just after 300 early reading books were also developed in the language. Additionally, at the governmental level, there is renewed interest in passing legislation to recognize Indigenous languages as a constitutional right. Efforts such as these to encourage the learning of Indigenous languages and to integrate them into daily life are tantamount to their survival.

Sources: Statistics Canada, "Aboriginal Languages in Canada," Dec. 22, 2015; James S. Frideres, *First Nations in the Twenty-First Century* (Don Mills, ON: Oxford University Press, 2011: 96); CBC *News Online*, "Nunavut Language App Brings Inuit Language to Life for Pre-Schoolers," March 9, 2017; Alex Ballingall, "Ottawa Planning to Recognize Indigenous Language Rights," *Star*, June 1, 2018.

produce this voice and when did we develop them? The evolution of our vocal anatomy is tightly bound to the development of language and other cognitive processes; in fact, in this area, definitions of voice, speech and language often overlap. In his *Dramatic Theories of Voice*, Andrew Kimbrough argues that studying our evolutionary history could give us new insight into theories of voice.[4] When examining the evolution of the physical voice, scholars often emphasize the commencement of the impulse to speak or sing.[5] Ultimately, research in this area is highly speculative, as there are no audio

Box 10.3 *Innov8*

The Virtual Linguistics Campus

For an indepth look at vocal anatomy and speech production, watch the following YouTube videos on speech anatomy and phonation: <youtube.com/watch?v=-m-gudHhLxc> and <youtube.com/watch?v=f62dqc-L36o>. These videos were created for the Virtual Linguistics Campus by Professor Handke's Linguistic Engineering Team from Marburg University, Germany. The Virtual Linguistics Campus is the world's largest online learning platform for the study of linguistics. Visit their YouTube channel at <youtube.com/user/LinguisticsMarburg/> to find a variety of interesting and informative resources.

recordings of prehistorical voices; additionally, the parts of the human body used to produce voice are made of soft tissue, muscles and cartilage and thus have decayed over time. We are therefore reliant, in large part, on an inconsistent fossil record.

The production and manipulation of vocal sound occurs in three stages: respiration, **phonation** and articulation. Respiration includes the process of inhalation and exhalation. Air is inhaled and travels down through the **larynx** and along the trachea to the lungs. The larynx, situated in the throat, controls the air flow in and out of the lungs, and it is covered by the epiglottis to allow swallowing to occur. In the reverse, breath is exhaled through the lungs, up the trachea and through the larynx. There, it comes in contact with the vocal folds, and this is when sound is created. The arytenoid cartilages aid in the opening and closing of the vocal folds. The vibration of the vocal folds produces sound, which then travels through the vocal tract. Reinforcement, enrichment and modification of the sounds occurs through a process called resonance, and the sound resonates through the pharynx and the oral and nasal cavities. Finally, the sound is manipulated by articulators, both passive and active, such as the teeth and the tongue.[6] Generally, humans produce sound for both speech and song on the exhalation; however, sound can also be produced on the inhalation as in the case of throat singing or extended vocal technique (see Box 10.5).

Discussion of the evolution of this vocal anatomy usually centres around three topics: the lowered larynx characteristic of humans; bipedalism and its connection to respiration; and social and cognitive developments. According to paleo-anthropologists, these advances began to occur after the hominid lineage split from that of the chimpanzee around 7 million years ago. All parts of the human vocal tract were **exapted**; that is to say, they originally served functions other than speech, such as eating and breathing. The larynx has three key functions:

1. to protect the lungs from food and other foreign matter by closing the epiglottis;
2. to retain the inhaled air to provide back pressure for activities such as lifting
   heavy objects; and
3. to produce vocal tone.

The human possession of a lowered larynx allows us to produce sounds other primates cannot. In other primates, such as the chimpanzee, the larynx is located up close to the back of the mouth, where the oral and nasal passages join. In contrast, the lowered larynx in humans allows for a hollow space, the pharynx, up between the larynx and the back of the mouth. This creates an upside down "L" shape in the human vocal tract which can be adjusted to allow for changes in resonance: a "shape shiftable chamber" through which the air passes and carries the sound.[7] It has been argued that the reason for the evolution of the lowered larynx in humans was to produce better vowels and more effective communication. It does also bring greater risk of choking, but evolutionary pressure to communicate outweighed this risk. Overall, the shape of the vocal tract allows humans to produce a unique range of vocal sounds.

The further development of habitual bipedalism, dated between 4 and 2 million years ago, around the time of the Australopithecines, provided the evolutionary opportunity for changes in respiration necessary for the production of vocal sounds. The bipedal gait freed the rhythm of breathing from that of movement: breathing and walking or running could occur on two different rhythmic planes. This freed up the thorax for greater depth and flexibility of breath and left the hands free, opening up the potential for gesture. Quadrupedal animals coordinate breathing with walk-ing and running, but bipeds were freed to breath as humans currently do, with the possibility of 10 percent inhalation and 90 percent exhalation. This gradually evolved into finer control of breathing, which James Hurford describes as "a relaxation of constraints paving the way for previously inaccessible evolutionary developments."[8] The gradual movement to habitual bipedalism also dovetailed with advances in the cognitive abilities of *Homo erectus* and *Homo habilis*, who, through their creation of tools, demonstrated the advanced cognitive abilities necessary for the development of language. It appears, then, that by the time of the *Homo sapiens*, the human vocal tract and fine control over it was quite similar to modern humans, with the beginnings of these developments rooted in *Homo erectus*.[9]

Just as important as the question of *when* humans developed this vocal anatomy is the *why*. Why would we speak or sing? In their book, *A History of Singing*, John Potter and Neil Sorrell provide us with four reasons for this impulse:

Box 10.4 Innov8

There is a great diversity of expression across cultures in Canada through music and song. *Reclaimed*, a weekly series hosted by Jarrett Martineau on CBC Radio explores the ways in which Indigenous artists in Canada are redefining their culture through contemporary music. The program is "equal parts celebration, resistance and reclamation" and aims to provide space for Indigenous musicians to create contemporary music while respecting music of previous generations. Listen to the program at <cbcmusic.ca/posts/19690/listen-to-every-episode-of-reclaimed-on-cbc-music> or follow the program on Twitter at @CBCReclaimed.

1. to support society and community and to maintain bonds of trust;
2. to cooperate in tasks necessary for survival;
3. to establish group identity; and
4. to express emotion, relieve stress and create empathy.

Humans have been singing songs to express our emotions for centuries, but even before the evolution of song, calls and signals were used to carry sound over large spaces more effectively than speech. In belief systems based on divine creation of life, ancient chants, mantras and songs served to connect humans to deities, and music was believed to be a divine gift. Both Curt Sachs and Stephen Mithen argue the case for song without words evolving in human culture before language. Sachs, in his well-known1943 book, *The Rise of Music in the Ancient World: East and West*, challenges the argument that music descended from spoken language. For him, the problem is that we cannot uncover the origins of singing through archeology. Therefore, it is less controversial to suggest that music began with singing. Mithen, in *Singing Neanderthals: The Origins of Music, Language, Mind and Body,* states that "without music, the prehistoric past is just too quiet to be believed."[10] He argues that in prehistoric times there was a great deal of movement, and singing is often connected to movement. Therefore, it could be argued that song likely developed earlier than speech. Ultimately, for our investigative purposes, it is not as essential to know which came first, speech or song; both require voice.

APPROACHES TO VOCAL TRAINING

There are many different approaches to the training and manipulation of the voice. The type, style and emphasis of the training provides us with insights on how the voiced is viewed. Most often, when we imagine vocal training, we imagine endlessly singing scales in preparation for a musical performance. Certainly, there is a long history of vocal training for both aesthetic purposes and for expressing meaning. Potter and Sorrell, in their book *A History of Singing*, describe many approaches to the training of voice in cross-cultural musical contexts. For the training of the voice outside of musical contexts, we can look at the disciplines of speech communication and theatre studies.

One important example of an approach to vocal training in speech communication is Lyle V. Mayer's *Fundamentals of Voice and Articulation*. In this book, originally published in 1953 and currently in its fifteenth edition, Mayer takes a technical approach to the voice as an isolated tool for ESL students, business people or teachers. Mayer's emphasis is placed, with the exception of breath, on the voice itself and on the articulation of sounds. Mayer highlights the value of a "good" voice and communicates to his readers the role of voice in achieving a kind of external power; that is to say, in communicating more effectively to get what you want. In contrast, a well-celebrated approach to voice in theatre studies is that of Arthur Lessac, who takes an overall mind/body approach to vocal training for actors. In his book *The Use and Training of the Human Voice: A Bio-Dynamic Approach to Vocal Life*, Lessac focuses on the whole body, which he refers to as a "body ecology." This approach involves the exploration of human skills and talents, be they physical, emotional, artistic, intellectual or intuitive, and provides a "problem solving resource," the function of which, Lessac argues, goes beyond the theatre and extends into other aspects of life.[11] Lessac focuses on movement and heightened awareness of the whole body and relies heavily on sensation rather than sound to assess vocal quality. Another oft-cited approach to vocal training is Patsy Rodenberg's *The Right to Speak*. Rodenberg's approach is used within theatre studies but has a much broader application. Rodenberg focuses on the development of a "natural voice" in a non-judgemental fashion. She emphasizes the impact feelings and experiences have in allowing the voice to come forward. This is a psychological perspective that ties in the discovery of emotional and physical habits with the development and training of the voice.

Lastly, an interesting approach to vocal training can be found in the programs of Canada's National Voice Intensive. These vocal training courses began in the early 1980s at Simon Fraser University and are now centred in the Toronto area. Originally designed for actors and performing arts teachers, their approach to vocal training combines many of the elements present in Lessac and Rodenberg; emphasis is placed on movement, with an equal focus on body, voice, image and text. The focus of the programs is to release existing habitual patterns, free the natural voice and provide students with a whole-body experience which empowers them to connect the sensation of voice to the power of the imagination.[12] These are only four examples of a wide range of vocal training approaches and techniques. The variety of approaches and the technical exercises they are associated with reflect the diversity of perspectives on the

---

Box 10.5 Think About...

Basic Vocal Training Exercises

Try these simple exercises while lying down on a mat or the floor in a comfortable position.

Begin by scanning the body and noticing areas where there is more tension and areas where there is more space.

Beginning at the feet, consciously tighten the muscles and then release. Continue this process through the body all the way up to the head.

Raise the arms up overhead and come into a full body stretch. Begin to yawn and sigh deeply on the exhale. Do this several times. Place your hands on your belly and allow it to rise and fall with breath.

At the end of the yawn, begin to relax the lips and introduce a hum. Repeat this five times. Relax the muscles of the face and allow the hum to create vibration through the cheeks and nose. Focus on this sensation.

Say the following words: moon, man, many, no, no one, no one knew me. Use your hum to exaggerate the m and n sounds.

Repeat the following sequence blending your hum with the word for each number. Breathe deeply into the belly before each hum.

HummmmOne

HummmOneTwo

HummmOneTwoThree

HummOneTwoThreeFour

HummmOneTwoThreeFourFive.

Relax the lips together. On the exhale, allow the lips to loosely trill or roll, as if creating the sound of a noisy boat on the water. Vary the volume, length and pitch of the sound, all the while keeping the lips relaxed.

---

relationship of the voice to the rest of the body and its connection to other aspects of life.

The approaches to training the voice discussed above provide us with examples of different assumptions about the nature of voice and its role within the body. Additionally, they reveal that the physical voice is often associated with the person; that is to say, our voice is often the primary form of contact we have with others. We are judged by our voices, and we make judgements about others based on theirs. In their discussion of vocal technique, both Mayer and Rodenberg describe circumstances in which individuals are judged for the tone, timbre, strength, volume, pitch and articulation (accents) of their voices. It follows that our physical voice is connected to our identity and becomes a vehicle through which we can satisfy our need to express ourselves. The voice as sound is part of a more personal voice: one that is connected

> **Box 10.6 Think About...**
>
> **How would you describe your own voice?**
> Choose five words that describe your voice from the following list. What positive or negative connotations are associated with the words you have chosen? Can you think of any other words often used to describe voice?
>
> | | | | |
> |---|---|---|---|
> | appealing | quiet | singsong | small |
> | breathy | strident | rough | throaty |
> | croaky | strangled | pretentious | disembodied |
> | shrill | raucous | smoky | tight |
> | thin | thick | flat | grating |
> | matter-of-fact | tremulous | nasal | guttural |
> | monotonous | wheezy | gruff | soft |
> | penetrating | gravelly | dead | wobbly |
> | high-pitched | hoarse | husky | |

to our identity, language and culture. We begin to feel it move, to hear it move, outside of the body, to connect with others. It follows, then, that any kind of work on the voice becomes work on the whole person.

VOICE AS SELF-EXPRESSION

Our investigation of voice now moves beyond the physical voice as sound to voice as an expression of our personal identity. This expression can come through the use of the physical voice, as in speech, or it can come through creative endeavours, such as artistic or literary works. This is the voice we try to find: an autonomous voice that is deeply connected to our inner truth. We express it to free ourselves from whatever binds us and to achieve a kind of catharsis. This static voice is deep inside us and we can spend our whole lives trying to uncover it.

The roots of this view of the voice can be found in many of the values of the Euro-Western romantic period, and it is often associated with the poetry of that period.[13] **Romanticism** itself was an eighteenth-century literary and artistic movement which spread throughout Europe. It embraced passion, individuality and new forms of expression. It demanded freedom for human beings to realize their emotional and cultural potential, and it celebrated the human soul and its mystical nature that connected directly with the divine. This movement emphasized inspiration and creative genius. Examples of artistic and literary works from this period include John Keats' "Ode to a Grecian Urn" (1820), Samuel Taylor Coleridge's "The Rime of the Ancient

Mariner" (1834) and the music of Chopin. What is important for us here is not the detail of the movement, but its emphasis on personal expression. Poetry has a long tradition of connecting us with divinity, whether an external divine or one within ourselves, our own truth. A "romantic understanding" is the idea that a poem is an

---

Box 10.7 Diversity in Action

Rita Joe Mi'kmaw Poet

Rita Joe (1932–2007) was a Mi'kmaw author from Whycocomagh, Cape Breton Island, Nova Scotia. When she was twelve, she entered the Shubenacadie Indian Residential School, where she was forbidden to speak the Mi'kmaw language. She relearned the language later in life through other Mi'kmaw speakers. Rita Joe's work speaks about the impact of residential schools and the complexity of Indigenous identities.

Rita Joe's most well-known poem, "I Lost My Talk," was first published in *Song of Eskasoni: More Poems of Rita Joe* (1988). Since then, it has inspired many artistic and literary works, and it has appeared in many publications, including the final report of the Truth and Reconciliation Commission of Canada (2015). In the poem, Joe emphasizes the impact of Mi'kmaw language loss on her cultural identity and calls attention to the effect of the English language on her understanding of the world. Joe concludes by offering her hand in reconciliation, opening the door to peace, harmony and justice. It is for this work and others that Rita Joe earned herself the title of "Gentle Warrior." The poem, "I Lost My Talk," can be found on the *Poetry in Voice* website at <poetryinvoice.com/poems/i-lost-my-talk>.

Rita Joe's poem was also the inspiration for the commissioning of the short film *I Lost My Talk* by the National Arts Centre in Ottawa . The film, which premiered on January 14, 2016, features a musical score composed by John Estacio and ten First Nations dancers performing a choreography by Santee Smith Tekaronhiáhkhwa, artistic director of Kaha:wi Dance Theatre. For further information on the film, visit the NAC website at <nac-cna.ca/en/lifereflected/ilostmytalk> or view an excerpt on the *Global News* website: <globalnews.ca/video/2552680/extra-i-lost-my-talk>.

Source: Originally published in *Song of Eskasoni: More Poems of Rita Joe* (Ragweed Press, 1988). This poem and others by Rita Joe can also be found in the *Anthology of Canadian Native Literature in English,* 4th edition, edited by Daniel David Moses, Terry Goldie and Armand Garnet Ruffo (Don Mills, ON: Oxford University Press, 2013).

Box 10.8 Think About…

Structuralism and the Sign

Structuralism is a set of theories brought to the forefront by Ferdinand de Saussure (1857–1913), a Swiss linguist who set out to describe language as a system. In particular, Saussure is well-known for defining social practices as systems of signs: language and communication, food and eating, clothes and clothing, bodies and gestures. Each sign is a representation of an object which Saussure described as a signified and a signifier. The relationship between the signified and the signifier (for example, the concept of a tree and the word tree) is completely arbitrary. Language, Saussure argued, is an arbitrary system of signs which does not label the world but instead constructs it. Additionally, it is not the essence of the object that determines its meaning but its difference from other things within the structure; for example, a chair is not called a chair because of its essential nature, but simply because it is not a tree. The world is therefore not something we discover, but instead something that we produce through language; this is why, in learning a new language, we also learn a new way of seeing and understanding the world.

---

expression of passion or profound genius working its way into form. As mentioned previously, many cultures have long traditions of creative expression through poetry both in oral and written form. The poems of Rita Joe, a Mi'kmaw author from Nova Scotia, are a great example of the expression of personal voice to establish identity and promote healing.

As Rita Joe expresses so eloquently in her poem "I Lost My Talk," it is through language that we most often express voice, and the two are inextricably intertwined. In her book, *Lost in Translation*, Eva Hoffman explains the complex relationship between language, identity and voice. Using the theories of Ferdinand de Saussure, the Swiss linguist (1857–1913) most famous for his work on **structuralism**, Hoffman discusses her experiences translating words from her first language, Polish, into her second language, English. She uses Saussure's concept of the sign to explain that as she cannot translate the nuance of word and experience from one language to another, she struggles to express her voice. Hoffman explains that "the signifier has become separated from the signified" and that this fracture leads to a fracture of voice. She states, "we want to be at home in our tongue. We want to be able to give voice accurately and fully to ourselves and our sense of the world."[14] Hoffman draws the conclusion that this difficulty with expression creates an unbearable inner conflict: an internal violence that is difficult to subdue. Works by authors such as Eva Hoffman and Rita

Box 10.9 Innov8

Do I Sound Gay? is an American documentary film directed by David Thorpe. In the film, Thorpe examines the history, stereotypes and cultural assumptions surrounding the "gay voice." The documentary chronicles Thorpe's experiences with speech therapists and vocal coaches. In the end, Thorpe concludes that he changed his voice himself to comply with social norms at the age of 17. This documentary investigates close connections between voice and the social construction of identity.

Joe reflect that if language is the primary way that we make sense of the world, and the primary way that we make meaning, inability to use our own language to express ourselves amounts to a systematic denial of voice.

Closely linked to Hoffman's discussion of her experiences with multiple languages are the linguistic theories of Edward Sapir (1884–1939) and Benjamin Lee Whorf (1897–1841) regarding linguistic relativity and linguistic determinism. These theories suggest that languages are deeply connected to culture and that they affect how we perceive, classify and describe the world.[15] It is, therefore, important to consider the question of how adequately we can express voice through language. Is it possible for language to adequately represent our thoughts and feelings? Additionally, what happens if the language we use to express ourselves is not our own, but instead is the language of another culture? How then, do we express voice? If language is the primary way in which humans make meaning, whose meanings are we making? These questions become even more relevant as we begin to discuss voice and its relationship to power.

"The 'grain' is the body in the voice as it sings, the hand as it writes, the limb as it performs." — Roland Barthes, "The Grain of the Voice," in Stephen Heath (ed.), Image Music Text (London: Fontana Press, 1977): 188.

The theories discussed above lead us to a different perspective: one that views voice as a kind of project constructed through our social and cultural experiences. This postmodern perspective challenges the romantic view of voice discussed above and argues that voice is not a "fixed thing that we possess," but is instead "an emotionally charged description of ourselves. Rather than being a timeless essence, what it is to be a person is said to be plastic and changeable within the bounds of certain social and cultural spheres."[16] In this view, voice is not completely autonomous, but is affected by external structures, policies, practices and rules. The ways that we express voice are only partly reflected by our own power and capacity as a person and are otherwise determined by linguistic, societal and cultural impositions. The question that arises here is this: how much of our voice is our own? In his well-known essay "Problems of Dostoevsky's Poetics," Mikhail Bakhtin explains this concern within the context of a literary work:

> All that matters is the choice, the resolution of the question, "Who am I?" and "With whom am I?" To find one's own voice and to orient it among other voices, to combine it with some and to oppose it to others, to separate one's voice from another voice with which it has inseparably merged — these are the tasks that the heroes solve in the novel.[17]

The ideas brought forward by Bakhtin can be extended to our own circumstance as we attempt to construct our own voice in relation to the voices of others. How we do this and why it matters to us how much of our voice is our own are addressed in the sections to come.

VOICE IN LITERARY PERSPECTIVE

As reflected in Bakhtin's well-known quote above, literary considerations of voice examine the complex relationship between characters and authors and how their voices are reflected in texts. In literary theory, two distinct areas of voice are most commonly discussed: narrative voice and authorial voice. Narrative voice or narrative mode consists of narrative point of view (who is telling the story) and narrative voice. Narrative point of view refers to the person's position in relation to the story being told: first, second or third person. Narrative voice refers to how the story is conveyed. This could include information such as how reliable the narrator is or the style of the actual text, such as stream of consciousness or epistolary. Narrative voice and authorial voice concern us most in fictional works, but we can extrapolate the theories used to discuss them to other genres as well.

The other area of voice of most concern is authorial voice; this is important because it speaks to the interpretation of the work and raises questions about the relationship between written texts, power and voice. Literary theorists have asked some very important questions around how much authority authors have and where that authority comes from. For example, Roland Barthes, in his famous essay "The Death of the Author," argues that "writing is the destruction of every voice."[18] Barthes argues that we tend to seek the explanation of a written work in the person who produces it. The assumption, then, is that if we understand the author, we will understand the work.

Barthes argues that once words are written, they take on a momentum of their own; the author slips away and their identity is lost. Further, Barthes suggests that our focus on the author as an autonomous individual is a way of concealing the economic system's powerful way of producing and reproducing itself. Lastly, he states that the production of literature represents not only a single personality but also a social world. Another important work came in the form of a speech by Michel Foucault at the College de France in 1969. In this speech, Foucault asked the very important question: "What is an author?" He questioned the authority of the author, and he argued that authorship was an ideological construct.[19] The discussions of both Barthes and Foucault suggest that we cannot appeal to the authority of the author when interpreting a text. Instead, the text takes on a life of its own and all that is left is the reader's interpretation to determine its meaning.

Is it important to completely understand every poem, novel, painting or film? Or is it enough that the author's voice has been expressed?

Arguments such as those articulated by Barthes and Foucault are complicated, however, by the human need for self-expression and the use of creative works to meet this need. It can also be argued that an author articulates an identity through their work for the purpose of achieving a kind of freedom. Here we make a return to the romantic definition of voice as a form of self-expression. From this perspective, we express ourselves not to deny anyone freedom but to find our own. Through authorship, we function as an authority to remind everyone that we are not instruments of society but autonomous, free people. This view of the author is understood as a source of newfound freedom for one who has characteristically not been free. This discussion reveals one of the fundamental splits around the politics of voice and identity: the first, that authorship affirms individuality and autonomy of identity; and the second, that authorship is a reflection of identities formed through complex webs of social practices that are constantly changing.

This discussion around the author and authorial voice is important because it speaks to larger issues such as identity, power and appropriation. It is necessary to consider in whose voice the text is written and to critically examine the ideologies that inform that voice. These questions become particularly important when the story is written by someone who did not experience it firsthand. On the one hand, it is admirable to wish to tell another's story so that it is heard. On the other hand, the story can never approximate the perspective of the person who experienced it. Those who are oppressed

> ## Box 10.10 Think About…
>
> **Discourse**
>
> Used specifically,
>
> 1) the thoughts, statements or dialogue of individuals, especially of characters in literary work;
> 2) the words in, or text, of a narrative as opposed to its story line; or
> 3) a "strand" within a given narrative that promotes a certain point or value system.
>
> More generally, discourse refers to the terms, methods and conventions employed in discussing a subject or area of knowledge or transacting a certain kind of business. Human knowledge is collected and structured in discourses; theology, medicine and law are defined by their discourses, as are politics, sexuality and literary criticism.
>
> Source: This definition comes from The Bedford Glossary of Critical and Literary Terms (2009: 116–117).

may not choose to have their stories told in the way they are told. Alternatively, a person may choose not to share their story at all, and instead stay silent. This leaves the story unwritten and therefore undefined. Because we do not know the story, we may speculate, but that speculation is never validated and therefore does not interfere with the individual's meaning. Additionally, the assumption that a person from one culture, ethnicity or social position may be more capable of telling stories supports an ideology based on inequity and superiority.

VOICE, DISCOURSE AND POWER

This set of assumptions around the capability of some individuals to better tell stories than others can be discussed further through the concept of discourse. There are several definitions of discourse; these are outlined in Box 10.10.

The concept of discourse provides us with a frame through which to explore issues around voice, identity, power and appropriation. Additionally, as each discourse has its own vocabulary, concepts and rules, the ways in which knowledge is structured in society can be revealed through its examination. Society is made up of discourse communities, some of which are more influential than others, and one of which usually serves the dominant ideology. As knowledge of certain types of discourse constitutes power, interaction of these discourse communities creates complex relationships in which there are often power differentials. It is in these circumstances that the voices of some individuals or groups may not be heard.

Just as we are often not aware of our own culture because we are in it, we are often not aware of our own participation in discourse communities. In their article, "Exploring Dominant Discourses: Creating Spaces to Find Voice and Cultural Identity," Boh Young Lee, Melissa Scott Kozak, Carla Nancoo, Hao-Min Chen, Katie Middendorf and Jerry Gale explain that dominant discourse contains ideological beliefs which shape our individual consciousness, experiences and behaviours as accepted ways of being. Those from privileged groups tend to accept messages in dominant discourses without awareness. People with social power tend to forget that they are privileged; they take it for granted and often pretend not to have power. Those of marginalized groups tend to internalize oppression, undermining their self-esteem and sense of empowerment but also developing personal and psychological characteristics that are pleasing to people with power. Lee et al. argue that cultural identity is self-perception of one's own position in different aspects of life, including ethnicity, gender, social class or sexual orientation. Therefore, they argue, "part of the journey of developing a cultural identity is recognizing the dominant discourse and discovering our inner voice."[20] Furthermore, identity is negotiated and constructed through dialogue, relationships with others and individuals' interactions with the external environment. Identity formation, then, and the expression of voice, may involve a process of negotiation and possible challenges to dominant discourses. This may mean examining our own truths as they intersect with those of the communities around us, looking for places where they do not mesh and challenging those places in order to find our own voices. One example of this kind of challenge comes to us through the music of Tanya Tagaq (see Box 10.11).

Another example of a challenge to dominant discourse is evident in the essay "Columbus and the Making of Historical Myth," in which Barbara Ransby examines the story of Christopher Columbus: a story she describes as "a myth which celebrates imperial conquest, male supremacy and the triumph of military might as necessary components of progress and civilization."[21] Ransby analyzes the dominant discourse around the story of Christopher Columbus through the examination of thirty social studies textbooks published between 1966 and 1990 in the United States. Ransby's analysis reveals that few textbooks mention the devastating impact of Columbus's exploration on the Indigenous Peoples already living on the Caribbean islands and instead celebrate it as the achievement of a great American hero. Furthermore, Ransby describes the exploration of the New World by Christopher Columbus as one version of a story which is used to justify the actions of white elites in the name of "progress" and to forward an ideology of white supremacy. Through her analysis, Ransby questions the objectivity of historical accounts, arguing instead that "history is ultimately written by the victors, and by those with the power and resources to publish, distribute

Box 10.11 Diversity in Action

Tanya Tagaq — Challenging Assumptions about the Aesthetics of Voice

Tanya Tagaq is an Inuit throat singer from Nunavut who has won many awards for her work, including the Polaris Music Prize in 2014 for her album *Animism* and several Juno awards (2015, 2017). Tagaq has taken the traditional art of Inuit throat singing, usually done in pairs, and transformed it into an original solo form. In this form of singing, the singer, using the lips, tongue, jaw, velum and larynx, creates more than one note at once through resonance and thus creates harmony. Additionally, sounds may be made on inhalation as well as exhalation.

Many of the techniques used in throat singing have been referred to as extended vocal technique and connected to artists such Meredith Monk, Diamanda Galas or Canadians such as Paul Dutton and Vahram Sargsyan. It is important to note, however, that throat singing techniques from Inuit, Tuvan or other cultures are deeply rooted in cultural traditions that have been alive for centuries. Tagaq's work is important in that it challenges our assumptions around the aesthetic quality of the "ideal" voice and encourages us to open our minds to the possibilities of the human vocal apparatus.<http://tanyatagaq. com/> or follow her on Twitter </twitter.com/tagaq>. Watch and listen to Tanya Tagaq's performance on TEDxMet: <youtube.com/watch?v=dumvYzfuT0w> or take in a performance by the Tuvan band Alash on TEDxMet: <youtube.com/ watch?v=V76psBrEypg>.

and thus validate the version of history which best serves the interest of the status quo."[22] Ransby's discussion of the history of Christopher Columbus reveals a societal circumstance in which certain individuals or groups control the stories that are told. The telling of certain stories at the exclusion of others connects to real power. If we are excluded, then our voice is excluded. We cannot therefore participate in the dominant discourse. As Mohan Dutta argues, it is important to ask, "whose agendas are represented in dominant discursive spaces? Whose voices are privileged within such spaces, and whose voices are erased from these spaces?"[23]

One important example of the exclusion of voices from dominant discursive spaces exists in the discourse surrounding the residential school system instituted in Canada during the 1880s. Through this system, which was part of an aggressive assimilation policy, many Indigenous children were forcibly removed from their homes and relocated to residential schools, where they were met with devastating abuse. Continued demands for recognition of the pain and suffering of Indigenous Peoples led to the establishment of the Royal Commission on Aboriginal Peoples (1996), the administration of a $1.9 billion compensation package in 2007 and more recently, the establishment of the Truth and Reconciliation Commission (TRC) in 2008. The goals of the commission, which published its final report in June 2015, were to "document and promote the extent and impact of residential school experiences; provide a safe setting for former students to share their stories; and produce a report to the federal government on the legacy of the residential school system."[24] Through the work of the commission, and the testimony of over 6000 people, the effect of the residential school system on Indigenous Peoples in Canada entered public discourse and thus formed a challenge to previous historical documents. In June 2015, the commission released a report with ninety-four recommendations regarding child welfare, health, justice, language, culture and education. Central to these recommendations is the understanding of the importance of sharing stories as providing a voice to Indigenous Peoples. As Nick Couldry argues, voice is "making an account of oneself" based on one's own truth.[25] If we do not feel that we have space to tell our story, then not only our individual truth, but also the truth of the community is lost and a kind of erasure occurs. The report of the TRC validates the experiences of Indigenous Peoples in Canada and finally gives voice to all those who suffered. In this case, therefore, voice becomes a kind of participation, not just of the personal, but of the political.

From here, we begin to consider voice and its relationship to social change. How can we create space for those voices excluded from dominant discursive spaces to participate? Any discussion of voice and social change involves the introduction of voice as a kind of dialogic process. If we are in dialogue, we must not only have voice, but we must also create space for voice. This space is created through silence and listening. Considering voice as part of a larger dialogic process means that it must be negotiated. Voice as represented in the quote from Bakhtin's "Problems of Dostoevsky's Poetics" is a kind of dialogue involving appropriation and choice. From this perspective, the construction of voice involves taking previous voices, integrating them into our own and choosing which voices we wish to bring forward. This dialogic process is central to the formation of identity, to any discussion of voice and to any form of individual or social change. The concept of dialogue has strong roots in literary and critical theory around voice; dialogue is seen as the prerequisite for an authentic relationship, offering space for the construction of meaning through authenticity. Through dialogue we work together to construct meaning. Authentic relationships are co-created through dialogic interactions, and space for mutual learning opens up. Central to any dialogue is a commitment to listening, and to opening up space for that listening through silence. Buber argues that human beings become persons through dialogue; listening, or "turning toward the other," is central, as an attentive listener is an invitation to speak. What constitutes dialogue and what determines the rules for dialogic engagement are determined by dominant social and cultural institutions around the globe.[26] It is to two of the processes that constitute dialogue, silence and listening, that our discussion now turns.

VOICE IN DIALOGUE: SILENCE AND LISTENING

In order to create space for voice, there must be periods of silence. According to Stuart Sim, one way to view silence is as the absence of noise. It is a physical condition, which, these days, is harder and harder to come by. Sim argues that noise pollution has become a "menace of 21st century life."[27] The amplification of sound has become widespread due to technology, and it goes where it likes; it cannot be blocked. It is important to recognize the space that noise takes up and its potential for negative effects. Additionally, silence can take on communicative value. That is to say, silence can be an essential part of conversational interactions, with culturally dependent uses that must be learned.[28]

A necessary distinction can also be made between being silent and being silenced. As mentioned previously, we create structure and meaning in our lives through language and story. The narration of our lives involves a process of editing and selecting: we voice some aspects of our lives and silence others. What is said through this narration is as important as what is left unsaid. Furthermore, it is not only the events of the story that are important but the meaning that is ascribed to them. Individuals may choose not to share details of their lives because they do not fit into cultural narratives. For example, a war veteran may not relate their story to family and friends because it is too horrific, or a rape victim may not discuss their experience because it makes others uncomfortable. On a larger scale, the reworking of tales such as the exploits of Christopher Columbus, as detailed by Ransby, the dismissal of experiences, as in the case of the residential school system in Canada, or the extension of discriminatory practices, as in the case of the Japanese-Canadian internment policies during the Second World War, essentially alter or obliterate the historical past of entire groups of people and create silences which serve ideological agendas.

Silence can also be viewed as an absence of action, as complacency or as a lack of participation. In some cases, this may be true; however, silence may also present itself as a form of resistance to certain activities and the institutional structures that govern them. The refusal to speak, tell a story or engage in artistic activity may make a comment about the activity and the structures that surround it. One great example of this is the work of John Cage, an American composer and musician. His well-known 1952 composition, 4'33" (pronounced "Four minutes, thirty-three seconds"

•••

Box 10.12 Innov8

A Better Man is a documentary film co-directed by Canadian filmmaker Attiya Khan. In this film Khan and her ex-boyfriend Steve review their two-year teenage relationship during which Steve repeatedly abused Khan. This review includes returning to past places of significance, such as their old high school and the apartment they shared, and visiting a domestic-violence counsellor. Khan's documentary is instrumental in empowering women to confront violence in intimate relationships. Additionally, the documentary emphasizes dialogue as central to both personal healing and social change. To learn more about Khan and the creative team, visit the film's website: <abettermanfilm. com/> or watch the documentary: <tvo.org/video/documentaries/a-better-man-feature-version>.

•••

or just "Four thirty-three"), is completely reliant on the incidental noise of the room to create its form; this forces the audience to listen attentively and wait in anticipation for the unexpected. Another example is Kasimir Malevich's 1918 controversial work of art entitled *White Square on White Ground*. Its pure white surface symbolizes silence and the refusal to offer a painterly composition. Overall, Sim argues, we must distinguish between silence as a condition or a response: an environmental issue or a metaphysical issue.[29] Regardless of this consideration, silence is an essential element and a practical requirement for our everyday lives. Without it there is little space for reflection and little space for listening.

Listening has been investigated in many disciplines; however, in examining listening within the context of dialogue, the work of Roland Barthes provides essential insight. In his essay "Listening," Barthes states that "hearing is a physiological phenomenon; listening is a psychological act."[30] This suggests that listening involves not only an auditory process but a deliberate action. How do we create space for silence and listening? In order to do this, we must examine existing structures and determine the types of structures that value voice. It is also necessary to address issues of inequality and to create space for people to participate.

VOICE AS PARTICIPATION

The starting point for any discussion of voice as participation is often the work of Paolo Friere, an author and educator from Brazil who believed that education based on dialogue and "critical consciousness" could raise individuals out of oppression. At a time when passing a literacy test was a prerequisite for voting in the presidential elections, Friere focused on educating disadvantaged labourers, arguing that education could bring about a critical awareness which would allow the poor and the oppressed to learn to analyze their own social, political and economic realities. For Friere, education was an instrument to achieving not only voice in the form of the vote, but also an enhanced critical understanding of the way the world works.[31]

So, what does it mean to use your voice? What are the elemental assumptions around this phrase? In regard to the example of Paolo Friere, using your voice can be equated to exercising the democratic vote. It can also be used to describe a circumstance in which an individual speaks out, usually against an opposing opinion or for a cause. Additionally, using your voice could mean manipulating or controlling a situation. Regardless of the exercise of voice, there are always certain assumptions around its use. First, there are the closely connected assumptions of confidence and risk. Making use of voice requires a certain degree of determination and courage, as there are almost always consequences for its use. Second, there is the expectation that if you use your voice, circumstances will change; usually the change will bring about good. Last, there is the belief that what you have to say is important and that it will make an impact: that is to say, the very act of using voice matters.[32]

VOICE AS PERFORMANCE

An extension of voice as a kind of participation arises through voice when it is viewed as performance. Performance is a term with a wide variety of definitions, depending on the context in which it is used. Many disciplines use this term to discuss culturally expressive actions or activities that are socially meaningful. In her book *Theories of Performance*, Elizabeth Bell argues that performance is both a process and a product, in that it develops, grows and changes, but ends in a complete event. Additionally, performance has a specific, creative purpose. Lastly, performance is traditional and transformative: on the one hand, it recognizes "former ways of doing, acting, seeing and believing," while at the same time, it transforms the present through its accomplishment.[33]

Performance is traditionally viewed as an artistic work that occurs at a specific time and in a specific place, such as a play, a musical concert or a poetry reading; however, the term performance is also used to describe other cultural activities, such as weddings, football games, awards shows like the Junos, or political protests. Performance is an embodied process that involves people coming together and acting in ways to make change. When discussion around performance is connected to events or activities that take place in public spaces with a view to resistance or social change, it is often connected to the expression of voice.

Box 10.13 Diversity in Action

Dandelion Dance is an inclusive dance school that invites girls with a variety of backgrounds and abilities to participate in creative dance works. The aim of the school is to make dance accessible and to allow girls to "develop empathy, break stereotypes, discover and explore their creativity and practice leadership." Through their work, the school challenges existing cultural assumptions about dancers and creates an opportunity for performance, self-expression and community building to come together. For more information on Dandelion Dance, visit their website: <dandeliondance.ca/>, learn about them on YouTube: <youtube.com/watch?v=PCmzn2Sf4pI> or watch them in this TEDxYouthOttawa performance: <youtube.com/watch?v=2Xq5_9UkzSA>.

Many excellent examples of this type of performance can be found throughout Canada. One such example is the march in Burnaby, British Columbia, on March 10, 2018. The march, which took place in protest of the $7.4 billion Kinder Morgan Trans Mountain pipeline expansion, raised concerns that the pipeline would cause environmental damage and threaten Indigenous ways of life. Another example is the student-led March for Our Lives protests that took place March 24, 2018, across Canada in support of gun reform in the United States. As one protestor's placard effectively stated, "You can put a silencer on the gun, but not on the voice of the people."[34] Rallies, walks and strikes are other examples of this kind of performance.

In his book *Communicating Social Change: Structure, Culture and Agency*, Mohan Dutta explains that "performance for social change embodies the politics of representing issues of social injustice, oppression, power, control, and resistance in public spaces through the use of aesthetic forms of representations." These processes of communication that disrupt the status quo open up "new possibilities for imagining states of being, feeling, living and thus bring about shifts in consciousness in how social realities are approached, lived in, reaffirmed and challenged."[35] The possibility of a changed reality means that performance is an act of voice: it is something we do. In completing the action, new meanings are constructed and change occurs. These types of performance engage the senses, challenge the ways in which public spaces are used and create opportunities to reshape existing structures within dominant discursive spaces.

CONCLUSION

In this age of technology, when new modes of communication are constantly evolving and social media provides ample opportunity for self-expression, what is the status of voice? Before the advent of social media, voice was formed privately through personal reflection and creative work. Now, voice is more often formed publicly through social media and other forms of online expression. This has led to a cacophony of voices that exist in a kind of communicative vacuum in which there is very little listening. That there is an oversaturation of voice, and that there is little awareness of how to critically discern and discuss information of importance, could be the crisis of voice we are currently experiencing.

In this chapter, we examine voice as a sound we use to create beauty or express meaning. We also review the evolution of our current vocal anatomy and consider voice as an essential aspect of the human impulse to speak or sing. Further, voice is considered as a project, as participation and as performance in a variety of contexts. Additionally, we reflect on how much of our voices are our own, how they are affected by internal and external influences and how voice functions as part of a larger dialogue that involves silence and listening. The resources available to create our voices, such as experiences, languages and stories, may constrain us, but they also provide us with opportunities: opportunities to participate in the social construction of meaning through dialogue with others. Once voice is considered as part of a larger dialogic process, the possibilities of its social impact are reached, and voice is seen as something that can free us even as it lays the foundation for change. Ultimately, it is the depth and complexity of voice that attracts us to its study, and through its consideration, we give it value. This chapter is a commitment to voice and to the hope that everyone finds within its exploration an element of inspiration that leads them on a path of discovery. Critical analysis of voice is a contribution to the self, to society and to the world.

CRITICAL REVIEW QUESTIONS

1. Why do you think that such a relatively small percentage of the world's people embrace and pursue the technical and artistic challenges associated with voice?
2. Why is it more important to consider why we developed the impulse to speak or sing than when?
3. What is the relationship between voice and language? What are your own experiences with languages and the expression of voice?
4. What does it mean to be part of a discourse community? What implications does this have for power and privilege?

5. What is the communicative value of silence in Canadian culture? Contrast this with your understanding of silence in other languages/cultures if you wish.

6. In what ways do you express your own voice? What, do you think, is the most effective way to use it?

RECOMMENDED READINGS

Nick Couldry, *Why Voice Matters* (London: Sage Publications, 2010).

Kate DeVore and Starr Cookman, *The Voice Book: Easy Exercises and Advice for Anyone Who Speaks or Sings for a Living* (Chicago, IL: Chicago Review Press, 2009).

David Novak and Matt Sakakeeny (eds.). *Keywords in Sound* (Durham and London: Duke University Press, 2015).

Harriet J. Ottenheimer, *The Anthropology of Language: An Introduction to Linguistic Anthropology*, 3rd edition (Belmont, CA: Wadsworth, Cengage Learning, 2013).

John Potter and Neil Sorrell. *A History of Singing* (Cambridge, UK: Cambridge University Press, 2012).

KEY TERMS

exapted: when an anatomical structure takes on a function for which it was not originally selected.

larynx: anatomical structure which houses the vocal folds.

phonation: production of a speech sound.

Romanticism: eighteenth-century literary and artistic movement which emphasized individuality, subjectivity and imagination.

structuralism: approach to linguistics which analyzes and describes the structure of language.

Notes

1. See Amanda Weidman, "Anthropology and Voice," *Annual Review of Anthropology*, 43 (2014) for a review of voice in Anthropology and related fields.

2. In *A Voice and Nothing More* (2006), Dolar argues for a third use of voice: an object voice. However, this third use of voice is beyond the scope of this introductory discussion.

3. Amalia E. Gnanadesikan, *The Writing Revolution: Cuneiform to the Internet* (West Sussex, UK: Wiley-Blackwell, 2009).

4. Andrew M. Kimbrough, *Dramatic Theories of Voice in the Twentieth Century* (New York: Cambria, 2011).

5. John Potter and Neil Sorrell, *A History of Singing* (Cambridge, UK: Cambridge University Press, 2012); and Clifton Ware, *Basics of Vocal Pedagogy: The Foundations and Process of Singing* (New York: McGraw-Hill, 1998) both emphasize the importance of volition or impulse as initiating the vocalization process.

6. For a more detailed description see Ware, *Basics of Vocal Pedagogy*.

7. James R. Hurford, *Origins of Language: A Slim Guide* (New York: Oxford University Press, 2014): 75–77.

8. Hurford, *Origins of Language*, 84.
9. There is some disagreement on whether or not Neanderthals also had this capability. Hurford, *Origins*, and Potter and Sorrell, *A History of Singing*, discuss this in more depth.
10. Cited in Potter and Sorrell, *A History of Singing*, 30). Stephen Mithen's arguments regarding the evolution of language and music have been heavily criticized; however, they do add space to the discussion around the importance of vocal expression to early hominids.
11. Arthur Lessac, *The Use and Training of the Human Voice: A Bio-Dynamic Approach to Vocal Life*, 3rd edition (Toronto: McGraw-Hill, 1997): 29.
12. For more information on Canada's National Voice Intensive, visit their website at <voiceintensive.org/home>.
13. Timothy Lensmire and Lisa Satanovsky, "Defense of the Romantic Poet? Writing Workshops and Voice," *Theory into Practice*, 37, 4 (1998).
14. Eva Hoffman, "Lost in Translation" [1989], in Nell Waldman and Sara Norton (eds.), *Canadian Content*, 7th edition (Toronto: Nelson Education, 2012): 124, 128.
15. Harriet J. Ottenheimer, *The Anthropology of Language: An Introduction to Linguistic Anthropology*, 3rd edition (Belmont, CA: Wadsworth, Cengage Learning, 2013): 32.
16. Chris Barker and Dariusz Galasinski, *Cultural Studies and Discourse Analysis: A Dialogue on Language and Identity* (London: Sage Publications, 2001): 2, 28.
17. Mikhail Bakhtin, "Problems of Dostoevsky's Poetics," in Caryl Emerson (ed.), *Theory and History of Literature*, 8 (Minneapolis and London: University of Minnesota Press, 1984): 239.
18. Roland Barthes, "The Death of the Author," in Stephen Heath (ed.), *Image Music Text* (London: Fontana Press, 1977): 142.
19. The entire essay can be found in *The Foucault Reader*, edited by Paul Rabinow (1984).
20. Boh Young Lee, Melissa Scott Kozak, Carla Nancoo, Hao-Min Chen, Katie Middendorf and Jerry Gale, "Exploring Dominant Discourses: Creating Spaces to Find Voice and Cultural Identity." *Journal of Cultural Diversity*, 20, 1 (2013): 24.
21. Barbara Ransby, "Columbus and the Making of Historical Myth" [1992], in Jerry P. White and Michael Carroll (eds.), *Images of Society: Readings That Inspire and Inform Sociology*, 3rd edition (Toronto: Nelson, 2013): 64.
22. Ransby, "Columbus," 68.
23. Mohan Dutta, *Communicating Social Change: Structure, Culture and Agency* (New York: Routledge, 2011) 186.
24. *CBC News Online*, "A History of Residential Schools in Canada," May 16, 2008 <cbc.ca/news/canada/a-history-of-residential-schools-in-canada-1.7022802008>.
25. Nick Couldry, *Why Voice Matters* (London: Sage Publications, 2010): 1.
26. Buber cited in Dutta, *Communicating Social Change*, 187.
27. Stuart Sim, *Manifesto for Silence: Confronting the Politics and Culture of Noise* (Edinburgh: Edinburgh University Press, 2007): 1.
28. The most well-known linguistic study of silence is by Keith H. Basso. See his *Western Apache Language and Culture: Essays in Linguistic Anthropology* (1990) for a full account.
29. Sim, *Manifesto for Silence*, 14.
30. Roland Barthes, "Listening," in *The Responsibility of Forms* (Los Angeles: University of California Press, 1985): 245.
31. For a full understanding of Freire's position, it is essential to read *Pedagogy of the Oppressed*, first published in English in 1970.
32. Couldry, *Why Voice Matters*, 1.

33. For a comprehensive discussion of the nature and definitions of performance, see Elizabeth Bell, *Theories of Performance* (Thousand Oaks, CA: Sage, 2008). This section, in particular, is from page 17.

34. Kyle Edwards, "Where March for Our Lives Protests Are Happening across Canada," *Macleans*, March 23, 2018 <macleans.ca/news/canada/where-march-for-our-lives-protests-are-happening-across-canada/>.

35. Dutta, *Communicating Social Change*, 195.

11

LITERATURE

VOICES OF DIVERSITY IN CANADIAN LITERATURE

Jennifer Chambers

> *As to ghosts or spirits they appear totally banished from Canada. This is too matter-of-fact country for such supernaturals to visit. Here, there are no historical associations, no legendary tales of those that came before us. Fancy would starve for lack of marvelous food to keep her alive in the backwoods. We have neither fay nor fairy, ghost nor bogle, satyr nor wood-nymph; our very forests disdain to shelter dryad or hamadryad. — Catharine Parr Traill, The Backwoods of Canada, 1836*

KEY OBJECTIVES

Sketch the origins and development of Canadian literature.

Discuss ways in which voice and power are related in Canadian literature and publishing.

Describe current and contemporary debates about appropriation of voice and diversity in Canadian literature and publishing.

Appreciate the diversity of experiences, voices and characterizations in Canadian literature that mirror a culture.

Consider and discuss the purpose and necessity of national literatures.

Canadian literature, at its best, is rich in diverse voices — of many races, ethnicities, socioeconomics, abilities, languages, genders and sexualities. There has often been a concern that it is a boring literature, representing a docile people, or that it is a literature and culture hijacked by either its British and French foremothers or its large and glamourous (if overbearing) American neighbour. What is the purpose of a national literature? What does it have to do with the people of the country, and how does it represent them — or does it? Can it?

With its turbulent history of colonization of Indigenous Peoples' land by European settlers, and the identities of predominantly British, French and Indigenous cultures, then the addition of Dutch, Eastern European, Scandinavian, Caribbean, African, Chinese, Japanese and multiple other populations, Canadian literature has a lot to account for. Undoubtedly, some of Canada's racialized and sexist policies are reflected in the voices published at a particular time. But if government policies reflect racism, sexism, classism, these elements will all be shown back to us — often subsequently, maybe generations later — in the literary works that voice those stories. It is, perhaps, a cautionary tale, as American poet Sharon Olds warns her parents in a poem, "Do what you are going to do, and I will tell about it."[1]

Literature can be a reflection of different identities, different perspectives, different voices. It offers us narratives of the beginnings of things, that we might understand where we have come from, and in early Canadian literature some of these narratives come in the form of Indigenous creation myths, explorer and travel narratives like Jacques Cartier's *Recits de voyages* and Frances Brooke's "first" **epistolary novel**. It offers us the messy middle of things, as in Joy Kogawa's novel *Obasan,* set in British Columbia and Alberta, recalling the 1950s internment camps of Japanese Canadians, Clark Blaise's story "Eyes," about how always strange it feels to be an immigrant in Montreal, Margaret Atwood's poetry collection *The Journals of Susanna Moodie,* which brought us back, in Canadian literature, to a lost pioneering voice.

The current tide in Canadian literature shows a wealth of diverse voices, but it is not without its growing pains. As Indigenous writers, women writers, immigrants and their children publish more frequently and gain recognition, there is a feeling — recurring, as it reared its head in the 1990s first, and again now — about how white and homogenous the publishing industry in Canada is, and about how strongly it influences whose voices get published, reviewed and win awards. There is a growing sense that for too long, many well-established Canadian writers have been using "**appropriation of voice**" in their narratives; that is, telling the stories of other cultures, races, socioeconomic circumstances — at the expense of allowing writers from those cultures with lived experience to have the same chance to write their stories, share them and enjoy the exposure and accolades that may follow.

BRIEF HISTORY OF LITERATURE IN CANADA

Canada is considered a relatively young country, and as such people like to assess its origins. Canada was inhabited by Indigenous Peoples for generations before European settlers came to colonize it. It is often said that for a country to "come into its own," or to mature, it must have a cultural, artistic identity. Post-Confederation (1867), the project of developing a Canadian literature became a hot topic among certain political figures in Ottawa. They developed a group called Canada First, which sought to develop a national literature by creating literary magazines to publish the voices of Canadians.[2] To do so, they thought, would be to promote patriotism, to enhance cultural values and ideals and to form a clear national identity. Their backgrounds in and affinity for a white Anglo-Saxon Protestant point of view undoubtedly influenced who got published, even in the nineteenth century, and there have been questions and problems with diversity in Canadian literature ever since.

Pre–1789

Many Indigenous Nations have a history of oral storytelling, and what remains of very early Canadian Indigenous literature ought to be considered, as some critics note, as "an existing indigenous tradition…disrupted — but not erased."[3] Some of the early Indigenous myths and tales have been collected by Saukamapee, Buhkwujjenene, Aisa Qupiqrualuk and Norval Morrisseau. They are often creation stories, survival tales or concern specific customs such as marriage. These tales, mostly oral in tradition, were told as entertainment but also as a way to "communicate ethical models from one generation to another; within these cultures they also explained natural events, spiritual beliefs, origins and uncertainties."[4] These early tales sometimes include trickster narratives. The trickster figure continues in Indigenous writing today. Sometimes they are represented by a coyote (or a raven), as both villain *and* hero in the same story, or at least a flawed, relatable character. The trickster figure represents the contradictory nature of humans and is often, in later incarnations, used comically to make us question the *status quo* or to highlight human foibles that we might think about them in new ways.

1760–1860

The first "Canadian" novel is credited to a British woman, Frances Brooke, whose husband John was stationed as a military general in Halifax, before they settled in Quebec, where he worked as the sole Protestant minister. The novel, *The History of Emily Montague*, was published in Britain for a British readership in 1769. It is an epistolary novel, that is, a novel written in letters, which was a literary trend of the day.

It tells the tale among six characters: Edward Rivers, a retired British military general in Quebec, who has settled there because his small pension will stretch further; his sister Lucy, who stands in for the audience as she lives in Britain and seeks knowledge about the new colony; Emily Montague, Edmund's romantic pursuit, a British woman in Quebec; Emily's friend, the coquettish Arabella Fermor, who is also friends with Lucy Rivers; and finally, Arabella's father, William Fermor, who writes political commentary to an unnamed British Earl back home. The novel offers a glimpse of early Canada through the eyes of a British woman intent both on selling the new colony as a place of wonder and on selling a lot of books. The Canadian landscape is described as beautiful and wondrous — as Arabella writes to Lucy, "the loveliness of this fairy scene alone more than pays the fatigues of my voyage; and, if I ever murmur at having crossed the Atlantic, remind me that I have seen the river Montmorenci."[5] There are of course elements that make Canada remarkable and different than Britain, namely French-Canadians and Indigenous Peoples, although both are treated mostly as stereotypes: the French-Canadian women being "handsome," while the men are considered tame and "not dangerous,"[6] and the Indigenous people described mostly along the lines of the "noble savage" stereotype, although being considered

> free as a people ... Lord of himself, at once subject and master, a savage knows no superior, a circumstance which has a striking effect on his behavior; unawed by rank or riches, distinctions unknown amongst his own nation, he would... possess all his powers as freely in the palace of an oriental monarch as in the cottage of the meanest peasant. 'tis the species, 'tis the man, 'tis his equal he respects, without regarding the gaudy trappings, the accidental advantages, to which polished nations pay homage.[7]

Brooke's novel, which follows a conventional romance plot, gives the first published account of the immigrant's experience moving to the new world. Well-received in its day, it continues to be published as the earliest work of Canadian literature.

As Canada was still in the phase of being or becoming the "new world," the next wave of literature includes narratives of exploration, written by Samuel Hearne, David Thompson, John Franklin and John Richardson. These explorers came as entrepreneurs with the Hudson Bay Company, or the fur trade, or as explorers seeking beyond the scope of what had been discovered. Many of the explorers relied on their connections with Indigenous Peoples to help them navigate the landscape and organize commerce.

The next generation includes travel literature, written by British people who made their way to Canada. Anna Winterson's *Winter Studies and Summer Rambles in Canada* is among the best known. Published in 1838, Winterson recognized her work as groundbreaking, writing,

While in Canada, I was thrown into scenes and regions hitherto undescribed by any traveler (for the northern shores of Lake Huron are almost new ground) and into relations with the Indian tribes, such as few European women of refined and civilized habits have ever risked, and none have recorded.[8]

Winterson's perspective shows that she finds Canada a "magnificent country," although "unhappy and mismanaged."[9] She chronicles the troubles of the low-brow colonial country with its ill-built towns and cities, but she endures the experience, even persevering through a chilly winter where the ink she wrote with freezes.

The first novel attributed to a *Canadian-born* author is Julia Catherine Beckwith's *St. Ursula's Convent; or, the Nun of Canada*, published in 1824 in Kingston. An epic tale, written in the ponderous, descriptive language of the day, some critics have called its "value…entirely historical, as a sort of musty landmark in Canadian literature."[10] Another early Canadian novel is John Richardson's *Wacousta; or, The Prophecy: An Indian Tale*, published in London and Edinburgh in 1832. It enjoyed greater success and continues to be printed today. The novel is part mystery, part historical narrative set in 1763, while Pontiac, chief of Ottawas, laid siege to Detroit and Michilimackinac. Wacousta, a veteran of the Plains of Abraham, English nobleman, and warrior of the Ottawas, synthesizes the three main elements of Canadians — French, English, and Indigenous — in one character. His story hearkens back to an earlier perceived injustice done to him by the English commander of the British at Detroit, for which he seeks revenge, by plotting to kill the English De Haldimar's children one by one.

In 1835, Thomas Chandler Haliburton, a lawyer, east-coast politician and writer, published "The Clockmaker" in *The Novascotian*. He wrote a series of sketches about a character Sam Slick, a clock salesman, who comments on the quirks of east coast Canadians, "Bluenoses," as he calls them, and is full of local colour descriptions and turns-of-phrase credited to Haliburton that remain quite commonplace today, such as "stick in the mud," "upper crust," and "quick as a wink." Haliburton's sense of humour reached a large audience. When a pirated copy was published in England, it was a smashing success, as the British audience was keen to learn about the foibles of colonials. Some people note that Haliburton wrote the beginnings of Canadian humour. At the time, Sam Slick was as well-known as some Dickens characters, and Artemus Ward named Haliburton "the father of American humour."[11]

The pioneering narratives of the Susanna Moodie were lost to history until Margaret Atwood wrote a collection of poetry in 1970 called *The Journals of Susanna Moodie*, based on Susanna Moodie's 1852 sketches, *Roughing It in the Bush*, about moving to Canada from Britain as a retired army officer's wife. The plot of land given to military veterans, and the way money could stretch in the British colony, lured many pioneers to Canada. Moodie's accounts stand out as she paints a stark, vivid picture of how difficult it was to move from a civilized, cultured motherland to a mostly forested, uncultured place, where the rules of civilization were still to be written. Although many of Moodie's sketches are still very readable today, and she interspersed many chapters with landscape poems, her conclusion was clear:

> Reader! it is not my intention to trouble you with the sequel of our history. I have given you a faithful picture of a life in the backwoods of Canada, and I leave you to draw from it your own conclusions. To the poor, industrious working man it presents many advantages; to the poor gentleman, *none!* The former works hard, puts up with coarse, scanty fare, and submits, with a good grace, to hardships that would kill a domesticated animal at home. Thus he becomes independent, inasmuch as the land that he has cleared finds him in the common necessaries of life; but it seldom, if ever, in remote situations, accomplishes more than this. The gentleman can neither work so hard, live so coarsely, nor endure so many privations as his poorer but more fortunate neighbour.
>
> If these sketches should prove the means of deterring one family from sinking their property, and shipwrecking all their hopes, by going to reside in the backwoods of Canada, I shall consider myself amply repaid for revealing the secrets of the prison-house, and feel that I have not toiled and suffered in the wilderness in vain.[12]

Moodie makes the case that those who are suited to life in Canada will be those who are suited to hard, manual labour, particularly toiling with the land, rather than, say, people who have been raised and educated to serve an already cultured and civilized people. Her arguments are class-based, but meant to be helpful, in terms of not casting Canada as a promising new world where anyone can thrive. Instead, she compares Canada, finally, to a "prison-house" for those who were sold on a simplistic vision without the knowledge of the wilderness they would have to "civilize." Of course, the pioneering vision of Moodie's is also very white, middle-class and follows the politics of Britain, which, as colonizer, saw Canada as its own without much thought to the Indigenous Peoples who had been living with and on the land for generations.

Margaret Atwood's collection of poems *The Journals of Susanna Moodie* was published in 1970, and we owe the recovery of Moodie's distinctive pioneering voice largely to Atwood's poems. Critics sometimes warn that Atwood's interpretation of Moodie is so strong as to have overshadowed Moodie's own voice. Atwood portrays Moodie as contradictory — both loving and hating the new world where she landed, but finally being unable to leave it once her son dies and is buried on Canadian soil.

Box 11.1 Think About...

To read "Death of a Young Son By Drowning" by Margaret Atwood, go to
<www.poetryinvoice.com/poems/death-young-son-drowning>.

Atwood's poems are very closely based on Moodie's sketches, and her idea of Moodie's personality "reflect[ing] many of the obsessions still with us" is part of what gives weight to our understanding of the early pioneers. Atwood describes Moodie as

> divided down the middle: she praises the Canadian landscape but accuses it of destroying her; she dislikes the people already in Canada but finds in people her only refuge from the land itself; she preaches progress and the march of civilization while brooding elegiacally upon the destruction of the wilderness.... She claims to be an ardent Canadian patriot while all the time she is standing back from the country and criticizing it as though she were a detached observer, a stranger. Perhaps that is the way we still live. We are all immigrants to this place even if we were born here; the country is too big for anyone to inhabit completely, and in the parts unknown to us we move in fear, exiles and invaders. This country is something that must be chosen — it is so easy to leave — and if we do choose it we are still choosing a violent duality.[13]

Atwood's idea that there is a "violent duality" to Moodie's vision of Canada is expressed in her poem "Death of a Young Son by Drowning," where the speaker of the poem is reminded of all of the ways that tie her to the son, despite the third-person objective title. Also in the poem, the speaker shows how the land has both swallowed that young son, and how she must now stamp out her place on that very land.

Moodie was of course an actual immigrant to Canada, but Atwood reminds us that even when we are born here, there is a sense of "otherness," of not entirely belonging because it is such a vast land, and we cannot know every part of it or everyone in it. As we move into the later part of the nineteenth-century and into the twentieth and even the twenty-first century, this thread of a theme — of immigration and immigrant voices, and of not belonging or trying to find a way in — remains a strong one in Canadian literature even today. Atwood's idea that there is a "violent duality" to Moodie's vision of Canada is expressed in her poem "Death of a Young Son by Drowning." For one thing, the title of the poem is written in the third-person objective, as though it were a newspaper headline, and yet the subject matter is very personal, and the poem itself universal in its themes. The poem begins,

He, who navigated with success
the dangerous river of his own birth
once more set forth

on a voyage of discovery
into the land I floated on
but could not touch to claim.

Atwood uses water and marine imagery throughout the poem to mimic the idea of drowning. Here, the speaker of the poem shows how her son was successful in the birth canal, but goes on to show how he was swept away by a strong spring current that brought him to his death. There is a universal theme of grief at losing someone, in this case a child, and the pain that follows. Having navigated herself to the new world, Moodie had a family on this new soil and in this new land, only to lose one of them so jarringly to drowning. Atwood expresses it in the poem as follows,

There was an accident; the air locked,
he was hung in the river like a heart.
They retrieved the swamped body,

cairn of my plans and future charts,
with poles and hooks
from among the nudging logs.

The imagery used here is both practical and sentimental. We feel the airlessness both for the boy who drowned, and for the mother who grieves, whose life will effectively never be the same now she has lost her son. The poem ends with the line, "I planted him in this country / like a flag." This final image is striking, for many immigrants do not feel joined to a place until they have buried someone there. In a sense, the burial ties them to the place, or stakes a place for them. In the poem, the speaker shows how the land has both swallowed that young son, and how she must now construct her place on that very land. In this way, we can sense repeatedly through the poem, the "violent duality" set up by Atwood about Moodie.

Rae Spoon and Ivan Coyote perform from their memoir Gender Failure *<youtube.com/watch?v=-n08vFSKIts>.*
"CanLit Is a Raging Dumpster Fire" by Alicia Elliot, Open Book <open-book.ca/Columnists/CanLit-is-a-Raging-Dumpster-Fire>.

1860–1950

As Canada became a recognized political and geographical entity during Confederation in 1867, when the British colonies Upper and Lower Canada turn into Ontario and Quebec and join with New Brunswick and Nova Scotia to become the Dominion of Canada, ideas about its sense of "nationhood" began to change. During the period after Confederation until after the First World War, there was the idea that Canadian-born citizens should be writing and telling the stories of Canada. Politician Thomas D'Arcy McGee believed that "there could be no new nationality without a national literature," and such a clear notion about the necessity for a national literature became the focus of many politicians and editors in early Canada.[14]

A group of male poets, namely Charles G.D. Roberts, Bliss Carman, Archibald Lampman and Duncan Campbell Scott, along with William Wilfred Campbell and Frederick Scott, became the first distinct school of writers, aptly named the Confederation Poets. They were a group of first-generation, Canadian-born writers remembered for their sonnets and lyrics about Canada. Their poetry was heavily influenced by Romantic and Victorian British and American writers, but the topics were usually Canadian and often nature-based. Each poet prided himself on craft and worked in an educated style. They set the standard in the nineteenth century for the kind of work — scholarly, traditional, conventional — that would be published in Canada's early journals.

Women writers of the nineteenth century were prevalent first in journalism and next in literary arts. Isabelle Valancy Crawford is sometimes the only woman poet listed among the Confederation poets. She penned the long poem "Malcolm's Katie: A Love Story," touted by critics to be of a "mythopoeic imagination" and "of the business of being a Canadian," on the one hand,[15] and of being "a preposterously romantic love story on a Tennysonian model in which a wildly creaking plot finally delivers true love safe and triumphant," on the other.[16] Such differences of opinion and interpretation are vast in Canadian literature, perhaps especially in early Canadian literature. Sara Jeannette Duncan wrote compelling articles for the *Globe* before embarking on a literary career. Her novel *The Imperialist* is considered by some critics to be Canada's first truly modern novel, although it was not widely loved by its audience given its political subject matter. Set in fictional Elgin, Ontario (a stand-in for Brantford), *The Imperialist* was published in 1904 and follows Lorne Murchison's bid for political office, as a representative of the British empire. The novel is noted for its historical portrayal of small-town life, romance and political life.

Northrop Frye, a Canadian critic, in the Conclusion to *The Literary History of Canada*, wrote:

The environment, in nineteenth-century Canada, is terrifyingly cold, empty and vast…. We notice the recurrence of such episodes as shipwreck, Indian massacres, human sacrifices, lumbermen mangled in logjams, mountain climbers crippled on glaciers, animals screaming in traps, the agonies of starvation and solitude — in short, the "shutting out of the whole moral creation."[17]

For all the work that was being done to create a Canadian literature, its merit, particularly in the early days of publishing, continues to be harshly judged for its sensational, stereotypical Canadian nature, and for following too closely British and American models of writing. London and New York were the largest, most-established places for Canadian writers to publish works, and even among early Canadian publishers, there appeared to be a deliberate maintenance of white, Anglo-Saxon, English literary traditions and conventions as Canadian literature developed. Many of these traditions and conventions were established by well-educated, white, males and were openly racist and sexist. Images of the "noble savage" when discussing token Indigenous characters or figures come to mind, as does open disdain for the Irish, the French-Canadian, the Catholic and people of colour.

Historically, many people cite the First World War as the moment when Canada came into its own, as Canadian troops helped to end the war in France, joining the allies to defeat Germany. Canadian losses were great, and there is a lot of poetry, both from Canadian soldiers who lived through the war, and from women writers supporting the war back home. Canadian soldier and poet John McCrae's poem "In Flanders Fields" lives on as perhaps the most famous poem of the day. Even during the war, "In Flanders Fields" was used as a motivational tool among British soldiers. Today, school children are still asked to memorize and recite it, and an excerpt from the poem has appeared on the Canadian ten-dollar bill.

With the need for settlers to move to the Prairie Provinces and the West Coast in order to build a transnational railroad, the Canadian government found itself with a conundrum: how to balance the needs of the country for settlers with its own elitist colonial mentality. As the government allowed immigration from more widespread countries, many of Canada's policies for immigrants were discriminatory, offering few choices for employment, integration and leaving people open for social exclusion. This is true for the Chinese immigrants who built much of the railroad and the Japanese who suffered after Pearl Harbor. Writing that confronts these contradictions will follow in the mid twentieth century.

In August 1927, five women from Alberta approached the Canadian Supreme Court to ask the question, "Does the word 'Persons' in section 24 of the British North America Act, 1867, include female persons?"[18] The case was *Edwards v. Canada*, which

Box 11.2 Diversity in Action

IN FLANDERS FIELDS

In Flanders fields the poppies blow
Between the crosses, row on row,
That mark our place; and in the sky
The larks, still bravely singing, fly
Scarce heard amid the guns below.
We are the Dead. Short days ago
We lived, felt dawn, saw sunset glow,
Loved and were loved, and now we lie
In Flanders fields.
Take up our quarrel with the foe:
To you from failing hands we throw
The torch; be yours to hold it high.
If ye break faith with us who die
We shall not sleep, though poppies grow
In Flanders fields.
— John McCrae

sought to answer the question of whether women could become senators in the government. Canada's Supreme Court ruled unanimously that women were not "qualified persons" in April 1928. However, the Famous Five — Emily Murphy, Nellie McClung, Irene Parlby, Louise McKinney, Henrietta Muir Edwards — did not give up, and "the Persons case," as it became known, was sent to the British Judicial Committee of the Privy Council, who overturned the decision in 1929. This case was controversial on both sides. On the one hand, it came down five years after the suffrage movement in the United States and made a shift toward gender equality in North America. In other words, it was culturally relevant and timely. On the other hand, it also meant that Britain was interfering in the Canadian constitution. This move was not popular since Canada enjoyed a peaceful relationship with Britain, while eking out its political autonomy. None of the Famous Five women went on to become senators, although they paved the way for others. Two of the women, Emily Murphy and Nellie McClung, were also Canadian authors.

Emily Murphy (1868–1933) would become the police magistrate and judge of the juvenile court in Edmonton, Alberta. She also wrote a series of works under the pseudonym "Janey Canuck." In *The Impressions of Janey Canuck Abroad* (1901), published under her maiden name Emily Ferguson, she overturns the early travel narratives of

British women coming to Canada, writing instead from a Canadian perspective about visiting the motherland, England. The persona of Janey Canuck is cheerful, fastidious and a character with one foot firmly planted in Canada. Even as she experiences England, she naturally compares it and thinks of the benefits of Canada:

> Riding on the omnibuses is a source of unflagging pleasure to me. The drivers have graduated in the rough college of practical experience and were veritable Doctors of Philosophy. They are sitting encyclopedias and are able to post you in all the "wrinkles" of sightseeing…. The omnibus horses mostly come from Canada … magnificent, sober-minded, incapable of surprises … they are a credit to our young colony.[19]

Here, Janey Canuck enjoys learning from her coachman about the sights in England, but she can't help but praise the Canadian-raised horses, using adjectives that might serve to describe Canadians themselves, or at least that Canadians might wish to describe them.

Emily Murphy has become a controversial historical figure because while her early works as "Janey Canuck" add to our sense of Canadian literature coming into its own, and she both raised awareness and changed the law about women being considered as "persons" by the state itself, some of her beliefs — fear about the drug trade in the west, for example, have been linked to racialized views about Chinese immigrants. In 1922, she published *The Black Candle*, an informative work of nonfiction based on her growing awareness of the prevalence of drug addiction in Canada. There are stark, racist links in the work to the Chinese community and their casual use and abuse of opiates. Also, Murphy believed in eugenics, the idea that only "fit" people should be allowed to procreate, while those "unfit" should not. Furthermore, Murphy worked to have the Sexual Sterilization Act passed in Alberta in 1928, a law that was meant to "protect the gene pool" by having mentally incompetent people sterilized.[20] Murphy reminds us that people are multifaceted and that changes in socio- and cultural historical ideas can alter the way people are remembered and judged for their literary works.

While the Famous Five were at work in the west, Canada's iconic, classic, arguably most famous novel, *Anne of Green Gables*, set in the east, was published in 1908. It became an instant bestseller, was reprinted multiple times within the first year and continues to be reprinted and adapted for film and television series more than a century later. Written by Lucy Maud Montgomery (1874–1942) and set in Prince Edward Island, the novel is about Anne Shirley, the orphan girl with the carrot-coloured braids who is erroneously sent to live with siblings Matthew and Marilla Cuthbert. They sought to adopt a boy from the orphanage to help on the farm, so they are very surprised by the chatty girl with the large vocabulary and wild imagination who arrives instead. The novel explores youth and imagination, social mores and experience, and without being overly didactic, champions family values. It has sold an estimated fifty million copies worldwide and been translated into at least thirty-six languages.[21] It continues to be arguably the best-known, best-loved of Canadian novels. Montgomery would go on to write a series of eight "Anne" novels,[22] and was prolific, penning more than two hundred short stories and twenty-one novels, poetry and journals. She is best known for *Anne of Green Gables* which made her a household name internationally and has been in print since 1908. Famous American author and humourist Mark Twain said of Anne, that she was "the dearest, most moving and delightful child since the immortal Alice." The pride Canadians can take in an endorsement by an American author comparing the Canadian character Anne Shirley to the English Alice in Wonderland shows how deeply Canadians desire international literary and cultural recognition.

Between 1915 and 1925, Stephen Leacock was the English-speaking world's best-known humorist. Today, Leacock is remembered for his humorous *Sunshine Sketches of a Little Town*, a series of vignettes set in the fictional town of Mariposa (known to be based on Orillia, Ontario) and following a deadpan narrator who can't imagine what the townspeople are laughing about. It portrays small-town Ontario as full of amusing eccentricities and pretensions, and picks up on the traditions set earlier by Thomas Chandler Haliburton. The Stephen Leacock Award for Humour was established in 1947 and continues to be awarded to the best humorous book by a Canadian author each year.

Box 11.3 Think About...

Alice Munro was awarded the Nobel Prize for Literature in 2013. She was the first Canadian to receive the award, and as the writer of fourteen original collections of short stories compiling hundreds of stories, she was recognized as "a master of the contemporary short story." Her stories are often set in Canada, and are apt character studies that use a conscientious, brilliant style to create searing plots that stick with readers long after they read her work. In presenting the award, Professor Peter Englund began, "It may seem like a paradox, but it is actually quite logical: what we call world literature is generally rooted in the local and individual."

What is the impact of a Nobel Prize in Literature to Canada and to Canadian literature? What is gained by such an honour?

To see the full text of the speech by Englund, go to: <nobelprize.org/nobel_prizes/literature/laureates/2013/presentation-speech.html>.

As immigration flourished in Canada, the literature reflects these changes. Consequently, the mid-twentieth century will see more diverse voices and stories emerge.

1950–2018

Some critics consider the period between the late 1950s and the mid-1970s as a "literary explosion" during which some of Canada's best-known writers emerge.[23] These writers include Margaret Atwood, Irving Layton, Mavis Gallant, Leonard Cohen, Dennis Lee, Alistair MacLeod, Mordechai Richler, Al Purdy, Michael Ondaatje, Michel Tremblay and Canada's one and only Nobel Prize winning author, Alice Munro. The beginnings of "Canadian literature" as a viable literature of its own emerge in the 1960s, when some of its first courses are offered at universities.

In 1981, Joy Kogawa published *Obasan*, a beautiful, lyrical novel about the Canadian internment of the Japanese people in British Columbia. Written from the perspective of Naomi, who was a young child when Japanese internment took place in Canada, but who is now an adult looking back, the dawning of what has happened and its implications happens for the reader alongside the protagonist. Kogawa's novel is based on actual Canadian history. When the Japanese bombed Pearl Harbor during the Second World War, a panic spread in British Columbia, where there was a large Japanese Canadian population. Suddenly, there was a feeling of unease and distrust toward Japanese people that led to the British Columbian government seizing the property and material things of Japanese people, and corralling the people into internment camps. The losses suffered by the Japanese were vast, and never recovered, even after the government abolished their racist, dehumanizing policies; the social damage was done.

With such a painful past, Naomi in *Obasan* is unsure about how to reconcile it with her present life as a school teacher in Alberta. Her activist Aunt Emily tells her: "You have to remember … you are your history. If you cut any of it off, you're an amputee. Don't deny the past. Remember everything. If you're bitter, be bitter. Cry it out! Scream! Denial is gangrene. Look at you, Naomi, shuffling back and forth between Cecil and Granton, unable either to go or to stay in the world with even a semblance of grace or ease."[24] Naomi feels caught between Aunt Emily's active voice, and her Aunt Obasan's quiet grace. Obasan accepts her fate with silence, even raising her brother-in-law's two children (Naomi and her brother Stephen) when the families are torn apart by prejudicial government laws. As the memories emerge for Naomi, she takes readers back to show us what "internment" meant, what it looked like and how it felt:

> I remember one time Mr. Nakayama came out east to take pictures of as many young **Nisei** as he could find to prove to the parents back in the camps that

their children were alive. How could they know whether the girls working as domestics were all right — whether the young people on the farms were eating adequately — whether the boys who had left the road camps were managing in the cities? The rumours were so bad.

Throughout the country, here and there, were a few people doing what they could. There were missionaries, sending telegrams, drafting petitions, meeting together in rooms to pray. There were a few politicians sitting up late into the night, weighing conscience against expedience. There were the young Nisei men and women, the idealists, the thinkers, the leaders, scattered across the country. In Toronto there were the Jews who opened their businesses to employ the Nisei. But for every one who sought help, there were thousands who didn't. Cities in every province slammed their doors shut.[25]

In 1942, over 8000 Japanese Canadians in British Columbia were detained. Women and children were taken and held in Hastings Park, in livestock buildings, and some were moved out to different remote ghost towns. Men were sent to work camps, in the classic separation of families that is often used in campaigns to demoralize and dehumanize groups of people. In 1943, the government was enabled to seize Japanese property and possessions — including homes, farms, cars, boats, belongings — and to sell them for government profit. The Nisei were Canadian-born, and while going back to Japan was an option offered to them, their lives were clearly now in Canada. Those who resisted internment camps were sent to prisoner-of-war camps in Petawawa, Ontario.

Forty-two years later, in 1984, a petition to the Canadian government was made for an apology and compensation to Japanese Canadians for the internment abuses. It took until 1988 before Prime Minister Brian Mulroney officially apologized in the House of Commons. NDP leader Ed Broadbent read a passage from Joy Kogawa's *Obasan* in Parliament in support of the petition, and many Canadians see Kogawa's novel as being particularly valuable in representing the pain and hardships to Japanese Canadians, and the abuses done to them by the British Columbian government in particular, but with no protection granted from the Canadian government. Finally,

Box 11.4 Innov8

Watch the CBC news report covering Prime Minister Brian Mulroney's Apology to Japanese Canadians on September 22, 1988, for the Japanese internment that took place from December 1941 until 1949: <youtube.com/watch?v=fxVZtQULIMQ>.

one of the significant changes to come out of the redress was the denunciation of the Canadian War Measures Act which had provided the means by which the government could legally remove Japanese people from their homes.[26] Japanese internment in Canada and the Canadian War Measures Act remain as strong reminders in our country's history of the effects of racism.

THE CULTURAL MOSAIC VS. THE MELTING POT

Bharati Mukherjee (1940–2017), an Indian-born writer, makes a strong case about racism in Canada. Mukherjee was born and raised in Calcutta but moved to the United States to attend the University of Iowa's famed Writing Program, where she met Canadian author Clark Blaise. The two writers married and first settled in Montreal, where they had two sons; they later lived for a short time in Toronto. In 1980, they moved to the United States, where Mukherjee took a position in the English Department at the University of California at Berkeley. In the introduction to her novel *Darkness,* published in 1981, just after she left Canada, Mukherjee wrote the following about her experiences in Canada, comparing them to those in the United States:

> In the years I spent in Canada — 1966 to 1980 — I discovered that the country is hostile to its citizens who had been born in hot, moist continents like Asia; that the country proudly boasts of its opposition to the whole concept of cultural assimilation. In the Indian immigrant community, I saw a family of shared grievances. The purely "Canadian" stories in this collection were difficult to write and even more painful to live through. They are uneasy stories of expatriation.
>
> The transformation as writer, and as resident of the new world, occurred with the act of immigration to the United States. Suddenly I was no longer aggrieved, except as a habit of mind. I had moved from being a "visible minority" against whom the nation had officially incited its less visible citizens to react, to being just another immigrant. If I may put it in its harshest terms, it would be this: in Canada I was frequently taken for a prostitute or shoplifter, frequently assumed to be a domestic, praised by astonished auditors that I didn't have a "sing song" accent. The society itself, or important elements in that society, routinely made crippling assumptions about me, and about my "kind." In the United States, however, I see *myself* in those same outcasts; I see myself in an article on a Trinidad-Indian hooker; I see myself in the successful executive who slides Hindi film music in his tape deck as he drives into Manhattan; I see myself in the shady accountant who's trying to marry off his loose-living daughter; in professors, domestics, high school students,

illegal busboys in ethnic restaurants. It's possible — with sharp ears and the right equipment — to hear America singing even in the seams of the dominant culture. In fact, it may be the best listening post for the next generation of Whitmans. For me, it is a movement away from the aloofness of expatriation, to the exuberance of immigration.[27]

Mukherjee makes clear that her experiences as a writer and citizen in Canada made her feel like an outsider, somebody who had expatriated from her homeland, but who could never quite permeate the new country. By contrast, when she lived in the United States, the assumptions about her may have been bold, but they felt consistent, and as such she felt more accepted and able to integrate. Therefore, she could join in the culture and society, even as an immigrant, as opposed to having her differences constantly pointed out in Canada.

Two notable ways of conceiving of immigration in North America are the metaphorical ideas of the **melting pot** and the **cultural mosaic**. Some people believe that the United States demands assimilation and therefore everyone who comes to America must strive to become "American," so they all join together in the same melting pot, promoting America. In a cultural mosaic, by contrast, people from different religions, countries and ethnicities are encouraged to maintain their affinities to their countries of origin and to be accepted into the Canadian culture all the same. One way of understanding Bharati Mukherjee's criticisms about Canada is to consider the cultural mosaic as alienating, without a clear way for newcomers to fit in and therefore always being perceived by Canadians as "Other." When Mukherjee says she "sees herself in" the other immigrants to America, it may be because the melting pot is clearer: you can fit in so long as you uphold American traditions. These ideas of the melting pot and the cultural mosaic are sometimes criticized as being too strange, an imagined way of considering a "nation," without statistical or measurable ways of conceiving of how multicultural one country is compared to the other.

INDIGENOUS WRITERS IN CANADA AND APPROPRIATION OF VOICE

In Canadian literature, the debate over appropriation of voice has been a long one. An early example includes Duncan Campbell Scott's nineteenth-century poems about Indigenous Peoples. Scott was one of the Confederation Poets as well as, by vocation, being the deputy superintendent for Indian Affairs. He is remembered as an intellectual, a civil servant, but the context of his work has led to his reputation being questioned if not sullied. Under his purview, the residential schools were expanded, a tuberculosis outbreak was overlooked, and treaties stripping Indigenous Peoples from their land were created.[28] Some critics believe "Scott's understanding of and compassion for the Indians, and of what was being done to them in the process of assimilation, grew from poem to poem — was itself a process of sorts — a result no doubt of his lifelong exposure to Indians and their culture."[29] His sonnet "Onondaga Madonna," with lines like "This woman of a weird and waning race, / The tragic savage lurking in her face," seems to voice racist stereotypes, and although it turns to consider the woman holding her baby, the "primal warrior," there is a feeling of ominousness, of hopelessness for the future of Indigenous Peoples. Scott's work is complicated by the fact that he knew what was happening to Indigenous Peoples because of assimilation, and, through his day job, he enacted discriminatory practices of erasure. Having said that, the literature of a given time offers a reflection of the cultural values and struggles, including racial and cultural discrimination. It is difficult to look back upon but serves as a record of where we were, where we are and where we aspire to be.

Another case of cultural appropriation comes through Archibald Belaney, or Grey Owl, as he was known. Born in 1888 in England, Archibald Belaney moved to Canada at the age of seventeen. Interested in Aboriginal Peoples, he befriended the Ojibwa in Northern Ontario, where he presented himself as the son of a Scot and an Apache woman. Through the Ojibwa and Iroquois Nations, he learned about nature, assimilated into the culture and became a proponent of conservationism — all seemingly positive things. His first book, *The Men of the Last Frontier* (1931), is part memoir and discusses the infringing industrialization of the land and its effects on wildlife. Through the 1930s, he published three more works, presenting himself as an Indigenous person and promoting conservationism in the face of losing the land and wildlife to sawmills. Upon his death in 1938, it was revealed in obituaries that Grey Owl had been born in England, of British parentage, which caused an international scandal.

Box 11.6 Diversity in Action

Appropriation of voice can happen in the context of gender — male authors writing from the female perspective, as in the case of eighteenth-century British author Samuel Richardson, who wrote in his 1740 novel *Pamela*, an epistolary novel written in diary form, from the perspective of maidservant Pamela Andrews. Pamela must stave off inappropriate sexual advances from Mr. B., the master of the house, after his mother dies. In Canadian literature, Carol Shields wrote the novel *Larry's Party* (1997) in the third-person perspective of a middle-aged man. Richard B. Wright wrote *Clara Callan* from the perspective of two sisters in 2001; it is considered a strong example of writing from the point of view of the opposite gender. It is also an epistolary novel.

"Appropriation of voice "is the representation of a culture and subjectivity that is not one's own but placed on the page as if it is/ can be and that this representation is of a subjectivity that's been historically marginalized, disempowered or disenfranchised."
— Hiromi Goto, "Appropriation of Voice: Part 1."

Through the case of Archie Belaney, questions on both sides of the appropriation of voice debate can be explored. The idea of power — of who gets to tell the story, whose story it is, how the story gets told and sold, and therefore how the story is received — is intrinsically swept up in the issue of appropriation of voice. In the case of Belaney, he revered the culture he was emulating and immersed himself in it, but it becomes controversial when the question arises of whose voices might have been repressed, whose stories left untold because his voice and his works were published. The question remains about Grey Owl of "whether he was a calculating fraud or simply a man who chose to reinvent himself within the context of the life he lived and continually re-imagined."[30] The question of appropriation of voice arose again in the 1990s surrounding Indigenous stories and characters being written by non-Indigenous writers.

Who gets to tell the stories of a nation, of a specific people within that nation? On the one hand, as Lenore Keeshig-Tobias writes in the article "Stop Stealing Native Stories" published in the *Globe and Mail* in 1990: "Stories are not just entertainment. Stories are power." She lists one film, one novel, and one collection of short stories, *Where the Spirit Lives*, *Bone Bird*, by Darlene Quaiff, and *Hobbema*, by W.P. Kinsella, charging them with "cultural theft."[31] She makes the case that "the Canadian cultural industry is stealing — unconsciously, perhaps, but with the same devastating results — native stories as surely as the missionaries stole our religion and the politicians stole our land and the residential schools stole our language."

Critics have noted that "too often…the private marketplace tends to publish the more established and dominant voices, and ignores minority voices. Furthermore… many works done by white artists about other cultures have served only to perpetuate stereotypes or, at best, to speak patronizingly on behalf of less powerful groups rather than letting these groups speak for themselves."[32] Lenore Keeshig-Tobias writes: "However, as Ms [Maria] Campbell said on CBC Radio's *Morningside*, 'If you want to write our stories, then be prepared to live with us.' And not just for a few months. Hear the voices of the wilderness. Be there with the Lubicon, the Innu. Be there with the Teme-Augama Anishnabi on the Red Squirrel Road. The Saugeen Ojibway. If you want these stories, fight for them. I dare you."

Indigenous Cree-Canadian writer Tomson Highway, "born in a snowbank" in December 1951, where northern Manitoba meets Saskatchewan in what is today called Nunavut, is a survivor of the residential school system who went on to work in social work before becoming an internationally successful playwright, novelist and classical pianist.[33] Highway's play *The Rez Sisters* riffs on French-Canadian playwright Michel Tremblay's successful play *Les Belles-Soeurs* and examines the lives of seven women on the Wasaychigan Hill Indian Reserve. His subsequent play, *Dry Lips Oughta Move to Kapuskasing,* was originally titled *The Rez Brothers* and continues the storyline. Highway, who speaks Cree, French and English, discusses his frustration with the English language as it is far more cerebral than the physicality of the French language or the humour of Cree.[34] His works are full of lightheartedness and humour, even while they criticize some of Canada's cultural policies, origin narratives and stifling religious values.

As previously mentioned, Joy Kogawa wrote a novel about Japanese internment in Canada from the perspective of a woman looking back on, and coming to understand, her upbringing. In 2005 Thomas King, a Canadian writer of Cherokee and Greek descent, wrote a collection of "Coyote" stories, *A Short History of Indians in Canada,* which question human foibles and history. His story "Coyote and the Enemy Aliens" puts the Japanese internment into an absurdist context that is masterfully written so that the bystander narrator is implicated in the "Whitemen's" pronouncement of Japanese people as "enemy aliens," while Coyote reaps the benefits by casually buying cheap, used trucks and goods that formerly belonged to the Japanese people. King shows the similar disenfranchisement of a people through Coyote's and the narrator's views of the Japanese "enemy aliens," as they go along with the stories they are told without question or action to support those disenfranchised.

DIVERSITYINACTIONDIVERSITYINA

Box 11.7 Diversity in Action

On August 20, 2016, singer and poet Gord Downie, during the final Tragically Hip concert in Kingston, Ontario, made a case for raising awareness about Indigenous issues in Canada when he called out Prime Minister Justin Trudeau, who was present at the concert, and said, "We're in good hands, folks. Real good hands," as the camera showed Trudeau in the crowd at the Rogers K-Rock Centre, clad in a Hip T-shirt. "He cares about the people way up north. That we were trained our entire lives to ignore." Downie's statement landed, as he was suffering with terminal brain cancer and a large audience of Canadians tuned in to watch his final show. His words rang true to the generation of people who grew up knowing little to nothing about the government-imposed Indigenous policies that led to widespread discrimination, abuses and cultural evisceration. With this last statement, Downie shone the spotlight on the plight of Indigenous Peoples in Canada and their long-ignored history.

Source: "'Trained Our Entire Lives to Ignore': Gord Downie's Call to Action for Indigenous in the North," CBC News, August 21, 2016 <CBC.ca http://www.cbc.ca/news/canada/north/gord-downie-praises-justin-trudeau-aboriginal-people-1.3729996>.

Although some years had passed since the 1990s and the appropriation of voice debate in Canadian literature, in spring 2016, it reared its head again. Hal Niedzviecki, editor of *Write* magazine, published by the Writer's Union of Canada, in the foreword to an issue highlighting essays and writing by Indigenous People wrote, "I don't believe in cultural appropriation. In my opinion, anyone, anywhere, should be encouraged to imagine other peoples, other cultures, other identities. I'd go so far as to say there should be an award for doing so."[35] Author Alicia Elliott, whose work was accepted and edited by Niedzviecki for the issue, was confounded by his position, which, she felt, completely contradicted the spirit of her own essay. While Niedzviecki opined that stereotypes will be rooted out and seen for what they are, Elliott had given an example in her essay where a story had won an award even though it relied on the stereotypes of drunken Indigenous characters and misunderstood their Potlatch ceremonies. Elliott pointed out that such stereotypes are not, in fact, rooted out, questioned or viewed as limited or problematic. Instead, they win awards.

Robert Jago sees the debate as a problem of power in numbers: "The dilemma, very simply, is one of numbers: non-native Canada has twenty-four times the population of Indigenous Canada, and occupies nearly 100 percent of senior positions in media organizations. No matter how small the incursion of mainstream media into Indigenous culture or politics, non-Native Canada overwhelms us."[36]

DIVERSITYINACTIONDIVERSITYINACTIONDI

Box 11.8 Diversity in Action

There are many exceptional novels written by Indigenous Peoples in Canadian literature. The following list highlights a handful of them.

Thomas King's *Green Grass, Running Water* follows four different plot lines of characters who masterfully meld together. It is part origin myth, part road novel, part family relationships oriented, culminating in a meeting at the ritual Sun Dance. It is humorous and entertaining, as well as thought-provoking.

Richard Wagamese's *Indian Horse* follows an Indigenous boy, Saul Indian Horse, who survives the residential school system to become a professional hockey player.

Katharena Vermette's *The Break* begins with a young mother looking out her window at night and witnessing violence against a young woman. Written from different characters' points of view, it explores sisterhood and family, as well as violence and the perpetuation of abuses.

Cherie Dimaline's *The Marrow Thieves* is a science fiction novel that places the reader in a world vastly affected by global warming. People have lost the ability to dream, and they hunt Indigenous Peoples for their bone marrow to help them recover this ability.

Joshua Whitehead's *Jonny Appleseed* is written from the point of view of Jonny, a Two Spirit/Indigiqueer character. Jonny is living off the rez in Winnipeg where he works as a webcam boy. It is a coming-of-age tale.

Writer and editor Hiromi Goto wrote about appropriation of voice in 2011:

> There are no clear lines to separate what is okay, from what is not okay. I do not believe in a kind of creative essentialism, for instance, that limits all writers to only write from their own lived experiences, their own cultural group, their own gender, sex, class, religion, etc. I don't feel like I cannot write a story from the point of view of a white male heterosexual character, for instance. What I ask myself is this: in the grand scheme of things, is my writing a story about this character going to take something away from the culture I'm representing, something they have always struggled to gain? In a kind of simplistic way, for me, it all boils down to air-time. If we look to published literature in N. America over the past 350 years, who had the most air-time? Who has not?[37]

What seems clear to most people is, as Goto suggests, that appropriation of voice comes down to a question of power — who has been given the power to write and

> **Box 11.9 Think About…**
>
> For more information and articles about appropriation of voice, Indigenous voices and Canadian literature, consider the following:
>
> Alicia Elliott, "The Cultural Appropriation Debate Isn't About Free Speech," cbc.ca, May 16, 2017 <http://www.cbc.ca/arts/the-cultural-appropriation-debate-isn-t-about-free-speech-it-s-about-context-1.4117142>.
>
> Alicia Elliott's Twitter thread following *The Write* Indigenous issue publication: <https://twitter.com/wordsandguitar/status/862044639263633408?lang=en>.
>
> Robert Jago, "On Cultural Appropriation, Canadians Are Hypocrites," *The Walrus,* May 18, 2017, updated August 22, 2017 <https://thewalrus.ca/on-cultural-appropriation-canadians-are-hypocrites/>.

publish stories? Whose voices have been left out because of discrimination? Taking stock and knowing the statistics, can't we do better and reset so that there is more balance?

BLACK LIKE CANADIANS

In 1997, Rinaldo Walcott published *Black Like Who? Writing Black Canada*, in which he documented the erasure of Black people from Canada's history and its ringing stereotype of Black men as criminals. Twenty years later, Walcott announced he was "quitting CanLit" because of its preponderance for maintaining the *status quo*, its continual surprise at Black literary expression and its slow progress at seeing Black writers as foundational to it.[38]

Walcott is not wrong in being disappointed at the literary establishment's inability to see the significant contributions of Black Canadians to the literary canon. The evidence of Black Canadian writers' works being critically well-received, award-winning and ongoing is significant: Dionne Brand's poetry and novels, Ian Williams' poetry and fiction, David Chariandy's novels and memoir, Austin Clarke's novels, Suzette Mayr's novels, Nalo Hopkinson, Claire Harris. Jael Richardson, an author herself, saw the need for a more diverse Canadian literature and its reflection in literary events, and in 2016, she launched the FOLD, the Festival of Literary Diversity. Held in Brampton, it includes community outreach with schools in the area, followed by a weekend of panels about and in discussion with diverse literary figures, or writing and publishing panels taught by people in the field. Richardson's FOLD includes a multitude of cultural, ethnic, sexualities, genders, abilities and the writings from these groups. It also invites people from the publishing industry to consider first page pitches and to offer information sessions about the industry. In this way, the FOLD is a two-way street, both introducing diverse writers and their works, and inviting the publishing industry to take part and listen in on these sessions.

In 2017, David Chariandy's novel *Brother*, set in Scarborough, Ontario, during the 1990s, received the Rogers Writers' Trust Award. Chariandy creates compelling characters in the protagonist Michael, his popular brother Francis and their hard-working mother. Chariandy's prose captures the feeling of place, as in the following passage:

> In Desiree's [barber shop], you postured, but you also played. You showed up every one of your dictated roles and fates. Our parents had come from Trinidad and Jamaica and Barbados. From Sri Lanka and Poland, and Somalia and Vietnam. They worked shit jobs, struggled with rent, were chronically tired, and often pushed just as chronically tired notions about identity and respectability. But in Desiree's, different styles and kinships were possible. You found new language, you caught the gestures. You kept the meanings close as skin.[39]

Scarborough has long been the starting place for immigrant families in Canada, and Chariandy writes lyrically about it, placing the reader right there with others in a sometimes awkward but endearing coming-of-understanding with what it means to develop and be a part of a community, however reluctant that initial community may be. In an interview, Chariandy explained the inspiration behind his novel:

> But I still wanted to capture what Scarborough was really like for a child in the early 1990s, particularly a child with a black mother and a South Asian father growing up at that particular time…. There was, at that time, a lot of anxiety about visible minorities moving into the area and changing the landscape. I grew up hearing these stories — about people I love and respect, who were profoundly creative and hardworking and simply had dreams of living a good life. These stories are often overlooked and ignored. I wanted to capture this narrative, one of resilience, creativity, tenderness and love.[40]

Chariandy is not the only author to take up Scarborough, once a condescended-upon suburb of Toronto, as his subject matter. Carrianne Leung has written two novels about it, *The Wondrous Woo* and *That Time I Loved You*, and Catherine Rodriguez wrote *Scarborough* in 2017. The generation who lived through Scarborough's less-than-stellar reputation comes back to write about it in ways that both expand readers' understandings and offer endearing depictions of it.

Box 11.10 Diversity in Action

A couple of articles show the growing pains of Black writers being included in the literary canon, at academic conferences, on panels both as the subjects of these panels and as academics working in the field.

Paul Barrett et al.'s article, "The Unbearable Whiteness of CanLit," outlines the experience of an academic panel on the topic of "Austin Clarke's Critical Neglect," and their own subsequent feeling of being completely neglected at the conference. In it, he quotes Clarke, who explained in a letter, "You have to be born here, preferably on a farm, and you have to write about growing up with cow-dung betwixt your toes, in order to be taken seriously by those people who think they know about writing and literature."

In Tania Canis's article "Diversity Is a White Word," she writes, "Terms such as 'diversity', 'multiculturalism', and 'culturally and linguistically diverse' (CALD) only normalise whiteness as the example of what it means to be and exist in the world."

Sources: Paul Barrett, Darcy Ballantyne, Camille Isaacs, and Kris Singh, "The Unbearable Whiteness of CanLit," *The Walrus*, July 26, 2017; and Tania Canis, "Diversity Is a White Word," *Arthub*, Australia, January 9, 2017.

GENDER IN CANADIAN LITERATURE

Scholar Carole Gerson, in working on early Canadian writers, found that the early anthologists had a lot to do with who got remembered in Canadian literature. She shows how anthologists work from previous anthologies, and so the writers represented in early Canadian literature, and even the poems or short works themselves, were often repeated on this basis. Women writers, a minority in early anthologies to begin with, were subsequently dropped and, once dropped, became increasingly hard to re-find. It took the effort of feminist scholars in the 1980s and 1990s to rediscover many early Canadian women writers. The same can be said of early women writers in England and America. Such work helped us to rediscover Isabella Valancy Crawford, Pauline Johnson, Sara Jeannette Duncan. Pauline Johnson (1861–1913), also known as Tekahionwake, is an early mixed-race Canadian poet and performer. She toured Canada and the United States reciting her poems and wearing traditional Indigenous costumes, having a flair for the dramatic arts.

While progress can be slow, and the case has been made that Canada's literature boasts a wealth of successful women writers, some critics see them as being held up as "tokens," rather than a reflection of the literary scene. Tokenism is the act of having one writer or character who is representative of a specific minority as a way of including that group without actually including them in a pluralistic, relevant, equal way. It's true that Canada's only Nobel Prize in Literature was awarded to a woman, Alice Munro, and arguably Canada's best-known international writer is Margaret Atwood, whose success from *A Handmaid's Tale* among other novels is far-reaching. Still, Carole Gerson believes that "when we see several female stars (in literature, film, music, broadcasting, politics or whatever), we tend to generalize the visibility of a few to signify equality or even majority, regardless of what the numbers tell us."[41]

In 2012, Canadian Women in the Literary Arts (CWILA) was initiated, whereby a group of Canadian women kept a public count of how many published works by women were reviewed, and whether the reviews were written by men or women. While initial numbers were "discouraging," with only between 23 percent and 40 percent of works by women being reviewed in the newspapers and literary journals they tallied, CWILA's work seems to have had some effect.[42] By 2015's count, there was near gender parity in reviews of books by men and women: 49% men; 48% women, as per their reports.[43] CWILA's work continues, although one would hope that soon it won't be required to have a gatekeeper on gender equality in literature.

DEPICTIONS OF SEXUALITY IN CANADIAN LITERATURE

In December 1967, Pierre Elliot Trudeau, then-Justice Minister, put forward a bill to decriminalize homosexuality. He famously said, "there's no place for the state in the bedrooms of the nation," and Canadians have enjoyed the forward-thinking vision of that statement ever since. In 2005, the federal government of Canada legalized same-sex marriage. As well, Toronto enjoys one of the most robust Pride Festivals celebrating LGBT2TQ+ identities.

A documentary about Canadian film called *Weird Sex and Snowshoes: A Trek Through Canadian Cinematic Psyche* (2004), directed by Jill Sharpe suggests through its title first, but in the film as well, that the Canadian imagination surrounding sex and sexuality can be a strange journey. In literature, Marian Engel's novel *Bear*, which won the Governor General's Award for Fiction in 1976, stands out as its plot is on the surface about a lonely librarian's sexual relationship with a bear. The relationship with the bear leads to a spiritual shift in the main character.

More recently, works like Suzette Mayr's novel *Monoceros* take on the discrimination against gay students and teachers in a Catholic high school. The novel covers the suicide of a bullied high school student, and the ripple effect of his death on the closeted male principal and his boyfriend, the guidance counsellor at the school, the boy's parents, other kids in his class and a drag queen. The narrative point of view shifts chapter by chapter, piecing together a richly poignant, at times humorous, portrait of how deeply one suicide can affect so many lives, and also questioning the limitations on sexuality imposed on faculty in Catholic schools.

When Raziel Reid's debut novel, *When Everything Feels Like the Movies,* won the

Box 11.11 Diversity in Action

One of the concerns in Canadian literature is that minority voices are not winning the literary awards, of which there are many in Canada. The table highlights some Canadian literary awards and the writers who have won them from the last four years. By this count, there are five different literary prizes over four years, so twenty winners total:

Male writers:	11
Female writers:	9
Indigenous writers:	2
Writers of colour:	8
Caucasian writers:	12

	2017	2016	2015	2014
Giller Prize	Michael Redhill	Madeleine Thien	André Alexis	Sean Michaels
	Bellevue Square	*Do Not Say We Have Nothing*	*Fifteen Dogs*	*Us Conductors*
Governor General's Award for Fiction	Joel Thomas Hynes	Madeleine Thien	Guy Vanderhaeghe	Thomas King
	We'll All Be Burnt In Our Beds Some Day	*Do Not Say We Have Nothing*	*Daddy Lenin and Other Stories*	*The Back of the Turtle*
Governor General's Award for Poetry	Richard Harrison	Steven Heighton	Robyn Sarah	Arleen Paré
	On Not Losing My Father's Ashes in the Flood	*The Waking Comes Late*	*My Shoes Are Killing Me*	*Lake of Two Mountains*
Rogers Writers' Trust Award	David Chariandy	Yasuko Thanh	André Alexis	Miriam Toews
	Brother	*Mysterious Fragrance of the Yellow Mountains*	*Fifteen Dogs*	*All My Puny Sorrows*
Griffin Poetry Prize (Canadian)	Jordan Abel	Liz Howard	Jane Munro	Anne Carson
	Injun	*Infinite Citizen of the Shaking Tent*	*Blue Sonoma*	*Red Doc>*

*As this chapter goes to publication, Billy Ray Belcourt, a 23 year-old Cree-Canadian writer, won the 2018 Griffin Prize for Poetry for his collection *The Wound Is a World.*

Governor General's Award for Children's Literature, it caused a ruckus across the Canadian literary and journalistic world. Reid's novel is loosely based on a true story out of California (the story of Larry Fobes King) but is set in Canada about a flamboyant gay middle schooler, Jude, who is relentlessly bullied and assaulted by a group of boys from his school. When Jude asks one of them, Luke, to the valentine's dance, then announces that Luke had, months before, actually come back to assist him to the hospital after a particularly cruel beating by Luke's friends, the bullies turn on Luke. At the dance, Luke shows up with a gun. One of the difficulties with Reid's novel is the portrayal of Jude, who is unapologetic, flamboyant, attention-starved and critical. In other words, he is not the easiest character to read or to like. However, Reid's novel stands out as a testament to just that; why do we ask our non-heterosexual characters to comply by the heteronormative culture? What happens when they don't? His work makes us consider the importance of empathy to deepening our understanding of one another.

Reid's novel is written using vulgar language and expressions, and portrays young people as highly sexualized. After Reid won the Governor General's Award, *National Post* writer Barbara Kay called the novel "values void" and considered the monetary award "wasted tax dollars."[44] Another group tried to have the award stripped from Reid. The novel ended up being chosen on CBC's *Canada Reads,* where gossip columnist Lainey Lui championed and defended it into the finals, where it lost. Overall, Reid's novel shows us how even in a country that prides itself on having adopted Pierre Trudeau's oft-quoted idea, in Canadian literature there is still work to do. Canadians like to think of themselves as "nice," peaceful and supporters of equality, but as we have seen, much work still needs to be done before we are truly inclusive.

CONCLUSION

The literary arts afford us opportunities in terms of diversity by allowing boundless portrayals of characters and voices so that our empathy for, and understanding of, one another grows. We can't always jump on an airplane and travel to see the people and places that interest us, and although most people know that each person carries unconscious biases, it can be hard to shift them. Literature allows us to explore the world through imagination, to reflect on how the world works and to consider how it is viewed by people other than ourselves. A national literature shows off the talents of a country in one artistic realm, while also mirroring the people, ideas, concerns of a particular time. As students of diversity, it is important to continue writing in, and listening to, a broad range of voices.

There is an embarrassment of riches to behold in terms of diversity in Canadian

> **Box 11.12 Think About...**
>
> **#weneeddiversebooks**
> Check out Jen Sookfong Lee's essay "On Respectable Narratives and Why Diversity in Literature Matters," *Open Book*, April 25, 2018 <http://open-book. ca/index.php/Columnists/On-respectable-narratives-and-why-diversity-on-the-page-matters>.

literature. There are Canadian writers of various races, ethnicities, religions, political stripes, genders, sexualities, classes. How well we are handling the wealth of Canadian literature may be the question. This moment provides us with a way forward: we must strive for fair representation through literature and in its publication. We know this, and we are reckoning with the cultural fires of the past that have involved eradication of, or ignorance about, diverse voices. Pioneering writer Catharine Parr Traill famously wrote that Canada was without ghosts. Now, in and through Canadian literature, we seem poised amidst many.

CRITICAL REVIEW QUESTIONS

1. Name three reasons the Canada First movement wanted to develop and establish a Canadian national literature. Do you think there is a value to having and supporting a national literature?
2. What specific problems do Duncan Campbell Scott and Archie Belaney, aka Grey Owl, highlight about diversity, particularly with regards to Indigenous Peoples?
3. What is CWILA? What prompted CWILA to initiate its counts? How effective have those counts been? (Check the website to see if there are updates).
4. Why did Rinaldo Walcott say he was "quitting CanLit"?
5. What made some critics feel that Raziel Reid's novel *When Everything Feels Like the Movies* ought to be stripped of its Governor General's Award?

RECOMMENDED READINGS

David Chariandy, *Brother* (Toronto: Penguin Random House, 2017).

Tomson Highway, "Why Cree Is the Funniest of All Languages," in Drew Hayden Taylor (ed.), *Me Funny* (Douglas & MacIntyre, 2006): 159–168.

Joy Kogawa, *Obasan* (Toronto: Lester and Orpen, 1981).

Suzette Mayr, *Monoceros* (Toronto: Coach House, 2011).

Kathleen Vermette, *The Break* (Toronto: House of Anansi, 2016).

KEY TERMS

appropriation of voice: representation of a culture or subjectivity different than the author's own, but passed off as though it were a true representation, particularly if the group being represented has been historically marginalized, discriminated against or disenfranchised.

cultural mosaic: metaphor used to describe the nationalism of Canada; built on a model of distinction, whereby immigrants to Canada are encouraged to maintain their cultures, ethnicities, traditions, while living and working in Canada.

epistolary novel: novel written sequentially through letters (epistles), journal entries, email messages, tweets.

melting pot: metaphor used to describe the nationalism of the United States; built on a model of assimilation, of bringing people together from other cultures, ethnicities, immigrant populations, to be a part of the "American" way of life.

Nisei: person born in the United States or Canada whose parents immigrated from Japan.

Notes

1. Sharon Olds, "I Go Back to May 1937," *The Gold Cell* (Knopf, 1987): 23.
2. The Canada First Movement was made up of men — George Denison, Henry Morgan, William Foster, Goldwin Smith, Robert Grant Haliburton — who had been born in Canada, who had attended college and who had written and published. W.H. New writes: "The normative values of the Canada First movement designed a Canada in which ethnic differences would be absorbed into an anglo-Protestant norm. But in different parts of the country these norms were simply not accepted" (*A History of Canadian Literature,* New Amsterdam, 1989: 85). Even after the movement officially dissolved, their ideas about the need to develop a national literature to enhance patriotism and develop an undeniable national character continued.
3. Donna Bennett and Russell Brown, *A New Anthology of Canadian Literature* (Oxford University Press: 2002): xvii.
4. W.H. New, *A History of Canadian Literature* (New Amsterdam, 1989): 16.
5. Frances Brooke, *The History of Emily Montague* (New Canadian Library, 1991 [1769]): 36–37.
6. Brooke, *The History of Emily Montague,* 37.
7. Brooke, *The History of Emily Montague,* 38.
8. Anna Brownell Winterson, *Winter Studies and Summer Rambles in Canada* (New Canadian Library, 1990 [1838]): 9.
9. Winterson, *Winter Studies,* 10.
10. Terence Scully, "Early Novel Has Not Survived Its Age," *St Ursula's Convent; or, the Nun's Story* Book Review, *Canadian Children's Literature,* 67 (1997): 78–79.
11. Adrian Mitchell, "Sam Slick, *The Clockmaker* by Thomas Chandler Haliburton, 1835," *Reference Guide to Short Fiction* (Gale, 1999).
12. Susanna Moodie, *Roughing It in the Bush or Life in Canada,* edited by Carl Ballstadt (Carleton University Press, 1995 [1852]): 515.
13. Margaret Atwood, *The Journals of Susanna Moodie* (Oxford University Press, 1970): 62.
14. Carl Ballstadt, "Thomas D'Arcy McGee as a Father of Canadian Literature," *Studies*

in Canadian Literature, 11 (1976) <https://journals.lib.unb.ca/index.php/scl/article/view/7827/8884>.

15. James Reaney, "Introduction," *Literature of Canada: Poetry and Prose in Reprint* (University of Toronto Press, 1973).

16. Roy Daniells, "Crawford, Carman, and D.C. Scott," *in* Carl F. Klinck (ed.), Literary History of Canada (Toronto: University of Toronto Press, 1967): 408.

17. Northrop Frye, "Conclusion," in Carl F. Klinck (ed.), *The Literary History of Canada* (Toronto: University of Toronto Press, 1965): 843.

18. "The History of the Persons Case," The Status of Women Canada, *Government of Canada*. September 23, 2016 <http://www.swc-cfc.gc.ca/commemoration/pd-jp/history-histoire-en.html>.

19. Emily Ferguson, *The Impressions of Janey Canuck Abroad* (Toronto, 1901) <https://archive.org/details/cihm_75218>.

20. Susan Jackel, Catherine Cavanagh and Tabitha Marshall, "Emily Murphy," *The Canadian Encyclopedia*, 28 (August 2015) <https://www.thecanadianencyclopedia.ca/en/article/emily-murphy/>.

21. Cecily Devereux, "L.M. Montgomery," *The Canadian Encyclopedia*, June 29, 2017 <https://www.thecanadianencyclopedia.ca/en/article/montgomery-lucy-maud/>.

22. The eight "Anne" novels by L.M. Montgomery are: *Anne of Green Gables, Anne of Avonlea, Anne of the Island, Anne of Windy Poplars, Anne's House of Dreams, Anne of Ingleside, Rainbow Valley, Rilla of Ingleside.*

23. Nick Mount, *Arrival: The Story of CanLit* (Anansi, 2017): 5.

24. Joy Kogawa, *Obasan* (Lester & Orpen Dennys, 1981): 49.

25. Kogawa, *Obasan,* 267.

26. The War Measures Act was passed in 1914 during the First World War. It allowed the government to by-pass parliament, and if necessary to suspend civil liberties in order to put in motion things deemed necessary for war through order-in-council. It was used during the Second World War as well. Because it was still in place, it was used to protect the government of British Columbia as it imposed the Japanese internment following Pearl Harbor.

27. Bharati Mukherjee, "Introduction," *Darkness* (New York: Penguin, 1985): 2–3.

28. Robert McDougall, "Duncan Campbell Scott," *The Canadian Encyclopedia* (January 18, 2018) <https://www.thecanadianencyclopedia.ca/en/article/duncan-campbell-scott/>.

29. Gerald Lynch, "An Endless Flow: D.C. Scott's Indian Poems," *Studies in Canadian Literature/Etudes en littérature canadienne,* 7, 1 (1982) <https://journals.lib.unb.ca/index.php/SCL/rt/printerFriendly/7971/9028>.

30. Karine Duhamel, "Review of *Apostate Gentleman: Grey Owl The Writer and the Myths* by Albert Braz," *Canada's History* (June 1, 2016): 55 <https://www.pressreader.com/canada/canadas-history/20160601/282218010140953>.

31. Lenore Keeshig-Tobias, "Stop Stealing Native Stories," *Globe and Mail*, January 26, 1990: A7.

32. Kelly Bondy-Cusinato, *The Voice Appropriation Controversy in the Context of Canadian Cultural Practices,* M.A. dissertation, University of Windsor (1995): 8 <http://www.collectionscanada.gc.ca/obj/s4/f2/dsk3/ftp04/mq30884.pdf>.

33. Tomson Highway, "Biography," *tomsonhighway.com* <https://www.tomsonhighway.com/biography.html>.

34. Tomson Highway, "Why Cree Is the Funniest of All Languages," In Drew Hayden Taylor (ed.), *Me Funny* (Douglas & MacIntyre, 2006): 159–168.

35. Robert Jago, "On Cultural Appropriation, Canadians are Hypocrites," *The Walrus*, May 18, 2017 <https://thewalrus.ca/on-cultural-appropriation-canadians-are-hypocrites/>.

36. Jago, "On Cultural Appropriation."

37. Hiromi Goto, "Appropriation of Voice: Part 1," *Hiromigoto.com*, January 10, 2011 <https://www.hiromigoto.com/appropriation-of-voice-part-1/>.

38. Paul Barrett, Darcy Ballantyne, Camille Isaacs and Kris Singh, "The Unbearable Whiteness of CanLit," *The Walrus*, July 26, 2017 <https://thewalrus.ca/the-unbearable-whiteness-of-canlit/>.

39. David Chariandy, *Brother* (Penguin Random House, 2017): Ch. 4.

40. Ryan. B. Patrick, "How David Chariandy Brought His Novel *Brother* to Life," *How I Wrote It,* CBC.ca, January 8, 2018 <http://www.cbc.ca/books/how-david-chariandy-brought-his-novel-brother-to-life-1.4310129>.

41. Savanna Scott Leslie, "An Interview with Carole Gerson," CWILA.com, December 20, 2013 <https://cwila.com/an-interview-with-carole-gerson/>.

42. Gillian Jerome, "The CWILA Numbers: An Introduction," CWILA.com, June 10, 2012 <https://cwila.com/the-cwila-count-2011-an-introduction-by-gillian-jerome/>.

43. "2015 CWILA Count Numbers," CWILA *Canadian Women in the Literary Arts* <https://cwila.com/2015-cwila-count-numbers/>.

44. Barbara Kay, "Wasted Tax Dollars on Values-Void Novel," *National Post*, January 21, 2015 <http://nationalpost.com/opinion/barbara-kay-wasted-tax-dollars-on-a-values-void-novel>.

12

CANADA'S NEWS MEDIA

THE CRISIS OF DIVERSE QUALITY

Peter Steven

> *Diversity in our media matters because our newspapers and television stations are supposed to reflect reality. If our mirror on society is distorted, our opinions get skewed.* — John Miller, Emeritus Professor of Journalism[1]

KEY OBJECTIVES

Describe the four major theories about media.

Understand the big issues confronting Canadian media today.

Explore the economic, political and technological forces that shape our media.

Understand the various forms in which Canadian news is delivered to its readers, viewers and listeners.

Assess the strengths and weaknesses of our news media.

This chapter sets out to examine both the good qualities and the problems within the Canadian news media.[2] We look at economic issues, technological factors, political dimensions and many aspects of Canadian culture. Throughout, we focus on the various features of diversity discussed in earlier chapters of the book. We begin by considering a range of theories about the media, the big issues being debated today and the giant organizations now shaping Canadian media. In the second part of the chapter we dive a little deeper into the characteristics of our print, TV, radio and digital news media.

CANADIAN MEDIA ADMIRED WORLDWIDE

Canada's media system has nurtured world-renowned artists and journalists, including film directors, writers, actors, musicians and war correspondents. In addition, the Canadian media enjoy high ratings at home and abroad for their serious journalism, their advanced tele-communications and their lively entertainment in radio, film and TV. The National Film Board of Canada (NFB) has long been admired for its high-quality documentaries and animation. CBC Radio draws respect for its journalism and social affairs programs. The *Toronto Star, Le Devoir* and other papers continue to publish essential reporting. And beginning in the 1970s, Canada achieved a reputation for its systems of satellite and digital communications.

But is that reputation still deserved? Has the excellent work that was produced in the past been maintained? For many, Canada's media still merit high praise. And yet, it is also clear that Canada's media system, like every other in North America and Western Europe, works primarily to legitimate this country's political and corporate elites and capitalism in general. Most of the time Canadian newspapers and TV function as a set of dominant institutions that push other voices and points-of-view to the margins.[3] Journalists within the system and groups on the outside sometimes manage to introduce alternative ideas but this requires an uphill battle. We can also compare Canada's media to that of the US, and other media practices around the world. To some degree Canada's record is stronger; in other areas it falls well short. In consequence, throughout the chapter I look at two related questions: What sorts of media do we have and how might we assess it?

This chapter centres on the Canadian media and how Canadians use it. We should recognize of course that all of us devour massive amounts of news and entertainment from the US, and that this profoundly shapes our society and our outlooks. But this should not be a tale focused solely on cultural nationalism, like a Canada Day love-in, where we celebrate all the media the country produces. Larger or more potent doses of Canadian content (CanCon) will hardly address the challenges we face. While questions about the overall value of Canadian media for both news and entertainment present us with many complex issues, on one point the evidence is clear. What we have now seems inferior to what existed ten or twenty years ago. Thus, we need to consider what could be termed "a crisis of quality."[4]

MEDIA AND ITS IMPACT ON SOCIETY

Think how you'd feel if your neighbour shouted out that a deadly measles epidemic had just erupted in the east end of the city, but you had no access to news media — no radio or TV, no papers, certainly no Internet. You might get some information from a nearby hospital or from the police. But they have their own jobs to do and can't be relied on to provide a well-balanced overview.

News people often tell us that a free media provides the oxygen for a healthy democracy. Reliable news helps us maintain our civil rights — to speak openly, to gather with others in public, to vote and run for office. But a free media also helps maintain our basic human rights — to food, safety and health. Without the ability to receive and distribute basic news information, we live in fear and danger — a long way from democracy.

In addition, the news matters because the organizations that gather and distribute news have become a major economic force in themselves. The Canadian news media employ thousands of people, gobble up tremendous resources and rake in countless benefits from governments. And through this economic power they attain political might as well. Some media owners stay in the business, even when losing money, precisely to maintain that political leverage.

Governments, schools, the military, churches, corporations and the courts all play a big role in shaping how we live our lives. But more than any of them the media have become the most powerful institutions in many societies today. Almost everything we know about the world comes to us through the media. Even if we ourselves get directly involved in an activity or an event, we look to the media to see it reported on, and hope our ideas and actions are taken seriously. From the media we not only receive information and ideas on big issues such as wars, politics and the economy. We also take in messages about other people and other cultures. Through watching others we absorb ideas about how to behave and what is acceptable, or unacceptable, in our culture. Sometimes we become aware of these media influences. Frequently we do not.

Many people believe that they are immune to the bad influences of media. "I grew up with it," they say. "I know when I'm hearing a biased report. I know the difference between the real world and the media world. I'm not affected." Nonetheless, companies with billions of dollars to spend in psychological research and advertising disagree. They feel confident that the media can affect us in all sorts of ways, sometimes subtly and without our knowledge.

That doesn't mean we're all dupes and zombies, brainwashed to behave uniformly and believe everything we see and hear. It does mean however that we need defences and tools to understand how the news media work. We also need the humility to recognize that we can be influenced even when we don't want to be. Adults are just as likely to adopt wrong-headed views of different cultures as young people if all they see over and over are simplistic images and explanations.

To get us started in thinking about the media in our society, let's consider three ways that the media and society relate: first, media reflect society; second, media affect society; and third, media affect other media.

Media Reflect Society

The best way to know what's going on in any society, many people believe, is to study its popular media. Accordingly, social trends, general fears and aspirations, the status of various groups and the power of ruling elites are reflected in the media. When you hear people talking about media as a mirror of society they are framing their comments in this context. With a "media reflect" approach, we might say, for example, that sexism in the presentation of a news story simply reflects what's out there in the world.

Other sorts of pressures and built-in structures at work in society affect how news gets reported and shaped. Racism in the news media, for example, often emerges as a result of general social attitudes and pressures on journalists. We can highlight many reasons why racist stories appear. These include journalists' and media owners' personal prejudices; the ethnic composition (overwhelmingly white) in the newsroom; the training of journalists; competition and marketplace pressures to serve the maximum number of readers, which in North America means the white majority; bureaucratic inertia in seeking out diverse news sources; and deep-seated news values that focus on conflict, violence, controversy and deviance.

Media Affect Society

While various theories about how the media may reflect the larger society provide us with valuable kinds of understanding, it's the debates over the media impact on society (its effects) that have generated the most heat and controversy. Thus, the second customary way of talking about the media is to express concern or admiration over its effects. These arguments about media effects have a long history, beginning in its modern form with the birth of cinema in the 1890s and its possible role in corrupting the morals of youth.

Do these types of statements sound familiar when people talk about media effects? Fashion: "everyone's wearing those Meghan Markle white coats now." Fears: "continual focus on crime stories causes readers and viewers to think that their neighbourhood is equally violent." Behaviour: "positive TV shows about men as fathers will influence real fathers to take more responsibility." Knowledge: "hearing a podcast about one's traditional music online will lead to a greater respect for one's culture." Discontent: "That new newspaper series on political corruption will trigger a change of government."

Power and the Media

The media reflect the power dynamics at play in any society. But the media don't simply reflect; they provide the symbols, images, ideas and frames that constitute power itself. Thus, the **dominant media** create some of the forms by which power operates. Not only that but the various media industries now constitute power centres themselves (along with courts, schools, police, etc.) due to their economic clout and central role in communications. Society's power holders construct a dominant ideology or way of thinking and viewing the world. The media are not separate from society; the media are part of it. So, because of these effects and their economic power, the various media are often referred to as cultural industries.

Media Affect Other Media

All media forms emerge from the genres and conventions that went before. No media form, no matter how closely it appears to flow directly from society, stands entirely on its own. There are always as many references to other media forms in any single TV show as reflections of the outside world. Even the most factually based newscast, such as CBC's *The National,* uses the conventions of newscasts as a genre, for example, an "anchor" who sits in an elaborate studio set.

Box 12.1 Think About...

Media Characteristics

The media is a modern concept. But contemporary use of the word media still carries a trace of its original Latin meaning of "medium" or "middle." The singular noun, medium, is a link or intermediate agent between places or things; thus, a medium in chemistry holds particles together, or a medium can be a device of transport, like a car, for reaching another place. Today, however, we now refer to "the media" as entities unto themselves (or even one homogenous thing). In this formulation media no longer act simply as devices or neutral carriers of ideas, but the source of those ideas and meanings. It's in this sense that the famous phrase from Canadian professor of literature Marshall McLuhan rings true: "The Medium is the Message."

FOUR THEORETICAL APPROACHES

Almost every Canadian has opinions about specific news programs, TV stations and Internet companies. In trying to see the big picture we might consider four approaches that media scholars usually encounter in their debates.

Free Markets

According to free market advocates, media should operate as businesses and companies should be rewarded by numbers of viewers and amounts of advertising. If US sources of news and entertainment are better and attract more Canadian consumers, they should be allowed to dominate. The state should not interfere, and the CBC should be forced to compete or should be dismantled. Canadian media, they argue, should not be forced to abide by Canadian content quotas. The biggest proponents of the free market approach are the large private TV networks (CTV, Global and TVA). Many conservative politicians and culture critics fiercely oppose any kind of state intervention into capitalist markets.

Nationalism

Canadians are dwarfed by the giant to the south. The US remains the most powerful country on earth, wielding political, economic and cultural power. Further, the US media and telecommunications sectors play a major role in the US economy, vigorously supported by political and economic aid from Washington. Therefore, the nationalists argue, it is only natural that the Canadian government should play an active role in supporting our media. Canadian media play a key role in shaping every aspect of our society. From newspapers to children's TV, Canadians need to see their lives reflected in our news media. Without Canadian media the country would quickly become a mere satellite of the US. Nationalists argue that with the rise of Amazon, Google, Netflix, etc. the power of US multinationals has only increased and the older forms of national intervention devised before the birth of the Internet are in urgent need of updating.

Media and Cultural Studies

This approach argues that the subject in question here (news, films, TV, radio, the Internet) should not be studied like any other economic or political phenomenon. When we talk about the media we are talking about social communication, cultural dynamics and the myriad forms of art. Humans do not "process" these things solely through their brains or within logical categories. A film is not the same as a political speech; a piece of music is very different from an economic analysis. Furthermore, even in the realm of media economics, the products of art (partly because they are generally unique) do not always operate like other commodities.

Media and cultural studies scholars ask questions such as: Why do Canadians watch the TV that they do? How do Canadian audiences use media in their lives? Although this approach obviously applies to the entertainment side of the media, it also helps explain our relations to the news media. That's because our interest in the news is also a social phenomenon. When it comes to Canada's regions, for example, as Paul U. Angelini argues in Chapter 2, people identify themselves in social and psychological terms.

Political Economy

Our media is the product of both economic and political decisions made by the government and by the owners of the dominant media. With its roots in a Marxist conflict theory approach (see Chapter 6), political economy develops critiques of both free market and nationalist approaches. Political economy scholars argue that the media in Canada have never operated solely by the processes of free markets or nationalism, and they believe that it should not. Proponents of these approaches argue for a more fully democratic or public control of the media.

Political economy writers focus on the very large forces that shape media, such as ownership patterns, the links between media owners and political elites and the ways in which government legislation shapes media practices — for example, by either stimulating production of Canadian media or working as mechanisms of censorship.

Filtering the News

The US political scholars Noam Chomsky and Ed Herman in their influential book, *Manufacturing Consent,* provide one of the best-known examples of the political economy approach, what they call the "Propaganda Model."[5] In it they develop the idea that the media practise a kind of filtering operation in creating the news. The news that we receive works primarily to get our consent to follow what the elites in society want. This serves to choke democracy. They suggest five types of filters:

> *1st Filter — Business interests of owner companies*: "You've certainly led one of the most extraordinary lives of the 20th century and it's been entirely of your own making. Can you accept the accolade that you are probably the most remarkable Australian in about 200 years?" — interview with Rupert Murdoch in the Murdoch-owned *Adelaide Sunday Mail.*
>
> *2nd Filter — Selling audiences to advertisers*: "The Coca-Cola company requires that their ads are placed adjacent to editorial that is consistent with

each brand's marketing strategy.... We consider the following subjects to be inappropriate: hard news, sex, diet, political issues, environmental issues." — memo from Coke's ad agency to magazines.

3rd Filter –Relying on information from agents of power: One group frequently referred to in Canadian economics stories is the Fraser Institute, a pro-free market "think tank," which is funded by Canadian and foreign corporate elites and has ties to similar groups in the US.

4th Filter — Flak, pressure on journalists and threats of legal action: Ben Makuch, a Canadian reporter for VICE Media refused to turn over background materials to the RCMP related to his interviews with a suspected terrorist. Allowing reporters to protect the privacy of their sources is a fundamental principle of democracy. The police do not agree. Makuch now faces a jail sentence.

5th Filter — Ideological belief in free markets: In 2004, Adbusters magazine filed a lawsuit against six major Canadian TV groups (including the CBC) for refusing to air Adbusters commercials. Most broadcasters refused the ads, fearing they would upset other advertisers.

BIG ISSUES FACING CANADIAN MEDIA

Diversity of Voices

Diversity stands out as the number one issue facing Canadian society and its media. As this book shows, we live in a multi-racial, multi-ethnic, multi-lingual country, accompanied by vast regional differences. We need media of all kinds that can facilitate communication among so many groups. Despite the great diversity of the country's regions, Canadian media is dominated by people and organizations in Ontario and Quebec. This is true for all the arts sectors, for all the most powerful news organizations and for all the biggest telecommunications groups. In the past, the government made it a priority to address regional issues by promoting universal access to basic communication. This was carried out in the nineteenth century with the creation of cross-country telegraph, rail and postal systems. Similarly, in the twentieth century Ottawa set up CBC Radio, then CBC TV, then satellite networks with a mandate to provide equal access in all regions. Today, Canada prides itself on being a multicultural nation. Indeed, it uses this ideology on the international stage to foster prestige and encourage trade, investment and business immigration.

Yet, what we see is a media system that barely reflects the real diversity of the population. In terms of regions Canada's media system has slipped badly thanks to ongoing cuts to CBC local news and public affairs. Diversity seems like a low priority in the leading newspapers, especially the *Globe and Mail*, which boasts of its links to

---

Box 12.2 Think About...

Media and Censorship

Chomsky and Herman's approach raises the issue of media censorship. In our era we find little evidence of regularized censorship in Canada. And yet:

- During the ten years of Stephen Harper's Conservative Party government (2006–2015) Harper demanded that all government scientists stop talking to the media about their work on climate change.
- Many federal and provincial governments routinely fail to provide timely access to information to journalists, although required to by law.
- All of Canada's media giants regularly apply systematic pressure on journalists not to jeopardize advertisers and government allies in their stories.
- Self-censorship among journalists and editors remains a significant trait of the media. For one reason they work as employees of large companies, often without strong union rights. In addition, most journalists share the views of their managers, and share similar economic and education backgrounds.

---

the cultural and political elites. The *Toronto Star* and *Winnipeg Free Press* do a better job at reflecting the concerns of a broader public, although not to the extent that editorially challenges the basic tenets of Canadian capitalism.

We can analyze diversity in many ways, but two key yardsticks measure diversity of media content and diversity of media control. In the first instance of media content we can ask: Who is represented on screen? Whose stories get told? and Who tells us these stories? We can also analyze how people are represented. For example, do working-class people only appear in stories about labour strikes? Are Muslim and Sikh characters usually presented as possible terrorists? This is the area in which media and cultural studies makes its contribution. We can apply these questions to both news stories and to fictional creations. Note as well that the analysis can be based on quantitative and qualitative measures.

More diversity would also include a broader range of opinion in current-affairs shows that feature guest panels of experts. Even lifestyle programs fail to reflect our demographic reality. Too often on TV and radio, non-white people are non-existent or introduced as lone standard bearers for their group. Too often so-called racial minorities are discussed only in terms of problems facing their communities. Too often news and documentary programs use the terms "main-street opinion" or "the heartland" as a shorthand for white people, implying that these folks are the real Canadians, the ones with a solid stake in our society, the backbone of the country.

The second major yardstick measures diversity in terms of media control. Here we can ask: Who are the media gatekeepers, the people who control access to the levers of power and to the tools of artistic and news creation? Who are the managing editors, directors and producers of news shows and fictional works? Who are the owners and boards of directors of Canada's big media groups? According to the 2016 census, 51.5 percent of people in Toronto and its suburbs identify themselves as non-white.[6] And yet, in every major study undertaken by media analysts the conclusion remains the same: Canadian media is overwhelmingly shaped by white men in central Canada. One study concluded that "local newscasts were dominated by stories about white people who saw the world through a prism of whiteness. These programs reinforced the construct of whiteness as the normative universe, a society in which essentially 'all others,' including people of colour — and especially Blacks and Indigenous Peoples — are constructed as 'problem' people."[7]

True diversity would entail a much broader range of editorial opinion and a fundamental change to hiring practices in the dominant media. Our journalism and communications schools are brimming with the full range of young Canadians — first- and second-generation students from Asia, Africa, Eastern Europe, South America and the Caribbean, as well as more women and Indigenous students than ever, but this diversity is not reflected in the news rooms.

"The CBC's own statistics," says veteran broadcaster Rita Deverell, "tell us that as of 2006, people with disabilities in the CBC are 2.1% of the workforce. That's in any capacity. And members of visible minorities in any capacity are 5.7% of the workforce."[8]

John Miller, a leading media historian at Ryerson University, conducted another major study that revealed the following: "Only 5 of 138 senior managers of the city's leading newspaper and television companies were non-white — a meagre 3.6 per cent. That's far behind the corresponding percentages of elected officials, public sector employees, the voluntary sector and government agencies, boards and commissions."

Box 12.3 Think About…

Selective News Coverage

"The Quebec mosque shooting received four times less coverage in major Canadian media than the Boston Marathon bombing, although the assault on the mosque was more fatal and happened in Canada. CBC's flagship news program *The National* spent five minutes of airtime on the mosque shooting the night it occurred — a stark contrast to the many hours of live reporting and commentary devoted to the London Bridge attack (in which three British Muslim men killed eight people) five months later."

Source: Azeezah Kanji, "The Persistent Gaslighting of Muslims about Islamophobia," *Toronto Star,* Feb. 8, 2018.

What about newspaper columnists? According to Miller, "only 16 of 471 columns, or 3.4 per cent, were written by visible minorities. Broadcasters fared a little better, but visible minorities made only two of 42 appearances as hosts — 4.8 per cent — and 56 of 244 appearances as on-air reporters, or 22.5 per cent." These numbers are unfortunately reflected in news coverage. "'Everyday life stories' on television news, for example, included visible minorities only 23 per cent of the time."[9] As for newsroom editors and producers, according to Miller's study only 6 percent were of a visible minority. For print columnists it was only 3.4 percent.

Gender Diversity Gap

Several studies have shown a significant gender gap in all sectors of the media and in the communications technology sector as well. One report looked at Canada's high technology businesses, including communication, and found that women make up at most 25 percent of the workforce. They stated that the "high-tech sector remains stuck in the past — and it could prove costly."[10]

In the world of gaming a more informal study revealed even greater problems. Because it combines computer programming and gaming, "you have … a double-male culture," says Rebecca Cohen Palacios, co-founder of the women-in-games initiative Pixelles. "Women in the industry still have to work harder than their male colleagues to prove their worth."[11] Some hope for change came in 2016 when the NFB announced that half of its films would be directed by women and half of its budget would go to productions directed by women.

Quebec as Distinct Society

The greatest gap in achieving diversity centres on the role of Quebec in relation to Canada as a whole. Ignorance of each society and culture, the infamous two solitudes, surely represents a great squandering — a throwing away of opportunities to expand, enrich and improve the country as a whole. In the 1960s the federal government set up programs to encourage student exchanges between English- and French-speakers, and thousands of young people jumped at the opportunity. Such schemes, modest as they were, later slipped into oblivion, along with language-translation grants.

Diversity then is a key topic of conversation in Canada: in Toronto, difference from the US; in Quebec, difference from the "English"; and among many ethnic and racial groups, difference from the white majority. This is only proper. But diversity should also be embraced as a strength. The knowledge of diversity, combined with ideas of what brings us together, our points of commonality, takes that one step further. And that combination appeals greatly to most working people. Unfortunately, it is rarely practised in our dominant media.

Media Concentration

Canada has created a media system that mixes public organizations and private companies, such as CBC and Rogers Communications. It strives to balance the rights of commercial companies with government regulations. This system ensures that Canadians receive some degree of universal and affordable access to media.

However, within the private sector only a few companies, controlled by a small group of people, dominate the business. To be precise, four companies control 85 percent of TV revenue and one company controls 33 percent of newspapers.[12] This leads to what's known as **media concentration**. Many international studies have shown that Canada labours under one of the most concentrated media systems in the world. This small group of very large companies can also be characterized by their use of "**convergence**," whereby they operate by both producing content and by distributing it. Furthermore, the powerful directors of these media giants constantly skip back and forth between business, government, banking and the oil companies. This combination of media concentration and convergence remains one of Canada's biggest problems, a major reason for the lack of diversity and therefore a key factor in a crisis of quality.

Economists describe Canada's media companies as an oligopoly. In a monopoly only one group controls that market. In an **oligopoly** *there are a few producers or sellers, but operating with only limited competition.*

Media for Profit

News and entertainment media that make profits their top priority have produced high quality, valuable work, most often when profits and commercial success are measured in the long term. Today however, corporate media have shifted their focus to short-term profits. This creates major problems because it discourages investment in quality or more innovative programs and initiatives, which may take longer to gain a foothold. The scramble for short-term profits fosters cost cutting in the reporting and communicating of news and has also led to a significant loss of journalists and editors. The result: fewer indepth reports and investigations. In the TV world these cuts have decimated local news programs, replacing them with truncated regional or national digests.

The Role of Technology

All of the media discussed here depend on sophisticated technology, often for their creation and always for their distribution. These systems require the skilled work of thousands of people along with billion-dollar investments. Within this media world new technological processes and practices continually disrupt the status quo. Today's great debates swirl around both the news and the entertainment media over whether these changes will be for the better. Many people believe that tech change is inevitable and usually leads to positive results. Others worry that new technology causes an erosion of media quality and job losses.

Most observers agree on three issues that shape the debate around new media technologies. First, the sophistication and expenditures required in all media technology means that few companies or public institutions can be involved. As noted above, Canada has one of the most concentrated media systems in the world. Second, the use of new technologies based on digital creation and distribution has meant that broadcasters and infrastructure companies have come together — this is referred to as convergence. For this reason companies such as Bell and Rogers now produce content and distribute it — they own the flow and the pipes. Third, because of the small number of companies, which operate as an oligopoly, and because of costs, a significant number of Canadians cannot afford to keep up. Thus, Canada suffers from what is known as a digital divide.

The Digital Divide

One of the persistent myths of the modern era is that "everyone is online." In fact, this is false. The digital divide refers to the gulf between those people who have computers and the Internet and those who do not. In thinking about the digital divide we need to consider three factors: access, cost and competence. Access refers to technical access or whether a person can receive high speed Internet in their home. According to some industry statements, as many as 96 percent of Canadians have access. However, in most small towns, rural areas and in the north, the service remains sporadic. Even in southern Ontario, many residents of small towns can't rely on high speed connections. Given these various factors, as many as 25 percent of Canadians do not have reliable access.

A second factor is cost and most reports compiled here and internationally show that Canada allows some of the highest rates in the G7 countries for Internet and cell phone service. Many families simply cannot afford the $100–$200 per month for services.[13]

The third factor is educational competence. This has become a major issue for many older Canadians unused to the increasing skills necessary to navigate the online world.

So much of government services, banking and basic shopping requires more and more advanced computer literacy. This applies as well for finding alternative online sources of news and even entertainment. Thus, when we take into account all three of these factors, we must conclude that Canada still suffers from a significant digital divide.

Is the New Media More Democratic?

The new digital media excels in its ability to create multi-media forms, using text, images, movement and sound. It is interactive, allowing two-way or multiple communication. It allows everyone to be a creator, not simply a passive spectator. It can be delivered to a mass audience around the world or to a very specific group. And, say its promoters, it will overthrow or radically change all of the **old media**.

Like television in the 1950s and radio in the 1920s, this technology has arrived with enormous expectations. For nationalists it provides hope that many more Canadian voices will be heard in the global village. It's also an opportunity for Canadians in widely diverse communities to know each other. For business, it holds great potential for both marketing and sales, as well as a chance to break beyond borders and join the race to globalization. From the perspective of governments and economists, **new media** companies mean thousands of jobs. For educators it shows real promise in making distance learning and online learning a reality. For believers in the profound value of the world's traditional "high art" it provides another chance to bring that culture to the masses, an opportunity that failed in the wasteland of television. For political activists it holds great possibilities for out-flanking the dominant media, in order to reach Canadians directly or form coalitions with new ideas for social change.

We might conclude that the so-called aggregator news sites, Google in particular, provide something truly innovative. Although none of them have their own journalists, they bring together and juxtapose news from a range of sources, then rank and display it, often creating startling forms of fresh knowledge. When you have the *Globe and Mail* and the *Daily Champion* of Lagos, Nigeria, both reporting on the same story, you benefit from a wider and deeper perspective on things. The presence of Google in Canada helps citizens link to dozens of new Canadian sources. However, we should note that in general, Google acts primarily as a funnel for even more US content.

Newspaper Financial Crisis

The newspaper still rules as the place where the most reporting gets done in Canada. Although many people read the news on Google or Facebook, the *source* of that news is most often a newspaper organization. Newspapers not only devote far more time to original news gathering than any other media, their coverage digs deeper and employs more full-time journalists. Consequently, TV and radio broadcasting, as well as the

> **Box 12.4 Think About...**
>
> **Too Big to Fail?**
> In January 2017 a Montreal group called the Public Policy Forum released a report on the state of Canadian newspapers and concluded that the federal government should give them $400 million per year in subsidies. The argument was that newspapers are too important to democracy to let them fail. This proposal received wide coverage in most media outlets but was quickly rejected by the government. Should the Canadian government hand over increased financial assistance to newspaper companies, because they are too important to fail?

Internet, remain dependent on stories generated by newspapers.

Unfortunately, Canada's commercial newspaper business is at present living through a profound disruption in its business model. Newspaper owners say that their world is collapsing. Since the start of the twentieth century, newspapers have been funded primarily through advertising. The country's advertising market now tops a whopping $12 billion per year. But, that advertising is now moving to the Internet and smart phones, an ad world dominated by Google and Facebook, which means a significant loss in revenue for newspapers.

Traditionally newspaper companies enjoyed high rates of profit, at times over 20 percent, which is much higher than rates in other economic sectors. According to most analysts, those rates have declined sharply since the 1990s. Still, as of 2017, newspapers enjoyed rates of profit above 7 percent.[14] Whatever we conclude about newspaper finances the companies that control this vital piece of our media believe that their profits are simply not enough and they continue to kill papers and slash full-time journalism jobs.[15]

THE MEDIA GIANTS

As of 2018 the following small group made up Canada's dominant media.

- Canadian Broadcasting Corporation (CBC / Radio Canada)
- BCE Inc. (Bell Canada, Bell Media, including CTV Network)
- Rogers Communications Inc. (tele-communications, broadcast and cable TV, magazines)
- Corus Entertainment Inc. / Shaw Communications Inc. (Global TV, cable TV, radio)
- Québecor Inc. (TV, cable distribution, newspapers)

- Power Corp (*La Presse* and many other newspapers)
- Irving Group (all of the dominant news media in New Brunswick)
- Thomson Reuters — *Globe and Mail*
- Torstar — *Toronto Star* — largest circulation paper in the country.
- Postmedia Network (*National Post* and many other newspapers)
- Newcap (radio stations)

Canadian Broadcasting Corporation/Radio Canada

At the centre of Canada's media universe sits the CBC, along with its sister French service, Radio Canada, and its Northern Service. The national radio network was born in 1936, after many years of experiments, controversies and competing ideas. Television soon followed in 1952.

The CBC is the product of many forces — nationalism, the needs of the Canadian state, class dynamics and the desire for media to serve the public, not simply the government or private interests. These forces remain as active today as in the 1930s. What we have, therefore, is a little of everything. Although supposedly an independent institution, at "arm's length" from the government, the corporation only receives funding on a yearly basis and the prime minister appoints its president. Therefore, the government of the day can exert its influence continually.

Yearly funding is approximately $1 billion. This may seem like a lot but it falls far short of what's required to fulfill its mandate. To do so the CBC has become in many ways the most sophisticated institution within Canadian society. It must serve a broad and diverse public, and it provides the most symbolic glue in maintaining the unity of the country. Not only does the government of the day expect the CBC to communicate its policies and play a key unifying role, most Canadians expect the highest standards of journalism and entertainment from "their" national broadcaster. That includes playing journalism's roles of investigation, analysis and uncovering wrong-doing, even in government. Canada's newspapers and other private media are not expected to play all these roles.

Within the institution of the CBC we can find bureaucrats who answer only to the federal government as well as senior producers who believe in Canadian nationalism above all else. But we also find producers, editors and creators who see journalistic principles as their highest goal, regardless of the consequences. For this reason, it is difficult to generalize about the functions of the CBC in Canadian society. At one moment it serves only as the mouthpiece of the state; at another it uncovers serious crimes and misdemeanors among the country's elites. It's an institution that can pay big salaries to Carol Off, one of the country's best investigative reporters, and to Don Cherry, for many years the $800,000-a-year voice of hockey violence.

Big Commercial Media

BCE, Rogers, Postmedia and the other major corporations listed above form an oligopoly whose major goal is to deliver profits to their shareholders. Along with the CBC, they control the telecommunications infrastructure, the media distribution forms, such as TV and newspapers, and the bulk of the media content.

All these commercial giants maintain close links with other power centres in the political world and the economy. Many directors of the companies have served (or will serve) in senior government positions or as directors in banks and energy companies. Finally, many of the CEOs and leaders in these companies rank among the wealthiest Canadians. For example, Canada's richest person is David Thomson, with personal worth of $41 billion and a controlling interest in the *Globe and Mail* and international media giant Thomson Reuters.

Dynasties: The Son Also Rises
Family ties and connections play a big role in Canadian media companies. The chairs of the boards or CEOs of Rogers, Québecor, Power Corp, Thomson Reuters, Corus and Irving are all the sons, grandsons or daughters of the company founders.

Tools of the Canadian State

In order to manage the competing demands of modern media and telecommunications the Canadian government employs three tools. The Broadcasting Act (1991) deals with radio and TV and considers issues of technology (such as cable TV and satellite delivery), program content and access. The Telecommunications Act (1993) deals primarily with phone systems and pays particular attention to the creation of reliable and affordable services. Both of these pieces of legislation use broad language to set out the government's principles and goals. Finally, the Canadian Radio-television and Telecommunications Commission (CRTC, 1976) is charged with interpreting these Acts and other laws. The CRTC is an arm's-length government agency and most of its work requires public consultation with all interested parties. The CRTC holds significant power to interpret the language in the Acts. For this reason, since the late 1990s, various government ministers have tried to exert more influence over important decisions. In 2010 Prime Minister Harper tried to influence the CRTC to allow the right-wing Sun TV a special licence. Some of the more important and controversial of the CRTC's rulings include that 35 percent of the music played by radio stations must be Canadian and questions surrounding the regulation of the Internet — should we tax US companies, such as Netflix?

Box 12.5 Diversity in Action

Alternative and Oppositional Media Sources

The giant media companies dominate, but they don't totally control what Canadians can read, see or hear. Dozens of small organizations, mostly non-commercial and free, provide valuable sources of news and opinion. Unfortunately, they don't have the financial resources to promote their work so most Canadians don't know of their existence. Also, most of these resources can only be found online, so not everyone has reliable access. Nevertheless, people with a need and an interest in getting beyond the dominant media can find different, much more diverse voices. All of the groups listed here feature the work of highly skilled reporters and editors. Although many work as volunteers on these projects, they are by no means amateurs.

Check out these: *Canadaland, The Conversation, The Georgia Straight, National Observer, rabble.ca, Ricochet, The Tyee.*

Indigenous Media: An Explosion of Voices and Different Perspectives

The Aboriginal People's Television Network (APTN) was launched in 1999. It reaches viewers throughout the north, runs on cable TV in the south and screens free online. The schedule includes a nightly *National News* program, which features timely stories from across the country. APTN also runs a high-quality slate of current affairs shows, including the ongoing documentary series *Wild Archaeology; Mohawk Ironworkers;* and *Samagan: Water Stories.*

A broad range of other important Indigenous media outlets include: *The Eastern Door, Kukukwes.com, Media Indigena, Unreserved* (CBC Radio), *Wawatay News* and *Windspeaker.*[16]

THE NEWS MEDIA

Most of us don't want to live as hermits. We recognize that knowledge about the world brings us status, or at least prevents us from looking ignorant. The only way to acquire this knowledge is to "keep up with the news." But in this process of keeping up — by reading, watching, listening — we also get drawn into all sorts of social ideas and feelings. We don't simply scan the information, we are influenced and affected by it. Whether we like it or not, and whether we know it or not, we enter into a relationship with the news.

The news presents us with many different types of information. And because it always comes packaged in some form of narrative or story, it always involves some elements of entertainment. Information and entertainment go hand-in-hand. You can't have one without the other. In fact, we could say that the news is never just news. It also participates in representing people and groups. It presents an image of us, or people like us (in our religious group, ethnic group, region, etc.). So, when many people read, or watch, or listen to news they also wonder if a picture or story about someone like themselves will affect them personally in society. Does the news validate me/us? Does the news denigrate me/us? Does the news ignore me/us?

What Is the News?

What is the *news* anyway? All of us likely have a good working definition, ingrained since the time we were young. The news is what reporters, presenters and editors tell us about current events. But if we stop to think more about this we find that a precise definition of the *news* becomes much harder to pin down. Here are four standard ingredients of the news that are largely agreed on by journalists and editors around the world:

1. *The Present Tense*: The news deals with the most recent events. Often these events are still unfolding, and the ongoing drama remains far from certain. Editors particularly like stories with a hook at the end to keep you tuning in tomorrow. Those stories seem to be newsworthy because they take place in a never-ending present.

2. *Big Consequences*: The news concentrates on events that affect many people. So, for example, every day people get killed in isolated car crashes, and those events rarely make the news. But if that death rate rises or falls sharply, or if one spectacular crash results in many fatalities, that might make it a "news-worthy" event. Yet, for all their boasts about covering the world, many news media outlets demonstrate an inward-looking attitude that often fails to take up international issues affecting their national audience.

3. *Sudden and Dramatic Change*: The news gravitates toward unusual events, events out of the ordinary, events that cause clear change. One old cliché of the news business tries to express this: "If a dog bites a man, that's not news. But if a man bites a dog, that's news!" And these events only attract interest if the change qualifies as dramatic. Two recent examples illustrate the concept: "Marijuana could be legal in Canada by July 2018." "Three injured in building explosion in Mississauga, Ont."

4. *The Story*: If you listen to reporters talk about their work they always speak of the *story* they are working on, the developing *story*, the big *story*. The news creates stories about events, stories that involve people and that arrange things into a chain of cause and effect, or narrative, order. The traits of timeli-

ness and consequences mentioned above only take shape when made into a story. If a news writer or editor wants desperately enough to make something news they can usually do it by creating a story. This means constructing the material to emphasize particular elements. These elements include conflict, such as a story-line that creates drama, crisis, resolution and clear consequences for people.

The Worthy and the Unworthy

"People tend to think that journalists are where the news is. This is not so. The news is where journalists are." — BBC journalist Martin Bell[17]

Journalists often use the term "news-worthy." Here's the funny thing. Many events seem to qualify as newsworthy because they include one or more of the four news characteristics listed above (the present, consequences, change and story). But for some reason they never get selected. Many events, involving millions of people, take place around the world daily, but they don't make it to the category of news. Is there a pattern of news values that can be discerned? Tony Harcup, an English journalism professor, has observed several categories that determine selection of stories in the dominant media. Here are some of his categories:

- the power elite (stories about powerful people or celebrities)
- bad news (stories with conflict or tragedy) / good news (stories such as rescues or cures)
- media agenda (stories that fit the news company's own agenda).[18]

In fact, many newspeople find Harcup's analysis embarrassing. After all, some of his categories, such as celebrity and media agenda, don't show the news business in the best light.

Missed, Overlooked, Ignored, Suppressed

Ignoring a story can be just as significant as selecting one. It can happen through ignorance, or through lack of interest, or intentionally. The following stories continually miss out as news; some might say they are systematically ignored by the media. That's because most media owners operate in close proximity to those with state power. In addition, reporters and editors by and large have not found the time or interest, and finally, many of these stories don't fit the standard definitions of news. We can see this most clearly by the usual exclusion of stories about:

- industrial accidents: in Canada, every single day a worker gets killed or in-

> **Box 12.6 Think About...**
>
> What are the pros and cons of the news media's interest in sudden and dramatic events?

jured on the job. These thousands of accidents rarely explode in big dramatic incidents. Rather, they take place in ones and twos, often in obscure workplaces.

- small-country events, both bad and good, that usually fall below the radar.
- mortality rates — especially for the world's poorest children: most children die not from war, but through preventable causes, such as dehydration and bad water.
- crime: violence against women. Like industrial accidents, crimes against women remain so common that they rarely make the news.
- white -collar crime: ordinary variety, rather than that of the spectacular variety, such as international money-laundering.

The next time you encounter an item in the media try to ask yourself these questions: Who decided this was news? Who made a certain event worthy? Why would it be considered worthy? Who chose to classify another event as unworthy, and why?

Fake News

The term "**fake news**" has entered our vocabulary particularly since the election of President Trump in the US. Sometimes it's a label that makes sense, but just as often becomes a dangerous phrase with no bearing on the truth. To evaluate specific news items we need to make some distinctions. First, we can admit that most media outlets, from the traditional paper to the latest blog, all have their political and cultural biases. As we have noted, most media in Canada are pro-capitalist and run by white men. Therefore, hard news items, headlines and opinion pieces all contain bias, which inevitably shapes and alters reporting in profound ways. Second, it is not hard to find news items that contain errors of fact. These can occur because the reporter was sloppy or was rushed for time or relied on only one source for information. Third, most news outlets contain large doses of opinion from regular columnists and others, and it is certainly not difficult to find opinion pieces that we strongly disagree with. None of these situations should be classified as fake news. For that term we should concentrate on those cases where the intent of the creator is to mislead or peddle lies. As this chapter shows, there are many reasons to be critical of the dominant Canadian media. That does not mean that we should discard everything it does.

There's another problem surrounding the fake news debates. The arguments tend to focus, as they should, on obvious lies or misinformation, for example that coming from Russia or Donald Trump. By doing this, however, the conversation seems to imply that there are simply two kinds of news: that which is true (objective and unbiased) and that which is fake. This true versus false dichotomy leads us to overlook the everyday biases built into the dominant media.

In these days of public relations specialists, spin doctors and plenty of old-fashioned quick-cure charlatans, fake news can turn up anywhere. It comes flooding in daily to the news organizations. This material can be in the form of text or of moving images, produced by individual pranksters, commercial firms or governments in the hopes that it will get picked up by a news outlet.

Since the rise of Donald Trump many government leaders, including Prime Minister Trudeau himself, have criticized the giants of social media, particularly Facebook and Google. They charge that these companies are not doing enough to root out, or at least label, false news. Facebook usually counters by stating that it isn't creating the news — it's only a "platform" — and therefore it can't be held responsible. Do you think Facebook and Google have some responsibility?

Box 12.7 Think About...

Four Reasons for the Rise of Fake News
A general decline in news media quality due to cuts of journalists and editors.
The mass closings of local newspapers and TV news programs.
The speed with which social media can spread rumours, conspiracy theories and false reports.

Governments, including some in Canada, have attacked the dominant news providers to the extent that we no longer respect journalists of any kind.
Some hope for optimism has recently emerged. On the issue of fake news, a 2018 international survey showed that 61 percent of Canadians had trust in the news media, a 10 per cent increase over 2017. Trust in journalists jumped even more, by17 percent. The same survey noted that a full 65 percent said that they were worried about fake news being used as a weapon.
Source: Susan Delacourt, "Journalists See 17 Per Cent Jump in Public Trust." *j-source.ca,* February 20, 2018.

CANADA'S NEWS FORMS AND GENRES: NEWSPAPERS, TV, RADIO, NEW MEDIA

Every news story can get told in many different ways. Media don't simply pass on information like the post office delivering letters. They not only transmit; they also transform. They shape events into genres or types of stories and create meaning to go with the information.

Newspapers

Hard News and Features

When we think about newspaper stories we probably think first of hard news. These items start with what's called a "lead" — a sentence or paragraph that lays out, right off the bat, the five W's — the what, where, who, when and why. The story overall resembles an inverted pyramid. It spells out the most vital information at the top and leaves the least important to the end. According to this model, readers who want only the basic information will find it right away in the first two or three paragraphs. Reporters write these items in the third person and never refer to themselves. The idea is to present the story in a form that looks as objective and unbiased as possible. There is much to be said for this clear, direct style. But language always carries other meanings. In this case the implication is that the content is obviously true. No one has selected or shaped the story. It implies that the world is simple.

Feature writing gives journalists an opportunity to write longer stories and to delve into the background or context. Although features usually deal with current events, in most cases they extend the timeframe. Features provide readers with more of the "whys" behind a news story or explain the significance of events. In addition, features are not locked into any particular style. Sometimes they delay the lead and start instead with an anecdote, sketch in a setting or describe a person. Features often read more like short stories because they use more narrative devices. For instance, they might withhold information, create conflict, follow one person, build to a climax or end with a "kicker" — a surprise or shocking ending.

Check out the following two good, worthwhile features. The first provides a hard news follow-up; the second offers us a human interest feature.

"Would Canadian Gun Laws Have Stopped America's Worst Mass Shooters?" (*Calgary Herald*, Feb. 16, 2018). This excellent piece was published a day after the latest mass school shooting in the US. It surveys Canada's gun laws in detail and provides opinion as to whether our laws would have worked as a legal deterrent to a potential killer.

"Explosion 100" (Halifax *Chronicle Herald*, Dec. 6, 2017). "To mark the centennial of the Explosion, The *Chronicle Herald* has prepared this special, 12-page commemorative edition that features exclusive survivor accounts, historical research and fresh perspectives on the disaster."

Headlines

The headlines for stories in newspapers and on TV often play a big role in how we understand the entire story. Quite often in fact we may only read or hear the headline. Headlines often reveal the editorial bias of the organization and sometimes contradict or subtly change the meaning of the story. For example, when the province of Ontario decided to raise the minimum wage to $15 per hour, both the CBC national news and the *Toronto Star* ran headlines that stated "Wage hike could cost 60,000 jobs, Bank of Canada says" (Jan. 3, 2018). Michal Rozworski, a reporter for the *Tyee* pointed out that, contrary to these headlines, the Bank of Canada actually offered "a <u>positive</u> conclusion about the effect of minimum wage increases on workers." Rozworski concludes that this represents a "recurring pattern of business-friendly bias."[19]

Another problem headline was more insidious. In 2014 Tina Fontaine, an Indigenous 15-year-old from Manitoba was murdered. Four years later, as her accused killer went to trial, the *Globe and Mail* and other papers decided to run big headlines, which stated "Tina Fontaine had drugs, alcohol in system when she was killed: toxicologist" (Jan. 30. 2018). This was not untrue. However, many readers questioned why this fact among hundreds of others in the case would be featured. It seemed to blame the victim and conform to the old stereotypes about Indigenous Peoples.

Think about who creates the content, the essential work of journalism — the researching, reporting and editing — versus those companies that distribute the content. (This is sometimes referred to as the flow versus the pipes). Google does not do journalism. Neither does Facebook nor Reddit nor Youtube. They distribute the content.

Investigative Journalism

One of the most important roles that newspapers play centres on their **investigative journalism**. As we have seen, most news stories are reactive. They consist primarily of reporting on events and things being said. Investigative work, on the other hand, requires a much more active and time-consuming practice. Investigative journalists

---

Box 12.8 Think About...

Young People and the News

Many older Canadians worry that young people take no interest in the news. They argue that young folks no longer read much and that they have abandoned TV, which remains the primary vehicle for news delivery. Is this your experience? Is there any truth to it? If true, what are the dangers? If not true, where do these opinions come from?

This huge topic ranges well beyond this chapter, but here are a few points to consider. First, there are few up-to-date empirical studies on Canadian reading habits, so most arguments rest on a tiny sample or remain anecdotal. Second, young people's lack of interest in the news may not be a new phenomenon. It's been the norm for several generations. In general, people only start to follow the news when they become more settled, with a job, an apartment of their own and family responsibilities. Third, it may be that all Canadians now read less than in previous years. We all find it easy to be distracted with the constant flood of news, entertainment and gossip — from the crucial to the trivial — that flows from our phones, pods and pads.

---

aren't satisfied to communicate the words of authorities. They seek out other opinions from people who don't have access to media. They also strive to move beyond a typical charge and counter-charge type of story. Most journalists believe that investigative work involves exposing something that has been buried — in many cases something that someone wants to keep hidden.

With each investigation journalists can try several methods. The Digger plows deeper than in regular news stories, in order to uncover facts and situations previously unknown. The Insider works with informants who have a story to tell about corporate or government problems. The Analyst spends countless hours sifting through public records, speeches and other media stories to expose discrepancies or contradictions. In more complex stories teams of journalists will use two or three of these methods.[20]

In recent years Canadian journalists working for TV, radio and newspapers, both traditional and online, have published major investigations on substantial issues. These include the *Toronto's Star*'s explosive series on police "carding" of African-Canadians, the *Fifth Estate* and Radio-Canada's *Enquetes* investigation into corporate offshore tax shelters; the *National Observer*'s lengthy series on the Irving Group of companies in New Brunswick, and a few investigations into murdered and missing Indigenous women and girls.[21]

Television News

It may come as a surprise to people under thirty but the vast majority of Canadians still get their news through broadcast TV. While Canada's upper class relies on the *Globe and Mail*, the *Financial Post* and *La Presse*, most Canadians tune in to the nightly newscasts of the three national broadcasters. And while the newspapers still carry out the bulk of news reporting, TV newscasts also engage in substantial amounts of their own reporting.

Two fundamental differences separate print news from TV news in Canada. First, as set down in the Broadcasting Act, TV news shows must strive for balance in their coverage of political issues. Newspapers have no such constraint from the government. Second, TV news is far more expensive to produce and distribute. These two characteristics can lead to very different treatments of the news and public affairs journalism. In North America, TV news comes in two flavours: the traditional set-time broadcasts and the 24-hour formats.

FORMS AND STYLES OF TV NEWS

Canada's major news shows are CTV's *National News*, Global's *Global National*, each with a nightly audience of 800,000, and CBC's *The National*, with 600,000 viewers. Within each news program, producers and editors think very carefully about the line-up of stories. A number of factors influence this. The first is time. For commercial stations, the normal 30-minute program will include four breaks for ads. This gives the show five segments, and each segment, except the last short one, needs four or five stories. Using this segment format, producers like to group stories that are similar in

---

Box 12.9 Diversity in Action

Investigative Reporting

"Canada's Toxic Secret" flashed onto the screen for a Global TV News report that uncovered serious chemical air pollution in Sarnia, Ontario (Global News, Oct. 12, 2017). The report marked the culmination of a joint investigation by Global, the *Toronto Star*, journalism schools at Ryerson and Concordia and many others. Journalists had analyzed more than 500 government reports, obtained through Access to Information requests. Almost immediately after the report hit the airwaves the Ontario government announced new funding for a health study on the impact of air pollution for residents in Sarnia's Chemical Valley.

Box 12.10 Diversity in Action

Quebec Newspapers Reveal a Distinct Society
Le Journal de Montréal, 1964, Québecor Media, largest French-language paper in North America, circulation 214,000 daily.

La Presse, 1884, online, Groupe Gesca, a subsidiary of Power Corporation of Canada. Generally federalist orientation, circulation, 212,000 daily. In May 2018 Power Corp. announced that it was rolling *La Presse* into a "not-for-profit news organization to be launched with a $50-million contribution." For analysis, see Jacqueline Nelson and Nicolas Van Praet, "La Presse Moves to Non-Profit as Desmarais Family Moves on," *Globe and Mail,* May 9, 2018.

The Gazette, 1778, English-language paper, Postmedia Inc., circulation, 163,000 daily.

Le Devoir (duty), 1910, Quebec Nationalist orientation, circulation, weekdays, 35,000, Saturday, 58,000. The only independent large-circulation paper in Quebec. The International Society for News Design has called *Le Devoir* the world's most beautiful newspaper.

tone and place. In other words, they don't jump back and forth between tragic and light or between local and international. Similar stories also create a flow that provides smooth transitions and encourages viewers to keep watching. In traditional newscasts, the significant hard news was followed by less important items. Today however, the newscast unfolds more like a variety show, supplying jolts and high points at key points throughout. Producers normally hold something back in order to create a "wow finish."

Canadians also consume significant amounts of news via local news shows and what is known as breakfast television. These offer a different format by mixing hard news, weather, traffic, interviews and happy talk. Breakfast TV looks different than the regular news. Five key features shape every show:

- most segments are broadcast live;
- the set resembles a living room or kitchen (not a news studio or office);
- the mix of serious and frivolous in a magazine format often creates radical jumps in subject and form from one item to another; and
- women make up the bulk of the audience.

Some breakfast shows, such as CTV's *Your Morning,* pull in higher ratings and achieve more commercial success than many other news or current events programs in the lineup.

Anchors and Reporters

TV news began life as nothing more than a radio script read by a serious man in a grey suit behind a plain, wooden desk. The newsreader, presenter, or anchor, to use the US term, remains a key element in TV news. They represent the station, the network and journalism in general. They must be likeable and appealing to audiences, acceptable to sponsors and a magnet for high ratings.

The only other group in TV news who get to approach the audience in direct address, that is head-on, are the reporters. This gives them the same type of authority as the presenters. Anyone else on camera, even important news-makers, must look slightly off-camera or speak sideways to a reporter. Reporters rank second only to the anchor as the public face of the news organization. As with their anchors, TV news organizations devote huge efforts to build up the image of their reporters. These folks don't need to be as photogenic as the anchors, and sometimes a weather-beaten appearance ads street credibility, but generally reporters look good on camera, sporting stylish hair and good teeth. Ads and slogans for the news department promote the reporters' work and push them forward as celebrity professionals. We take these genre conventions for granted. They just seem natural. Even after all of the experiments in TV news presentation over the years, think how startled we'd be if the anchor appeared wearing shorts or reading the news outdoors in a lawn chair.

Back in the studio, sets have evolved from the barest and drabbest spaces possible to the most elaborate theatrical concepts. The scale of the set seems to reflect the resources of the station and its connection to a vast electronic world of news gathering. A back wall of TV monitors and international clocks is a favourite design. Numerous people rushing past in the background give the feeling of perpetual activity. The news never stops. Of course, we never see people just sitting at desks and writing the scripts. That

---

Box 12.11 Think About...

The News Screen

Not only has the studio changed. The TV screen itself has gradually become more and more elaborate. In the 1980s video effects made it easier to combine images on-screen. Since the 1990s the TV news presentation resembles the computer screen. Now the presenter gets framed off-centre to make room for computer graphics, maps, logos, menus and reports from off-site reporters. This slightly unbalanced image conveys an impression of action, up-to-the-minute, suddenly exploding events. "Wow," we think, "these folks are really scrambling to keep us informed." Ironically, of course, newscasts generally attract older audiences who often experience this as too much clutter and glitz.

would indicate that the news broadcast is as much a created product as a series of constantly breaking outside events.

TV Images

Although literacy rates in Canada are very high, for millions of people, watching TV is easier than reading a newspaper or navigating text and images on a digital screen. This lower barrier to access means that TV remains the dominant news and entertainment medium. Most of the time on TV, dramatic images make for the most important stories. If a station has acquired such images, they will be repeated several times during a broadcast. They can be used as promotional teasers, shown during the story and then again in a program recap. A clear example of this appeared in the news coverage of the huge wildfires that swept through Fort McMurray, Alberta, in 2016. We remember the dramatic images. This repetition of dramatic images occurs most often in the 24-hour news programs, such as CBC's *News Network* and CITY TV's *CP24*. When TV is working to its full potential with appropriate, well-shot, thoughtfully edited images the news has real power — the power to grab and hold an audience.

Public Affairs TV

Public affairs shows take us beyond the daily news headlines. Some use a magazine style, mixing light and serious stories and a mix of forms. Others stick to interviews and panels. Some shows provide analysis and discussion but focus on the recent news. Others serve up more active forms of journalism, including investigative reports. As with Canada's general interest print magazines, primarily *Macleans* and *l'Actualite*, public affairs TV presents much more of a mix in story types than we see in standard news programs. A serious political report can be followed by a celebrity piece or a lifestyle item on new fashions.

The interview provides the glue for all these shows. These range from soft, easy-pitch questions to the so-called accountability interview, where the host pushes back against vague or untruthful answers. Some media and communication scholars study these interactions in detail as part of an academic field called "discourse analysis." This type of study doesn't simply examine the words being used but body language, the tone of voice and the overall relationship between interviewer and interviewee. Canada can claim its share of tough journalists who specialize in this type of interview. But too often, TV journalists stick to the easy questions and played it safe.

Expert panels serve as another common feature, particularly on the cheaper shows. Sometimes these experts can bring a fresh viewpoint to bear on the news story. Other times (and much too often) the panels give us the same faces over and over; too often the panels consist only of other journalists from the same media organization. TV

Ontario's *The Agenda,* hosted by the veteran journalist Steve Paikin, gives viewers the most thoughtful and extended interviews on Canadian TV. Compared to some interview shows on US and British TV, especially the BBC's *Hard Talk,* Paikin never becomes aggressive. His guests rarely get angry with the conversation; however, he often asks tough questions that demand straightforward answers. TVO is funded as an educational network and thus can avoid some of the pressures faced by the CBC or other networks to balance news and entertainment. *The Agenda* can boast the best record for including women in its expert panel discussions, at times reaching a 50/50 ratio.

The two most important public affairs shows on Canadian TV have battled each other for ratings and influence since the 1970s. CBC's *The Fifth Estate* and CTV's *W5* consistently provide the best in TV investigative journalism. Over the years they have employed some of the most skilled reporters in the country. Each program includes three to six stories, all presented by a journalist in a documentary format. This is expensive television that combines months of sophisticated research with dramatic images and skilled editing.

Radio News: The Land of the Mini-Snapper

More people worldwide listen to radio news than any other medium. Compared to other forms it's the least expensive, especially for listeners, and it can be portable and sent over long distances or tough terrain. Reporters can gather material with little fuss, under the radar of authorities. In Canada, CBC Radio remains the dominant source of radio news. No other group, public or private, comes close. Although technically independent, CBC stations must walk a fine line in the way they treat news. They can't stray too far from the mainstream or they risk losing their government funding. At the same time, they face increasing pressures to make more money. Many educated middle-class Canadians prefer the news and current affairs offered on CBC Radio to any other news source. If we agree with polls, which show that the majority of Canadians share attitudes and ideas of the centre-left, CBC Radio provides a comfortable home-base for news. According to right-wing commentators, the CBC shelters a nest of communists.

Mainstream radio news generally bursts out in short programs, often five minutes or less. Each newscast consists of several items usually running about thirty seconds. Regular newsreaders, who introduce themselves, provide consistency and link the items with short transitional phrases. For stations with reporters, the reader usually sets up the story and then throws it over to the staff reporter.

Unlike newspaper hard news stories, based on the inverted pyramid, radio and TV items need to be much shorter. And not only must they grab your attention right away, they must hold your interest for the entire story. For that reason many radio and TV clips end with a strong, clear phrase called a "snapper." The CBC also offers longer news reports, often updated every hour. The location stories usually also include sound effects and location audio of background sounds to lend ambiance and mood. For instance, while a reporter describes a scene in downtown Regina, you'll hear streets sounds, other voices, maybe car horns.

Public Affairs Radio

Public affairs on Canadian radio comes to us in three formats, serious current affairs shows, all-news stations and talk radio. Here again, the only service for serious material is provided by CBC/Radio-Canada. Current affairs at CBC Radio follows magazine formats similar to the mix of items seen on TV programs. This means a variety of items of varying length, separated by snippets of music (usually instrumental). These include prestige interview shows such as *As It Happens*, hosted by Carol Off, and *The Current*, with Anna Maria Tremonti. These experienced journalists come well-informed and well-prepared. Guests have been carefully selected to be articulate. Long-form interviews cover international and national stories.

If the serious radio might be termed sober, a lot of talk radio can best be described as laced with wild emotions. In place of serious discussions and interviews pitched to an informed audience, talk radio often gives us loud hosts and a call-in format, emphasizing strong opinions. Most talk radio does no news reporting and doesn't require anyone to leave the studio. That makes it cheap to produce — especially with a phone-in format. In these shows an occasional interview or eye-witness account can bring to light an important event or piece of information. Sadly, however, very little news makes its way onto these shows. And consequently, because talk radio counts as "public affairs" and therefore fulfills the station's obligation to offer some public service, it has pushed genuine news to the margins.

Talk radio projects an entirely different sense of the country. It is dominated by right-wing hosts, confidently unafraid of making their views known. This is the home of backlash, anger and ignorance. Canada's leading TV critic, John Doyle, observes: "Turn on most commercial radio in the morning and you're listening to a bunch of people laughing hysterically ... and, in general, being obnoxious. That's why a lot of those shows have the word 'zoo' in the title."[22] Some exceptions stand out from the crude right-wing shows. Vancouver Co-operative Radio, for example, describes itself as "a non-commercial, co-operatively-owned, listener-supported, community radio station. Located in the Downtown Eastside, Co-op Radio strives to provide a space for under-represented and marginalized communities."[23]

New Media News

The adoption of computers in our society has disrupted every aspect of the media. In the creation of different forms, the digital has affected cameras, sound recording, editing and distribution, for both audio and images. In addition, Canadians now view media on a wider array of digital devices, including home computers, tablets and mobile devices. In today's digital world of news, we can make a distinction among three groups: 1. creators (such as reporters at CBC); 2. editor/packagers, usually called aggregators (such as Google and reddit); and 3. distributors (such as Rogers cable).

In recent years Canada has seen the arrival of news groups that operate solely within the online, digital world. Some of these use a magazine format, with a mix of news, reports and opinion and a stable of reporters. *Vice* and the *Huffington Post* (both with Canadian content, but controlled from the US) are the largest and enjoy the best access to commercial capital. Others, such as the *Tyee, rabble.ca*, etc. have devoted followers but suffer from tiny budgets compared to the dominant media. *Vice* in particular has enjoyed success for both its print and video operations and has achieved significant name recognition among young people. It bills itself as "the world's preeminent youth media company." The news and video features cover a wide range of topics. However, the owners have often stated that Canada is boring; thus, the overall tone tends not only to be irreverent but impatient with what they term the "politically correct." Unfortunately, this has translated into what many have described as a "boys club" atmosphere in the workplace and a string of sexual harassment charges against senior management.[24] Nevertheless, *Vice News* employs many excellent reporters and editors, both men and women.[25]

New Media Forms and Styles

Many studies have shown that people read computer (and mobile) screens differently from print. Even with the modern smaller format newspapers there is less space on a computer screen. This discourages the reading of longer articles, which require constant flicking from screen to screen. In addition, most news homepages in digital formats contain more distractions, such as ads, navigation tools, etc. These present drawbacks for serious journalism, especially long-form features and investigative reports.

On the other hand the experience of reading digital news forms provides many more opportunities for the reader or viewer to follow-up on issues. Hotlinks in the text and side panels of related or previous articles provide opportunities to dig deeper into multiple issues. Most news pages also offer a link to search other articles by the same journalist. Many pages include audio and infographics. Other services, such as Google Maps and Wikipedia, with only one or two clicks away, can also encourage a faster and deeper understanding of a news issue. Of course, due to screen size there is a difference between reading on a standard laptop screen and a mobile device.

One important US study of how people get the news makes the distinction between "readers" and "watchers." The authors believe that "the web has largely pulled in 'readers' rather than 'watchers.' While those who prefer *watching* news predominantly opt for TV and listeners turn to radio, most of those who prefer *reading* news now opt to get news online."[26]

CONCLUSION

In our examination of the news we've seen that genres or types of media, such as a hard news item in a newspaper or breakfast TV, function both as art forms and as industry practices. The modern media always contains an aesthetic element and a commercial one. In addition, the news means different things in different media. Finally, we've seen that the news is selected, shaped and created by journalists, editors and media owners.

While there is much to celebrate in the Canadian news media, we continue to face significant problems, which add up to a crisis of quality. These problems centre on the growing concentration of ownership and decision-making in the dominant media. This profit-based system has led to cuts of journalists, along with closings of newspapers, TV and radio stations. In addition, many of our papers and TV programs provide less news than in the past and the cuts to international coverage, in a world that is increasingly interdependent, should be especially troubling to everyone. For all these reasons, Canada's news media has failed to reflect the diversity of the country. The flowering of alternative news sources on the Internet and radio create some hope for a more inclusive and diverse media landscape. In particular, the explosion of high-quality Indigenous news and analysis allows Canadians to be much better informed than in the past.

CRITICAL REVIEW QUESTIONS

1. Why should we talk of the dominant media rather than simply the big media or the mass media?
2. In what ways is Canada experiencing a "crisis of quality" in the news media?
3. Does the Canadian news media do a good job at reflecting the diversity of the country?
4. Is bias or a strong point of view the same thing as fake news?
5. What are some of the differences in news delivery between print, TV, radio and online?

RECOMMENDED READINGS

Noam Chomsky and Edward Herman, *Manufacturing Consent: The Political Economy of the Mass Media* (Pantheon Books, 2002).

Rita Shelton Deverell "Who Will Inherit the Airwaves," *Canadian Journal of Communications,* 34, 1 (2009).

Marc Edge, *Greatly Exaggerated: The Myth of the Death of Newspapers* (New Star Books, 2014).

Cecil Rosner, *Behind the Headlines: A History of Investigative Journalism in Canada* (Oxford, 2008).

Peter Steven, *About Canada: Media* (Fernwood Publishing, 2011).

KEY TERMS

dominant media: a small group of media institutions, both private and public, which has the power to push others with fewer resources to the side, the power of broad influence and the power to exclude other voices.

fake news: stories in the media that have been deliberately designed to mislead or items that are knowingly false. A common example is a commercial notice or public relations item designed to look like a regular news story.

investigative journalism: journalism that seeks to go beyond or beneath the everyday news; in general it takes more time and money and it often seeks to uncover wrongs in society.

media concentration and convergence: the operations of the dominant media; concentration refers to the fact that most media power is centred in a small number of players; convergence refers to the situation where these groups are able to both produce and distribute media products.

old media/new media: old media includes newspapers, film, radio and television; new media refers to all those forms that rely primarily on digital production and distribution, for example online newspapers, blogs, podcasts, etc.

oligopoly: a small group of companies that can control a market through limited competition.

Notes

1. John Miller, "Step Up to Plate," *The Journalism Doctor*, Oct. 28, 2017 <thejournalismdoctor.ca>.
2. This chapter concentrates on the news media. Space limitations do not allow an exploration of magazine and book publishing, nor our entertainment industries.
3. I use the term dominant media (rather than mass or mainstream media) to emphasize the power of these media institutions to push others with fewer resources to the side. Dominant media has the power to influence and the power to exclude other voices.
4. For more on the Canadian media's crisis of quality in both the news and the entertainment media, see Peter Steven, *About Canada: Media* (Fernwood Publishing, 2011).
5. Noam Chomsky and Edward Herman, *Manufacturing Consent: The Political Economy of the Mass Media* (Pantheon Books, 2002).

6. Alex Ballingall, "A Majority of Torontonians Now Identify Themselves as Visible Minorities," *Toronto Star,* October 25, 2017.

7. Frances Henry and Carol Tator, *Deconstructing the "Rightness of Whiteness" in Television Commercials, News and Programming* (Prairie Centre for Excellence on Immigration and Integration, 2003). See also Marsha Barber and Ann Rauhala, "The Canadian News Directors Study: Demographics and Political Leanings of Television Decision Makers," *Canadian Journal of Communication,* 30, 2 (2005).

8. Rita Shelton Deverell, "Who Will Inherit the Airwaves," *Canadian Journal of Communications,* 34, 1 (2009).

9. See John Miller et al., *Diversitycity Counts 2: A Snapshot of Diverse Leadership in the GTA, 2010.* (Diversity Institute, Ryerson University, 2010). See also John Miller <thejournalismdoctor.ca>.

10. See Ramona Pringle, "Gender Gap Shows High-Tech Sector Still Stuck in the Past," CBC News, February 12, 2018 <cbc.ca/news/technology/diversity-tech-jobs-pringle-1.4528149>.

11. Rebecca Cohen Palacios, "Women in Gaming Talk about the Hurdles," CBC News, March 13, 2015 <cbc.ca/news/canada/montreal/women-in-gaming-talk-about-the-hurdles-1.2994491>.

12. See the "Canadian Media Concentration Research Project," 2016, based at Carleton University's Journalism School <cmcrp.org>.

13. Peter Nowak, "Internet, Phone Bills in Canada Too High, Says Consumer Study," CBC News, March 23, 2015.

14. See Marc Edge, *Greatly Exaggerated: The Myth of the Death of Newspapers* (New Star Books, 2014).

15. The Canadian Media Guild has tracked job losses. A summary appeared in their submission to the federal government's Heritage Ministry in 2016. See <canadiancontentconsultations.ca/system/documents/attachments/82d693aa3d84f254f20fe2e9c6e68915e9ba5348/000/004/836/original/Canadian_Media_Guild.pdf?1481214475>.

16. Oscar Baker III, "5 Independent Indigenous Media Sources to Check Out Online," CBC News, July 11, 2016 <cbc.ca/news/indigenous/independent-indigenous-media-list-1.3609578>.

17. Quoted in Tony Harcup, *The Ethical Journalist* (Sage, 2006), 53.

18. Tony Harcup, *Journalism: Principles and Practice* (Sage, 2004), 36.

19. "Media Got the Minimum Wage Story Wrong," *Tyee,* January 5, 2018.

20. The best history of investigative reporting in Canada is Cecil Rosner, *Behind the Headlines: A History of Investigative Journalism in Canada* (Oxford, 2008).

21. See in particular, Jim Rankin, "Race Matters: Blacks Documented by Police at High Rate," *Toronto Star*, February 6, 2010; Bruce Livesey, "House of Irving," *National Observer,* March 30, 2017; Harvey Cashore et al., "The Untouchables," CBC the *Fifth Estate,* March 3, 2017; Lindsay Kines, "Police Target Big Increase in Missing Women," *Vancouver Sun,* July 3, 1998. Regarding the ongoing tragedy of Indigenous women, the media record seems poor overall. For a summary of the media treatment see, for example, "Media Portrayals of Missing and Murdered Aboriginal Women," *Media Smarts,* n.d. <mediasmarts.ca/diversity-media/aboriginal-people/media-portrayals-missing-and-murdered-aboriginal-women>.

22. John Doyle, "CTV's *Your Morning* Is an Exercise in Harebrained Inanity," *Globe and Mail,* March 24, 2017.

23. The National Campus and Community Radio Association has 108 member stations, some in very small places <www.ncra.ca>.

24. Emily Steel, "At Vice, Cutting-Edge Media and Allegations of Old-School Sexual Harassment.

A media company built on subversion and outlandishness was unable to create 'a safe and inclusive workplace' for women, two of its founders acknowledge," *New York Times,* December 23, 2017. See also Reeves Wiedeman, "A Company Built on a Bluff," *New York,* June 10, 2018.

25. Other forms of new media also show a lack of diversity. In the world of podcasting, for example, a Toronto freelancer Katie Jensen has developed several projects to correct the "imbalance of women and people of colour in podcasting," Amy van den Berg, "Fighting the Lack of Diversity in Podcasting," *Ryerson Review of Journalism,* Nov. 6, 2017.

26. Amy Mitchell, Elisa Shearer, Jeffrey Gottfried and Michael Barthel, "Pathways to News" (Pew Research Center, July 7, 2016).

CONTRIBUTORS

Paul U. Angelini has been teaching at Sheridan College since 1988. He has developed and delivered courses in politics, diversity, sociology and philosophy. He is contributing editor to *Our Society: Human Diversity in Canada*. He holds a master's degree in political studies from Queen's University.

Michelle Broderick completed her PhD in anthropology at the University of Toronto and has taught a variety of courses at both the college and university levels. She works in institutional research at the University of Toronto.

Leslie Butler is a community college professor who has taught journalism, history, politics and communication for thirty years. She holds a master's degree in journalism from the University of Western Ontario and master's degree in English from University of Waterloo.

Jennifer Chambers holds a PhD in English from the University of Alberta. She specializes in Canadian literature and has published and presented on early Canadian women writers, the role of the English professor in contemporary fiction and film, and gender and sexuality in the early twentieth century. She teaches in the Creative Writing and Publishing Program at Sheridan College.

Sara J. Cumming has her PhD in sociology with a specialization in gender, inequality and social policy. She is a professor of sociology at Sheridan College and the co-chair of Applied Sociology in Canada.

Lee Easton is an associate professor in the Department of English, Languages and Cultures at Mount Royal University. He teaches film studies and comics studies with a focus on gender, sexuality and identity. He is co-author of *Secret Identity Reader: Essays on Sex Death and the Superhero*.

Shane Gannon is an associate professor in the Department of Sociology and Anthropology and associate dean in the Faculty of Arts at Mount Royal University.

His research and teaching interests include queering (post-)colonial sexual histories of South Asia and exploring the role of citizenship in sexual governance.

Kate Hano has a BA in psychology and sociology from St. Jerome's University and an MA in sociology from the University of Waterloo. Kate's PhD is in geography, with a focus on accessibility of all-inclusive resorts in the Caribbean for physically challenged individuals.

Alexander Hollenberg is a professor of storytelling and narrativity at Sheridan College, where he specializes in narrative theory and ethics. He has published widely in such journals as *English Studies in Canada, Narrative, Style* and *Studies in American Indian Literatures.* He is collaborating on a project on Indigenous narrative resistance in Canada. Alexander earned his PhD in English from the University of Toronto.

Jessica E. Pulis is a professor of criminology at Sheridan College. Jessica's research specializations include social regulation, corrections, young offenders and the experiences of marginalized persons, in particular women and girls and Indigenous peoples, in the criminal justice system. Jessica earned her PhD in sociology and legal studies at the University of Waterloo.

Peter Steven is a professor of film studies at Sheridan College. He received his PhD in radio/TV/film from Northwestern University. He is the author of several books on film and the media, including *About Media: Canada, The News* and *The No-Nonsense Guide to Global Media.*

Tamara Wasylenky-Stern has a BA in linguistics and an MA in applied language studies. She is a professor of language and literature at Sheridan College. Through her teaching and research, Tamara continues to explore voice as a critical lens through which to understand the stories that shape our world.

INDEX

Bolded page numbers indicate Key Term definitions. *Italic* page numbers indicate tables and figures.